The Rorschach: A Comprehensive System, in two volumes
  by John E. Exner

Theory and Practice in Behavior Therapy
  by Aubrey J. Yates

Principles of Psychotherapy
  by Irving B. Weiner

Psychoactive Drugs and Social Judgment: Theory and Research
  edited by Kenneth Hammond and C. R. B. Joyce

Clinical Methods in Psychology
  edited by Irving B. Weiner

Human Resources for Troubled Children
  by Werner I. Halpern and Stanley Kissel

Hyperactivity
  by Dorothea M. Ross and Sheila A. Ross

Heroin Addiction: Theory, Research and Treatment
  by Jerome J. Platt and Christina Labate

Children's Rights and the Mental Health Profession
  edited by Gerald P. Koocher

The Role of the Father in Child Development
  edited by Michael E. Lamb

Handbook of Behavioral Assessment
  edited by Anthony R. Ciminero, Karen S. Calhoun, and Henry E. Adams

Counseling and Psychotherapy: A Behavioral Approach
  by E. Lakin Phillips

Dimensions of Personality
  edited by Harvey London and John E. Exner, Jr.

The Mental Health Industry: A Cultural Phenomenon
  by Peter A. Magaro, Robert Gripp, David McDowell, and Ivan W. Miller III

Nonverbal Communication: The State of the Art
  by Robert G. Harper, Arthur N. Wiens, and Joseph D. Matarazzo

Alcoholism and Treatment
  by David J. Armor, J. Michael Polich, and Harriet B. Stambul

A Biodevelopmental Approach to Clinical Child Psychology: Cognitive Controls and Cognitive Control Theory
  by Sebastiano Santostefano

Handbook of Infant Development
  edited by Joy D. Osofsky

Understanding the Rape Victim: A Synthesis of Research Findings
  by Sedelle Katz and Mary Ann Mazur

Childhood Pathology and Later Adjustment: The Question of Prediction
  by Loretta K. Cass and Carolyn B. Thomas

Intelligent Testing with the WISC-R
  by Alan S. Kaufman

Adaptation in Schizophrenia: The Theory of Segmental Set
  by David Shakow

Psychotherapy: An Eclectic Approach
  by Sol L. Garfield

Handbook of Minimal Brain Dysfunctions
  edited by Herbert E. Rie and Ellen D. Rie

Handbook of Behavioral Interventions: A Clinical Guide
  edited by Alan Goldstein and Edna B. Foa

Art Psychotherapy
  by Harriet Wadeson

Handbook of Adolescent Psychology
  edited by Joseph Adelson

Psychotherapy Supervision: Theory, Research and Practice
  edited by Allen K. Hess

Continued on back

A "renegade" theory since its inception, personal construct psychology has fought an uphill battle for respect and acceptance. PERSONAL CONSTRUCT PSYCHOLOGY is an exciting step forward in establishing this, George A. Kelly's pioneering approach, as an integral part of the psychological mainstream. The therapeutic implications of the theory are extensively elaborated here for the first time. Eminent second and third generation construct psychologists now face the challenge of extending and clarifying the work of a major theorist. PERSONAL CONSTRUCT PSYCHOLOGY documents their success so far in a tribute to the integrative and anticipatory power of the approach. Editors Landfield and Leitner have gathered together an impressive collection of important articles, including an exploration of consciousness through children, the teaching of personal construct psychotherapy, and a very special examination of recently discovered tapes of George Kelly conducting his therapy. An intriguing guide for students and professors, PERSONAL CONSTRUCT PSYCHOLOGY is also a challenge to scientists and professionals to give more careful consideration to the potential value of this personality theory.

About the editors

ALVIN W. LANDFIELD, currently Professor of Psychology at the University of Nebraska-Lincoln, received his Ph.D. from Ohio State University in 1951. Dr. Landfield has published extensively and is a member of the American Association of University Professors, the Nebraska, and American Psychological Associations, and the Society for Psychotherapy Research.

LARRY M. LEITNER recently completed his Ph.D. in Clinical and Social-Personality Psychology at the University of Nebraska. He is an assistant professor at Miami University, Oxford, Ohio.

PERSONAL CONSTRUCT
PSYCHOLOGY

PERSONAL CONSTRUCT PSYCHOLOGY
PSYCHOTHERAPY AND PERSONALITY

Edited by

A. W. LANDFIELD
University of Nebraska
Lincoln, Nebraska

L. M. LEITNER
Miami University
Oxford, Ohio

A WILEY-INTERSCIENCE PUBLICATION

JOHN WILEY & SONS, New York • Chichester • Brisbane • Toronto

Library of Congress Cataloging in Publication Data:

Main entry under title:

  Personal construct psychology.

  (Wiley series on personality processes ISSN 0195-4008)
  Includes bibliographies and indexes
  1. Pesonal construct theory. 2. Personality.
3. Psychotherapy. I. Landfield, A. W., 1924–
II. Leitner, Larry Milton. [DNLM: 1. Personality.
2. Psychotherapy.   WM420 P466]

BF698.P356   155.2   80-16938
ISBN 0-471-05859-9

Printed in the United States of America

10 9 8 7 6 5 4 3 2 1

"It is a luxury to be understood"

Ralph Waldo Emerson

Series Preface

This series of books is addressed to behavioral scientists interested in the nature of human personality. Its scope should prove pertinent to personality theorists and researchers as well as to clinicians concerned with applying an understanding of personality processes to the amelioration of emotional difficulties in living. To this end, the series provides a scholarly integration of theoretical formulations, empirical data, and practical recommendations.

Six major aspects of studying and learning about human personality can be designated: personality theory, personality structure and dynamics, personality development, personality assessment, personality change, and personality adjustment. In exploring these aspects of personality, the books in the series discuss a number of distinct but related subject areas: the nature and implications of various theories of personality; personality characteristics that account for consistencies and variations in human behavior; the emergence of personality processes in children and adolescents; the use of interviewing and testing procedures to evaluate individual differences in personality; efforts to modify personality styles through psychotherapy, counseling, behavior therapy, and other methods of influence; and patterns of abnormal personality functioning that impair individual competence.

IRVING B. WEINER

University of Denver
Denver, Colorado

Preface

This volume may be considered a major elaboration of Personal Construct Psychology into the area of psychotherapy. The thrust of the volume is as much theoretical as practical since the authors challenge scientists and professionals to give more careful consideration to the potential value of personality theory; in this case, a theory written by the late Professor George A. Kelly.

Sometimes construct psychology has been described as a brilliantly reasoned theory that was 20 years before its time. It also has been described in less laudatory ways. The theory did not sit well with those who were angry with their environments. Certain events seemingly could not be reconstrued. The theory also did not satisfy the eternal craving for simple and permanent answers to the nature of human beings. At the same time, the theory did not have sufficient content for those who sought mysterious and hidden complexes within the human psyche. Then, of course, emotions were handled too abstractly. And, despite the protests of Professor Kelly, psychologists misinterpreted Kelly's "scientist" and also insisted on equating a personal construct with a limited methodology. George Kelly seemed to be correct about how important it is for humans to place their experiences in frameworks of *their own* meaning (and feeling, and value).

Despite roadblocks of counterinterpretation, construct psychology has gained support within the scientific community. Many construct-related volumes have been published since 1965. Three international Congresses have been held and a Clearing House for Research serves more than 300 members. Personal Construct Psychology is alive and kicking. This will become obvious as you read the chapters.

The chapters are arranged in three parts: Basic Theory, Psychotherapy, and Personality and Social Interaction. Although the chapters seem to fall naturally into these divisions, all chapters nonetheless have implications for understanding personality, social interaction, and psychotherapy.

I. BASIC THEORY

A brief overview of Personal Construct Theory is presented in the first chapter. After a characterization of the theory within Rychlak's four dimensions for describing personality theories, the philosophy of constructive alternativism is discussed, along with the fundamental postulate and 11 corollaries. The chapter ends with a brief examination of the nature of change within construct theory. Chapter 2 is a spirited and classical statement from George Kelly on the nature of human beings. The chapter is reprinted from a volume entitled *The Goals of Psychotherapy,* edited by A. R. Mahrer, published by Meredith in 1967. We wish to thank Prentice-Hall, Inc., for permission to use the chapter.

Chapter 3 takes us to London where Ravenette discusses consciousness, scientific philosophy, and children. His chapter begins with a profound statement made by a 13-year-old girl. The statement was elicited by construct methodology devised by the author. He then takes up the theoretical issue of consciousness, philosophy of science, and the nature of construct theory. Following this, he leads his reader to the practical level of Graham, a 10-year-old boy. Ravenette introduces more unique methods for getting at the contrasting ways of how Graham views his world. The interviewing methodology is followed by Ravenette's therapeutic intervention—a statement to Graham about how he understands him.

II. PSYCHOTHERAPY

Kelly's "optimal person" is elaborated by Epting and Amerikaner in Chapter 4. They examine some of the ways Personal Construct Psychotherapy relates to the highest level of personal development—that is, the best self, the truly healthy personality. Issues concerning optimal functioning include the nature of open systems; the transcendent experience; the nature of human potentials; the nature of love, obligation, and responsibility. The chapter also includes techniques useful in facilitating optimal functioning.

Chapter 5 is a very special one. Recently, we received 40 hours of tapes on which George Kelly is the therapist. We traced the whereabouts of the client and have received permission from him to use the tapes. In this chapter, Neimeyer will review the ways in which George Kelly conducted his therapy.

Having learned something about how Kelly went about his task as psychotherapist, we can now compare his work with that of one of the third-generation construct therapists. In Chapter 6, Leitner discusses his relationship with Sue, a highly disturbed person. Leitner systematically employs his understanding of construct theory, even to the point of interpreting a mistake and then correcting it according to the logic of George Kelly. Sue responds to treatment, something not predicted by experienced clinicians.

Chapter 7 begins with a discussion of the complaint, followed by an analysis of the expectations clients and therapists bring with them to the first session. The concept of expectancy is central to construct theory. Then, a dozen illustrations from the author's practice are given which introduce certain concepts and strategies of construct treatment. The chapter concludes with a discussion of client-therapist congruency.

In Chapter 8, McCoy discusses the situation of Western women who married Hong Kong Chinese men when they lived abroad (usually during a professional education and after the men had adapted to the Western life-style of the host country). When these couples move back to Hong Kong not only are they required to make the usual expatriate adjustments, but they also encounter special difficulties. The different expectations of Chinese and Western marriages are highlighted. In discussing her counseling with several of these culture-shocked marriages, McCoy illustrates construct change through the use of Rep Grids.

Karst has written two major sections for Chapter 9: (1) the general relationship between theory and technique with special attention to fixed-role therapy and other theoretically derived techniques; (2) reconstruing other therapeutic techniques—for example, hypnosis, operant conditioning, systematic desensitization, and so on, within a construct framework.

The teaching of Personal Construct Psychotherapy is the subject of Chapter 10. Fransella has written a chapter about her recent six-month adventure—teaching psychotherapy to a variety of professionals in London. When asked to write the chapter, she stated that the idea was an exciting one, but that we might be taking a gamble. The reader may judge for himself.

III. PERSONALITY AND SOCIAL INTERACTION

In Chapter 11, Doster attempts to show how the behavioral and intra-individual approaches can be combined within construct theory. In other words, an attempt is made to integrate what seems to be happening in the interaction with the meanings attributed to it by the participants.

Carr focuses on research literature relevant to the Commonality and Sociality Corollaries in Chapter 12. These corollaries are the keys to understanding what goes on in the therapeutic relationship, predictive of eventual outcome. This literature review covers his own work in the United States as well as research programs overseas.

In Chapter 13, Mancuso and Handin describe a project in which mothers were instructed in the process of taking into account their children's construct systems (Sociality Corollary) in order to regulate the arousal generated by failure to anticipate (First Postulate and Choice Corollary).

The final chapter by Landfield represents an attempt to distill from many years of experience as a Personal Construct Psychologist certain observations and their interpretations which seem most vital for understanding how persons, including the author himself, both function and malfunction. The unifying conception is perspectivism, which is contrasted with literalism and a related idea, chaotic fragmentalism. This dimension of *perspectivism* versus *literalism* is presented in varied contexts. The chapter may be considered an elaboration of Personal Construct Theory, one with far-reaching implications for the fields of personality and psychopathology.

A. W. LANDFIELD
L. M. LEITNER

Lincoln, Nebraska
Oxford, Ohio
August 1980

Acknowledgments

We wish to thank the following for their kind permission to reproduce material quoted from other volumes:

Prentice-Hall, Inc., for permission to reprint George A. Kelly's "A Psychology of the Optimal Man" in *The Goals of Psychotherapy,* edited by Alvin R. Mahrer, 1967, pp. 238–258; John Wiley & Sons, Ltd., for permission to reprint a section from D. Bannister (Ed.), *Issues and Approaches in Psychological Therapies,* 1975, pp. 10–13; the *Dutch Review of Psychology* for permission to quote from J. C. J. Bonarius, "De Fixed Role Therapy van George A. Kelly," 1967, **22,** 482–520; the American Psychological Association for permission to reprint tables from the *Journal of Abnormal Psychology,* 1970, **76,** 361–369. Finally, we are especially indebted to clients who have given permission to use material from their therapy sessions.

A. W. L.
L. M. L.

Contributors

MARTIN AMERIKANER Department of Counselor Education University of Houston, Texas

JOHN E. CARR Department of Psychiatry and Behavioral Sciences, University of Washington, Seattle

JOSEPH A. DOSTER Department of Psychology, North Texas State University, Denton

FRANZ EPTING Department of Psychology, University of Florida, Gainesville

FAY FRANSELLA Department of Academic Psychiatry, The Royal Free Hospital, University of London, England

KENNETH H. HANDIN Saint Catherine's Center for Children Albany, New York

THOMAS O. KARST Department of Psychiatry, Medical College of Ohio, Toledo

GEORGE KELLY *

A. W. LANDFIELD Department of Psychology, University of Nebraska, Lincoln

L. M. LEITNER Department of Psychology, Miami University, Oxford, Ohio

JAMES C. MANCUSO Department of Psychology, State University of New York, Albany

MILDRED McCOY Department of Psychology, University of Hong Kong

ROBERT NEIMEYER Department of Psychology, University of Nebraska, Lincoln

A. T. RAVENETTE Education Department, Borough of Newham, London, England

* Deceased

Contents

PERSONAL CONSTRUCT
PSYCHOLOGY

PART ONE

Basic Theory

CHAPTER 1

Personal Construct Psychology

A. W. Landfield and L. M. Leitner

This chapter begins with a discussion of several dimensions along which any personality formulation may be understood. Personal Construct Theory is described briefly in relation to its underlying philosophy, fundamental postulate, and corollaries. Generalizations about the nature of psychotherapeutic change, or reconstruction, conclude the chapter.

Personality theories evolve as an attempt to understand more deeply and/or systematically the human condition. Although the ultimate validity of each theory will rest upon its usefulness in helping individuals understand the human dilemma, there are other interesting dimensions along which theories may be described. Rychlak (1968), using the dimension of realism-idealism, states that a realistic theory encompasses the idea that the world of perception and cognition has an immutable existence which is independent of the perceiver. Standing in contrast to realism is the theory of the idealist who feels that it is not profitable to speak of a world that is independent of the perceptions and cognitions of the perceiver. Knowledge, to the idealist, is primarily an act of inventing reality, not discovering it. As will be seen later, Personal Construct Theory makes some concessions to realism but will be predominantly idealistic.

A second dimension refers to the contrasts objective-subjective. Rychlak states that the objective abstraction transcends the individual abstractor and can be grasped and understood by all individuals in a specified class. Subjectivity implies that it is nearly impossible to generalize our abstractions, and it is difficult for other individuals to grasp them. Within Personal Construct Theory, there is an appreciation that the person's views can be highly idiosyncratic. However, the theory itself is quite objective. Restating this point, it is an objective theory about each person's individualized and possibly subjective theory of man.

A third dimension on which theories vary is their theoretical perspective (Rychlak, 1973). Rychlak refers to the frame of reference, or orientation, of a theory. An introspective theory takes as its frame of reference the object being studied and formulates its theoretical constructs from that vantage point. For example, the introspective theories of personality form their theoretical constructs from the point of view of the person. In contrast to this are the theories with an extraspective frame of reference. These theories describe the person from the point of view of an external observer; less emphasis is placed on the internal experience of the object being studied. Personal Construct Theory falls on the introspective side of this dimension.

Another way of categorizing personality theories is by looking at their image of man. Essentially, we can divide this issue into whether the theory views the person as an active organism who has some control of his own destiny, or as a passive respondent to past history, environmental contingencies, instinctual drives, and the like. In this regard Personal Construct Theory espouses a more active image of the human being.

Summarizing in relation to Rychlak's dimensions, the person within construct theory is actively inventive in trying to control his destiny. In this process, he can be both objective and introspective. Although one might construe these characteristics as oppositional to each other, there is no reason to assume such an oppositional relationship within a Psychology of Personal Constructs. It is the blending of these two characteristics that allows the person to sensitively confront the events of his life.

PERSONAL CONSTRUCT THEORY

Kelly (1955) begins his writing with a basic philosophical assertion out of which stems the whole theoretical structure of his position. This assumption, called constructive alternativism, essentially states that all of our present interpretations of the universe are subject to revision or replacement. Kelly asserts that the universe is real but that different persons construe it in different ways. Moreover, this universe owes no allegiance to any individual's (or theory's) construction of it and can always be reconstrued. Whatever nature may ultimately prove to be, ". . . the events we face today are subject to as great a variety of constructions [interpretations] as our wits will enable us to contrive" (Kelly, 1970, p. 1). In taking this stance Kelly does not deny that one construction of the universe may be better suited to man's purposes than another. He also does not deny that we may, at some point in the very distant future, see reality in its utmost reaches. However, he does state that even the most obvious occurrences of everyday life might be totally transformed if we were inventive enough to construe them differently. A classic example of constructive alternativism can be seen in the evolution of physics. Newtonian and Einsteinian physics are different ways of explaining many of the same events. However, physicists prefer Einstein's formulation because it can anticipate more events than Newton's, not because it is truer or more right. In Kelly's terminology it has a broader range of convenience (application). All other things being equal, the broader the range of application, the more useful the theory.

The philosophical position of constructive alternativism stands in marked contrast to an assumption frequently made in psychology—accumulative fragmentalism. This latter philosophy argues that truth is collected piece by piece and this process paints reality for the psychologist. When enough pieces have been collected, the nature of persons and the universe will become manifest. In contrast, constructive alternativism emphasizes the interpretation of events. It is the process of interpretation and reinterpretation, rather than the accumulation of facts, which will help us approximate the reality of the world. As Kelly put it, man is always free to reconstrue that which he cannot deny.

In this process of construction and reconstruction, the person actively tries to encompass his inner and outer worlds, psychologically, by means of personal dimensions of awareness anchored by contrasts in meaning. These dimensions of awareness, or *personal constructs,* are formed by the processes of differentiation and integration; that is, the ways in which events are similar and different from others. The person experiences his life by noting series of events from which he abstracts the recurring themes and their contrasts. This dual process of abstracting and contrasting defines *construing*—a process which may encompass what we know as feelings, values, and behavior. Construing, which can be understood at different levels of verbal awareness, is a uniquely bipolar process. In regard to the bipolarity of constructs, the experience of a communality of certain events implies a negation of some other aspect or aspects of that experience. For example, the concept of lightness would make little sense without its companion—darkness. Although we do not consciously think much about darkness while appreciating lightness, there must be a negation, in some measure, of lightness. Without this negation, lightness would have no meaning.

A final point about construing emphasizes the idea that a bipolar interpretation is not a refutation of continuous scaling, where perceptions are distributed across many points of a scale. Continuous scaling can be construed as using one's bipolar understandings in combinations. Kelly (1955) argues that there is no essential difference between the basic natures of binary and continuous scaling (pp. 63, 141, 299, 302). Scientists have no problem reinterpreting their continuous data into binary structures.

The essential nature of *or* reason for construing is *anticipation.* Personal constructs are structures which facilitate "the *better* understanding of future events" (Bannister & Mair, 1968, p. 13). This better understanding of future events can be illustrated by an interpersonal situation. Imagine that you are experiencing insensitivity from an acquaintance for the first time. At the point of this experience, an expectancy or prediction about the other person can be generated. Although you could dismiss the experience altogether, until it happens again you might wonder about its possible recurrence (a weak prediction). You might also become convinced that it will happen again (strong prediction). To use another illustration, a construct theorist would state that any attribution of characteristics to another person implies the unstated expectation that the person will possess those same characteristics tomorrow. The feelings of doubt that most of us experience when someone we know suddenly changes give testimony that our person perceptions have anticipatory implications. If we were not anticipating regularities in behavior, why should we become upset about sudden change? Anticipation is a central assumption within construct theory.

By emphasizing the anticipatory nature of human enterprise, Kelly has freed his theory from the constricting stimulus-response and drive theories of personality. Kelly's opinion of the conditioning and drive theories of human functioning can be seen in the following statement:

The construct of "energy" is really an outgrowth of certain fundamental assumptions that physicists have found it convenient to make. By assuming that matter is composed of basically static units, it became immediately necessary to account for the obvious fact that what was observed was not always static but often thoroughly active. What made the units active? Why "energy" of course! Psychologists therefore, by buying the notion of "energy," had implicitly bought the same assumption of static units which had first made "energy" a necessary construct for the physicists. (1955, pp. 35–36)

By assuming that man is born "alive and struggling" (Kelly, 1955, p. 37), Kelly avoided the need for drives to "push" or stimuli to "pull" the human organism into action.

The importance of anticipation is set forth in his primary metaphor—*man-the-scientist*. By this Kelly means that the person, like the scientist, is continually asking questions of her or his world in the hope of understanding it better.

Kelly perhaps chose "the scientist" as an explicit metaphor for man because in our time the scientist is par excellence the person who has elaborated the act of asking penetrating questions in ways which have provided answers and further questions of astonishing beauty and power. Kelly's interest was not to turn everyone into a formal scientist, but rather to draw attention to the essential human function of questioning, and to encourage the elaboration of ways of clarifying and pursuing our questions which are most often acted rather than stated, implicit in our assumptions and deeds rather than consciously recognized and pursued in full awareness. (Mair, 1977, p. 284)

Underlining further the importance of anticipation, Kelly embedded it in his fundamental postulate "A person's processes are psychologically channelized by the ways in which he anticipates events" (Kelly, 1955, p. 46). Beginning with this postulate and its emphasis on the importance of anticipation, Kelly developed a comprehensive, scientifically testable theory of personality based on an active image of human functioning—a rare accomplishment in psychology.

We now have a statement of a fundamental postulate for which we have high hopes. Perhaps there can spring from it a theory of personality with movement as the phenomenon rather than the epiphenomenon, with the psychological processes of the layman making the same sense as those of the scientist, a dynamic psychology without the trappings of animism, a perceptual psychology without passivity, a behaviorism in which the behaving person is credited with having some sense, a learning theory in which learning is considered so universal that it appears in the postulate rather than as a special class of phenomena, a motivational theory in which man is neither pricked into action by the sharp points of stimuli nor dyed with the deep tones of hedonism, and a view of personality which permits psychotherapy to appear both lawful and plausible. Let us call this theory *the psychology of person constructs*. (Kelly, 1955, p. 49–50)

Man-the-Scientist

Even as Kelly employed the metaphor of man-the-scientist, he did not visualize anticipation as *necessarily* mechanical, verbalizable, exact, logical, complexly organized, or unemotional. Anticipation, scientific or otherwise, can also be imaginative, unverbalizable, approximate, illogical, simply organized, or highly emotional. Moreover, anticipation can vary within the contexts of time and abstraction. John Hoad (Landfield, 1977a) states:

Kelly did not mean to rob the person of his life right now. Anticipations can be of the now variety: for example, "This is the best way of handling a situation right now as I project things into the future." One may speak of global versus detailed kinds of anticipations. An example of the global anticipation might be an "anticipatory conviction" about being adequate for whatever happens in the future, perhaps even one's eventual confrontation with death. Statements such as "I can ride with the punches" link longer-term, global predictions with anticipants of the "right now" (p. 352)

As the person uses his constructs in the anticipation of events, he tests the utility of his constructs through validating evidence. *Validation* refers to personal anticipations which are borne out. Paradoxically, even though the psychologist speaks of validating his own hypotheses, he may speak nonreflexively of reinforcing his subject. Kelly, appreciating this paradox, felt that the critical experience for both psychologist and subject was better stated as validation (the subject's decision) rather than reinforcement (the psychologist's manipulation). Kelly chose not to confuse manipulation (reinforcement) with the experience of validation. A preoccupation with our own manipulations and personal views of reinforcement may cloud our perception to the possibility that events may be construed differently by the subject and his investigator. This point is illustrated by the psychologist who failed to comprehend why Billy, an eleven-year-old boy, did not hate his father. Billy loved his father in spite of the fearful beatings he received from him. "Billy must be denying his hatred," the psychologist assumed. However, Billy's strange attitude made more sense when he stated that father only beat him when he was bad (fairly), and besides, he was tough! Taking the beatings really proved it. It was important to be tough in his highly delinquent neighborhood.

Eleven Corollaries

Kelly elaborates his fundamental postulate with eleven corollaries. These corollaries combine with the fundamental postulate to provide the major structure of Personal Construct Theory. These corollaries will now be stated without an extensive elaboration.

According to the *construction corollary*, "a person anticipates events by construing their replications" (Kelly, 1955, p. 50). This corollary essentially emphasizes the abstracting process of the mind in interpreting the world. Since, in concrete terms, no two events are identical, it is only man's ability to abstract which enables him to see repetitive themes in the world. "An event is replicative of another only if one is willing to accept the abstracted similarity of the two" (Kelly, 1955, p. 53). By abstracting and seeing replications, the person places structure and meaning onto his world. He construes.

The *individuality corollary* states that "persons differ from each other in their construction of events" (Kelly, 1955, p. 55). This corollary, which stems directly from the philosophy of constructive alternativism, raises an important clinical issue—an issue related to the confounding of the client's system of meaning and value with that of the therapist. This confusion of meaning systems is illustrated by the patient who "beats his head against the wall."

He does this despite the obvious pain and the alternatives of hope extended to him. How can one hold onto that which apparently is not working? Within Personal Construct Theory, there is an explanation for this type of observer dilemma. The observer may be making the error of assuming that the constructs of the observed person are similar to his own in content or organization. Moreover the observer may be functioning within a simplistic view that life can be neatly reduced to clear-cut pleasures and pains. Within Personal Construct theory, one may direct his life toward many anticipations other than simply pleasures and pains. A person may willingly anticipate suffering for the sake of his expanding loyalty, bravery, love, freedom, antagonism, or identity. (Landfield, 1980, p. 73).

Kelly's *organization corollary* states that "each person characteristically evolves, for his convenience in anticipating events, a construction system embracing ordinal relationships between constructs" (Kelly, 1955, p. 56). This is an important corollary. A system of interrelated constructs is formed. This evolution of personal constructs into a personal construct system allows the construer to minimize incompatibilities and inconsistencies. The person can consequently minimize the possibility of making contradictory anticipations from different constructs. Moreover, even if two people use the same verbal symbol, they may organize it differently within their construct systems. For example, two people may construe a person as "introverted" as opposed to "extroverted." However, for the first person, "introverted" may be related in the system to "insecure" and "shy." In the second person's system, "introverted" may be related to "snobby" and "stuck-up."

The key to organization is the *ordinal* relationships that are formed. Some constructs are more superordinate while others are subordinate. A superordinate construct is one which subsumes another construct in its context. A subordinate construct is one which is subsumed by another construct. A construct which is superordinate to another construct is more abstract and important for the individual's construction of the world. The most superordinate of constructions are called *core* constructs. They "govern a person's maintenance processes" (Kelly, 1955, p. 55). Core constructs in the area of interpersonal relations can be called *core role* constructs. These are the most superordinate of our values and very much define our relationships with others. A person will act in relation to his core structures as if his life depended on it. As a matter of fact, within Personal Construct theory, suicide is viewed as the individual acting to protect his core structures from further invalidation. Thus suicidal behavior can also be seen as an act of dignity rather than "just" hostility turned inward (Kelly, 1961; Landfield, 1976). Now core constructs can be contrasted with less important *peripheral constructs*. These can be altered quite easily without serious modification of the core structure.

The *dichotomy corollary* states that "a person's construction system is composed of a finite number of dichotomous constructs" (Kelly, 1955, p. 59). This corollary essentially states the bipolar nature of one's construing. The relation between these two poles is one of contrast.

The *choice corollary* states that "a person chooses for himself that alternative in a dichotomized construct through which he anticipates the greater possibility for extension and definition of his system" (Kelly, 1955, 64). This may be exemplified. If the person understands life in the context of security versus adventure, he will opt for the pole which will give him greater meaning and greater possibilities for anticipating events. In one situation he may foresee adventure as providing the life experiences of value to him. In another situation he may choose the more conservative pole of security, particularly when there is more at stake for him. The person who has had few supportive relationships may choose to elaborate the negative ends of his dimensions, observing others within a critical context. Functioning from the negative poles of his constructions may help him feel less vulnerable and more able to cope with the vicissitudes of his life. In this process of choosing in the direction of greater definition, expansion, and extension of his life, the person makes what Kelly called the *elaborative choice*. Note that this choice does not force the person into motion; it merely determines the direction of the action. Being alive assumes that the person is in motion.

The *range corollary* states that "a construct is convenient for the anticipation of a finite range of events only" (Kelly, 1955, p. 68). In other words, a construct does not apply to everything. Constructs have a *range of convenience* (application). The range of convenience of a construct is the scope of the construct's relevance. Those events which fall outside the range of convenience of both poles of a construct are irrelevant for that construct. Those events for which the construct is maximally applicable define the construct's *focus of convenience*. For example, the focus of convenience of a construct like "happy-sad" may be in certain interpersonal relationships. However, it may apply, albeit not as well, to a person's understanding of pets. The price of yak milk in Tibet is probably outside the range of convenience of this construct. A construct which can subsume a wide variety of events (large range of convenience) is called a *comprehensive construct*. A construct which has a very narrow range of convenience is called an *incidental construct*.

The *experience corollary* states that "a person's construction system varies as he successively construes the replications of events" (Kelly, 1955, p. 72). Since a total understanding of the universe or even of one's personal universe is not possible, invalidation and reconstruction are a part of each person's life.

The *modulation corollary* states that "the variation in a person's construction system is limited by the permeability of the constructs within whose range of convenience the variants lie" (Kelly, 1955, p. 77). Essentially this corollary determines how the variations in the system occurring under the experience corollary are determined. In order to understand this corollary, the reader must know what construct theorists mean by permeability. The permeability of a construct is determined by whether it will admit into its range of convenience new events which are not yet construed within its framework. The variants in the corollary are the constructs that replace each other. These constructs are subordinate to a more superordinate construction and it is the permeability of this superordinate structure which governs the amount of variation the system will tolerate. Change is therefore governed by the permeability of one's superordinate structures.

The *fragmentation corollary* states that "a person may successively employ a variety of construction subsystems which are inferentially incompatible with each other'' (Kelly, 1955, p. 83). In other words, incompatibilities at one level of the personal construct system may be compatible at a higher level of personal theory. Employing this type of conception ''may help to explain how a marital argument can lead to the dissolution of a marriage in one instance and to an affirmation of the relationship in another case. In the first instance a marital partner might construe ambivalent feelings as validating a poor relationship. In the second case ambivalent feelings might be interpreted as supporting the importance of the other person and the need for better communication'' (Landfield, 1977b, pp. 142–143). The modulation, fragmentation, and organization corollaries point to the idea that behavioral consistency must be comprehended at different levels of the person's construct system or life organization. Psychologists who pursue behavioral consistency at the level of behavioral bits will certainly conclude that there is little stability to be found in human personality (Landfield, 1977b, pp. 139–143).

The *commonality corollary* states that ''to the extent that one person employs a construction of experience which is similar to that employed by another, his psychological processes are similar to those of the other person'' (Kelly, 1955, p. 90). This corollary, with its implications for interpersonal and cultural communication, stands in a supportive relation to the sociality corollary.

The *sociality corollary* states that ''to the extent that one person construes the construction processes of another, he may play a *role* in a social process involving the other person'' (Kelly, 1955, p. 95). This corollary is so important that Kelly almost entitled his theory ''role theory.'' However, for Kelly, role has a very special meaning, as may be seen by its technical definition in this corollary. A less technical definition of a role is ''an ongoing pattern of behavior that follows from a person's understanding of how the others who are associated with him in his task think'' (Kelly, 1955, pp. 97–98). In other words, the person performs an interpersonal task *based on his understanding of another person's construct system.* This is very different from our traditional notion of role as simply a behavioral description. For Kelly, role relationships are the ideal in life. Psychotherapy without the utilization of role relationships on the part of the therapist is impossible. In regard to the importance of role, note that under the organization corollary, it was stated that a person's most superordinate constructs are called core role constructs.

Construing Constructs

Constructs may be characterized in a variety of ways. They may be described as propositional, constellatory, preemptive, differing in levels of verbal awareness, loose to tight, dilated to constricted, and so on. Beginning with the *propositional* construct, it may be used independently of other ways of understanding an event. For example, describing someone as ''socially outgoing'' need not imply anything about one's view of that person's intelligence, happiness, or competence on the job. Restated, ''socially outgoing'' can be seen as orthogonal to other dimensions of experience. In contrast to this example, another person might equate ''socially outgoing'' with intelligence, happiness, and competence. In this latter case "socially outgoing" is found in a tight cluster of other perceptions. Such a fixed cluster of dimensions is called *constellatory*. Although Kelly interpreted the freedom of propositional construction as healthier than the dogmatism of constellatory ways of experiencing, he also understood that even propositional or orthogonal construction could be overused, signifying a lack of integration of constructs into a system and a concomitant inability to make decisions (Kelly, 1955, p. 155).

Another way of conceptualizing construct relatedness involves construing the person as capable of assuming, hypothesizing, and fragmenting his life (Landfield, 1977b). Relationship without an exception points to assumption; relationship with exceptions suggests hypothesis. A lack of relationship among one's bipolar constructions defines fragmentation. The excessive use of assumption would seem to be correlated with rigidity. A hypothesizing orientation to life would seem most useful if one is to cope with a complex and changing world. Fragmentation implies a disorderly and confusing way of life. The overuse of constellatory construction can be linked to assumption, whereas the overuse of propositional construction could lead to confusion.

Preemptive construction can be seen in a statement such as "Schizophrenia is a biochemical disorder." In this statement physiologists preempt the events subsumed under the term schizophrenia for their exclusive construction. Other constructions of this event are not accepted. We are acquainted with a person diagnosed as "manic" who was denied badly needed psychotherapy because his problem was "just" biochemical. This is just one illustration of the sad use of preemptive construction in the field of mental health.

With regard to *levels of verbal awareness*, many of our most vital constructs are preverbal and difficult to put into words. Moreover, certain of our significant constructions, for example, emotional ones, are sometimes better communicated in gestures and sounds. It should be remembered that constructs may vary along dimensions of verbal awareness and modes of expression.

Constructs can also vary from *loose to tight*. A loose construct is one that leads to varying predictions but still maintains its identity. The concept of "good mental health," used as a public or common construction, can be seen as quite loose. The same behavior which may have "bad" implications for one person may not have such "bad" implications for others. A particular person might also employ the concept of mental health loosely. For example, a particular behavior labeled as "high maladjustment" on one occasion might be ignored on another.

When a construct is loose an event may sometimes be subsumed under one pole, sometimes under the other. By way of contrast, tight constructs lead to unvarying predictions. Even those elements at the outer edge of the construct's relevance can be consistently categorized as belonging to either the like or the unlike grouping. "In a healthy person, the structures tend to be tight. He has regular habits with respect to such matters as eating, sleeping, and so on" (Kelly, 1955, p. 484). Possibly the most loosened constructs that can be put into words are those represented in a dream. The dream may seem to change while it is being told. After it is told, the dreamer may swear that the beginning could not have occurred the way he described it. "The loose construction is like a rough sketch which may be preliminary to a carefully drafted design. The sketch permits flexible interpretation" (Kelly, 1955, p. 484).

Another dimension used by construct theorists to construe constructs is the dimension of *dilation to constriction*. Dilation occurs when a person broadens the perceptual field so that he can reorganize it on a more comprehensive level. For example, a person is dilating his perceptual field when he gazes at the stars at night, contemplating the intricate beauty of the universe and the wonders of infinite time. The person who sees invaders from Mars may also be engaging in a process of dilation. In contrast to dilation, constriction occurs when a person narrows his perceptual field in order to minimize apparent incompatibilities. This can be nicely illustrated by the therapy client who had dedicated himself to becoming the world's leading authority on buffaloes in western Nebraska. The entire area of interpersonal relationships was out of bounds.

Concepts of Transition

The following conceptions, considered briefly, have special implications for the clinical relationship: threat, fear, anxiety, guilt, aggressiveness, hostility, the CPC and creativity cycles, and impulsivity. Kelly began by defining *threat* as an awareness of an imminent and comprehensive change in core structure. Paraphrasing this statement, threat occurs when the person anticipates, *at some level of awareness,* that something is going to happen to him which will have far-reaching implications. Essential to this definition of threat is the idea that "change can be threatening." Moreover, these far-reaching changes do not have to be negative in value. If a person has defined his life-role in terms of sickness, the prospect of a successful therapy could be traumatizing. It can also be stated that a person can be most threatened during a period of life transition. The person does not have a clear notion of where he lives in relation to his basic conceptions. Moreover, he might be completely dislodged from his central system of meaning. In this context of transition, the person is most vulnerable. The troublesome years of adolescence provide the most common illustrations of transitional threat. Then there is the special case of threat in which a person is challenged to move backward toward a past, a past that he has been moving away from. This challenge to "regress" comes from the person's own perception that others with whom he interacts either resemble his past behavior or expect him to behave in past ways. Even the minimal and unverbalized awareness of these past exemplifications and expectancies can precipitate feelings of discomfort and bring about attempts to avoid these threatening others. In some instances, the person may even try to change the other's behavior and to punish him (Landfield, 1954; 1955).

Fear is defined as the awareness of imminent incidental change in one's core structures. Although this is still an awareness of imminent change in core structures, the change is more incidental; that is, it is not as far reaching. *Anxiety* is the awareness that one's constructs don't apply to the world around him. The events that the person is facing lie mostly outside the range of convenience of his construct system. The person does not have sufficient structure to understand the events around him. The system fails! A change is called for. However, due to feelings of threat, or imminence of change in core structure, this change may not occur.

A person experiences *guilt* when he perceives an apparent dislodgment from his core role structure. The person has done something which he perceives as being in direct contradiction to his central role constructions. He has violated what is most sacred to him, what defines himself most importantly as a human being. A person is *aggressive* when he is active in elaborating his personal construct system. In a more private way persons who read this chapter might begin to rapidly extend, define, and broaden their constructs of psychology. This is aggressiveness. A person might also become interpersonally aggressive by energetically sharing his ideas for new developments and change with his friends and colleagues. If such rapid elaborations lead others to feel uncertain about him, they might become anxious (if it is vital to comprehend him). If his rapid elaborations become too demanding, they might view him as hostile. However, within Personal Construct Theory, the person might not be labeled as hostile. He would be seen as *hostile* only when he persisted in attempts to obtain validational evidence in support of a social prediction which has already proved itself to be a failure. The temper tantrums of a child provide an excellent illustration of hostility—a desperate and anxious attempt to make one's conception of the world come out right.

There are two processes of change which Kelly referred to as the *creativity* and *C-P-C cycles*. These cycles have important implications for psychotherapy. As we discuss these cycles, the reader should keep in mind that these cycles are not necessarily highly conscious processes. In other words one should not confuse the awareness of the client with the conscious theoretical awareness of the construct psychologist.

The C-P-C (circumspection, preemption, control) cycle relates to decision making in the context of known alternatives. The process begins with circumspection. At this stage the person is perceptually open; he scans a variety of relevant alternatives. Circumspection is then followed by preemption. At this second stage the person chooses some alternative; in this instance, a most applicable construct or dimension of experience. Once an applicable construction has been determined, the person enters the control phase by choosing a construct pole which will allow for the greater extension and elaboration of the system.

Although the C-P-C cycle may seem overly complex, it does lead to a different conception of impulsive behavior. *Impulsivity* is construed as a shortening of the circumspective stage. Very quickly the perceptual field is preempted, a choice point established, a decision made, and an action ensues. This delimiting of the circumspective stage may occur because the person experiences anxiety. Rather than interpret impulsivity as a loss of control, it is more helpful to view such behavior as an anxious effort to gain control—to give meaning and structure to one's life. In contrast to impulsivity, one can define *indecisiveness* as the excessive lengthening of the circumspective stage.

Whereas the C-P-C cycle focuses on decision making in the context of known alternatives or dimensions of experience, the creativity cycle emphasizes that which is new—creations that emerge from loosened construction. This cycle begins with playfulness and a rejuxtaposition of elements without an immediate need to find the best alternative. Since the immediate aim is not precise prediction and decision making, there is less at stake for the person in regard to being right or wrong. Nevertheless, the final stage of actual creation does involve tightened construction with more precise implications. Although the creative "production" is not defined by vagueness or confusion, the "process" of creative thinking begins with a relaxation and loosening of the commandments of formal logic and systematic analysis. The loosening phase of the cycle can be facilitated in therapy by such techniques as free association, dreaming, playing with feelings, and by imagining oneself as different persons within a community (Mair, 1977). Even as systematic analysis may follow the loosening phase, tightened construction can emerge without planning and deliberation. This point is well illustrated by the young man who suffered from acute anxiety. He complained about his inability to complete the sexual act with his "beauty queen" wife. The therapist prescribed playfulness for the couple, a playfulness which did not have to lead to the sexual act. Demands that the marriage be consummated were suspended for several weeks. The therapy successfully terminated when the couple's playfulness culminated in sexual inter-course without deliberate planning as to how or when the sexual act should take place.

PSYCHOTHERAPY AND RECONSTRUCTION

The psychological reconstruction of one's life is the ultimate objective of the personal construct therapist. Reconstruction also defines the development of all human beings. This emphasis on reconstruction is so important that Kelly considered dropping the term psychotherapy. However, psychotherapy does focus on change in relation to a professional person. At the same time, the change that is related to psychotherapy is not different from change occurring within other contexts of experience. Using the phraseology of construct theory, one may state that reconstruction is superordinate to the construct of psychotherapy, psychotherapy being but one method of achieving the process of psychological reconstruction.

Reconstruction can occur in several forms. Among these forms are *construct use change, new construction,* and *system change.* Beginning with construct use change, one can define four subtypes of change (Paine, 1970, pp. 7–9): contrast reconstruction, dimensional change, construct shift change, and construct application change.

Contrast reconstruction, sometimes called slot movement, refers to a shift from one side of a construct to the other. The phenomenon of "flight into health" exemplifies this type of change. The sudden reversal from liking someone to disliking that person also illustrates contrast reconstruction. Although this change in sidedness can be superficial, easy to achieve, and often unstable, resulting in what Kelly called "slot rattling," it can also be significant and stable change in the context of system reorganization. For example, developing a greater appreciation for the complexities of interpersonal communication might result in reidentifying a disliked person as a friend.

Dimensional change takes place along a scale on which magnitude of position can be shown. One might identify a person as friendly, yet perceive the person as more friendly and less friendly on different occasions. This kind of reasoning is not a refutation of the dichotomous nature of construing (Kelly, p. 141). For Kelly, the dimensional scale is comprised of complex combinations of dichotomies. Thus the statement that a person is less friendly implies that within certain limited contexts of friendship elements, the person is not friendly. Perhaps he did not smile on a particular occasion. He may not have been attentive at a particular moment. And, as stated previously, the person need not be highly conscious of the specifics of such decisions.

Construct shift change refers to movement from one construct to another in the construing process. For example, in the context of a family dinner, one may focus on the "good humor" of a friend. However, in the context of a business argument with this same friend, one may focus on his "weakness." Another way in which this kind of change can be understood is to say that "Sometimes an individual will shift from one axis of 'looking' at an acquaintance to another axis of 'looking' " (Paine, 1970, p. 8).

Application change refers to what Kelly called the "range of convenience" of a construct. For example, it might not make sense to label a child as financially responsible or irresponsible. If this were the case, the adult-centered construct would have a restricted range of application; children would be excluded from it. Taking another example, a person might state that he evaluates only a few acquaintances from the viewpoint of being either "emotionally close" or "emotionally distant." If the person in this latter example were to apply his bipolar construct of emotional distance to those acquaintances previously excluded, a change in construct application would have occurred.

New construction refers to the formation of new constructs and the redefinition of old ones. These new constructs may be tentatively formed as incidental in nature. However, they can become more permeable and their applications gradually expanded until the person can use them to replace certain obsolete core structures. Interpersonal experimentation and the use of dream material are two ways of encouraging new construction.

System change refers to alterations in the relationships between and among an individual's bipolar construct dimensions. New relationships may form; old ones may disappear. Then there may be a tightening or loosening of construct relationships. One type of system change involves "controlled elaboration." In this instance reconstruction occurs principally through clarification of the internal consistency of the system. "The purpose is to make the system—or large sections of it, rather—internally consistent and communicable so that it may be tested out and its validity or invalidity discovered. For example, a client may keep repeating the idea that he would like to have sexual relations with his boss's wife. The therapist may help the client by saying, 'Let us think through how this would be done and how it would turn out in the end' " (Kelly, 1955, p. 585).

As one can readily see, several types of construct change may occur in tandem. Of course the most fundamental change would involve new construction and a reorganization of the system. The chapters which follow will highlight many of these changes. In concluding this brief review of Personal Construct Theory and its application to psychotherapy, it seems appropriate to share a statement by Kelly with regard to psychological treatment. We have chosen a quotation from a letter to Han Bonarius in which Kelly comments on Bonarius's first experience using a specific approach called "fixed" role therapy (Kelly, Chapter 8). Essentially, fixed role therapy involves the construction of a role sketch that the therapy client experiments with, both inside and outside the therapy hour.

Kelly, in commenting on Bonarius's use of fixed role therapy, has captured the spirit of all construct procedures:

It seems to me your TV viewers must have been getting a lot of vicarious experience during the course of your therapy sessions. The fact that they, perhaps more than the client, started out skeptically and were highly critical of each move you made during therapy, suggests that the experience provided sharp contrasts for them along lines they had not anticipated before. Thus it may have added more dimensions to their own thinking about the nature of psychotherapy than it did for the client. Perhaps if they had enacted the parts they thought you and your client should have played, the experience might have been even more valuable for them.

Much will depend, I suspect, upon whether your client now thinks he has a fixed pattern for living, or whether he realizes that his life is amenable to reconstruction and experimentation. If only the former, he may find the fixed role of Geert less and less effectual as life moves on toward its more mature stages. If the latter, however, he may find himself able to take the initiative in changing his outlook and role whenever the old ways no longer serve their purposes. When he comes back, I would hope that he would have begun to see Geert as a stage in his development, not merely a solution to Peter's problems.

The fact that you yourself found the experience deeply moving is as it should be. You did not say in what respect you found it moving, except that you implied that you felt you were far out on a limb trying something for the first time with all your sophisticated colleagues watching and likely feeling threatened by your daring approach to something as sacred as psychotherapy is supposed to be.

The fact that rehearsals during psychotherapy sessions often go badly is not necessarily a discouraging sign, as I suspect you now realize. It is not perfection in the role that one seeks, but the definition of the challenge it offers the client, and the sense that through experimentation, the imperfections can be worked out. Thus a session in which there is a great deal of fumbling with enactments may actually be the one in which new constructions are being formulated for the first time.

The initial writing of the fixed role continues to be, in my estimation, the most demanding part of the whole process. It is here that the therapist must be most imaginative and must see the client's position in the broadest perspective. Moreover, it is at this stage that the therapist's own faith in the client's future will either enliven or depress the whole enterprise. If the therapist substitutes for this faith his own dogmatic notions of what the client really should become, he in effect denies that there is any constructive solution or that there is any such thing as a creative approach to treatment. It is very easy to see the fixed role not as an experiment with life, but as a panacea. Once this mistake is made, the whole undertaking becomes superficial and depressing. (Bonarius, 1967, pp. 516−517)

REFERENCES

Bannister, D. & Mair, J. M. M. *The Evaluation of Personal Constructs*. London & New York: Academic Press, 1968.

Bonarius, J. C. J. De fixed role therapy van George A. Kelly. *Ned. Tijdschr. Psychol.*, 1967, **22,** 482−520.

Kelly, G. A. *The Psychology of Personal Constructs*. New York: Norton, 1955.

Kelly, G. A. Suicide: The personal construct point of view. In N. I. Farberow & E. S. Shneidman (Eds.), *The Cry for Help*. New York: McGraw-Hill, 1961, pp. 255−280.

Kelly, G. A. A brief introduction to personal construct theory. In D. Bannister (Ed.), *Perspectives in Personal Construct Theory*. London: Academic Press, 1970, pp. 1−29.

Landfield, A. W. A movement interpretation of threat. *Journal of Abnormal and Social Psychology,* 1954, **49,** 529−532.

Landfield, A. W. Self predictive orientation and the movement interpretation of threat. *Journal of Abnormal and Social Psychology,* 1955, **51,** 434−438.

Landfield, A. W. A personal construct approach to suicidal behavior. In P. Slater (Ed.), *Explorations of Intrapersonal Space,* vol. 1, London: Wiley, 1976, pp. 93−108.

Landfield, A. W. Addendum. In A. W. Landfield (Ed.), *Nebraska Symposium on Motivation, 1976, Personal Construct Psychology*. Lincoln/London: University of Nebraska Press, 1977, pp. 345−360. (a)

Landfield, A. W. Interpretive man: The enlarged self-image. In A. W. Landfield (Ed.), *Nebraska Symposium on Motivation, 1976, Personal Construct Psychology*. Lincoln/London: University of Nebraska Press, 1977, pp. 127−178. (b)

Landfield, A. W. Personal construct psychology: A theory to be elaborated. In M. Mahoney (Ed.), *Psychotherapy Process: Current Issues and Future Directions*. New York: Plenum, 1980, pp. 61−83.

Mair, J. M. M. Metaphors for living. In A. W. Landfield (Ed.), *Nebraska Symposium on Motivation, 1976, Personal Construct Psychology*. Lincoln/London: University of Nebraska Press, 1977, pp. 243−290.

Paine, C. Reconstruction and Personality Change with Personal Construct theory. Unpublished Ph.D. dissertation, University of Missouri, 1970.

Rychlak, J. *A Philosophy of Science for Personality Theory*. Boston: Houghton Mifflin, 1968.

Rychlak, J. *Introduction to Personality and Psychotherapy*. Boston: Houghton Mifflin, 1973.

CHAPTER 2

A Psychology of the Optimal Man

George A. Kelly

Any discussion of the goals of psychotherapy is likely to proceed in both of two directions. First it will lead its participants to speculate about the kind of creature man ought to make of himself. Then against this ideal, often so vaguely formulated that it provides no clear guidelines for continuing the discourse, the participants usually feel they must turn about and assess as realistically as they can those internal limitations of man that may prevent the attainment of this or any other human objective.

While these are the directions such a discussion ordinarily takes, there are many twists and turns that may be attempted in order to avoid or reshape the two issues. Among these is the especially attractive argument that man need seek only to become himself. By taking this position some psychologists attempt to resolve both matters at once—the question of what man should become and the question of what there is about his own self that blocks the fulfillment of his aspirations. Their stand, they hope, permits them to go on and say that psychotherapy needs no direction other than that spontaneously taken by their clients. Psychotherapy is something to be encouraged, but never directed.

Although this posture of absolute respect for human nature in all its present forms appears to remove the onus of deciding what man should do with himself—and along with it the awful sense of responsibility for what is happening in human affairs everywhere—it seems to me to beg the question each of us asks himself sooner or later. In the end, man the person is left wondering in his loneliest hours what on earth he has been doing with himself, and man the psychotherapist, who has acquired an easy virtue with his clients by lapsing into permissiveness, will come to hold himself no less accountable for the outcome of his efforts.

This is the way I see it. Before this chapter is finished I may find myself accused of using this same psychological dodge. I shall not, however, accede to the charge!

PSYCHOTHERAPY AS AN ONTOLOGICAL VENTURE

The statement "to become oneself" makes sense only if you believe that man is presently something that he has not yet managed to become. The reasoning is a little tricky, for it requires that we distinguish between what is existing in some active state of being and what exists only latently, and, therefore, remains to be realized. The whole of oneself is presumed to include both levels of reality, but "being," in its strictly ontological sense, refers only to the former, to what is actually now existing.

The teleological construct of a human potentiality that has no actual "being," yet manages to serve as the sole activator of human destiny—and therefore as the infallible guide to psychotherapy as well—is more than a mite confusing. At worst, it encourages us to go around peering into dark corners looking for something which, by our own definition, is not there. At best, it sets us out in pursuit of something we would not be able to see even if we were lucky enough to catch up with it.

Now there is no harm in talking about things that cannot be seen. We do it all the time. But when we do it we are depending on inferences rather than direct observations. Even the modern materialists, with all their emphasis upon keeping one's eyes open to what is going on, are caught "observing" their inferences now and then, as if, like the dachshund who chased a "strange animal" around a tree, they had bumped into their own constructs. Indeed, if they, or any of us for that matter, were to take full account of themselves from beginning to end they too would likely come to the conclusion that their "direct observations" follow hard on the heels of their own adventures. Thus, in some degree, the observations of the most wide-eyed observer must be regarded as inferential—and therefore constructive—in nature.

It is when we forget this psychological fact that our inferences get in the way of our efforts, for constructs need to be evaluated not so much in terms of their visibility as in terms of what they lead us to do. It is against this criterion that the notion of a guiding human potentiality does us a disservice. We are tempted to go around looking for a certain golden key which, once it has been discovered, will unlock the door to all of human destiny.

Instead of arguing that man's potentialities are the guiding force behind his achievements, it seems more forthright to turn the proposition around and say that man is continually in the process of redefining his potentialities through the sheer audacity of his achievements. Having put the proposition in this way we can take a good look at what man has accomplished thus far and then venture to say something about what generally happens to human hopes and how it is that man's presumed limitations can so effectively block his efforts.

After looking at the unfolding record of man's achievement, one thing we can say is that whatever the range of human potentialities may ultimately turn out to be, there are probably a lot more of them than any individual can, even in his most expansive moments, reasonably hope to exploit in a lifetime. Some possibilities, therefore, have to be abandoned outright. Then there are some talents that one never suspects, although they might have been inferred from his achievements. Or if he does suspect them, they are conceived too late in life for him to do anything about them. Then again, besides these, some objectives are pretty likely to get in the way of others. Any attempt to achieve them negates the contrary ones. This forces the abandonment of still more of one's potentialities. In the end, even if a man carefully defines his objectives in terms of what seem to be his emerging potentialities, there still are limiting choices to be made.

Who is to make them? Stephen Leacock's man, who mounts his horse to ride off in all directions, will eventually find that some of his choices have been made by his horse. In the course of his headlong ride he, willy-nilly, abandons some of his brightest prospects in his galloping pursuit of the obvious. This is a common tragedy, as many a man past 65 realizes, now that he has taken the time to think about it.

Ever since Eden it has been clear that man has capacities for both good and evil, and with them the burdensome yet exciting responsibility of distinguishing between the two, as well as between a lot of more transitive alternatives. The post-Eden man is held responsible even for the decisions of his horse. Most people, I am sure, are more or less convinced of this, in spite of the empathic amorality of their psychotherapists.

But the ontological decision that man must make, the decision to be something, need not be hemmed in by what he presumes are his potentialities, any more than it can be foreordained by them. Just how broad his field of choice is man will never know until he assails the impossible. One thing is sure—if he starts his venture into reality by circumscribing himself with prior assumptions about potentialities, or lack of them, nothing very exciting is going to happen. Rather, the initial question—the point of departure for the genuinely adventuresome person—is, What should he try to be? Or simply, What ought he to be?

I am well aware of the allergy psychologists have for "oughts." This is because many of them regard all commitments as coercive. Perhaps in too many cases their own early commitments proved to be intolerable. But to state our problem the way we have is far less coercive than to argue that man can aspire to nothing more than to be himself. The "ought" we propose is a venturesome "ought," an audacious one. It becomes coercive only when one surrenders his right to state the predicates of his sentences and resigns himself to the "oughts" that others impress upon him. In any case, the initiative in man's enterprises lies with decision and commitment rather than with impulse and fulfillment.

Psychotherapeutic movement can thus be said to get under way when a man starts questioning for himself what his immediate objectives may be and is thus led to initiate actions that challenge whatever previous notions he may have held as to what his limitations were. This is the first step in redefining his potentialities. He sets out to be what he is not.

The long-range objective of the psychotherapeutic effort is an extension of this first step. It, as well as that of any other worthwhile human undertaking, is not to conform to oneself, whole or fragment; or to society, lay or ordained; or to nature, whatever the latest version of that happens to be. This objective is for man continually to determine for himself what is worth the price he is going to end up paying for one thing or another anyway, to keep moving toward what he is not—surmounting obstacles as best he can—and to keep on doing both as long as he has anything to invest. To render and utilize technical aid in this ontological venture is the special transaction we call "psychotherapy."

EXPERIENCE AND VITALITY

The human enterprise does not follow a Euclidian line from point A to point B. No matter how carefully a man lays his plans and no matter how earnestly he announces his commitments, both plans and commitments are, almost from the very moment they are initiated, subject to reappraisal. An adolescent seeking to become a man, or a student aspiring to become a scholar, will change his notions about manhood or scholarship many times before he attains much of the status of either. This is not to say that his original plans were futile or that he must be unfaithful to his commitments. Even a plan which is abandoned outright may have served a purpose in leading one to the point where he could see more clearly what he should have planned instead.

So also with a commitment. A person who, from experience, knows what it means to be dedicated to a cause—even a bad one—may thus come to judge for himself what on earth is worth the ultimate price he must pay, that price being, of course, his own life. It is hard to say this of one who has never ventured to have the experience of commitment, although he too will certainly end up paying the same ultimate price, whether he wants to or not. And suppose, from his vantage point, the experienced man sees for the first time what lies beyond his original objectives and then commits himself to that instead, thus discarding the ill-phrased literalisms of his earlier commitments. Can it be said that he has proved disloyal to his undertakings? I think not.

I am not saying that it is experience that changes man, but rather, that man changes himself through a process called experience. Nor would I want to say, as the stimulus-response psychologists do, that external events shape the man. That denies human vitality altogether and reduces life to a prolonged reverberation of outside occurrences.

Psychotherapy needs to be understood as an experience, and experience, in turn, understood as a process that reflects human vitality. Thus to define psychotherapy as a form of treatment—something that one person does to another—is misleading. Psychotherapy takes place when one person makes constructive use of another who has offered himself for that purpose. The professional skills of the therapist, as well as much of his repertory as an experienced human being, are brought into the transaction. He offers as much of both as he thinks can be used. But it is the client who weaves them into the fabric of his own experience.

Just as human progress, as we have said, follows a circuitous course rather than a Euclidian line, so should personal experience be regarded as a circuitous affair. The teacher who had had only one year of experience—repeated 29 times—had indeed made little headway in life. Human progress is not accomplished so much by the persistence of effort along a single line as by the exploration of paths leading to fresh vantage points from whence one may chart and rechart his course.

Experience, then, is not measured by years or the accumulation of events all handled in the same way, but by the revisions of one's outlook, revisions, of course, that take into account the outcomes of prior commitments. If one merely vacillates without taking into account what has occurred as a result of his previous ventures, or if he fails to put forth any serious effort to gain new perspectives, he may, to be sure, acquire some interesting scars to show his grandchildren, but he will end up surrendering his life without ever having experienced it.

What we have said about experience and the essential role of human vitality goes for psychotherapy too. Being a form of experience, it, too, follows an exploratory course, with many reappraisals based on the outcomes of yesterday's commitments. Goals get changed and changed again. Yesterday's useful insights become today's stubborn resistances and tomorrow's trivial cliches. The enterprise into which the client plunged himself last week may mark a crucial turning point in his life, long awaited by his therapist, yet it may be something that ought never to be repeated. Indeed, some of life's most precious moments ought never to be repeated. This, too, is one of the considerations to be kept in mind in any attempt to state the goals of psychotherapy.

HISTORICISM IN THE PSYCHOLOGY OF THE OPTIMAL MAN

To put it simply, it is not what the past has done to a man that counts so much as it is what the man does with his past. The psychotherapist can scarcely fail to be amazed at how differently two of his clients may make use of what has happened to them. If he is alert he will be aware of wide differences in the way they make use of him too. Men are not so much shaped by events—including what the psychotherapist says during interviews—as they are shaped by the meaning they ascribe to such noises. This is not to say that one is perfectly free to ignore what is going on. He is not. But man is always free to reconstrue that which he may not deny.

It is true that events of the past intrude themselves into our present and that to some extent, what we experience at any one moment is only the current phase of a process that began a long time ago, and will be likely to continue for a long time to come. But more and more, man takes a hand in directing the course the process takes. The history of things that happened before he was born may point to the circumstances in which one now finds himself, but they do not dictate what he may do about them. What a man does with his history and its legacies is up to his own ingenuity and whether or not he wishes to exercise it.

The phenomenological psychologists, of whom I certainly am not one, usually take the view that it is only the experience of the passing instant that is of essential psychological significance. But I would argue that it is the whole story of mankind that is of greatest psychological significance. It is significant, not because it tells us what has happened to man, but because it tells us what has happened by the hand of man. I am talking about a history that tells us what man has done, not one that claims to say what he was made to do. Once history is interpreted in this way we need not limit ourselves to the phenomenal moment in order to see man in dynamic perspective.

While the historical record provides us with a version of what man has actually done, it does not set the limits on what he could have done, nor on what he can do, nor on what he will do. The story of all science, for example, is, as I see it, a story of man's past psychological efforts unfolded in vast perspective. Those efforts produced, among other great things, what we know as the body of science, in itself an amazing display.

But this is not the most exciting part of the story that history has to tell us. This is only prologue. Infinitely more exciting is what potentiality these audacious feats suggest is locked up in the unrealized future of man. While the man of yesterday was developing a physicalistic science that tested itself by experiments and its ability to predict their outcomes, he was, without intending to do so, stating the basic postulates of a psychology for the man of tomorrow. Slowly he demonstrated not merely that events could be predicted, but, what was vastly more important, that he was a predictor. It was not only that hypotheses could be generated, experiments controlled, anticipations checked against realizations, and theories revised, but that he—man—was a hypothesizer, an experimenter, an anticipator, a critical observer, and an artful composer of new systems of thought. What he did, physically, portrayed what he was, psychologically.

Out of the saga of human achievement we can shape a postulate for a massive psychology of man. It runs like this: a person's processes are psychologically channelized by the ways in which he anticipates events. The bold pursuit of inferences that follow up on this postulate can serve to trace for us the outlines of a theory of personality we may call the psychology of personal constructs.

None of this is to say that the factual substance of our present-day science draws any outer boundaries around man's capabilities, nor does it convince me that the scientists I know are optimal men. On the contrary, if examined closely, what man has accomplished in science, and in other forms of scholarly enterprise, points to the presence of psychological processes that have never been fully unleashed. The history of mankind, whether particularly scientific or generally literary, throws psychological light on the processes of man; it is not an iron chain of events that binds him forever to what he is—to that, and no more.

Some students, impressed by the accomplishments of scientists, try to make the most of themselves by acting like their heroes. Acting like a scientist is child's play. What one observes in scientific effort is not something to be imitated outright, but rather something to be examined and construed. Properly construed, it may open new vistas that no scientist has yet envisioned.

As one abandons childlike imitation of scientists and launches into the exploration of the horizons opened up by them he is not likely to be regarded as a fellow scientist. Especially is he not likely to be so regarded by the psychologists of our day who are themselves still pretty much in the imitative stage of their mental development. But no matter; whatever one does that turns out well in the end is likely to be claimed by the "scientists" eventually.

Making use of the record of past events, whether in one's own biography or in the history of human progress, is not, then, a matter of looking for something to imitate, any more than it is a matter of reading the writing on the wall. The value of the record lies in its being subject to construction, for it is by construing events, not by subordinating oneself to them, that light is thrown on human possibilities not yet envisioned.

In psychotherapy, particularly, it makes a great deal of difference how the historical past is used. A therapist who is aware of the sweep of man's accomplishments, as well as what particular men have done about their handicaps, will envision the goals of his efforts quite differently from one who thinks in terms of disease entities, childhood traumata, or the closed economies of psychodynamic systems. As for the client, if he is one who regards his past as the successively emerging phases of his personal experience, each leading to a new outlook, he will make use of his therapeutic opportunities in a much different way than will one who recounts his past only to show what it has done to him and who looks at other men only to see who can tell him what to do.

THEORIES OF PSYCHOLOGISTS AND MEN

So far what has been said is that the goals of psychotherapy cannot be taken as self-evident, that man must determine them for himself, that they are subject to continual revision, even during the course of the interview series, and that, in any effort to reach goals, the past is something to be utilized rather than to be undone. This is background for saying next that the goals of psychotherapy cannot be entirely separated from the human processes and stages through which they are to be pursued. But in saying this we have simply elaborated our basic postulate: a person's processes are psychologically channelized by the ways in which he anticipates events.

Perhaps it is clear by now that we see no valuable distinction between the theorizing of psychologists, who may want to be seen as scientists, and their clients, who usually prefer to be seen as human. Both may be regarded as scientists, if you please, as well as men, for both seek to anticipate events. Both have their theories, in terms of which they attempt to structure the onrush of occurrences. Both hypothesize. Both experiment. Both observe. Both reluctantly revise their predictions in the light of what they observe, on the one hand, and the extent of their theoretical investment, on the other.

Nor do we see psychotherapists as applied scientists, in the sense of exploiting what the pure scientists have found out, that is, using science in an unscientist-like manner. For us the course of therapy, like the course of all human enterprise, including scientific enterprise, is essentially exploratory, both for the therapist and for his client. This means that therapy is fraught with revisions, revisions that are undertaken by both client and therapist and by the two of them together. In short, psychotherapy is itself a form of experience, as we have defined experience.

Thus it is that the objectives of the psychotherapist must include the skillful facilitation of those human processes upon which all of us, scientist and client alike, depend as we move from stage to stage in the great human adventure. Goals, processes, and stages are often indistinguishable from each other. Indeed, the initiation and continuation of a lifetime effort to conjure up ever-fresh visions of what is worthwhile is itself a goal of psychotherapy. This is not the kind of goal at which you can hope to arrive and then stop looking further. It is, instead, a continuing series of commitments and revisions of commitments. Most of all, it is a commitment to experience, with the stock-taking that honest experience requires. The person who profits from the therapeutic transaction is one who has started to make headway in this ceaseless enterprise.

Furthermore, it is probably futile, without due allowance for the circuitous routes man must follow, to specify the ultimate goals he hopes to attain, except, possibly, in some such imprecise terms as "heaven," "brotherhood of man," or "Utopia." Who knows where man will eventually arrive? Certainly not the certified therapists! Thus for man, whether he is seen as on his own or as clutching the hand of his somewhat befuddled therapist, ends and means often turn out to be indistinguishable from each other.

The tangible end of therapy is to implement the means by which the ultimate and intangible end of mankind's efforts can hope to be achieved. This is to say that while the therapist cannot quite put his finger on what his client should eventually achieve, he can at least put his finger on the processes by which his client might hope to achieve it. And he can implement those processes without knowing their ultimate outcome. To do this much is a perfectly tangible end of his psychotherapeutic effort. For what kind of a therapist would claim he knew where the ultimate end of man lies, or even what epitaph should be written on his client's tombstone? At best, all the wise therapist can hope to say is, "There, at last I think my client and I are hot on the trail of something." As for the client, at the end of his last psychotherapeutic session he can hope to say little more than something like this himself. Indeed, if he tries to say too much more than this, he probably needs to schedule some further sessions—with another therapist.

So the way a person lives his life cannot be divorced from how he anticipates the future (our basic postulate again), and vice versa. A man spends his time making as much money as he can. What does it mean? Perhaps he is trying to insure his family against every conceivable hazard, or himself from the haunting fear of disclosing his own insufficiency. Whatever it is, his money-making makes sense only in the light of his anticipations. But it also works the other way around. He may end up his life as a wealthy, grasping man, himself his family's worst hazard and, as a person, revealed as insufficient in more ways than when he started. The goal he so faithfully pursued turns out to be defined, not only by his ambition, but also by what he did to fulfill it. So for us all! The events we attempt to anticipate may turn out to be contaminated by what we did to ancitipate them. In the words of our fundamental postulate, a person's processes are channelized by the ways in which he anticipates events.

The same goes for psychologists, who are known to have human characteristics too. Two therapists may state their goals in a similar way, yet have little in common, either in their methods or in what they eventually accept as confirming their predictions. For example, one American psychologist I know places primary psychological value on human "efficiency," while another says he hopes to aid in the fruition of a "fully functioning person." The two statements appear to be similar. Yet from listening to the two men I am convinced that what they would do to achieve their goal and when they would think they had reached it differ vastly.

Indeed, what one would do to his client would, I am sure, be considered unconscionable by the other, and, perhaps, vice versa. My point, therefore, is that psychotherapeutic goals have to be understood as part of the psychologist's functional involvement with a theoretical position in which his working assumptions about the nature of mankind, and of his client, have been made to stand out as clearly as possible. What I am saying about understanding the psychotherapist is very similar to what I said about understanding man in general.

So how shall we state the objectives of psychotherapy? It is obvious by now that I do not intend to make up a list of "goals" to be checked off against the names of my colleagues who also write about psychotherapy, though from other points of view. Without a clear understanding of their theoretical positions it is impossible to know what they mean when they recite their own lists. So also for me and my client. Without some clear understanding of the fellow's outlook, that is to say, without some notion of the way he personally construes events of his past and present, it is uncertain what he will be doing to attain the goals either he or I envision, and what contaminated meaning those goals will eventually come to have. Goals can be distorted in the most grotesque ways by the means one employs in his effort to achieve them.

ONE PSYCHOLOGIST'S ASSUMPTIONS

We turn now to the things that must be said before any further statement of my own therapeutic goals can be fully understood. I believe that everything man does follows lines laid down in his effort to anticipate what will happen. We have already stated this as our basic postulate, though in somewhat different words.

Since this is our logical point of departure it is important that there be no misunderstanding about what such a statement means to us. One's anticipation of the onrush of events may not be expressed definitively; it may be expressed as a posture toward the future, possibly a future we would prefer not to portray too clearly or too realistically. A friend of mine, while driving her car, customarily closes her eyes when she gets caught in a tight spot. This is an anticipatory act; she suspects something may happen that she would prefer not to see. So far, it hasn't happened, though it is hard to understand why. Fortunately, in recent years she has given up driving a car; and that, too, is an anticipatory posture. Neither of her postures can be said to be very practical, but it would be hard to say neither of them was anticipatory in nature. As a matter of fact they seem very clearly to me to be anticipatory.

Most people anticipate death in a somewhat similar manner. This certainly does not mean that they go shopping for bargains in coffins. But in some persons especially we can see a great deal of what they do and say as an anticipatory posture toward death. Like my friend, they seem both to invite it to come and get them to try to postpone it as long as possible, even to the extent of denying themselves the full life.

If we press this part of our theorizing into areas at the fringe of psychology's normal range of convenience we can say that contractions of the stomach, the beating of the heart, or the drooling of Pavlov's dog can easily enough be regarded as anticipatory. There is no reason to limit the notion of anticipation to what can be verbally communicated or logically projected.

We can, if we wish, extend this construct of anticipation to some other frontiers. We can speculate about the implications of saying that anticipation is one of the characteristic features of man, or saying that man is such and such a creature who does his best to cement the future to the past and thus grasp time in his own two fists, a Herculean task if there ever was one!

Some people are led to believe that man, in letting himself be guided by his ways of anticipating events, renders himself subservient to things that have not happened yet. But this is not true. Events do not control man's behavior before they occur, any more than they do afterward. The control of his behavior remains man's own prerogative, though limited, of course, by the amount of ingenuity he brings into play. If events, either past or expected, appear to manipulate a man it is only because, so far, he has figured out only one way to cope with them. He will continue to dance to the tune he thinks he hears them play until he contrives some other way of listening for the succession of notes.

Man never waits to see what will happen; he always looks to see what will happen. Even my motorist friend is looking for something, though she shuts her eyes to do it. Many of us close our eyes when we are looking for something, though not usually when we are looking for an opening in freeway traffic. While man always looks to see what will happen, he is occasionally surprised out of his wits by what turns up. But if he had merely waited I doubt that he could ever have been surprised—not even faintly amused. Sometimes, to be sure, he is caught looking intently in the wrong direction. And there is many a time when he fails to be surprised because he overlooks what is going on under his nose.

All of this is, of course, my own particular assumption about the nature of man. Moreover, it is the way I, too, look to see what will happen, for, unlike most psychologists I know, who view themselves as scientists and their subjects as something else, my theory of personality applies to me as well as to people I don't like. It is the way I look to see what is going on in psychotherapy. It works moderately well, so far. I anticipate it will work better after I have explored its implications further.

While right now this anticipatory approach seems like a particularly reasonable way to go about the job of being a psychologist, especially a psychotherapist, undoubtedly I will change my mind in some ways, for changing one's mind as a result of pursuing his commitments is, as I have already said, an essential feature of honest human experience. Just where I will end up with this business I cannot foresee, but at least, as the reader may all too readily agree, my posture is one of anticipating some changes I cannot yet spell out. But if I am to describe the goals of psychotherapy as I see them today, it is imperative that the reader know something about my present assumptions, tentative though they may be, and that he not accuse me of failing to make any commitment to these assumptions. I am determined to see where they lead, and, having seen where they lead, I am equally determined to modify or abandon them in the light of what my quest reveals.

A PSYCHOLOGICAL DEFINITION OF LIFE

While our topic is the psychology of the optimal man, with particular reference to the goals of psychotherapy, it will do no harm to extend ourselves for a few moments and talk about life. This takes us outside the range of our assignment, and perhaps outside the range of psychology. But if we can venture a definition of life, whether human or otherwise, perhaps we can introduce an assumption of such far-reaching significance that what we attempt to say later about man in particular will be enhanced and clarified.

Let us start out with a definition, or an assumption, if you prefer, though all definitions are assumptions. Let us say that life is a way of using the present to link the future with the past in some original fashion. Now that we have started, let us pursue the implications of what we have said. We can say next that without life the present makes no difference in the future; only the past governs what will happen. Since, without life, there is no active anticipation of the future, the notion of a future does not even stand for anything until after it is too late to call it "future" any more. And without a future the present makes no sense either, for what is the present but the boundary between past and future? No future, no present! And without a present there is no point of observation from which to differentiate time.

Already we can see some psychotherapeutic implications of these extra-psychological inferences. Some clients do make only minimal use of the present for anticipating their future. Most psychotherapists have dealt with such a client. He seems to have only the most precarious foothold on this vantage point for looking out on what goes on. He is disengaged from reality. Even his life appears to be held in a state of suspension.

But to return to our extra-psychological discussion of the nature of life. We could define it otherwise. We could describe it, as many psychologists describe man's behavior, simply as the outcome of past events. But to do this is to lose one's grip on the future, particularly the future of human affairs, and, through the concurrent loss of the present, to deny oneself the vantage point for viewing or doing anything at all. I do not like the idea of giving up all this, not even to be called a scientist. It is too much like giving up the human enterprise in order to make of man something utterly predictable. But if the human enterprise is to be abandoned to the sequelae of past events, why bother to predict anything? If I am to give up one or the other, I would prefer to give up stimulus-response psychology, except, possibly, for explaining trivialities, or in those moments when I am in too much of a hurry to pay attention to what I am saying.

Everything we try to say about life seems to reflect upon psychology. Let us continue, therefore, to speculate about life. Suppose we were to take our fundamental postulate, the one we intended as a starting point for a psychology of man, and make a biological postulate out of it. Let us have a try. We shall then say something like this: It is the nature of life to be channelized by the ways events are anticipated. While I am not prepared to defend this assumption with great skill or the weight of much evidence, it does intrigue me and I cannot help but wonder where we would be led if we ventured to start from such a premise. Particularly, I wonder what a psychotherapist would be led to do or what goals he would envision for the outcomes of his efforts.

Salivation, for example, takes place in a manner that suggests the anticipation of food, or perhaps hunger—I am not sure which. Perhaps what is anticipated is an activity we call eating. Whatever it indicates, Pavlov seems to have demonstrated it and there is no reason we should not be grateful even though we are not quite sure what it was he demonstrated. The momentary rest the heart takes between beats can be construed as preparing it for its next effort. That, also, is consistent with observation.

But we must keep it clear in our minds, as long as we are following the implications of our tentative biological postulate, that it is not the impending event that makes a creature's mouth water or its heart rest up. It is the beast itself which does those things, and it does them as it does because this is in line with its particular ways of anticipating events. If the events were anticipated differently its heart and glands might very well function differently. Whether the anticipated events actually do take place later or not, for example, whether the food arrives or the next beat occurs, is another matter.

This is not the place to press any argument about "lower order processes" in great detail, or to answer the frequently asked question, "But does Personal Construct Theory have any practical application to rats?" It is sufficient for a paper dealing with the goals of psychotherapy merely to suggest the notion that possibly, quite apart from psychology, life itself is essentially an anticipation of events to come. This is a more venturesome postulate than the one from which the psychology of personal constructs was launched. But from it may spring some additional ideas about the whole of psychology, as well as about the goals of psychotherapy.

It follows, for example, from such a super-assumption that an overall technical goal of psychotherapy might be to enhance this essential feature of life by making the most of man's moment-to-moment expectations. This is to say that psychotherapy should make one feel that he has come alive. This, presumably, would be a good thing to have happen. But the expression really does not mean much unless behind it lies some assumption about the nature of life, such as is embodied in the biological postulate we have suggested.

One may, of course, question the appropriateness of our assumption on the grounds that it does not seem to correspond to our personal experience. For example, what about those rare and delectable hours when we can lie in the grass and look up at the fleecy summer clouds? Do we not then take life, savoring each moment as it comes without rudely trying to outguess it? Does one not feel very much alive on such occasions? Certainly! But this, too, is an anticipatory posture. To be sure, it is not the frantic apprehension of popping little events. It is rather a composed anticipation of a slowly drifting universe of great and benign proportions.

Still, what we have managed to say about the anticipatory nature of life, and the goal of therapy it implies, remains much too general. Perhaps the specifics it embraces will become clearer after we have returned to the line of inference stemming directly from our psychological postulate.

CRITERIA FOR A GOOD THEORY: SCIENTIFIC OR PERSONAL

A theory is a useful device, useful because one can derive from it all sorts of consistent notions about how to proceed in a variety of situations. Everybody has at least one tucked away somewhere, although many are reluctant to exhibit them, and some even deny that they have them, insisting instead that all their notions are revealed to them by direct observation of nature. I suppose one could regard this claim as itself a theory, but I intend to avoid any dispute that might ensue from pressing the point.

Generally it is supposed that a theory must be a comprehensive formulation; that is to say, it should be a statement of the essential feature of a large family of assumptions. There is some difference of opinion as to whether these assumptions all have to be logically inescapable in the theoretical formulation, or if the theory need serve only to provoke a fresh lot of semieducated guesses about the nature of things, without coming right out and saying precisely what these guesses should be.

But whatever the opinion, the fact of the matter is that every theory, scientific or personal, has embedded in it a great many assumptions that are not initially apparent to those who read it—or even very clear at first to the person who formulates it. These embedded assumptions are likely to have much to do with what eventually happens to the theory and the people who use it; this is true whether it is a theory used publicly by a group of scientists or a personal one used intuitively by a certain man in managing his daily affairs. All of this makes one of the objectives of psychotherapy the exploration of hidden assumptions in the client's construct system.

It is tempting to say that the foremost requirement of a good theory is that it should be true. But, in any literal sense, this is an impractical specification. We already know that most of the theories formulated in the past have served their times and proponents only to be displaced by others which, at some later juncture in the course of human thought, seemed better. We have reason to suspect, therefore, that almost any theory we formulate today is going to end up like its predecessors and, sooner or later, be supplanted. If we rejected all theories that were not known to be accurate portrayals of bedrock truth we would find ourselves with nothing to live by.

This is not quite the same as saying there is no truth. It is, rather, grounds for the stand that, whatever the truth is, no one, least of all a scientifically trained psychotherapist, ought to claim that he has quite caught up with it yet. Even if we don't catch up with it, however, each of us can gain on it. And that, too, is something that may hopefully be said of personal theories as well as scientific ones.

Clients approach truth by the same kind of successive approximations that scientists employ. Psychotherapy helps them do it.

Good theorizing does not unwind itself endlessly without being checked. To test a theory one acts in accordance with its implications to see what will happen. In a broad sense, this is what we mean by scientific experimentation, though to be good science we think there should also be appropriate controls to discipline the conclusions we draw. If, under the aegis of a certain new theory, events become more predictable and many desirable things can be made to happen that failed to occur before, we are justified in saying the theory has a good measure of truth in it.

But experimentation is no special prerogative of the accredited scientist. It is, first of all, man's device. And because it is a human technique for getting closer to truth—employed more or less by all of us—it becomes the concern of any proper psychotherapeutic effort.

A theory, then, scientific or personal, ought to cover a lot of situations, to be fertile with coherent practical suggestions about what one might do in those situations, to be a reasonable approximation to the truth, serving the person at his present stage of development, and should always lead to constructive experimentation and revision. When we say specifically that these are the criteria of a good personal theory we are establishing some further objectives for psychotherapy to attain.

It should be noted that we have not said that insight is a goal of psychotherapy. That implies catching up with the truth. Too often, when such a notion is impressed upon a client, he functions well enough for a while after "completion" of his analysis, but eventually bogs down in some orthodoxy.

PSYCHOTHERAPEUTIC GOALS AND PSYCHOLOGICAL PROCESSES

Already the point has been made that psychotherapeutic goals cannot be appraised independently of the processes by which one seeks to attain them. Nor can either processes or goals be fully understood apart from the deeply underlying constructions employed by the client and his therapist. We have therefore discussed the underlying theories that men live by, whether they claim to be scientists or not. Then we discussed our own, and the emphasis it places upon anticipatory processes, very broadly conceived, in the life of man. And we have mentioned, too, the part that experimentation plays in checking one's construction of events, whether that construction is scientific or personal.

But our discussion has necessarily been very general, for when one brings up the matter of goals in psychotherapy he immediately involves himself in making value judgments and these tend to be more philosophical than technical in nature. Nevertheless, to understand what goals I value most, it should be helpful to mention more of the particular processes through which I think these goals can be attained.

In generating the theory of the psychology of personal constructs out of its basic postulate we are led by a series of inferences that need not be detailed here to say that one's ways of anticipating events can be regarded as his personal constructs.

Each construct is a two-ended affair, that is, it is a reference axis rather than a punctate designation of an object or an entity. When events are plotted against such an axis or within a system of such personal axes alternatives become identified and it becomes possible for a person to make some choices between them.

Only within his personal system is one ever free to make a choice in his own behalf, and only along the coordinate lines he himself has managed to erect is he ever free to initiate movement. Man's freedom, then, can be said to have ontological meaning only within the anticipatory framework he has devised; his personal construct system defines the only liberties he is ever able to claim. Adam and his girl friend found this out when they decided to look into the matter of good and evil. They shifted the basis of their actions from obedience to knowledge, thus achieving freedom and all the responsibilities that go with it.

There is no sense in prodding a client toward the choice of a therapeutic goal that does not yet fall within his coordinate system of personal constructs, any more than it would have made sense before The Fall to drag Adam and Eve off to a revival meeting—they wouldn't have known what all the shouting was about. One of the intermediate goals of psychotherapy, then, is to help the client devise a construct system through which he is free to move toward something worthwhile.

Given a pair of alternatives adequately defined within a client's personal construct system, how does one know which he will choose? It may seem doubtful at first, but I am inclined to believe he will always make what may be called the "elaborative choice." That is to say he will choose that alternative, aligned to one of his construct dimensions, which appears to provide the greater opportunity for the further elaboration of his anticipatory system.

Two men will not necessarily make the same choice even though they may construe the alternatives the same way, nor will one man make the same choice at one time that he makes at another. It is still the man that makes the choice, not the alternatives that dictate it to him. At a certain stage in one's development it may be more promising to choose to do something that will help him define his position more clearly and thus consolidate his gains, just as a military commander who has seized the initiative must often pause to consolidate his position. But at other times one will choose to extend his system so it will embrace more of the unknown and bring more of the future within his grasp. The two kinds of action, because they are both efforts to develop the anticipatory system, are really not so different. Both are examples of the psychological principle of the elaborative choice. Of course, it seems that some clients are always consolidating their positions and others are always overextending them. But these are differences in strategy; the basic process remains the same.

Another process question is, Finding himself caught up in shifting circumstances, how does one decide what to do? This is the fix that most clients are in when they come running for psychological assistance. But in a less spectacular way it is a fix in which each of us finds himself a thousand times a day. The first step, of course, is to construe what we see. To do this we go through a circumspection phase, sometimes in a split second, without actually spelling out anything to ourselves, and sometimes in a period unduly prolonged by see-saw efforts to define the issue. This is a period of "trying on for size" the various constructs available in our personal repertory.

If one does not have many constructs circumspection may not take long, and he may achieve the somewhat enviable reputation of being "a man of action." If circumstances appear to be changing faster than he can keep up with them one may plunge through this phase of his decision cycle. This is the way to get the reputation of being impulsive. The Hamlets of this world, with their complex repertories, may not be able to tolerate the delay a full exploration of their repertories would require, and sometimes they may unexpectedly act on impulse before their complex circumspection process has finished weighing the issues.

In any case, the next step in the decision cycle is preemption. One construct is allowed to preempt the situation and define the pair of alternatives between which the person must make his choice. From then on, unless he backs up, the issue appears—whatever else may have some applicability to the situation—to be "this and this only."

Finally comes the commitment, and at this point the principle of the elaborative choice takes over. The whole decision cycle may be called the C-P-C cycle, after the terms we have used for its phases: circumspection, preemption, and choice. One of the intermediate objectives of psychotherapy is to help the client make appropriate use of this cycle whenever important action is required.

NEW CONSTRUCTS FOR OLD

New constructs are obviously invented, not discovered. But how? There are several ways, but one of the most interesting is through a process we have termed the creativity cycle. Here a warning is in order. If one defines construing as a process that follows conventional principles of logic and conceptualization, or if he has already classified the psychology of personal constructs in his own mind as "a cognitive theory," what follows won't make much sense.

Some construing is consistent. It may not be logical but it can still be consistent. Of two objects one is always construed as darker than the other, or heavier, or more beautiful; that is to say, whenever the construct dimension is applied to a pair of objects the outcome is the same. This is tight construction. Language labels, for example, once they are pinned on constructs, tend to tighten their usage. Mathematics is a particular language system that seems to have the maximum tightening effect. Of course, mathematics is supposed to be logical, too, but that is another matter. Tightening may or may not be a good thing. So may language. Certainly there are moments in psychotherapy when the conventionalities of language get in the way of the client's efforts, and there are other moments when they establish just the base he needs for extending his probe of the unknown.

But there is loosened construction too. The inconsistency of the dreams one tries to recall in the morning is a good example. Language may play a part in such dreams but it usually fails to keep their construction tight. Some of us don't have to be asleep to construe loosely. We can even make our spoken words clatter along with our loose construction in a way that would give Noah Webster the jitters.

Actually, construction can be tight or loose, regardless of whether words are tied to constructs or not. Many of the so-called physiological processes, which follow construction to our way of thinking just as much as the so-called conscious processes do, involve very tight construing—the regular beating of the heart, for example. On the other hand, free association, a supposedly conscious verbal process, has a loosening effect that many of us have found quite helpful in our short-sighted moments.

When we construe tightly we can subject our constructs to experimentation and to various other kinds of tests, but it is very hard to rotate them into new positions so as to get any new slant on our personal affairs. A tight construct tends to be brittle, and it stands firm or is shattered by the outcome of the predictions it invokes. It is almost impossible to test a loose construct, or, to put it better, a construct loosely used. In an elastic sort of way it seems to apply to almost everything—or to almost nothing—that happens. That, too, can be good, for if every idea we ever laid hold of remained rigid and either stood firm or collapsed in the face of every test it got, mental process would all be guesswork, and any progress that happened to take place in human thinking would depend on the sheer accident of hitting on something useful.

The creativity cycle we envision is one that employs both loosening and tightening in a coordinated fashion. The cycle starts with a loosened phase in which construction is vague, elastic, and wavering. Out of this fertile chaos shapes begin to emerge and one seeks patiently to give them definite form until they are tight enough to talk about and to test. This notion of creativity does not suggest that one simply alternates between loose thinking and tight thinking, as he may appear to alternate between nighttime thinking and daytime thinking. These are not simply two separate exercises, but phases of the same creative process, just as I am convinced dreaming and alert critical thinking are essential phases of the basic process by which we keep ourselves from ending up as schizophrenics or automatons. It is when man tries too hard to separate his loosened construction from his tightened construction that he becomes unhinged and loses his ability to live creatively.

None of this has anything much to do with "creativity" as a particular trait possessed by "gifted" people, or that stultifying preoccupation which has been misnamed "the psychology of individual differences." We are talking about a human process, not about discriminable classes of mankind. Of course, we are willing to concede that some of us reach further into the outer chaos that surrounds us, and some further into the cosmos we have carved for ourselves than others. And it is true, we know, that some go "loose" and stay that way, as, for example, those patients of early psychoanalytic technique who succumbed to its persistent loosening demands. It is true, also, that some of us get so tight and literal that when our thinking is finally shattered by its predictive failures we collapse into a protective looseness from which we dare not recover. But these are not traits; these are predicaments. They are some of the unfortunate outcomes of the psychological process all of us invoke when we try to solve our problems.

One of the important interim goals of psychotherapy is to help the client make optimal use of his ability to think both loosely and tightly and to employ those two phases of the creativity cycle in a proper relationship to each other. Moreover, therapy should enable a person to span an optimal range of loosening and tightening without breaking up the process into disjunctive thinking.

ORCHESTRATION OF PSYCHOTHERAPEUTIC TECHNIQUES

Unlike most personality theories, the psychology of personal constructs does not limit itself to any pet psychotherapeutic technique. More than any other theory, it calls for an orchestration of many techniques according to the therapist's awareness of the variety and nature of the psychological processes by which man works toward his ends.

In presenting the goals of psychotherapy as we see them we have laid initial stress on man as a creature who forges his own destiny rather than allowing himself to drift with the tide of human affairs. The term "personal constructs" refers to the guidelines by which he pinpoints anticipated events and along which he establishes the dimensions of the freedom he hopes to exercise and the pathways of movement he seeks to follow. There are many interesting processes man uses in reaching his ends, some of which we have attempted to describe. All of them fall within the purview of the technically versatile psychotherapist.

Man uses many kinds of resources too in attaining his goals. One such resource which men occasionally find useful is a psychotherapist. In addition to the goals that his client ought to seek, however, the therapist needs to have a goal of his own which he ought to try to use well.

CHAPTER 3

The Exploration of Consciousness: Personal Construct Intervention with Children

A.T. Ravenette

By way of introduction, let me present an excerpt from an interview with Jane. Jane is a 13-year-old girl who is living with a family that is well-known to the Social Services Department because of her mother, who is chronically depressed. Jane attends school sporadically and with considerable reluctance, and it is for this reason that she was referred to the Child Guidance Clinic. In the process of systematically exploring some of her ways of making sense of school, it became apparent that Jane felt she was the kind of girl whose thoughts, feelings, and actions made no difference to anyone at all. Since such a state suggests a denial of effective social interaction, I decided to explore it more fully. She agreed that she was the kind of girl who felt she made no difference to anyone, but would prefer to be the opposite. In other words, there was an indication of some need for change. Since, however, the solution was to some extent in her own hands, there was the possibility of some advantage in remaining isolated. I asked her, therefore, to tell me what was "bad" and "good," "good" and "bad" about each of these two states.

To make no difference to anyone is *bad* because "that makes you a child of air." To make no difference is *good* because "then they don't treat me bigger than everybody else. I just like to be like everybody else." To make a difference is *good* because "everyone knows I'm there." To make a difference is *bad* because "they might think I'm like somebody I'm really not. They might think I'm big."

I would like you to consider for a moment the complexity, scope, and poetry of Jane's answers to these very simple questions. If you sense a little of the quality contained in this extract and retain a memory of it throughout this paper, you will have a key to what I am trying to say.

I have started with a specific instance from practice and shall follow with an extended theoretical discussion about my twin themes of consciousness and theory. In the second part of the paper I shall reverse the balance by giving a detailed account of an interview followed by a very short restatement, by way of quotation, of my two generalities. The centerpiece will show the relationship between the Personal Construct Theory of George Kelly, and both theory and practice.

CONSCIOUSNESS

"When I once told a friend that it was my intention to explain consciousness, he exclaimed, 'But consciousness is everything!' After thinking about it, I agreed with him" (Deikman, 1973).

It is my suspicion that if any one concept has underwritten the theory and practice of psychotherapy in child guidance (and therefore the prescriptive rights as to who should or should not practice psychotherapy), that concept would be "the unconscious" together with its elaboration "unconscious motivation." Doubtless at the time Freud formulated the concept it was both a necessary and appropriate reaction to an excessive reliance on rationality (which is not its opposite). Unfortunately, the consequent overvaluation led it to be used as a key explanatory concept for both the height of man's creativity and the depths of his iniquity. With the passage of time such explanatory excursions have been found wanting, but the corresponding revaluing of consciousness has been late in developing.

My immediate concern is to look at the *conscious vs. unconscious* dichotomy insofar as it has practical, rather than conceptual, implications. The underlying theme in this pair of opposites is "knowing" and "being aware" on the one hand, "not knowing" and "not being aware" on the other. Although these expressions refer to psychological processes, the adjective "unconscious" has, by way of the metaphor "unconscious mind," been changed into a noun, "the unconscious." It is instructive that although the expression "the unconscious" has passed into common language, no comparable metamorphosis has taken place for the expression "conscious."

I would hold it to be axiomatic that no person can ever be fully *conscious* of all of his psychological or physical processes. Nor can he ever be fully aware of all that he knows. He is therefore always *unconscious* of many things. It does not follow, however, that there is some entity in reality which can be labeled "the unconscious," and to infer that such an entity exists is one of the tricks that language often plays on us. Unfortunately, its usage as a noun leads to a distortion in thinking through the concretization of what are, in fact, hypotheses. That of which we are unconscious is not experienceable and, as Govinda (1977) says: "A reality that is not experienceable is only an abstract concept, a product of our speculation, a hypothesis."

This semantic confusion, although very serious in its own right, is of less importance than the lack of balance when the notion "consciousness" is relegated to the background because of the corresponding overemphasis and over-reliance on "the unconscious."

In the first place, consciousness itself is undervalued. What a person knows and the sense he makes of things take second place to what some other person—the therapist, for example—knows, namely unconscious contents and unconscious processes. Invariably, however, these unconscious contents and processes are theory based in the mind of the therapist, not experientially based in the client—they cannot be if they are unconscious. I might put this more aphoristically: "If I wholeheartedly and deeply adhere to the notion and power of 'the unconscious,' then the contents of my 'unconscious' are to be found in the 'conscious' mind of my therapist. Unfortunately he won't keep quiet about it.'' If, in fact, we give primacy to unconscious factors for explanation, interpretation, and treatment, it is patently of little relevance to carry out deep and systematic inquiries into a person's consciousness.

In the second place, and perhaps surprisingly, the complexity which the client actually is, tends to be ignored. Descriptions of a person that are given in terms of unconscious processes are indeed often very complex. The complexity, however, is complexity of theory, not of the person. Moreover, since any theory reflects a simplified version of reality, explanations in terms of theory are given basically in relation to a simplified version of the client. The client, in his own reality, is too easily replaced by theoretical abstractions.

In the third place, there is a serious danger, for theoretical rather than experiential reasons, of distrusting the client's use of his own intellect and the veridicality of his own perceptions, especially when these are manifested in his reports of himself and others, and the events of his life. If it is the influence of the unconscious which is all important, then what figures in consciousness must inevitably be distorted either for self-defense or self-delusion.

In essence, the use of ''the unconscious'' and ''unconscious motivation'' places the user at risk, either at best in playing ''one-up'' with his client, or at worst in invalidating the client's sense of self as a knowing person. In my view these criticisms arise from the overvaluing of the unconscious pole of the *conscious versus unconscious* dichotomy, not from the dichotomy itself; my observations on consciousness which follow represent an attempt to redress the balance between the two poles.

Consciousness includes being aware, and being aware means being aware of something.

Consciousness includes knowing, and knowing also implies an organization of what is known.

Because a person is conscious, he is committed to making some sense of the phenomenal world of people, objects, and their interrelationships. He can also reflect on the sense he has already made and in doing so he is opening the way to adaptation or change.

It is easy to be misled about the depth and quality of a person's consciousness. In the ordinary give-and-take of social interchange, we expose these depths only to those we know well. With casual acquaintances and colleagues we will, as likely as not, keep our thoughts to ourselves. And to the person who seeks to intrude on our thoughts and feelings without a recognized right we will give as little as we can get away with. On this basis it is easy to assume that consciousness is shallow and superficial, is made up of the trivia of communicative habits, or the banalities of secondhand attitudes and opinions. If, however, we turn our attention to ourselves, we would need to note that our consciousness includes a vast range of thoughts and feelings, actions and aspirations, hopes and fears, questions and moral judgments. What is true for each of us is no less true for everyone else. We should not assume that a ready verbalization is the hallmark of consciousness, or that because a thing is not expressed we are not aware of it. Nor should we assume that what is asserted is identical to that of which we are conscious. We know from self-experience that consciousness has many levels, and not all are mutually consistent. The relation between what is asserted and what is known is a function of the relationship between speaker and listener. Indeed, I have heard it said that the only two occasions when a person tells the truth is when he trusts and when he wishes to hurt.

Knowledge is also organized. It develops out of the interplay and elaboration of similarities and differences, and the complementarity of opposites. Out of these contrasts arise associations, implications, the awareness of regularities and contingencies, and hence the ability to understand, to anticipate, and to predict. In this sense, consciousness, seen as the organization of knowledge, is also meaning.

Consciousness is also dynamic. Its scope broadens to include new events and deepens to illumine more fully old ones. Its organization changes as an outcome of experience. Just as the organization of knowledge is shaped out of the interplay of opposites, so the organization itself changes out of the interplay between the individual and his environment. The environment here includes all that is felt to be other than self: objects, persons, and their interrelationships. The person also is a part of that network of relationships, as are the contents of knowledge he has of himself: his own thoughts, feelings, actions, and processes.

When we look at consciousness from this standpoint we can see it as a source of great psychological wealth, hidden perhaps by the dross of superficiality which is frequently all that is apparent. We should be prepared to go below the outer appearances and explore the depths of consciousness. We should ask, "What does this person know? How is his knowledge organized? What is the sense he makes of things?" We may then have some understanding of the problems with which this individual is confronted. Moreover, we should recognize that the very posing of questions of this nature includes the possibility of influencing both the contents and the organization of consciousness itself.

THEORY

I shall now turn to a discussion of theory, the second of my two themes, and in the development of the argument it will become apparent that there are important parallels between theory and consciousness.

Any theory is made up of *axioms* (statements that are not provable, but have a self-evident quality), *categories* (which are the verbal labels by which we record our discrimination among things), and *laws* (which are statements of the ways in which categoriies are related). To know a theory is to know the axioms, the categories, and the laws. A theory arises out of the attempt to produce order out of chaos: it gives organization to knowledge; it offers an understanding of the past and the hope of anticipating what is to come.

It is implicit in what I have just said that there are two different aspects to theory, its construction, and its use. These two aspects are related to the academic search for knowledge on the one hand, and the pragmatic application of a theory to do a job of work on the other. From the academic standpoint, theories are to be constructed (preferably in ways that are disprovable through the dynamics of research activity) with the aim of producing in public and linguistic terms a verbalized version of how the universe in question works. By contrast, from the pragmatic standpoint, theory—whatever its shortcomings—is there to be used for dealing with problems. When we are committed in this way to action, theory gives salience to some information at the expense of other information. It simplifies, at a price, the true complexity of reality in order to make provisional understanding possible. It opens up certain lines of action while sealing off others. Thus some form of theory, implicit if not explicit, is crucial if we are to cope with the problems with which we are presented. Theory, however, should not be mistaken for truth.

While it is certainly the case that the pragmatic use of theory may lead to its modification, it is important that the academic approach should not be confused with the pragmatic. The essential activity of each is necessarily different. That there is a relationship between the academic and the pragmatic is obvious, but its ramifications go beyond the scope of this paper.

There is a component of theory which I have so far deliberately omitted. Every theory is based on metaphor. (cf. Mehrabian, 1968). The metaphor is an assertion by analogy that some aspects of what is relatively well-known can give meaning to what is relatively less well-known. The metaphor is not derived logically; it seems to arise of its own accord out of the theorist's perception of situations. In this way it may well carry meanings, thoughts, and feelings which are sensed at a very low level of awareness and which may have been derived from the very roots of consciousness. (May I point out that I have just used as a metaphor for consciousness the growth of a tree or plant. The word "roots" gives the key to the analogy.) Theorists seldom state their metaphors and it is not always easy to spot them; nonetheless, they represent unverbalized and unacknowledged aspects both of the assumptive framework of the theorist and perhaps also of the times themselves. Much of psychoanalytic theory, in its concern with the flow of energy, is derived from the metaphor of 19th-century hydraulics. Other aspects use biological metaphors involving the separation of compartments of an organism by its membranes. Some aspects involve metaphors from topology. The key metaphor, however, is conflict between the individual's own wishes and those of society, among various parts of the individual's own psychological makeup, and metaphysically between life (or love) and death. The acceptability of a theory is a matter of both a head reaction through reason and a gut reaction through feelings. The former is decided by a theory's comprehensiveness, its apparent validity, its logical consistency. The latter is determined by the way an individual senses the underlying metaphors.

Just as in my general discussion of theory I distinguished between two approaches, so, in discussing the pragmatic approach, I propose to make a further distinction. Because this distinction is not commonly made, but is, in fact, somewhat revolutionary, I shall come to it gently.

We are familiar with the great public theories, or accounts of man: Freud and Jung, the behaviorists, Allport, Rogers, and others, each of which offers answers to the question, "What is man?" The pursuit of answers to this question is, of course, an essential component of the academic approach to theory. We seem to take it as axiomatic, however, that having arrived at generalized answers for the generalized man, these answers are also true for individual man. I would suggest, however, that if we really apply these answers to ourselves, we do not readily say of any of them, "Yes, this is I." How could we, if they are to some extent mutually contradictory? Moreover, the fact that we can stand outside any theory means that the theory is not big enough to account for ourselves. Despite these obvious comments we do not easily see that each of us, in fact, makes his own sense of things, of people, of events, of himself. Each of us creates his own theory about people, not in the academic sense of formal theory construction, but at the pragmatic level of getting along in the world. Thus my distinction between theories at the pragmatic level is between the great public theories and the personal, private theories that each one of us constructs out of the raw material of his experiences.

From the distinctions I have now drawn it can be seen that there are close parallels and similarities between consciousness on the one hand and theory on the other. Each involves the structure, categorization, and organization of knowledge. Each is a tool for coping with problems. Each represents a means of adapting to phenomena. Each is purposive. When we now take the step of fitting ideas of consciousness into the idea of a personal personality theory, we have arrived at George Kelly's Personal Construct Theory (Kelly, 1955; Maher, 1969) to which I can now, at last, turn.

Personal Construct Theory

Everything I have said up to now points to Personal Construct Theory, and everything that follows is based on it. I shall not attempt a formal exposition, however, but use some of the themes I have already developed in relation to consciousness and theory to reflect some of the essential features of Personal Construct Theory. In particular, I have chosen metaphor, categories, organization, function, and dynamics, but there will be resonances of other themes as well.

Kelly developed his theory in the double context of academic learning and psychotherapy. From these two contexts he recognized a similarity between the activities he followed with his research students and his activities with his therapy clients. In each, he would invite them to define the issues with clarity, to undertake careful observation, to formulate and test hypotheses, and to modify the hypotheses in the light of their outcomes. At the same time, he made an interesting observation from psychology textbooks. He noticed that when, in the introduction, the writer described the activities of the psychologist, he presented the image of the scientific enterprise. When, however, the writer came to the chapter on personality, he described man in rather different terms: motivation, needs, unconscious forces, motives, and so forth. Kelly saw no reason at all why the creative theory about man which the psychologist applied to himself should not also apply to the man in the street: "Let us, then, instead of occupying ourselves with *man-the-biological-organism* or *man-the-lucky-guy* have a look at *man-the-scientist*" (Kelly, 1955, p. 4).

The metaphor for man, therefore, is *man-the-scientist* and from this, certain implications follow. The theory is self-reflexive in that it does not distinguish between the formulator of theory and the people about whom the theory is formulated. Moreover, although Kelly has written a theory in public terms about man in general, the theory is built around the idea of each individual man as a theory builder—that is, it is couched in terms that include the idea of a personal or private theory. Just as the research psychologist carries out his own research program to elaborate on and exemplify his theories, so the man in the street carries out his research program, which is the business of everyday living.

Kelly states this formally, together with a statement about organization, in the following way: "Organization Corollary: Each person characteristically evolves, for his own convenience in anticipating events, a construction system embracing ordinal relations between constructs" (Kelly, 1955, p. 56).

More generally, and in less precise language, he says:

> Man looks at his world through transparent patterns or templates which he creates and then attempts to fit over the realities of which the world is composed. The fit is not always very good. Yet without such patterns the world appears to be an undifferentiated homogeneity that man is unable to make sense out of at all.
>
> Let us give the name *constructs* to these patterns that are tried on for size. They are ways of construing the world. They are what enable a man, and lower animals too, to chart a course of behavior, explicitly formulated or implicitly acted out, verbally expressed or utterly inarticulate, consistent with other courses of action or inconsistent with them, intellectually reasoned or vegetably sensed. (Kelly, 1955, pp. 8–9)

The word "construct" is important within the theory since it represents Kelly's formulation of the categories whereby the world is discriminated. He expresses it formally in the following way: "Dichotomy Corollary: A person's construction system is made up of a finite number of dichotomous constructs" (Kelly, 1955, p. 59).

The essence of a construct is that it is two-ended: it is made up not of simple attributes but as pairs of attributes that are opposite, not necessarily in a logical or semantic sense, but in terms of the individual's own terminology. The construct is the means whereby an individual categorizes and discriminates the event with which he comes in contact. It is not merely an intellectualism, but involves thoughts, feelings, and moral judgments. It also offers alternative courses of action. Kelly also makes the point that the construct has a limited range of applicability—that is, it is not equally relevant over the whole range of a person's experience. Let me illustrate the nature of a construct with an example. An adolescent boy describes some of his acquaintances as "rough." The opposite, in his language, is "queer," meaning, in his terminology, "effeminate and potentially homosexual." The construct "rough-queer" is applicable only to boys of about his own age, not to girls, nor to adults. In relation to action, if the boy has no other means of discriminating among boys he is likely to have difficulties in his definition of himself. If he does not wish to be "rough," which has the implication of trouble with the police, his only other choice might be "queer," with equally disastrous implications.

Personal Construct Theory is also dynamic. It postulates that man is always active in his affairs and does not wait to be stimulated or motivated. Further, his personal construct system is itself open to change as the outcome of experience. Kelly states these two issues in his Fundamental Postulate and in his Experience Corollary. "Fundamental Postulate: A person's processes are psychologically channelized by the way he anticipates events" (Kelly, 1955, p. 46). "Experience Corollary: A person's construct system varies as he successively construes the replication of events" (Kelly, 1955, p. 72).

Thus, if my observations on "consciousness" and "theory" given earlier are seen as twin pillars, then Personal Construct Theory, as portrayed in these quotations, can be seen as a unifying keystone or link between the two.

Pragmatics: Personal Construct Theory and Change

The application of a Personal Construct Theory approach must inevitably be shaped by the nature of our involvement in our professional work. It needs to be clearly recognized that we only become engaged in work with children because others have complained about them—a child's actions, the expression of his thoughts and feelings, his interactions with others, are such as to cause parents, teachers, social workers, and others to be worried. The adults then seek help, usually saying that something is wrong with the child and asking us to put it right. When the adults are troubled, it is a reasonable inference that the child is troubled, too. It is seldom, however, that the troubles the child complains of are the same as those that upset the adults. The overriding generalization from these observations is that a referral to a child guidance clinic or a psychologist means that things are somehow going wrong in relation to the child. It is our commitment to do something about it, either with the child on his own, or with the adults who are part of his life, or with their interactions.

I have pitched the question of "complaint" at a low level of abstraction since that provides a more practical account of the referral process. Similarly, despite the precision with which Kelly presents Personal Construct Theory, in practice, a broader formulation along the following lines is more useful. A person's behavior depends on how he makes sense of things and on his viewpoint. When troubles arise it is likely either that his ways of making sense are inadequate, or that he has adopted a point of view that leads to false perceptions. If we construe trouble as interactionist rather than intrapsychic, we would say that the sense that individuals make of each other does not match the sense that these same individuals make of themselves. The aim of therapeutic intervention, then, is to generate a change in behavior by initiating a change in these ways of making sense or points of view. The first step is the exploration of these points of view.

The metaphor *man-the-scientist*, which lies behind the theory, immediately suggests lines of action whereby change might be initiated. The scientific process involves skilled and dispassionate observation, and this in itself implies a modification or enlargement of consciousness. In a clinical setting, a child might be asked to report in detail the experiences that he has when he wets the bed or has a temper tantrum. Sensations and feelings can be located in the body and information requested as to how these change. He can be invited to describe the psychological, temporal, or situational sequences within which the troubling behavior arises, and to develop guesses or hypotheses to account for this behavior. These tasks involve the extension and elaboration of a child's knowledge. They may also show up gaps or inconsistencies in his ways of making sense (cf. Raimy, 1975). Out of all these activities a change of viewpoint or consciousness can become possible. More important, however, underlying all this work lies the expectation that the child can become responsibly active in the enlargement of his consciousness and in the solving of his own problems.

These are some of the general strategies which arise from the theory. My special aim, however, is to advocate the exploration of consciousness since this is fundamental, especially if we see misperceptions of identity as the central issue.

The contents of a child's consciousness do not stand in line ready for inspection. They are available only when deliberately looked for, and only then if the child knows where the interviewer is going and the nature of the information he requires. In order to explore consciousness, therefore, it is necessary to ask questions, and the art of skillful exploration is at the same time the art of skillful questioning. If we use as a metaphor the notion of the map, we can say that the child, out of his experience of life, has developed maps whereby he can plot his way through everyday events. Our task is then one of finding out the nature of his maps. Any map is created as a projection from a round surface to a flat, and maps are described by their projection as well as by their content. Kelly described Personal Construct Theory also as a theory of projection (cf. Ravenette, 1972a).

We need to specify those areas of experience where troubles arise and then question the child systematically. This process will include the child's awareness of internal and external events. Consciousness, as I describe earlier, includes thoughts, feelings, potential actions, and moral judgments; we must make reference to these in our questions. Out of such an investigation a number of things may happen. The child himself frequently shows a sense of personal responsibility for his dilemmas and a serious involvement in the interview. He is frequently surprised at the amount and quality of his own knowledge and this enhances his feelings of self-worth. He is usually able to give a coherent sense of his own identity, and to hint at the unspoken metaphors that color many of his actions.

Knowledge of this nature is crucial if we wish to bring about some change in the interactions between adult and child, and Kelly gives this a theoretical basis in his Sociality Corollary. "Sociality Corollary: To the extent that one person construes the construction processes of another, he may play a role in a social process involving the other person" (Kelly, 1955, p. 95).

Very simply, without some understanding of the other person, the interactions are likely to be tangential. But the understanding must be of his understanding, not of him. This is a subtle distinction. I can now illustrate this approach.

A Case in Point

Graham is a 10-year-old boy about whom the head teacher was worried. He presented no behavioral or learning problems in school but had had frequent absences because of illnesses which had involved hospitalization. Despite many investigations, however, nothing abnormal had been found. For a period of time, Graham had become exhausted in school by midday and the head teacher had allowed him to go home. The parents were worried and the family might equally well have been referred to the Child Guidance Clinic. The head teacher knew, however, that he would have the opportunity of sharing the interview and in that way would acquire at first hand an understanding of the boy from the things he said. The presence of the head teacher reflects the application of the Sociality Corollary. By sharing the exploration of Graham's sense of himself and others, the head teacher might later be able to play a more meaningful role in relation to the boy. The interview lasted for a full hour but I shall restrict my account to those interviewing techniques that will not be well-known, and to responses from Graham that reflect more directly on himself than on his construction of the rest of the world.

The Interview

Graham could not tell me why I had been asked to interview him, but agreed that people might be worried about his frequent illnesses. He said that he himself was not worried by his illness but that his parents and relatives were. I asked him where he had his pains; he showed me his right side. He said that his legs would ache around the ankles and the pains would move up his legs. He had stomachaches and headaches.

When I asked him to describe boys, not himself, who might have the same pains as himself, he was at a loss to say anything. Yet he could not readily accept that he was therefore different from all other boys. All he could say of boys who never had pains was that they were fit. They could not become boys who had pains unless there was some difference in their bodies—for example in their blood.

I want to make the point here that to ask Graham questions about what he knew was already to force him into thinking carefully about himself and others, and to stretch him to the limits of his own consciousness. He was not a static entity giving information without undergoing any change, but a boy operating a personal theory. By necessity, the interview itself drew his attention to gaps and inadequacies in his theory (cf. Raimy, 1975). The evidence so far suggested that Graham's identity was firmly rooted in an awareness of his physical body rather than in some psychological sense of self.

Graham's drawing of his family showed him in contact with his dog, but isolated from his two brothers who were six and eight years older. His mother and father appeared to one side of the picture, facing each other, mother with a garden hoe in her hand, father eating his dinner. (According to the head teacher, the mother was aggressively the boss in the family, and was also involved in running a troop of Girl Guides. He could say nothing of the father.)

TROUBLES IN SCHOOL. The technique used with Graham is concerned with a child's awareness of situations in school with a special emphasis on troubles and upsets. I have described earlier versions elsewhere (Ravenette, 1977a) and the current practice is more complex. The child is invited to choose three out of eight drawings of situations in school. The pictures are postcard size. The drawings are in black ink on white paper. They are loosely drawn in relation to detail, but they are fairly well structured in relation to theme. Each situation is used as the focus for a detailed inquiry and the child is told in advance what the questions are:

1. What do you think is happening?
2. Who do you think is troubled or upset, and why?
3. How do you think this came about?

These questions tap the ways in which a child makes sense of troubled situations in school. He is directed to reality, and is asked to show his awareness of psychological, situational, or interactional sequences.

4. If this child were you, what would you think? What would you feel? What would you do? What difference would that make to anyone? As a result of all of this, would you feel good or bad? And why?

These questions put the child fairly and squarely into familiar situations and demand of him an awareness of his own thoughts, feelings, and potential actions. Perhaps the most important of these questions is about the difference he makes to others since this issue is at the heart of a child's sense of potency in the world.

5. If the child were not you, what sort of a boy would you say he was?

This question allows a child to entertain the possibility of alternative identities, and therefore the possibility of change (Ravenette, 1977b). By implication, he will also be giving some idea of the kind of boy he is not, as well as the kind of boy he feels that he is.

Let us follow Graham's responses:

Picture 1 (outside the school railings; adults and a pram; children between school and gate). (1) The children are coming home from school and meeting their mothers. (2) Three are upset, but he eventually settles on just one of them. He had done something wrong in school, he had not done his work. (3) He looks sad, he did his work wrong, he wasn't trying. (4) If Graham were this boy he would feel miserable. He would go home and tell Mum. He would think, "I wasn't trying." After a long pause he said this would make no difference to anyone. He would feel bad, he would feel ashamed. (5) If Graham were not this boy, the boy would be lazy, not trying hard enough.

Picture 2 (children standing in serried ranks in a hall; adults on a dais; figures around the walls, one at a piano). (1) This is in assembly. (2) The boy at the wall is upset. (3) The other boy started it, he joined in. (4) If Graham were this boy, he would feel stupid. He would sulk. He would think, "You are stupid." He said this would make no difference to anyone. As a result of his action he would feel bad because he had messed up someone else's assembly. (5) If Graham were not this boy, the boy would be a boy who mucks about, who does a lot of wasting of his and other people's time.

Picture 3 (children sitting in two rows of desks; teacher standing in front, book open, looking at children). (1) They are having a lesson. (2) The boy at the front is upset. He is just looking down, he is being told off. (3) He has not been doing his work properly. (4) If Graham were this boy, he would feel unhappy. He would sulk. He would think, "I am stupid." This action would make no difference to anyone. As a result he would feel bad. (5) If Graham were not this boy, it would be a boy who mucks about a lot and doesn't do as he is told.

A sixth question was also asked for each of these situations. Was the boy in question 5, the boy who was not Graham, the kind of boy who could have the same aches and pains as Graham? Each time he said no.

From these responses, Graham appears to be a boy who is open to very negative thoughts and feelings about himself, but for whom the expression of these thoughts and feelings makes no difference to anybody. Even sulking is a compromise between admitting and acting on bad feelings. He seems to draw a moral difference between a boy like himself who *feels that he is bad,* and by contrast, the boy who is not Graham who *actually is bad*—he mucks about, doesn't work, and wastes people's time. This boy, the alternative identity, could not have the same physical badness that plagues Graham. Is it the case that a moral link between sin and suffering is already being forged in Graham? Or is it simply that his proper and ordinary bad feelings are not allowed to exist unless channelized into a physical rather than a psychological form?

PORTRAIT GALLERY. Whereas the previous technique aims to explore Graham's sense of self within the school setting, the Portrait Gallery (Ravenette, 1972b) is concerned with the elaboration of feelings. Two schematic faces are drawn, one to stand for a sad boy and one for a happy boy. The child is asked to distinguish which is which and to say three things about each. He is then presented with blank faces and asked to fill in each of them in turn to represent other feeling states, and say three things about each of them.

Graham's responses were as follows:

Sad: (1) Naughty, he gets told off. (2) Doesn't get what he wants. (3) Doesn't do as he's told, therefore he gets smacked, therefore he is sad.

Happy: (1) He doesn't get told off all the time. (2) He is good: Mum asks him to do something, he does it, he sets the table. (3) He doesn't want things straight away, he waits, he knows he will get it later.

Angry: (1) He gets angry when he doesn't get what he wants, he wants it straightaway. (2) He gets angry if he is talking to somebody and they don't talk back. (3) Someone calls him names, he gets angry, he starts fighting.

Worried: (1) If he has hit someone; his mother is after him with the slipper, he knows the slipper hurts. (2) Like his brother has gotten some money. If he takes it without telling; if his brother comes around and says, "You took my money." (3) He stole something from a shop; the shopkeeper knows who took it and goes to the parent.

Things go wrong with his body, like aches and pains: (1) He feels worried; he is
afraid he might have an operation. (2) He feels horrible inside. (3) He loses
color in his face.

Despite the simplicity of the technique, there is a wealth of personal content in
Graham's responses. Sadness goes with badness and having to be patient for his
needs to be met. Happiness seems not to exist in its own right, but only as a
consequence of meeting the demands and values of the parents, or in the absence of
sadness. Graham's sense of his family suggested that they preached, if not
practiced, a puritan morality within which bad thoughts and feelings are also
immoral and which may well be at variance with the values of the neighborhood.
Inadvertently he gave the lie to happiness when he admitted to anger for not getting
what he wanted. When we also see that he got angry at being ignored, do we
recognize shades of that isolation which he so graphically portrayed in his family
drawing and might we not hazard the guess that he was frequently angry there, but
to no purpose?

THE GOOD AND THE BAD OF IT. The final technique uses the basic idea that in any
state that is held to be good, there is the possibility of something disadvantageous,
and in any state that is considered to be bad there is the potentiality of something
that is to a person's good (Tschudi, 1977). We obtain agreement with the child of
what is bad for him at the moment, or what stands in the way of his being all right.
We then ask what he would prefer it to be. This gives two contrasting states, and we
ask of him what is "bad" and "good," "good" and "bad" about each. It will be
remembered that it was through this technique that Jane, with whom I introduced
this paper, showed something of the quality of her awareness.

Graham conceded that what was wrong with him was:

"I have aches and pains that people do not understand."
The *bad* thing about this is that it really hurts the body.
The *good* thing about this is—after a pause Graham said "experiments." When I
asked him for whom this was good, he said "the pathologists." This would be
good because it helps the body.
And after a long pause he added, "to help my blood."

By contrast he would prefer:

"To be fitter, run around a lot, and take part in things."
The *good* thing about this is taking part in things a person has never done.
The *bad* thing about this is it makes one get tired, the muscles get all tied up, one
can't walk.

These questions pushed Graham to the limits of his awareness of the implications
of his condition, forcing him to verbalize links that he probably never considered
before. As at the beginning of the interview, Graham, as someone who is ill, was a

body that could attract the attention of people who are important to him. He was also an object which can be used, ostensibly for his own good, but, as he saw it, for the benefit of the pathologists. The contrasting pole to that of the body is not, as might be expected, a soul or a mind or a person, but a social interaction, "taking part in things." Where, one is forced to ask, was the psychological self which seemed somehow to have been lost, or perhaps never existed?

It seemed necessary to offer Graham a contribution which might bring together some of the themes that appeared in response to my questions. Such a contribution does not have to be absolute truth, but it should say something meaningful about the situation. It should also contain a psychological understanding which Graham can be free to accept or reject, but which he would find it difficult to ignore. To this end my remarks ran something like this:

> I know a boy who is like you but who is not you. Whenever this boy feels, thinks, and does things that are bad, he feels it doesn't make any difference to anyone. Because this also makes him feel bad inside himself, the only way he can show it is by having a lot of aches and pains. This means that people take notice of him. This does not have to be true of you, but perhaps a little bit of it is.

I thanked him and sent him back to his classroom.

Résumé of "A Case in Point"

It needs to be pointed out that the problem for which Graham's behavior was a solution was not the problem for which the head teacher sought help. Nor, incidentally, was Graham's behavior, in itself, a problem. The problem for the head teacher was that he could not understand or have an effect on that behavior. As will be seen, some resolution of the head teacher's problem seemed to have arisen out of his sharing the interview.

Graham's own difficulties were of a different order and what follows is an inferential reconstruction. In terms of Graham's own sense of things, he lived in a family where morality was important and where at the same time he felt isolated (part of which is to make no difference to anybody). Moreover, the acknowledgment or expression of bad thoughts and feelings was unacceptable. What the family did accept was badness of the body as expressed in physical illness or disorder (aches and pains, and bad blood). Physical illness therefore provided a channel for expressing "badness" and at the same time it provided a means both of making some impact on people and of being acknowledged in return. The price, however, may have been the atrophy of his sense of self as a "person" in favor of a more limited vision of himself as a "body." The exhaustion that was manifested in school may well have provided a means of escaping from a world in which demands were made on him as a person.

The construction which I gave back to Graham at the end of the interview contained some of these ideas.

The Sequel

I was discussing the implications of the interview with the head teacher, and after about 10 minutes there was a knock on the door. It was Graham, who wished to ask the head teacher a question. This might have seemed a trivial incident until the head teacher turned to me, beaming, and said that the boy had never before been to the office to ask for anything. Perhaps, he continued, the boy feels good that for the first time someone has understood him, to which I must add that the boy himself sensed the possibility of a new role relationship with the head teacher.

Twelve months later the head teacher reported that all continued to go well.

Conclusion

This brings my formal exposition to an end, but I want to bring it to a completion very simply with two quotations, which, as I indicated at the beginning, would represent a synthesis of much that I have been trying to express. I do not see our work as curing peripheral psychological ills, but rather as intervening in the very fabric of life itself. Thus our frame of reference should extend beyond the circumscribed ambit of child guidance and link with broad streams of thought that have universal implications.

My first quotation comes from the Eastern metaphysical traditions through the words of the Lama Anagarika Govinda (whom I have already quoted):

Thus all reality is built upon polarity, the polarity of part and whole, of individuality and universality, of matter and energy, differentiation and one-ness etc. [to which I would add conscious and unconscious]: and there can be no question of ''higher'' and ''lower'' values between these polar, mutually complementary qualities. The concept of value depends on the merits of the momentary situation, the particular circumstances. Wherever there is an imbalance between the two poles, the one that is in danger of being outweighed represents the greater value.

My second quotation comes from a Western poetic source. T. S. Eliot, in ''Little Gidding,'' the last of the Four Quartets, wrote these three lines:

> And the end of all exploring
> Will be to arrive where we started
> And know the place for the first time.

REFERENCES

Deikman, A. J. The meaning of everything. In R. E. Ornstein (Ed.), *The Nature of Human Consciousness*. New York: Viking, 1973, pp. 317–326.

Govinda, L. A. *Creative Meditation and Multi-Dimensional Consciousness*. London; Unwin Paperbacks, 1977.

Kelly, G. A. *The Psychology of Personal Constructs:* Vols. 1 and 2. New York: Norton, 1955.

Maher, B. *Clinical Psychology and Personality*. New York: Academic, 1969.

Mehrabian, A. *An Analysis of Personality Theories*. Englewood Cliffs, N.J.: Prentice-Hall, 1968.

Raimy, V. *Misunderstanding of the Self*. San Francisco: Jossey Bass, 1975.

Ravenette, A. T. Projective psychology and personal construct theory. *Journal of Projective Psychology*, 1972a, **18** (1), 3–10.

Ravenette, A. T. Psychologists, teachers, children—How many ways to understand. *A.E.P. Journal* 1972b, **3**, (2), 41−47.

Ravenette, A. T. Personal construct theory: An approach to the psychological investigation of children. In D. Bannister (Ed.), *New Perspectives in Personal Construct Theory*. London: Academic, 1977a, pp. 251−280.

Ravenette, A. T. Exploring alternative identities: An essay in personal construct theory and therapy with children. Paper given to the Institute of Child Psychology, 1977b.

Tshudi, F. Loaded and honest questions. In D. Bannister (Ed.), *New Perspectives in Personal Construct Theory*. London: Academic, 1977, pp. 321−350.

PART TWO

Psychotherapy

CHAPTER 4

Optimal Functioning:
A Personal Construct Approach

Franz Epting and Martin Amerikaner

We have chosen the label *optimal functioning* to describe our concept of the positive, desirable pole of an uncomfortably ill-defined continuum of psychological functioning. A variety of terms have been used by many writers in attempts to describe this area. Healthy personality (Jourard, 1974) implies sickness as a contrast and involves a medical model. "Adequate personality" (Combs et al., 1976) suggests "coping," "normal," and other mid-range labels which miss the potential for high-level, extraordinary functioning which is both possible and actual in the population. The notion of "self-actualization," used by several prominent theorists (Goldstein, 1939; Maslow, 1968; Rogers, 1961), comes closer; however, from the Personal Construct Theory position described below, "self-actualization" is seen as limited by implying that positive functioning is a process of enacting or bringing into being what is lying dormant in the "self" of the person. Rather, the emphasis here is on "creation" and "invention" rather than "discovery."

This view of persons is developed within the Psychology of Personal Constructs as formulated initially by George A. Kelly in his two-volume work (1955) and in his subsequent papers, "A Psychology of the Optimal Man" (1967, reprinted as Chapter 2 in this volume) and "The Psychology of the Unknown" (Kelly, 1977). It is our intent in this chapter to base our comments on optimal functioning as closely as possible on Kelly's original ideas rather than to create a new theory. The personal construct approach always emphasizes the process of human functioning, rather than describing stages, traits, or states of the person. Interest is focused on people during their most exceptional moments, and on the processes that characterize the functioning of people who are often consistently reaching the optimal level.

An important point to understand in dealing with the optimal person from a constructive point of view, one that was alluded to earlier, is that self-fulfillment is not exactly the right way to conceptualize the problem. It isn't that a person should *not* fulfill himself or herself, but that having self-fulfillment as the primary goal may be too limiting. Optimal functioning may necessarily turn out to involve a transcendence of the self—becoming what one sees as a possibility beyond the present self. Similarly, an equally limiting idea is to see the self as a container of the potentials that a person possesses. It is then up to the person to lay hands on these potentials in order to actualize them through either a full exploration of self or a systematic satisfaction of preprogrammed, biologically based needs (Maslow, 1967). Personal Construct Theory tries to convey the idea that the self to be fulfilled is primarily invented and often reinvented by the person rather than discovered or uncovered.

The nature of these inventions, however, is neither random nor arbitrary (though it may appear so to the outside observer). The person may reach potentials, discover limits, and create successful means to surpass these only by undertaking an active inquiry into possibilities. Only through actively pursuing these outer "growing edges" are people able to know what their potentials are. These potentials are not static or predetermined "things"; they change as the person's inventions (constructs) change. In Kelly's terms, "man is continually in the process of re-defining his potentialities through the sheer audacity of his achievements" (Kelly, 1967, p. 241).

Another consideration in the issue of a person's potential choices and actions is the recognition that the sheer number of possibilities that are open to and well within the grasp of most people is far greater than what can be achieved in any one lifetime. Therefore, assessment, reassessment, and responsible choices must continually be made concerning which potentials will be fulfilled. This dilemma is often encountered in the excitement and fear of new possibilities appearing on the horizon, with the recognition that choosing movement in one direction implies moving away from many others. The person's situation becomes one of having the responsibility for making a thorough self-appraisal and then choosing the paths that will (and will not) be followed. An emphasis here is on the "real" nature of active choosing—the real quality of a changing world, the real consequences of choosing one or another path, and the real responsibility a person maintains for his/her constructions of this world. In recent years, many writers in counseling and psychology have developed activities to facilitate "value clarification" (cf. Simon, 1974). From the personal construct perspective, these exercises help people articulate their current construction of themselves and the paths open to them, help them understand the implications and organizations of their "developing self" constructs, and ideally help them actively move toward commitment and away from deadened resignation or confused, "stuck" inactivity.

From this position, the direction that an optimally functioning person takes is not necessarily based on what is "really possible" as defined by others, or on the restrictions set by a currently defined set of potentials; rather, the direction is based on what the person *should* be or what that person *ought* to be. Only by facing the implications of *ought* and *should* is the person able to commit those resources needed for the tremendous job of fulfilling the chosen potentials. The *ought* that is referred to here is described by Kelly (1967, p. 242) as "a venturesome ought—an audacious *ought*." It is very close to the idea of *ought* and *should* that Maslow (1971) speaks of in discussing "fusion knowledge," where what is, in fact, should be. Maslow's position is that the optimally functioning person is what he or she should be. The person desires and is attracted to what he ought to have, and/or avoids that which she ought not have. This is, of course, defining *ought* and *should* from within the person's own system, rather than having it imposed from the outside. We are discussing a sense of rightness, of certainty, of "fit" that develops from the person's own experience, not from the list of rules he or she has internalized from parents and other representatives of society. We are also not referring to those that have been condemned by therapists as the tyrannical "shoulds" which must be outgrown or discarded in the process of personal growth. Neither are these "oughts" or personal certainties we are describing necessarily of a purely verbal nature; they are felt as well as thought. This underscores an important distinction between Personal Construct Theory and "cognitive" theory. The overall dimension is similar to the knowledge Gendlin works to facilitate through "experiential focusing" (Gendlin, 1977). The *ought* we are describing is defined by consequences; it is that which will, in the long run, lead to continuing fulfillment and development of the person. In construct theory terms this is called validation of the elaborative choice.

FULL CYCLES OF EXPERIENCE

The activities and behaviors which contribute to personal development (to movement toward potentials) are not based on externally defined practical or factual realities. Neither are they determined by developmental stages or an emergent biological value hierarchy. Rather, growth, as experienced by optimally functioning people, is characterized by the process of consistently completing what Personal Construct Theory has described as "full cycles of experience."

The main thrust of this section will focus upon this cycle. It is through such cycles of seeing experiences through all the way to some sensible or satisfying conclusions that a person is able to become truly enlivened. It is the completion of such cycles which results in the richer, more complex, and ever-growing personal construct systems that are characteristic of optimally functioning people.

The first step in such a cycle is the *Anticipation* of what is coming from the future to greet us in our present moment. It is the forecasting of events in such a manner that we actually look to see what is coming next. As you probably know, in construct theory we conceive of these anticipations as occurring along dimensional lines. In addition, these dimensions of meaning used to anticipate events are described as both bipolar and dichotomous.

This anticipation can be done in either a consciously aware, vigilant mode or in a more relaxed, contemplative spirit. Additionally, we frequently anticipate events through actions other than simply thinking about them. We behave in a certain way based on the expectations that we have about an event. For example, the physical arousal an athlete experiences before an important event and the "butterflies" before a performance are psychophysiological anticipations, based on the meaning that the events have for the individual. As noted above, construing is not particularly cognitive.

The second phase of the cycle is *Investment*. The person invests himself or herself wholly in the matters that are to be anticipated. This means that optimal functioning involves the risks of full involvement, of really "diving in and getting wet"; the person must become immersed in the problem. This can be stated as *self-involvement*. This involved self-investment happens in a very personal way. It is experienced at the person's "center," that place where the person feels most alive and most vitally "me." A particularly forceful device that has been employed in Personal Construct Psychology to facilitate this aspect of growth is to invoke an invitational mode in a person's approach to life. Here, the world is approached with an open, inviting stance, "as if" there were new and different alternatives to present patterns. This open, creative posture allows the new ideas and experiences necessary for fresh self-investment to pass through previously closed barriers. In this way, the person can become truly experimental and inventive with life, if only for very brief periods of time.

This combination of anticipation and self-involvement is called commitment; it is on this commitment that the third phase of the cycle, *Encounter,* is based. Encounter does not mean a collision with events. It implies an active knowledge of what one has met which lets that knowledge make a difference. This is an engagement, in which the person acts on, or *constructs,* the encountered event in a dialogical fashion. There is an open interaction between "person" and "events," not a rigid or destructive forcing of the person's perspective of the event, not an overly passive flooding of the person by the events. Counselors may recognize this aspect of encounter as related to "assertiveness," although the open, constructive attitude is characteristic of the person's immersion in all aspects of the experience and is not limited to the interpersonal relationship usually emphasized in assertiveness training (see also Kelly's discussion of "aggressiveness," 1955, Vol 1). To be fully involved in the encounter phase, the person must be truly open to the experience, so that the event is not diminished, distorted, or made meaningless through intellectualization or other "distancing techniques." That which becomes known through such authentic encounters profoundly affects the self.

Beyond the encounter phase are two further stages in the full experience cycle. The fourth is *Confirmation and Disconfirmation.* This phase has to do with making some assessment concerning the commitments made during the encounter and the resulting evidence which either supports or refutes what the person has created as his/her construction of the encountered experience. Following Kelly's metaphor of the person-as-scientist, the optimally functioning person/scientist must be able to assess from the evidence what has just happened. How do the "test hypotheses" stand up to the data? This does not mean, however, that optimal functioning can be equated with a simple measure of the frequency of accurate predictions. We are describing intense, compelling, and even possibly upsetting experiences, in which the constructions created by the person are necessarily new and tentative. "Rightness" is therefore not the issue; rather it is the "style" or process of construing, and the degree to which confirmation and disconfirmation is possible.

The fifth and final stage of this cycle is the *Constructive Revision.* After the evidence has come in, the person faces the implications of what has just occurred. On the one hand is the possibility that some areas of the person's life are more compatible than before; aspects that were discrete or in opposition may move toward integration. Previously inaccessible material (not clearly understood experiences) may become more fully synchronized with the rest of the person's life. It is in constructive revision that all of the greater moments of life which are often recognized and labeled as "growth experiences" take place. From these we are enlivened and invigorated, and feel more fully grown. On the other hand, the person may now realize that certain beliefs or life stances cannot be maintained, and drastic, painful changes are needed. This is also optimal functioning, although it is of an unpleasant variety. The recognition of the need to change, to relinquish old constructions, and the subsequent actuality of revision are, of course, what were risked at the outset of the cycle. Though often painful, the new, revised system stands in "growthful" contrast to the person who, in the light of continually disconfirming evidence, refuses to budge, clings to original constructions, and seeks to "extort" validating evidence from an unwilling environment.

A final point on this last phase must be made. Though noted as the time when great enlivening moments occur, it should not, in itself, be equated with growth from the personal construct position. Growth is described by the entire cycle, and the full sequence is necessary, although the "fruit" of observable change may occur only in the final phase. Growth is the entire process, and the lives of optimally functioning people are marked by the continual nature of their involvement with the cycle.

To recap this whole sequence, the process that we emphasize as characteristic of high-level, optimally functioning people is called the "experience cycle." It includes *commitment,* which is affirmative anticipation plus self-involvement; *encounter;* and a process of *confirmation* or *disconfirmation*. This does not, however, complete the task, for it must be followed by *reconstruction*. "The cycle of human experiences remains incomplete unless it terminates in fresh hopes never before envisioned" (Kelly, 1977, p. 9). For Kelly, completing the full cycle of experience is a key to human progress. When a person involves himself in the life of another person and makes unequivocal predictions, he is committed. He must then be open to the "evidence" and face the events of his life. This description of optimal functioning is focused on a continuing process and is not limited to a particular sphere or aspect of a person's life. As life goes on and the person keeps growing, the construct system with which any given cycle begins is richer and more complex than it was earlier. This, however, never does necessarily make the cycle "easy," or less intense, or less enlivening. The transcendence and reinvention of the current self in the face of a continually changing world seems to be an ongoing process throughout the lives of optimally functioning people.

RELATIONSHIP TO OTHER PERSPECTIVES

As we have described a personal construct description of optimal functioning, we have emphasized the importance of immersion in life events through a process called the experience cycle. Aspects of this cycle, and of the style of life of people who are frequently engaged in these full experiences, have been noted by other writers in theorizing about optimal functioning, although the labels are often different. The willingness to engage in encounter, to affect and be affected, is what Rogers (1961) seems to consider the "openness to experience" characteristic of "fully functioning" people. Experiencing such openness, the person is fully aware of all organismic experiences and all messages communicated to and from the environment without resorting to defensive distortion to block awareness of threatening material from the environment. Existential philosophers and psychologists (Ellenberger, 1958; Gendlin, 1973; Jourard, 1974) use the term "authenticity" to describe the process of free choice of action as opposed to automatic responding in life situations. Such authentic action is characterized by clear perception of change in the world, openness to acceptance of change, and willingness to act in the light of change. Bugental (1965) describes authenticity as being "fully aware in the present moment, in the present situations" (p. 102), with full awareness eloquently defined as "being devoted to intercourse with the panorama [which is] a kind of interpenetration with that to which we attend" (pp. 400–401). Though Personal Construct Theory emphasizes an anticipatory phase prior to this full engagement, certainly the experience of committed encounter described earlier is closely related to these latter comments on authenticity. The importance attributed to authenticity for optimal functioning is concisely stated by Jourard: "Authentic being is a sign of healthy personality and it is the means of achieving personality growth" (1974, p. 168).

The finishing of the cycle, through confirmation-disconfirmation and revision, is based on a willingness to see and make use of all relevant "data" in understanding what has happened. These completions are similar to the concepts of "closure" and "finishing of unfinished situations" described in Gestalt therapy (Perls, 1969). The Gestalt approach emphasizes the use of nonverbal, kinesthetic cues (e.g., "What are your hands doing now? What does your stomach feel like now?") to help in understanding and completing situations. Certainly this is consistent with the personal construct position of being open to all "data" in the confirmation-disconfirmation and revision phase.

The importance placed on anticipation and on revising one's construing to better understand and anticipate future events suggests a time orientation which focuses on movement toward the future. Adlerian theory (Adler, 1964), in which the person's movement toward individually chosen "life goals" figures prominently in that person's degree of feeling "encouraged" or "discouraged," is also a future-oriented perspective. Similarly, for Allport (1961) the sense of moving toward the future is central in the functioning of "mature" adults. His term "proactive" is meant to distinguish behavior that influences and acts upon the environment in the pursuit of goals from behavior that is merely "reactive" to the environment. For Allport, "propriate functioning" develops as a person matures, especially the future-oriented propriate functions, which center on striving, long-range purposes, and distant goals (Allport, 1961).

Another dimension which figures in optimal personality functioning over time is the organization of personality, and specifically the idea of hierarchical organization. In Kelly's view, construct systems are made of relatively core and relatively peripheral (i.e., superordinate and subordinate) constructs. Core constructs hold central importance in the maintenance and development of the system, as they subsume the more subordinate constructs which extend to the periphery. For Kelly, optimal functioning is characterized by construct systems that have developed hierarchically, with a relatively stable core structure. Day-to-day adaptation to the world would then occur principally in the periphery, with relatively little stress placed on the superordinate core structure. As Kelly suggests:

> Core constructs are those which govern a person's maintenance processes—that is, those by which he maintains his identity and existence. In general, a healthy person's mental processes follow core structures which are comprehensive but not too permeable. Since they are comprehensive, a person can use them to see a wide variety of known events as consistent with his own personality . . . He can see himself as a complex but organized person. If his core constructs are too permeable, however, he is likely to see too many new events as having a deeply personal significance. He may become paranoid, as he interprets each new event as intimately relating to himself. Or he may become hypochondriacal as he sees each new event as relating to his health.
>
> Peripheral constructs are those which can be altered without serious modification of core structure . . . The reformulation of a peripheral construct is a much less complicated affair than the reformulation of a core construct. Peripheral constructs can be broken up in therapy without precipitating serious anxiety. (Kelly, 1955, pp. 482–483)

Extending this view for a moment, a concept of "boundaries" borrowed from systems theory (von Bertalanffy, 1968) is relevant here. Optimally developed systems maintain open, yet adequate boundaries which recognize a distinction, a separation, between the person and the outside world, such that not all aspects of the interpersonal world are construed as having implications for self-constructions. Concurrently, however, the boundaries remain open to interaction and encounter with the world, and allow the person to continually test out and revise new constructive hypotheses pertaining to his or her world. A source of personal difficulty would then be personality system development characterized as nonhierarchical, so that any change within the system or stress from the outside is likely to produce relatively large-scale change throughout the system. If such a system has poorly developed boundaries, then a wide variety of experiences might be expected to induce rapid and extensive shifting in the person's self-construction. At the other end of this boundary development continuum, a person with too rigid or impermeable boundaries, which effectively close the person off from new experience or new data from the changing outside world, would be "locked into" his or her fixed set of constructions. This person has little opportunity to revise hypotheses until or unless some event occurs which is powerful enough to break through the boundaries and therefore induce massive, rapid, and possibly chaotic revision of the system.

The last dimension to be discussed in this section concerns the twofold "rhythm" or dual-process nature of optimal functioning. It is consistent with Personal Construct Theory, as well as several other positions, that maintenance as well as growth/change processes are important to optimal functioning. The experience cycle, by definition, involves openness to and continual seeking out of new experiences and a willingness to be changed by them. Concurrently, however, the immediately preceding passage quoted from Kelly concerning core and peripheral constructs points out the importance of a relatively stable core structure. From this position, growth and stability are not in opposition to one another, but rather are complementary processes which function in relation to one another; both are basic to optimal functioning. Though some proponents of personal growth experiences may emphasize only the growth and change dimensions and may seem to support a change-for-change's-sake perspective, the ongoing maintenance of relative integrity and stability is of central importance as well. Striking a similar note, Maslow's (1968) growth-motivated person is primarily motivated by needs for self-actualization and cognitive understanding; but that person must continually maintain ways of satisfying the deficit needs as well. Similarly, Allport's (1961) mature individual maintains self-esteem, self-image, and so on, as well as moving toward long-range purposes and goals, known as "propriate strivings." Combs, too, emphasizes the dual nature of optimal functioning in his suggestion that the development of what he calls "adequate personality" is marked by "maintenance and enhancement of the self . . . [both of which] relate to exactly the same function—the production of a more adequate self" (Combs et al., 1976, p. 57). Both change and maintenance are seen as important for optimal processes, and lack of either can be problematic. On the one hand aimless, chaotic, and disintegrative change is likely when maintenance does not occur. On the other hand stagnation, boredom, and isolation from the continual change in the outside world are the likely outcomes when devotion to maintainance keeps the person unwilling to risk change.

In summary of this section, then, it was noted that from a starting point of describing the experience cycle as basic to optimal functioning, other dimensions of personality process could be articulated from Personal Construct Theory. These dimensions included openness to exchange and interaction with the environment, the importance of completion, a future time orientation, the hierarchical organization of personality, the development of open but adequate boundaries, and the description of change and maintenance as interrelated processes, both of which are characteristic of optimal functioning. The relationship of these ideas to other theories was also noted. Additionally, however, we underscore the value of Personal Construct Theory, with its dynamic qualities and systematic theoretical basis, as being an excellent position from which an integrative theory of optimal functioning can be developed.

THE ROLE OF THE PSYCHOLOGIST

What, in all of this, becomes the role of the psychologist? As Kelly (1969) notes, the distinction between the person-as-scientist and the scientist (psychologist)-as-person is blurred, and when both are functioning well, there may be no fundamental distinction at all. As Kelly put it, Personal Construct Theory is "the way I, too, look to see what will happen, for, unlike most psychologists I know, who view themselves as scientists and their subjects as something else, my theory of personality applies to me as well as to people I don't like" (1967, p. 250). He also comments that he *anticipates* that the theory will work better after exploring its implications further.

There are several implications of this posture for professional psychologists which are basically challenges to live as if the theoretical has actual meaning for life. This includes the challenge to ourselves as psychologists to encounter all aspects of our work, including our clients, our colleagues, our teaching, and our research, with the openness and willingness to commit ourselves described in the experience cycle. A further challenge is to explore through life, as well as research, the implications of hypotheses, while maintaining a willingness to revise time-honored and cherished hypotheses (i.e., to reconstrue in the face of the data). This is akin to Jourard's (1971) image of the psychotherapist as a "fellow seeker" (p. 155). From this professional and experimental base, the psychologist becomes a person who might be able to define the parameters of the ways that people might go in the direction of optimal functioning. Professionally, this becomes the process of extending and elaborating theory through creative, innovative research. Perhaps, with individual clients, the psychologist might help define some of the parameters of *the general way* that a given person should go, even though the psychologist, as an outsider, will not be able to know ahead of time what, in terms of content, is the way for that person to develop optimally.

In fact, the person himself or herself is not very likely to know ahead of time what this direction should be. The person is only able to know by beginning to act, so that through full experience some light begins to be shed on the matter. It may be that the person's *anticipations* of these emerging events are not really crystal clear; the person, nevertheless, is able to, and does, form some posture toward them (Kelly, 1967, p. 245). As mentioned earlier, that is not necessarily done through verbal or logical processes. These anticipations and enactments are more often accomplished through active living and not merely by introspective reflection and contemplation. The issue concerns a person's ability to anticipate events at least in some general way. People should be able to anticipate and commit enough to know whether or not they have been surprised by what eventually really does happen. This process of moving into action based on anticipation and commitment requires courage and, quite often, more than a minimal sense of humor. This process applies as much to the psychologist as it does to the client.

For Kelly (1967, p. 251), "It is the nature of life [itself] to be channelized by the ways events are anticipated." In other words, this is an enlivening process with an anticipatory stance toward the future, as has been discussed earlier. It is by casting his or her dimensions of meaning toward the future, living into the events and reconstruing as necessary, that the person is able to gain freedom from constricting personal systems that have outlived their anticipatory usefulness. Through this process it becomes possible to transcend obvious events and discard the constricting attributions that bind the person here and now, and to the past. The exploration and invention of new anticipatory orientations and commitments is a central aspect of what we understand to be the process of liberation.

In his discussion of psychotherapy, Kelly (1967, p. 255) states that "one of the intermediate goals of psychotherapy, then, is to help the client devise a construct system through which he is free to move towards something worthwhile." We take this to be the same as moving in the direction of optimal functioning. We would add that with some clients, movement may best be initiated by helping the client move through the entire experience cycle in spheres of his or her life other than the critical issues for which therapy is sought. The goal is to provide and support practice with the difficult, scary, and enlivening experiences of stumbling through, to completion, all phases of the cycle. Successfully completing encounter and reconstruing in relatively less threatening life issues can serve as a supportive base for moving toward more central issues, and thus help the client begin "moving toward something worthwhile."

An alternative way of saying this is that it becomes a matter of helping the person to face the choice outlined by his or her system; this choice, as we discussed earlier, is called the elaborative choice. The most helpful way to effect such a choice is to facilitate a process of *circumspection* (C), whereby the person considers all apparently relevant aspects of his or her situation, then moves to *preemption* (P), wherein one of these possible dimensions of meaning is chosen. Only then does the person *choose* (C) the one end of a bipolar dimension that will be his or her commitment. This C-P-C cycle is by no means automatic; it is possible to delay or to short-circuit the cycle in such a way that either no effective action is taken or too much action and not enough preliminary consideration rule the day.

Another question to consider here is how the personal system might gain the richness of constructions that will be needed in order to circumspect wisely. This brings us to what Kelly termed the *creativity cycle*, where one starts with a *loosened* construction of the world, such as in dreams and other altered states of consciousness, and ends with *tightened* constructs that enable the person to see the implications of specific ideas. For Kelly (1967, pp. 257−258), "one of the important interim goals of psychotherapy is to help the client make optimal use of his ability to think both loosely and tightly and to employ these two phases of the creativity cycle in a proper relationship to each other. Moreover, therapy should enable a person to span an optimal range of loosening and tightening without breaking up the process into disjunctive thinking." When considering the broad area of optimal functioning, we consider that these statements are applicable to a wider range of events than psychotherapy situations. It is interesting to consider how optimal education systems, patterns of family interaction, friendships and lover relationships, all designed and lived out to enhance personal growth, can facilitate a person's ability to move freely from loose to tight construing.

For example, classroom interactions designed to enhance the creativity and personal growth of students would encourage all aspects of the creativity cycle and full cycles of experience. Students would learn to develop and respect their powers of loose construing by working with dreams, meditation, "brain-storming," and dialogue, as well as the tighter processes of disciplined observation and categorizing, controlled manipulation of variables, and systematic review of relevant literature. From this perspective, the study of any academic area (science, social studies, etc.) would call for continual involvement by students in projects and creative experiments which require individuals and/or groups to move back and forth from loosely created responses to questions such as, "I wonder what would happen if . . ." and "What would it be like if . . ." and "How could it be that . . .," to more tightened, testable, or researchable hypotheses. The complete project would involve fully encountering the decided-on activity (by collecting the data or creating the model or interviewing the group under study, etc.) and actively going through the confirmation-disconfirmation and reconstruing processes described earlier. It may be worth noting that this emphasis on creativity and process does not deemphasize the importance of systematic and often painstaking "hard work." Rather, it looks toward better balance of the several phases of creative learning by directing teachers to reconnect and facilitate the loosened processes from which the tighter constructs grow in creative work. From this perspective, the teacher's role comes to resemble a process guide and consultant with less emphasis placed on supplying and "stuffing" academic content into passive student receptacles.

Similarly, relationships with significant other people can facilitate or inhibit movement from loose to tight construing of self, the partner, and the relationship. A crucial dimension here is the degree to which each person is willing to accept the continuity of change. For example, Jack can support the loose construing—in the forms of fantasy, daydreams, and so on—that Jill needs to do in the first stages of personal growth, if he feels comfortable with the very real possibilities of Jill's changing significantly in her perceptions of and goals for herself and their relationship. If, however, these possibilities upset, intimidate, or terrify Jack, he will tend to cling often desperately, to old constructs of himself and of Jill. Unwilling to accept or create change himself, he will work to inhibit or eliminate the possibility of Jill's construing their relationship freshly and creatively. Within the context of a relationship, then, this is an example of Jack's "hostile" (Kelly, 1955) attempts to force the environment (Jill) to revalidate constructs that have lost predictive value, and in the process he has acted to inhibit Jill's own creative growth processes.

THE PROCESS OF CONSTRUING

Speaking more generally now about the role psychological understanding plays in optimal functioning, Kelly (1977, p. 4) states "to serve as a theory one's psychological formulations must not only give him mechanistic prediction and control over the familiar acts of man, but provide access to human potentialities not yet realized." In dealing with theory in this connection he states further that "this means that a theory must be constructive, not merely representative." Kelly (1955) has noted that Personal Construct Theory parallels "professional" scientific theorizing, and thereby points to the importance of an individual's own theory of his/her world being an active, constructive process. As part of the full cycle of experience discussed above, the very act of construing is a way of providing access to human potential, a way of inventing the dimensions along which this potential may be developed by the person. It is the basic creative aspect of optimal functioning.

The act of construing is a way of reaching beyond that which is presently known, and thereby it is a method for transcending the obvious. The person, in Kelly's view, is reaching beyond the obvious to something that he or she has not known before. Kelly (1977) asserts that a person coming from a position of relative ignorance is able to reach out for knowledge no one has yet attained. We might add that this reaching out is not an automatic act; it is in itself a creative process, and the willingness to immerge with the unknown is part of what we are describing as optimal functioning. The transcendent function of constructive experience becomes more comprehensible when one realizes that even our most obvious understandings are themselves creations of a human constructive process rather than any real kind of objective truth.

As stated earlier, the ingredient that makes all of this work is the venture into the world with real action. It is only through a person's investing his/her whole being in a situation and actively anticipating what is going on that this person can find (or better, invent) the commitment that will enable real experience to happen. It is this active-commitment posture being a part of the full cycle of experience which allows the person to assess outcome, reconstrue as necessary, and decide if it will be worth the continuing price that will have to be paid for the venture. In a process of redefining potential, the person is able to choose that for which he or she will pay the ultimate price, that of spending an entire life pursuing the implications of this decision. Of course, this is all done with no guarantee that things will go "as they should." A deliberate choice, which impels continuing cycles of experience (which may prove the choice to be a wrong one), has some advantages over a constant drift where the oughts are imposed from the outside, and life is lived only for what others expect or demand.

Other positions have pointed out the consequences of short-circuiting what we call the full cycle by leaving out one or more phase of it. This is especially evident when the anticipations concern core life decisions. For example, Adler (1964) considers the anticipatory decision to pursue "mistaken goals" of personal superiority as leading to discouragement and lack of cooperation. Using different terminology, transactional analysis (Steiner, 1974) suggests that life decisions to pursue and validate a "life position" other than the central one of "I'm OK—you're OK" is basic to the development of life problems. In these early decisions, *anticipation* and *commitment* are certainly present, but the tenaciously held certainty about one's position in relation to others becomes a kind of dogma to be defended, and eliminates the hypothesis-testing stance, with possibilities of confirmation or disconfirmation which the personal construct position considers central to optimal functioning.

The process of "identity formation" described by Erikson (1963) and developed by Marcia (1966) also focuses on the processes leading to important life decisions. The model suggests that identity formation may follow several paths, leading toward identity achievement, foreclosure, or diffusion. Achievers have experienced a period of crisis and have resolved this crisis through commitments in several life domains (e.g., work, family relationships, politics, religion). The forecloser is also committed to a particular path in each of these domains, but the person has not experienced the crisis period leading to authentic personal choice; instead, the forecloser experiences these choices as having "always been there" or "having been made for him (or her)," often by parents. The diffuser has experienced neither crisis nor commitment and lives as if adrift, with no direction or long-range involvements. From the personal construct position we can see a parallel to the several aspects of the full cycle of experience. Erikson's theory would suggest that achievers are in the "healthiest" or most optimal position, and there are some data to support this idea (cf. Waterman et al., 1970). The achievement process seems to involve *encounter* with the life questions, wrestling with experience, openness to being affected, and a resulting *choice* and *commitment,* a long-term resolve from which the internal sense of "ought" described earlier can emerge and serve as a guide. Foreclosers make their decisions without encounter; they confirm their hypotheses without the inefficient bother of life-data, and their "oughts" are externally derived. Diffusers have decided (or act as if they've decided) to stay removed from the cycle rather completely. No anticipations, no threat of encounter or being affected, and thus no commitments develop at all. Though the diffused person may describe this style of life as some form of freedom, from the personal construct position it is more aligned with alienation, since freedom exists only in the context of active, committed choice. (See Kelly's [1977] discussion of the relationship between freedom and determinism on this issue.)

Without belaboring the point, we see that other theoretical positions have articulated the importance of how life decisions are made, and the implications of short-circuited decision processes for later functioning. Personal Construct Theory goes further, however, by emphasizing the full cycle process as a necessary and continual orientation to the world which permeates the life-style of optimally functioning people.

Ultimately, the criterion against which all of these ventures, decisions, and commitments are to be judged is life itself, as experienced by the person. We mean here the vitality-in-living, the "zest for life" derived from one's projects, as Sidney Jourard (1974) so aptly put it. In other words, this refers to the enlivening versus the deadening effects on the person of potential encounters with other people and events.

SOCIAL PROCESSES

A major aspect of optimal functioning for Personal Construct Theory concerns the social context, or, in other words, the relationships in which people engage. As in earlier discussions, the emphasis is placed on constructive processes, but the primary focus here is on the constructive processes of others. For optimal functioning in relation to another person, one must strive to see the world from the point of view of the other. The ability to take the role of the other and really to comprehend what things are like from the other's perspective places a person in a very special relationship to the other. The actions one decides on are based on the understanding one has gained concerning who the other is as a person, rather than orienting toward that person as an object to be manipulated. This is what we mean by creating a constructive relationship. As has been frequently pointed out, the creation of this constructive relationship does not mean that agreement or harmony will follow, but it does mean that actions within the relationship are undertaken with the knowledge that one is dealing with another actively construing human being who in some way is similar to oneself, yet in other ways quite different.

This constructive approach to relationships, which might be considered a key aspect of optimal functioning on a social level, is also of benefit for individual processes because of what it implies about the nature of the social reality against and within which each of one's own constructs will be validated or invalidated. Since most of a person's constructive activities center around the general social and interpersonal context, we have a better chance of truly validating or invalidating our own constructs if we understand the social processes (the meaning of the other's messages) through which this validation must take place. If I am construing a person as cruel versus kind and am then tightening this construct in order to test it, I had better be able to adequately interpret the other's actions based on his/her intended meaning, or else it will be very easy for me to draw the wrong conclusion. Of course, this occurs far too often. In a sense, this constructive relationship defines a major requirement for the openness to encounter and subsequent validations and revision processes of the experience cycle. A closed posture allows only one's own meaning to be attributed to the other's actions, and the self-fulfilling "hypotheses-validation-in-a-vacuum" process that follows is a sure road to keeping from true completion of the experience cycle. We might also add that relationships themselves, which are special kinds of reciprocal constructions, must, to be high-level, mutually enlivening experiences, go through full experience cycles, including the revisions of hypotheses based on authentic encounters. This is close to what Jourard (1974) describes as the continual "reinvention" necessary to make long-term, intimate relationships remain alive and life-giving.

A final topic in the social domain that we will briefly mention in the context of optimal functioning is the area of dependency. Kelly believed that it is far better to distribute one's dependencies, rather than concentrate them on one or two people. It is very unlikely that any one or two people will have the ability and/or resources to satisfy the diverse numbers of interpersonal needs experienced by any individual person. From this vantage point, it is better for all concerned to spread their dependencies over a relatively wide range in order to assure some realistic possibility of having the most important of these met (Kelly, 1969).

FACILITATING OPTIMAL FUNCTIONING

We conclude this overview of a Personal Construct Theory perspective of optimal functioning by discussing several techniques which may prove helpful in facilitating personal growth and optimal processes. The methods discussed either have been devised with construct theory as a basis, or are seen as congruent with the theoretical perspective. Clearly, the list is not exhaustive, but rather suggestive of some methods for facilitators to consider.

Self-Created Experiments as Growth Exercises

As mentioned earlier, completing the experience cycle is seen as an important aspect of optimal functioning, and practice in the process is considered valuable. In this procedure (suitable for classes on personal growth as well as counseling or growth groups) each member is asked to select a life problem with which he or she wants to work. The instructions include limiting the problem to a rather small, clearly defined area. From here, hypotheses are formed in terms of anticipations, which are then "translated" into operational terms (if the original anticipations were not already operational). Each person sets up a small experiment in living to furnish information about his or her hypotheses. These hypotheses might include sentence stems such as the following:

1. "I predict that if I do _____ , then my (roomate, mother, girlfriend, etc.) will respond to me _____ ."
2. "If I try _____ , the difficulties I will encounter will be _____ ."
3. "When I change my behavior in this way _____ (or during the time I am attempting to change my behavior), I will feel _____ ."
4. "When I successfully complete this change, the outcome in terms of my personal and interpersonal life will include _____ ."

The evidence is also anticipated—that is, what exactly will serve to support or refute the hypotheses? Journals are kept to record the hypotheses, evidence, and all other aspects of the experiment. As the project continues, the person can record the process of encounter and use the journal entries to assist in the final phases of assessing confirmation-disconfirmation, and reconstruing as necessary. The goal here is to help people systematically approach a problem area, to develop a strategy for dealing with it, and ideally to gain valuable experience in the process of completing the experience cycle.

Perception of Change

In a procedure described elsewhere (Epting, 1974), which is useful when working with individuals, groups, and classes, the person is asked to write a self-characterization in the third person as he or she was five years ago, is now, and hopes to be five years in the future. The person is also asked to describe the changes that he or she sees and to what he or she attributes these changes. The technique helps people gain heightened awareness of the flowing and/or stagnant dimensions along which they construe change to occur, and brings into focus the possibilities of experimenting with new dimensions. Discussion of the "five years in the future" section serves to emphasize the active future orientation and can serve to stimulate anticipations, hypothesizing, and experimenting as outlined in the first exercise. "What can you do now to begin moving toward the future fantasy? How will you know if you are making progress? What obstacles or problems do you envision?"

Photographic Self-description

As mentioned earlier, personal constructs are not necessarily cognitive or verbal in nature. Photographic self-description (Amerikaner, et al., 1978), a method designed to facilitate assessment and counseling processes with individual clients, couples, and groups, underscores this point. Individuals are asked to create a series of photographs which describe how they see themselves (and/or their partners in the case of couples). The resulting pictures, mounted on poster board, are used to help both clients and counselors understand nonverbal aspects of self-description. Moving away from the verbal to the visual, the images illustrate both symbolic and literal dimensions along which individuals have come to understand themselves. The pictures can be worked with individually or as a set, and provide an additional source of data for counselors and facilitators who may rely too heavily on verbal methods. When extended to working with couples, the task includes photographs of the partner; the pictures and subsequent discussion both generate valuable data on the current level at which the partners are "construing the constructions of the other," as well as simultaneously serving to improve empathic understanding within the relationship.

Multiple Role Group

The idea of "invention" has been emphasized as our preferred way of describing how optimally functioning people go about the business of creating their roles and projects. From this perspective, techniques are valuable which help people recognize the range of possibilities and their responsibility for choosing their own paths. The multiple role group is an approach to exploring and expanding role possibilities. In one case, a men's group explored the masculine role by displaying many potential dimensions of "maleness." In this group, members built alternative conceptualizations of masculinity as role figures with actual names. Each role figure had a major theme; for example, one was a rather dashing fellow named Jim Diamond. Sam Lampton was much more down to earth, a farmer close to his land and crops. There were scholars, artists, and businessmen as well. Precautions were taken to avoid stereotypes and oversimplified caricatures. Members enacted these roles and the group's task was to compile constructive descriptions. The method serves the varied purposes of safely "playing" with invention, facilitating both "loose" and "tight" construing, encouraging alternative constructions of "one" phenomenon (e.g., the male role, the teacher role), and enhancing the group members' potential for constructive relationships (as defined above) with those with whom they engage in role relationships.

As was noted earlier, these few exercises are simply examples of how a variety of the aspects of optimal functioning presented in this chapter can be focused on and facilitated. Though not derived from construct theory, other techniques drawn from the general counseling literature are certainly to be examined and used when appropriate for the facilitation of optimal processes. For example, the basic counseling skills of "active listening" (e.g., Egan, 1975) are fundamental to the high-level constructive relationships discussed earlier.

Learning the empathic processes basic to "construing the constructions of the other" through laboratory experience in constructive communication is therefore of value to a much wider range of people than counseling trainees. Other examples of useful techniques that are congruent with the personal construct position include the elicitation of early memories, through which we can begin to understand and untangle the conflicting and/or constricting constructions within which individuals keep themselves stuck and afraid of moving toward the future. Encouraging future fantasies, as used in values clarification and career counseling, can similarly help in the articulation of the dimensions which are serving as core self-constructs in the client's current construct system. Moving to another perspective on assessment, in which the construing of significant other people, such as family members, is included, we can benefit by using techniques developed by family therapists. One energizing and affectively engaging example is the process of "family sculpting." Here, each family member has an opportunity to physically position all family members in relation to one another. The procedure serves as a powerful method for assessing how shared, often unspoken family rules and closed constructions serve to keep individual family members from the exploring, encountering, and reconstruing that have been emphasized here as crucial to personal growth.

SUMMARY AND CONCLUSIONS

In the course of this paper we have attempted to elaborate Kelly's theoretical position in the development of a description of optimal functioning, and we have pointed out both similarities and differences with other leading formulations of optimal functioning. Much more attention was devoted to similarities since we believe that a personal construct approach can serve as a way of integrating these other theories into a comprehensive and more adequate description of what it means to be functioning at this high level.

In our description we emphasized the full cycle of experience and pointed out how this process is not merely cognitive, but an active, constructive orientation of the whole person toward his or her world. Emphasis was placed on a future-oriented invention and reinvention of possibilities as opposed to a discovery and uncovering of hidden potentials. In addition our description of optimal functioning made use of both the C−P−C cycle and the creativity cycle as well as the roles that sociality and dependency spread play in completing a description of the optimally functioning person.

Some implications of this position for the professional psychologist and psychotherapist were discussed which included a brief discussion of several techniques that may be helpful in facilitating movement toward this optimal level of functioning. The overall aim of our efforts in this paper is to provide a description of optimal functioning which will enable all of us to do more with our theoretical description in this area, in terms of operationalizing them for empirical investigations and practical application to the lives of men and women. It is our contention that this personal construct formulation can make significant contributions in this regard.

REFERENCES

Adler, A. *Social Interest: A Challenge to Mankind*. New York: Capricorn, 1964.

Allport, G. *Pattern and Growth in Personality*. New York: Holt, Rinehart and Winston, 1961.

Amerikaner, M., Shauble, P., and Ziller, R. Images: The use of photographs in personal counseling. Symposium presented to the American Personnel and Guidance Association. Washington, D.C., 1978.

Bugental, J. F. T. *The Search for Authenticity*. New York: Holt, Rinehart and Winston, 1965.

Combs, A., Richards, A., and Richards, F. *Perceptual Psychology: A Humanistic Approach to the Study of Persons*. New York: Harper and Row, 1976.

Egan, G. *The Skilled Helper*. Monterey, CA: Brooks-Cole, 1975.

Ellenberger, H. A clinical introduction to psychiatric phenomenology and existential analysis. In R. May, E. Angel and H. Ellenberger, (Eds.), *Existence*. New York: Basic Books, 1958.

Epting, F. An exploration of personal change. Paper presented at Association for Humanistic Psychology, Annual Meeting. New Orleans, 1974.

Erikson, E. *Childhood and Society*. New York: Norton, 1963.

Gendlin, E. Experential psychotherapy. In R. Corsini (Ed.), *Current Psychotherapies*. Itasca, IL: Peacock, 1973.

Gendlin, E. Experential focusing and the problem of getting movement in psychotherapy. In D. Nevill (Ed.), *Humanistic Psychology: New Frontiers*. New York: Gardner, 1977.

Goldstein, K. *The Organism*. New York: American Book, 1939.

Jourard, S. *The Transparent Self: Self Disclosure and Well-Being* (revised ed.). New York: Van Nostrand, 1971.

Jourard, S. *Healthy Personality: An Approach from the Viewpoint of Humanistic Psychology*. New York: Macmillan, 1974.

Jourard, S. Marriage Is for Life. Paper presented to American Association of Marriage and Family Counselors. St. Louis, 1974.

Kelly, G. A. *The Psychology of Personal Constructs:* Vols. 1 and 2. New York: Norton, 1955.

Kelly, G. A. A psychology of the optimal man. In A. Maher (Ed.), *The Goals of Psychotherapy*. New York: Appleton-Century-Crofts, 1967.

Kelly, G. A. In whom confide: On whom depend for what. In B. Maher (Ed.), *Clinical Psychology and Personality: The Selected Papers of George Kelly*. New York: Wiley, 1969.

Kelly, G. A. The psychology of the unknown. In D. Bannister (Ed.), *New Perspectives in Personal Construct Theory*. New York: Academic, 1977.

Marcia, J. Development and validation of ego-identity status. *Journal of Personality and Social Psychology*, 1966, **3**, 551−558.

Maslow, A. A theory of meta-motivation: The biological rooting of the value life. *Journal of Humanistic Psychology*, 1967, **7**, 93−127.

Maslow, A. *Toward a Psychology of Being*. New York: Van Nostrand, 1968.

Maslow, A. *The Farther Reaches of Human Nature*. New York: Viking, 1971.

Perls, F. *Gestalt Therapy Verbatim*. Moab, UT: Real People Press, 1969.

Rogers, C. *On Becoming a Person*. Boston: Houghton-Mifflin, 1961.

Simon, S. *Meeting Yourself Halfway*. Niles, Il: Argus Communications, 1974.

Steiner, C. *Scripts People Live*. New York: Grove Press, 1974.

Von Bertalanffy, L. *General System Theory*. New York: Braziller, 1968.

Waterman, C., Buebel, M., and Waterman A. Relationship between resolution of the identity crisis and outcomes of previous psychological crises. *Proceedings of the Annual Convention of APA*. 1970, **5**, 467−468.

CHAPTER 5

George Kelly as Therapist:
A Review of His Tapes

Robert A. Neimeyer

George A. Kelly's contribution to psychology was not limited to his theory of personality, although it is this aspect of his work that seems most widely recognized, at least in the United States. Nor was it limited to the development of a single psychometric technique (the Role Construct Repertory Test) or a single psychotherapeutic strategy (Fixed Role Therapy) as some clinicians seem to conclude. Unfortunately, the preoccupation of psychologists with these aspects of his work has obscured, until recently, much that is original and still provocative in Kelly's thought. One such underexplored horizon in Personal Construct Theory (PCT) is its broad approach to psychotherapeutic change. Admittedly, important publications dealing with this topic have begun to appear (e.g., Landfield, 1971; Fransella, 1972; Bannister, 1975; Epting, in press), but by and large these have consisted of research reports or discussions of the general principles underlying PCT therapy rather than treatments of the specific clinical procedures (e.g., loosening, reassurance, enactment) which Kelly set forth in Volume 2 of his cornerstone (1955) work. This chapter was written to redirect attention to several of these procedures by analyzing excerpts from Kelly's own clinical practice which illustrate their use. As we shall see, a consideration of these procedures will often lead us back to an examination of the theory in which they are embedded, and which alone gives them cohesiveness and direction.

THE DATA

The material for this analysis is provided by tape recordings of Kelly's therapy with Cal Weston,[1] conducted only a few years after the initial publication of Kelly's 1955 work. Of the total number of interviews Cal had with Kelly, fewer than half remain; whether these represent an intentionally retained or random record of the therapy is

[1]The client's name and all other identifying information have been fictionalized to protect his identity. The author and editors wish to express their profound appreciation to the client, who, 20 years after this therapy was completed, gave his permission for the discreet scholarly use of the audio tape recordings.

unknown. The incompleteness of the taped record and the poor quality of many of the recordings impose certain limitations upon the type of analysis that can meaningfully be conducted. In particular, an attempt at evaluating the "outcome" of therapy or its overall "effectiveness," based only upon this partial record without follow-up, would seem unsound. A more responsible approach would focus upon the "process" of the therapy, although the thoroughgoing longitudinal analysis of such process also is frustrated by the fragmentary nature of the recordings. For this reason, I have confined myself primarily to the consideration of relatively molecular interchanges between client and therapist, and have attempted to interpret these in light of the therapeutic strategies Kelly outlines in his writings. Less frequently, but just as important, I will attend to Kelly's overarching goals for the therapy as they are implicit in his actions, and will suggest the theoretical convictions that influence his formulation and treatment of this specific case.

PHYSICAL CONTEXT FOR THERAPY

Kelly has written in some detail of the setting in which he preferred to conduct therapy (1955, pp. 627–631). Electronic recording of sessions was becoming a feasible and increasingly common technical aid to therapy by the mid- to late 1950s, and one that Kelly obviously found useful in his own practice. We know from an introductory remark by Kelly that he secured the client's permission for recording early in the first session, probably by introducing it as an aid in helping him to "go back over each interview and study it carefully" (1955, p. 628). The microphone, though not concealed, was inconspicuously situated so as to minimize the distraction it might cause the client. Auditory clues also suggest that Kelly separated himself from the client by a desk, establishing, as he preferred, a distance of "six to eight feet" (1955, p. 629) between therapist and client. It is worth noting that such features of Kelly's therapy represent more a reflection of the historical context within which he worked than essential characteristics of Personal Construct Therapy itself. Therapy obviously can be conducted sensitively and effectively at somewhat closer range, and without interposing a desk or other object between interactants, which might restrict the therapist's awareness of the client's nonverbal expressions. Interestingly, Kelly did seek to personalize the therapeutic interaction by offering the client a cup of coffee at the commencement of each session, reflecting his concern that the setting be one that facilitated personal discussion.

INITIAL ELABORATION

Kelly's client, Cal Weston, was a 28-year-old university student still pursuing his undergraduate degree after having spent some time in the military. Although no taped record of session number one remains, it is clear from remarks in later sessions that Cal's initial complaint centered on his inability to choose a career and his long-standing academic problems. Kelly evidently spent the first interview encouraging Cal to sketch in some detail the dimensions of the presenting problem from his own viewpoint.

The second semiweekly session begins with Kelly's inviting Cal to *elaborate the complaint* (1955, Chapter 18)—that is, to consider the wider implications of his presenting problem as they might have become clear since the first interview.

> *Kelly:*   Would you recapitulate the problem as you see it now, at this point?
>
> *Cal:*   The problem is trying to find my goal in life; I've had a difficulty in finding myself . . . my wording slips . . . The problem is I've never had to study before, and I've been getting C's and B's. Now I'm failing language because I'm not studying.

Kelly's approach here differentiates his therapy from models of treatment that take the client's complaint *literally* and then develop a therapeutic "contract" that specifies as the goal of therapy the elimination or alleviation of the sharply delimited presenting problem. On the other hand, Kelly does not *dismiss* Cal's version of his difficulties as distorted or irrelevant to the actual dynamics of the case. Rather, Kelly takes the client's complaint seriously, but regards it as the point of entry into his larger *construct system,* on the assumption that Cal's constructions of himself and others may be problematic in a broader sense than is strictly implied by his initial complaint. Some vindication of this assumption is provided by Cal's updated reiteration of his difficulties. At first, he *dilates* or enlarges his perception of the problem to include his difficulty in finding himself and his goal in life, then *constricts* or narrows his construction to include primarily academic concerns. Constriction, used in this way, temporarily can serve to reduce the anxiety that would accompany the recognition of a more broadly defined problem, though it is seldom a workable strategy for avoiding it indefinitely (Kelly, 1955, p. 901).

In describing his attempted solutions to his problems as he formulated them, Cal dwelt upon his need to study more for the courses he was failing, while giving little attention to those subjects which he didn't "need" to study. Kelly questioned whether this was not the kind of rationale that had been an "open manhole" for him in the past, but Cal assured him that his "insight" that he needed to study seemed different from the traps he has set for himself previously. Kelly pursues this:

> *K:*   And this really does seem different than other times?
>
> *C:*   So far . . .
>
> *K:*   I sense that this was a happy discovery rather than a depressing one. Am I guessing right?
>
> *C:*   Happy, yes, if it does provide a solution.
>
> *K:*   And if not, if it's another false alarm, will it make you feel worse than ever?
>
> *C:*   No, at least it will have been tried.
>
> *K:*   So even if it doesn't yield better grades, it has already provided a kind of yield in self-respect and comfort.
>
> *C:*   But not yet as far as I'd like it to be.

Kelly's concern over whether or not he is "guessing right" in his hypothesizing about the nature of Cal's "discovery" points up his understanding of the first major task confronting the psychotherapist: to demonstrate his *acceptance* of the client, not simply by creating the proper "emotional" atmosphere, but by accurately subsuming the constructs by which the client operates (1955, p. 589). He goes on to explicate this point in dialogue with Cal.

K: You see, it's important for me to know *how* these ideas work for you, what it means to you. I could jump at a conclusion as to what they might mean, but this is the reason I ask . . . Is studying the answer?

C: To getting my grades up, yes. To finding myself, no.

Up to this point in therapy, Kelly has occupied himself with elaborating Cal's construction of the complaint and the alternative solutions he envisions or has attempted. Having glimpsed the breadth of Cal's problems and the inefficacy of his means of dealing with them, Kelly now begins to shift his attention to Cal's conception of therapy itself. Kelly did not consider it essential that the client share the clinician's perception of the change process. However, he did recognize that "the client's conceptualization of psychotherapy represents a body of constructs whose permeability determines how extensively he can envision therapeutic change in himself" (1955, p. 567). For the individual whose construction of therapy is *impermeable*—that is, incapable of incorporating new understandings as therapy evolves—change may be limited to small-scale technical adjustments within the preexisting construct system. On the other hand, the client whose conception of psychotherapy appears more flexible is more likely to undertake a larger-scale, ongoing reconstruction of her or his approach to life. Because such conceptions on the part of the client provide a regulating framework within which progress can take place, Kelly considered it important to subsume Cal's construction of therapy within his own more comprehensive interpretation of their interaction. He approaches the exploration of this area in a concrete, rather than an abstract, manner by asking Cal about his expectations regarding the person of the therapist.

K: Let me ask a little more intimate question. What kind of therapist did you hope that I would be?

C: I don't know. I came with the anticipation that I would get some therapeutic help. The kind doesn't matter.

Cal's response to this question reveals little about his construction of psychotherapy, so Kelly adopts a second approach.

K: Another kind of question that it might be helpful to think about for a moment: If we are to be successful in this undertaking together, do you have any picture of what kind of person you would be, at the end of the sessions?

C: I hope I wouldn't fly off, and not have this temper. If I let off feelings I'm supposed to be better off. It seems to me it would be better if I didn't have them, if I weren't tense.

As Kelly notes in his writing, questions of this sort illuminate the client's expectations regarding therapy, since the answer "throws considerable light upon what he expects the therapist to do for him" (1955, p. 988). From Cal's viewpoint, a chief aim of therapy would be the alleviation of his chronic tension, a tension that sometimes erupts in explosive outbursts directed at physical objects in his environment. One source of this tension seems to be the conflict he experiences over his choice of career: teaching versus the ministry. Both were professions chosen by his father, who despite his diligent work did not find a satisfying position until he was in his 50s. Kelly explored with Cal the "central respects" in which he did, and did not, "want to follow in these same footsteps."

K: Well, this adds up to some kind of vocational conflict anyway.

C: Yes, and Dad has very little time to be a member of the family. His major relaxation is the TV. I don't know what he'd do without it.

K: Well, this is interesting, isn't it? You've come back to your father's kind of vocational interest—teaching, that sort of thing, the ministry—but throughout much of your life you've been avoiding his kind of grinding scholarship.

C: Yeah.

K: And you are a little frightened at your own delay in finding an occupation, because you see *his* delay. . . . The austerity of certain features of his life is a little frightening, a little disturbing to you. And at the same time you share certain of his enthusiasms, the occupations. Am I on the trail of something there, or, rather, are you? . . . Has this increased the conflict in your own mind?

C: I'm not sure I'm following you entirely . . .

K: Is it like a person who would like to explore the North Pole, but doesn't want to get his feet cold? (Both laugh.)

C: That's a possibility I hadn't thought of, that I might be interested in the field of education, but might not be willing to become a scholar.

K: Well, you just don't want to have to grind that way. If you could just find a way to find yourself in that profession, without having to do all that to get there . . . Does that fit, or is something missing?

C: When I try to think back on what we've said here, nothing comes through. Maybe I've been too relaxed, not listening hard enough.

K: No, what we've tried here is a type of interpretation that doesn't quite fit. Let's lay it aside.

C: It comes a little too quickly, a little too smooth.

K: I think so too. And maybe our interview comes a little too smooth so far, and yet it seems as if this possible breakdown is what was being said in here. But there are other levels of understanding.

C: I would definitely agree that what I want is a life involving the educational field, but not the long hours my father has had to put in in order to achieve that. Money is also a problem.

K: And this formulation doesn't take that into account . . .

C: . . . But it takes into account more than I thought . . .

K: But this is just an hypothesis, you see, that we look at, try on for size, and understand that when we attempt a formulation, either of us, whether you attempt one or I attempt one, we look at it. These are always tentative until they really seem to work, until they work for us.

This exchange highlights Kelly's characteristic use of humor to render less threatening a potentially disquieting interpretation, as well as the active, hypothesizing role he plays during the interview. Since his entire theoretical edifice is erected on the metaphor of "man-as-scientist" (1955, p. 4ff.), it is hardly surprising that Kelly accords to the client in psychotherapy the status of "co-investigator," whose own experience helps to validate or invalidate the propositions that either propound. Much of therapy, from a personal construct perspective, can be analogized to scientific inquiry (Kelly, 1955, pp. 940–941). A primary therapeutic goal is the elaboration of a personal "theory" which enables the client to impart structure and coherence to his or her past life, and which embraces "hypotheses" or constructs that allow for the anticipation of future realities. As such hypotheses are formulated, the therapist assists the client in designing "experiments" to be conducted in the "laboratory" of the interview room or to be "field-tested" in the course of every-day life. Together, the two evaluate the results of such experiments and grapple with their implications for the client's existing construct system. This scientific analogy—sometimes explicit, sometimes only implicit in Kelly's therapy—serves as an organizing framework for clinical practice that sets construct theory therapy apart from more traditional approaches which seem predicated upon very different root metaphors: "man-as-biological-organism," in the case of Freudian analysis, and "man-as-behaving-animal," in the case of orthodox behavior therapy.

DEFENSES

Just prior to the beginning of the fifth interview, Kelly records a prologue on his interpretation of "defensiveness" and its relation to Cal's "vulnerability," which apparently has become more salient during the four preceding unrecorded sessions.

When we talk about defenses within Personal Construct Theory, we are saying essentially that the construct system does not support the kinds of insights we think the person ought to be able to see, and indeed it might set up construct dimensions along quite unexpected lines . . .

He notes Cal's inability to "carry through the implications of his own present helplessness" and his reliance upon the therapist, and observes that Cal's academic problems persist because "it has not occurred to him that the task is for him himself to get on with the establishment of whatever habits he thinks are necessary." He continues:

Personal Construct Theory, then, is concerned with these defenses, not just as kinds of perversity toward the therapist, but as genuinely vulnerable points in the construct system. Some confusion, some anxiety, some hostility may help protect the individual.

Kelly then moves on to the passivity and avoidance of responsibility that has characterized Cal's approach to his problems, and notes:

There is implicit in this kind of thinking, the stimulus-response outlook toward psychology. He feels that if he could just get the right stimulus, then his responses would take care of themselves, and he keeps looking outside of himself for the stimuli. Now this is the kind of trap that S-R psychology sets for the individual himself. Often it is very helpful to look at things in S-R terms if you are yourself outside the situation. But in dealing with your own problems, to sit around and wait for stimuli to prod you—which is what S-R theory often does, I fear—really puts you in a position where you cannot move. Personal Construct Theory, of course, would lead one to look for interpretations of his stimuli, and if he doesn't like what his responses are, to review his interpretations, as well as the stimuli themselves.

It is interesting that Kelly finds himself confronting *therapeutically* what he had long confronted *theoretically*—the implications of a form of psychological discourse inimical to his own more person-centered outlook. Both the more extreme behaviorist formulations of the 1950s and his own psychotherapy client seemed to subscribe to a kind of naive philosophical *realism,* which understood an individual's reactions to be determined by the contingencies represented in her or his environment. Both underemphasized the capacity of the person to creatively construct alternative conceptual templates which would impute new meanings to the "stimuli" one encountered, and which would permit one to establish alternative modes of being or acting in the world. Kelly's position, on the other hand, fundamentally was built on the latter view. Kelly termed this philosophical position *constructive alternativism,* the assumption that

All of our present interpretations of the universe are subject to revision or replacement . . . We take the stand that there are always some alternative constructions available to choose among in dealing with the world. No one needs to paint himself into a corner . . . no one needs to be the victim of his biography (1955, p. 15).

Both of these themes—the client's vulnerability and his tendency to embody an unsophisticated rendition of S-R psychology—surface during the next two interviews.

LOOSENING AND TIGHTENING

Cal opens the fifth session with the remark, "I'm not in as good a shape as last time," and proceeds to discuss an "explosion" which was "triggered off" in him as he was typing letters of application to various seminaries the day before. He found himself "making a pile of errors" which resulted in his "exploding" and breaking his glasses. Even a day later, he reports that his muscles are "quivering, uneasy."

In construct theory terms, this incident can be understood as the outcome of severe *anxiety* attendant on too much structural *loosening* in the client's previously *tight* constructions. Kelly defines anxiety as "the recognition that the events with which one is confronted lie outside the range of convenience of one's construct system" (1955, p. 495). In other words, anxiety is experienced when one becomes immersed in events that appear incomprehensible and jeopardize one's ability to anticipate what might happen next. For the client who lives exclusively in the realm of *tight* construction (i.e., for whom events have fixed, explicit, prescribed and unalterable meanings), psychotherapeutic change may induce considerable apprehension. Previously tight constructions are temporarily *loosened,* made elastic and tenuous, in order to "set the stage for creative thinking that is to come later. The loosening releases facts, long taken as self-evident, from their rigid conceptual moorings" (Kelly, 1955, p. 1031). Although such loosening serves several important therapeutic functions (Kelly, 1955, p. 1033), it represents only one phase of the "Creativity Cycle" which must terminate in revised tightened construction if it is to offer the individual fresh and more viable alternatives in everyday life (Kelly, 1955, p. 528−530).

As Cal reports the impact of his explosive outburst the day before and his confusion about its meaning, Kelly asks: "Is this like other experiences you've had?" This question represents an immediate attempt on Kelly's part to *retighten* Cal's construction in order to alleviate the overwhelming anxiety he is experiencing. In essence, the question urges Cal to begin the task of *construing* the apparently uninterpretable experience. Since constructs are by definition dimensions that abstract similarities among some aspects of one's experience and differentiate these from others (Kelly, 1955, pp. 50−51), the act of elaborating the similarity between two events represents one means of producing a tighter structure within which both can be viewed (Kelly, 1955, p. 1074). The task of structuring this area of Cal's experience occupies the bulk of the fifth session, during which Kelly treats Cal very gently so as to avoid precipitating him into the same unmanageable anxiety with which he walked in. He concludes by saying:

K: I think at this point the thing to do is for me to understand just the experience itself well enough, so that you begin to feel more and more free to tell me what is going on in your own feelings and your own outlook.

C: Right now, each time we come to a stop, a halt, temporary as it may be, I feel a little relaxed. And then as soon as you start talking again, trying to find the key, that is, trying to bring things together . . . I feel a tenseness building up in me even with this.

K: This is the reason, you see, that I think it is not appropriate for me to try to put things together too much . . . you'll have to help me understand you by being as clear as you can (another attempt by Kelly to keep Cal temporarily dealing only in explicit, tightened constructions), and by correcting me whenever I seem to be misinterpreting you. This is our first job. We're not going to try to solve a whole bunch of problems all at once, as if we could.

REASSURANCE

The opening of the sixth session, held later the same week, makes it clear that Cal's tension has not subsided entirely during the intervening days, although no major eruptions of anxiety have occurred.

K: We'll give you the ball today, to start with . . .

C: I have noticed developing . . . a nervous tenseness throughout my upper legs, upper arms and chest and abdomen.

K: Yeah. . . . Now let me suggest something at this point because, while I don't know everything that may be involved in this—it may be due to studies or lack of studies; it may be due to things happening on the outside; it may be due to things that neither of us is quite ready to appraise—but let me throw this into the picture as a matter of a wee bit of reassurance. Sometimes in therapy as we begin to reopen closet doors that have been shut, even though we haven't opened anything with very creaky hinges (Cal laughs), as we do this there sometimes are impulses that slip through. One finds himself acting impulsively where once he may have had some control. For if we are to go through this house and take a look at all the closets and all the plumbing, it may be that some articles will fall down . . .

C: A few skeletons might rattle, hmm?

K: Well, I don't know if they're skeletons or not, but you know, a storage closet that has been packed full for some time, and you open the door . . .

C: A Dagwood storage closet, you mean . . .

K: Yeah, you've got the idea . . . it doesn't mean that this answers our questions about it, but at least I think you can feel some assurance that things like this do happen at stages . . .

Two features of this passage are noteworthy. First, Kelly operates in a *metaphoric mode* at this juncture, as he often does throughout therapy. Although Kelly did not give metaphor a formal place in his theory or his therapy, it might be understood as the act of importing a construction used to interpret one domain of experience in order to structure another, perhaps underdimensioned domain in a new way. In this case, he analogizes Cal's outbreak of anxiety to articles tumbling out of "a storage closet that has been packed full for some time" when its door is opened in the course of therapeutic exploration. Kelly elaborates this metaphor with the client in order to reassure him that his experience is to some degree predictable, and this introduces the second noteworthy feature of this excerpt. *Reassurance,* in construct theory terms, is

. . . a simplified superordinate construction placed upon the clinical situation. It is communicated to the client so that his behavior and ideas will temporarily appear to him to be consistent, acceptable and organized. It is never more than a temporary expedient . . . yet it does have its place in therapy (Kelly, 1955, p. 699).

For Kelly, reassurance represents a minor palliative technique that can be useful, if used judiciously, in reducing the anxiety that may accompany a precipitous breakdown in the client's construct system. It is not without its hazards, however, since it may tend to confirm the client's vulnerability and foster dependency upon the therapist (Kelly, 1955, p. 651).

THE NATURE OF THERAPY

Having buttressed Cal's existing structures through reassurance, Kelly refocuses attention to the nature of psychotherapy. This move seems to follow from his perception that the client will experience recurrences of anxiety until he abandons the passivity implicit in his "stimulus-response" conception of therapy and sets about the task of building more adequate constructions of his life role. A necessary propaedeutic to such constructive revision would be his sharing more actively with Kelly the fundaments of his own outlook.

K: You see, what goes on in therapy is often not very much a matter of what the therapist does. Because the goings-on, the important goings-on, the center of action and behavior and thinking and reorientation is in your noggin, not in mine. That's the theater of operations.

C: That's what (my previous counselor) said. He said that he was there strictly to probe and prod when my own investigation dies down, or hits one of those "brick walls" as I call them.

K: Yeah. That was an interesting figure you used of the "brick walls," and we want to remember it. But that's the way it felt, wasn't it?

C: Yeah, something real solid. There's nothing much more solid than a brick wall.

K: Yeah. Not only does it stop you, but it makes you detour, makes you go around . . . or do you feel yourself just flattened up against it, sort of?

C: Well, I don't know, I can't recall any of the instances clearly . . .

K: Okay. It's just that I want to understand it as well as I can, and as you get words to describe it for me or as you get additional feelings that enrich the meaning of this, guide me along with you on it.

Kelly has digressed here momentarily to explore Cal's metaphor of the "brick walls" he runs up against at points of impasse in therapy. The careful examination of such idiosyncratic images is consistent with Kelly's injunction that therapeutic communication be conducted within the personal language system of the client in order to carry maximum richness and impact (1955, p. 642). He then returns to his discussion of therapy.

K: I don't see therapy—it may be of help for you to know this—I don't see therapy as simply a matter of probing, my probing. I see it more as a matter of my coming *first* to understand your outlook as well as possible, and for that, you see, you have to take quite a bit of initiative and educate me. And once we've got the outlook, once we've got the pattern, the way you handle things, the way you do things, then we can start to inquire to see whether these are effective, to see whether these are working, to see what the gaps seem to be. And we can join with each other in a series of inquiries, but it . . . isn't quite probing.

C: Well, I think what I meant was that as I would do the probing myself . . .

K: Ok.

C: . . . the investigation, and that the role of the psychologist would be that when I hit something and didn't want to go any further, he would try to *stimulate* me with questions to *cause* me to *respond* in one way or another.

K: Ok . . . now we'll learn to work with each other as we go along.

It is clear that Kelly is still confronting Cal's recalcitrant conceptualization of therapy in stimulus-response terms. Despite their "theoretical" differences, however, they appear to be making some progress, as the following interchange suggests.

C: One of my problems in the past is that I haven't opened up at all to anyone else. So the ability to tell you what you want to know is not there 'cause it's never been used.

K: I sense this. When I tell you, "Come on, come on, give out with real feelings," you open your mouth but the words don't come out the way you want them to. I know you're trying; and you'll notice I don't nag you too much. Could I ask you this, just for my own help: Have you opened up with me more than with most people, or more than anyone else?

C: Yes.

K: This helps me understand at what level you're operating. You're really on the frontier of opening up right now.

C: I don't know if I'm on the frontier, but I'm much further towards the frontier . . . than I have ever been with anyone else before.

THE REP TEST IN PSYCHOTHERAPY

In his prologue to the fifth session Kelly had contemplated administering a Role Construct Repertory Test (Rep Test) to Cal during that hour, should the appropriate opportunity present itself. Cal voiced his anxious concern about his "explosion" at the outset of the interview, however, and Kelly, sensitive to the client's immediate needs, decided to postpone testing. By the sixth session, Kelly obviously had evaluated both the advantages of testing (e.g., its potential for elucidating previously undisclosed facets of the client's construct system) and its disadvantages (e.g., its threat to the therapeutic relationship [1955, pp. 978–982]), and had decided that in Cal's case the former outweighed the latter.

Kelly's Rep Test is actually the designation of an entire collection of flexible psychometric techniques (cf. Fransella and Bannister, 1977; Neimeyer and Neimeyer, in press) which can be adapted to the study of virtually any topic of psychological interest. In its clinical employment, however, the Rep Test usually represents a concept formation task which requires the respondent to compare and contrast sets of significant others who occupy certain prescribed roles in his or her own life (e.g., mother, close friend). In addition to its utility in illuminating the principal construct dimensions by means of which the client structures the interpersonal world, the Rep Test may minimize the threat entailed in testing by giving the client more opportunity to express her or his point of view than many tests allow. Kelly's use of the technique in Cal's case illustrates its clinical employment. Kelly introduced the Rep Test by saying:

Maybe today is a good time to do something more formal and less involving and less tension provoking. You remember I mentioned we might do kind of a formal exercise to give me some better understanding of how you see things. I don't think you'll find this particularly threatening; if you do, by all means tell me.

Kelly then proceeded to read to Cal a heterogeneous list of role titles, asking him to designate the figure in his own life who occupied, or most nearly occupied, each of the roles.[2] Even Cal's responses to this minimally demanding task are of considerable clinical interest. For example, he hesitated in naming his mother and father, pausing "to stop and think" about how he referred to them before responding. When Kelly asked him to designate the name of his girlfriend, Cal replied nervously, "You're safe there," adding that no one presently came close to occupying that place in his life. In providing the name of an "ex-girlfriend," Cal remarked after some delay that he would "have to go back 13 years or so" to find a name. Similarly, when asked to supply the name of a neighbor, he indicated that there was "no one within two miles" with whom he spoke. Unusually long pauses (sometimes of a couple of minutes) followed Kelly's request that Cal designate someone who "appeared to dislike" him, a person for whom he felt "sorry," someone with whom he felt "most uncomfortable," the "most successful" person he knew personally, the "happiest" person he had known, and an individual who appeared "to meet the highest ethical standards." Clearly, even this preliminary phase of Rep Test administration offered abundant documentation of the sense of interpersonal isolation that Cal must have experienced poignantly, although it had seldom found expression up to this point in therapy.

When Cal had provided the names of individuals who most nearly filled each of the role titles, Kelly began the "construct elicitation" phase of the administration. He handed Cal cards on which he had written three of the 22 names that Cal had supplied, and instructed him:

Look at these three people. Tell me if you see some important way in which two of them are alike, but which distinguishes them from the third.

Cal was then to sort the remaining figures into two stacks, indicating whether they fit the first or second pole of the constructs that had been elicited. For example, Cal described two teachers and the person he would "like to get to know better" as

---

[2]Detailed procedures for the administration, scoring, and clinical interpretation of the Rep Test are provided by Kelly (1955, Chapters 5 and 6).

"elderly, successful" and contrasted them with the neighbor, the uncomfortable person, and both of his parents, whom he construed as "like a young student." His construction of his mother and father as more like students than successful adults is clinically significant, as are his allocations of other elements to the constructs he provided. Later in the structured interview, for instance, he assigned his mother and a former friend to the "disappointment" pole of a construct, contrasting them with figures who had "helped" him. As he was doing so he explained: "That's the way I put them impulsively, but I don't appreciate the implications." Remarks of this kind are consistent with Kelly's assertion that psychodiagnostic testing must be understood as an interpersonal event affecting the perception of the client as well as the therapist; that it operates "as a confrontation likely to have therapeutic repercussions" (1955, p. 980).

Unfortunately, the fact that most of Cal's sorts were not audibly recorded on the tape precludes the kinds of sophisticated "structural" analyses of the Rep Test that are available (Fransella & Bannister, 1977; Neimeyer & Neimeyer, in press). It is noteworthy, however, that Cal rarely construed this set of role figures in terms of "psychological" dimensions bearing on their personalities, feelings, or outlooks, but instead concentrated on their success, age, social roles, and whether or not he respected or disliked them.

After the session had ended, Kelly privately recorded a few observations concerning Cal's responses. He noted that the client's Rep Test displayed "a good deal of concretism," and "certain kind of rigidity" related to Cal's frequent need for a "third category" into which to sort the figures, rather than assigning them in clear-cut fashion to one pole or the other of the constructs he had used. In construct theory terms, this suggests the narrow *range of convenience* of most of Cal's constructs; that is, their inability to apply meaningfully to many of the important persons in his life. Kelly also noted that several of the female figures were "pretty remote," and implied that the concretism of Cal's interpersonal construing and his estrangement from people in general and his parents in particular could be explored more actively in upcoming sessions.

SELF-DESCRIPTION

Both the administration of the Rep Test and Kelly's earlier questioning concerning Cal's conception of therapy represented attempts to lift into focus aspects of the client's construct system which were neglected in the discussion of his presenting problem per se. Kelly employs a third such strategy early in the eleventh session, by inviting Cal to elaborate his construction system through self-description.

> *K:* What kind of picture do you think you've given me of you, as compared with the kind of picture I would have if I really knew you?
>
> *C:* . . . when I'm feeling real good, my portrayal would be blacker than the way I'm feeling. When I'm feeling lousy, it's probably a little lighter shade of gray than I actually feel.

K: . . . what kind of *person* do you think I see when I look at you?

C: I'd say a person who's probably confused a little bit, who's unsure of himself.

K: Go on; you're doing fine.

C: . . . I can't dig up anything else.

Kelly's intent in asking for such a self-description is to provide the client with the opportunity for conveying the larger sense of *self* within which his present problems are anchored. If the therapeutic enterprise is to be effective, the clinician needs to have a perspective on the client's resources as well as his vulnerabilities, and this requires "elaboration of the construction system as a whole, not just those unfortunate constructions which are applied to problem areas" (Kelly, 1955, p. 985).

ENACTMENT

In Cal's case, however, this direct approach makes minimal headway. Kelly then switches tactics and attempts a *casual enactment* procedure targeted at achieving similar ends.

K: If you were to . . . imagine yourself in my place, and I were asked to describe Cal Weston to someone, with some care, what do you imagine you would say? You're Dr. Kelly, describing Cal Weston to a close associate in whom you have confidence, and you wish to sketch accurately and with some depth, some sensitivity, the Cal Weston that has been seen for eleven interviews now . . . I'll be the friend; you're Dr. Kelly.

C: Outside of what I've said, I don't know if I could say anything; I can't think of anything.

K: "I'm seeing a fellow by the name of Cal Weston." This could be your first sentence. Now what sentence comes next?

C: (Long pause.)

K: What kind of a patient is this, Dr. Kelly?

C: I'm trying to think of something, but I'm not getting anywhere fast.

K: You mean you can't describe him, Dr. Kelly? (Long pause.) How well do you think you know your patient, Dr. Kelly?

C: I don't know how that would be answered. I'm just drawing a blank in my mind, that's all. Nothing.

Kelly's approach to this therapeutic exercise typifies his use of casual enactment techniques, informal role-playing procedures which can be used spontaneously in therapy with therapist and client enacting the parts. This specific scenario that Kelly suggested invites Cal not only to take perspective on his problems, but also to indicate his interpretation of Kelly's outlook (Kelly, 1955, p. 1152). Cal, however, has considerable difficulty playing Kelly's part, a fact that is hardly surprising given the concretistic character of his interpersonal construing as evidenced on the Rep Test. Kelly attempts to control Cal's tendency to drop out of cast by staying in cast himself and interpreting even his silences as if they occurred in his role as "Kelly" (1955, p. 1154). Even this tactic is unsuccessful, however, and Kelly steps out of cast to discuss his client's uneasiness.

> *K:*   How do you feel about this kind of exercise? Is it disturbing?
>
> *C:*   *No.* I just get nothing.
>
> *K:*   Do you have some doubt about how I would really describe you?
>
> *C:*   I don't know how you would describe me . . . to make a description, I'd have to remember what I've talked to you about in the past . . . and I can't remember anything . . . the only thing that I've been able to construct so far is that I came in to see you, and, uh, felt I had a problem when I came in, logically enough. But the development beyond this is zero.
>
> *K:*   What did this fellow talk about, Dr. Kelly?
>
> *C:*   (Pause) Well, for one thing, whenever you mention me as Dr. Kelly, I get an uneasy feeling. I don't like it. But to carry on with the idea . . .
>
> *K:*   Well, we can change this. Go on . . .
>
> *C:*   I'd say one of the problems was the problem in school, not being able to achieve and maintain a standard which the individual feels he should.
>
> *K:*   Um-hm. This was his main, or his initial comment?
>
> *C:*   Yeah. The discussion was about the individual and his problems in school, his family background, educational background. (Pause.)

In resuming the enactment, Kelly formulates his question at a lower level of abstraction, merely asking Cal as "Kelly" to recapitulate the material that had been discussed in the sessions. This tactic meets with some limited success, but Cal soon bogs down again, leading Kelly to modify further the roleplay in order to make it less anxiety-provoking.

> *K:*   Well, let's say that you're Dr. Jones, who has been seeing Cal Weston. Does that make it a little easier? It takes some of the "personal" out of it.
>
> *C:*   Yeah, but still there's an uneasiness in that you're asking me to make a judgment which I'm not qualified to make . . .

They then discuss Cal's concern that his emotional involvement in the therapy makes it impossible for him to present a "true picture" of what has transpired from the therapist's point of view. Before dropping out of cast entirely, however, Kelly frames one last inquiry in enactment form.

> *K:*   May I ask one more question of you in your role as Dr. Jones? Dr. Jones, what kind of *person* do you think this man is?
>
> *C:*   What do you mean?
>
> *K:*   What motivates him? Or let me put it this way—what is it like to meet him? What kind of *feeling* do you get when you meet him?
>
> *C:*   I doubt that I could answer that.

K: Is it a little threatening to ask this question?

C: I don't think so (loudly); I just don't see how I can reflect on myself and describe myself from that sort of view.

Cal goes on to explain the difficulty he encounters in taking up Kelly's perspective.

C: I'd have to . . . guess at how someone else might see me. But I would have no idea, no basis for describing the person that was doing the seeing, or how he would see me.

K: Do you feel that you have no basis for knowing how I see you, or do you have a *sense* of how I see you?

C: I'd never thought of it. I think if anything, I tried to keep an idea like that out.

K: Why?

C: Well . . . what I expect of you is an objective, rational study of my problems, provided you can find them, the roots of them, and trying to help me sort them out through questions and discussions. At least that's what I assume . . . the role of the psychologist is. What was the question again? (Laughs.)

K: What kind of a *sense,* what kind of an *impression,* what kind of *feelings* do you think I have about you? Or did you have the feeling, or the conviction that I would have as few feelings as possible and be as analytic as possible?

C: *And* the development of any emotional friendship with you would tend to lead me to answer any questions . . . with a bias towards maintaining that friendship. . . . I'm not in a position (to play your role). I would be assuming some of the points of view you might have, and to develop those points of view I'd have to come to know you a little bit, and know how you think and how you feel. I've tried to prevent anything like that from happening, so that I wouldn't feel emotionally involved in our personal relationship. That's strictly— professional. You're the doctor. I'm going to keep this strictly on an "M.D./ guy with a cut throat" situation.

K: What kind of situation?

C: "Cut throat." I tried to come up with something rather radical.

In exploring in some depth the nature of Cal's resistance to the enactment, Kelly has arrived at a much clearer understanding of Cal's conception of therapy and the role he expects the therapist to play. As he frequently does, however, he validates his interpretation of the client's viewpoint before moving on.

K: This discussion we're having now is good. Now let me see if I understand. This is my examination now; you see if I can pass it. In a sense you are saying, "I'm going to keep Kelly at arm's length, so that he'll be a kind of doctor, so that he can cut my throat if it's logically required. I'll keep him at a distance so that I can tell him the worst about me, so that I can bare myself to the worst that can happen. For if I get too close, I'll be afraid of losing him, and I'll start having a kind of personal relationship."

Cal confirms that Kelly has captured his point of view, and adds that the distance he has interposed between himself and Kelly has made it difficult to put himself in the therapist's shoes.

THE NEED FOR STRUCTURE

Having attained some provisional closure on the topic of Cal's conception of therapy, Kelly then highlights a prominent theme that had run through their discussion: the conflict between rationality and emotion.[3] In elaborating on this theme, Cal confesses his apprehension about his feelings "taking over," and his need to be "somewhat rational" in order to understand where his emotions were "taking" him. Kelly summarizes Cal's concerns in a geographic metaphor.

> *K:* I think I get more of a sense of how you feel. It isn't that you don't want to go into this uncharted (emotional) area, but you want to make sure that when you do go in that you don't flounder, that you don't become lost, that you can still relate it to something that you do know, that you do consider firm on the outside, back in the realm of rationality.
>
> *C:* Yeah. I don't want to go into this thing and then be at a complete loss as to what we've covered, to have you play back the record or something so that I can understand what's happened . . .
>
> *K:* So you're saying essentially . . . "For God's sake, don't throw me into chaos all at once!"
>
> *C:* Yeah, yeah, yeah! That's it! I hadn't thought of it from that point of view, but it fits; it fits what I've said very clearly.

From a personal construct perspective, the sine qua non of human existence is the capacity of persons to forge personal structures or *construct systems* which render life meaningful and impute to it a measure of predictability. As Kelly notes, the fit between an individual's constructs and the "realities" of which the world is composed is not always very good, "yet without such patterns the world appears to be such an undifferentiated homogeneity that man is unable to make any sense of it" (1955, p. 9). One overarching goal of Kelly's psychotherapy is the *extension* of the client's construct system into previously undifferentiated, apparently chaotic domains of experience.

For Cal, the area of his emotionality represents such an unstructured domain. Feelings, particularly those that bear upon his relationships to others, are anxiety-producing for him because he lacks the constructions that would make them comprehensible. His cognitions and affect act as two tightly compartmentalized "systems of control"; in construct theory terms they represent "fragmented subsystems" (Kelly, 1955, pp. 83–90) having little apparent relationship one to the other.

---

[3]This is not the place to discuss in detail construct theory's unique rejection of the "feeling versus thinking" dichotomy, both poles of which it would encompass in its central notion of "construing." Enlightened discussions of this topic, however, may be found in Bannister (1977) and McCoy (1977).

In order to be effective, therapy would have to help Cal evolve more workable *superordinate* or higher level constructions which could encompass both his thought and his feeling, allowing him to experience them as integrated, rather than contradictory, systems.

In his metaphoric statement to Cal, Kelly acknowledges the client's lack of structure in the area of his emotional life and his need to venture into that "uncharted" domain only gradually, working outward from the better understood realm of rationality. This interpretation clearly strikes a responsive chord in Cal, who goes on to elaborate the image of his rationalistic life-style as a familiar "prison" out of which he is venturing for the first time.

After the interview, Kelly comments on Cal's need for structure, as well as the character of his role of relationship to Kelly as therapist.

He did do a very good job of expressing the apprehension he has about getting into the area of feeling. It comes up a little more clearly how he expects to bare his breast to the surgery of psychotherapy, and how he's afraid if he gets into the area of feeling he will be so self-protective that he will manipulate the situation. Certainly it makes more clear how he has used the mechanism of *constriction* to keep his world down to the proportions of a prison cell, and his need for dependence upon something which is rational because the vast area of potential *anxiety* is too much to be faced all at once. It illustrates also the patient's need for *structure* before he ventures too far into chaos. This indicates, then, that if we are to go into the area of feeling, we had better give him some structural material, some way of thinking about it or dealing with it, so that he will not be completely lost as he ventures into the area.

His inability to portray the part of the therapist indicates something more, too. The *concretistic* nature of his concepts is such that he cannot lift them and apply them to an interpersonal situation where he plays the part of the therapist. In other words, his constructs do not have sufficient *ranges of convenience* to be used when he gets away from certain concrete, particular situations. Thus, by limiting the range of convenience of his constructs and constriction (meaning limiting the realm of things with which he deals, limiting the realm of *elements),* he has kept himself reasonably safe. The task of therapy now, of course, is to start moving out away from these prison walls by extending the ranges of convenience of his constructs so that he can apply the thinking he already has to new and unfamiliar material, but also to provide such additional structure . . . that he can move into the seas. He is not in any position yet to think about *role constructs,* seeing the world through other people's eyes. I might get fooled on this, but I don't think he is. So I suspect maybe the next time we'll have to do some thinking about what the person does when he does feel chaotic, or how he deals with chaotic feelings. I'm not sure how to approach that in this case, since we've got both constriction and limited ranges of convenience of the construct system. I suppose the thing to do would be to deal with some particular situation in which he felt chaotic, or even maybe produce a miniature one in the therapy room, and show how some construct or some dimension of evaluation can give a little clarity and dimension to the experience, when otherwise it would appear to be completely amorphous and dimensionless.

PREVERBAL CONSTRUING

By the 21st session Kelly has carried his investigation of Cal's interpersonal construing to deeper levels, and has begun to grapple with his *preverbal* constructions as they bear on the therapist and other important figures in his life. In Kellian terms, a preverbal construct "is one which continues to be used even though it has no consistent word symbol" (1955, p. 459) and is apt to deal with those sorts of elements of which the young child could be aware (1955, p. 461). In attending closely to the threat that Cal verbalizes at the prospect of becoming close to him, Kelly has begun to suspect the operation of an unspoken but very fundamental construction that governs Cal's relationships to others. Early in the session Cal contended that the psychotherapy client can be taken "strictly as a collection of various facts and fictions, worthy of critical inquiry," and has added, "I don't think it's necessary to go beyond that." Hearing a theme similar to that expressed during their earlier enactment, Kelly seeks an elaborated understanding of Cal's remark:

K: So any kind of *tenderness* I might express toward you, anything of that order . . .

C: No, because . . .

K: Because this is not necessary?

C: Well, it may or may not be.

K: I see.

C: Uh, if the tenderness is . . . shown because of an emotional feeling toward the individual that is trying to prevent, what, an unpleasant occurrence for him . . . just out of kindness on your part, then no . . .

K: So if it's merely tenderness in the sense of being, uh, being kind of butter-fingered, in the sense of being unwilling to get in there and go to work on the job, if it's an evasive kind of tactic . . .

C: Yeah.

K: It has no place there. Now this makes sense with other things you've said, I think. You don't want tender-mindedness in the sense of being so tender that you can't come to grips with reality, come to grips with your problem.

C: Yeah. What I was thinking, though, uh, was being tender or kind, or nice simply because you don't want to be nasty . . .

K: Yeah, yeah. And that is just a kind of a, kind of a superficial social mannerism, huh?

C: Yeah.

K: Hardly worth the time and effort it takes to carry on the interview. 'Cause other people have been kind to you in this sense.

C: Oh sure, sure.

K: Uh, kind of *politeness,* just politeness.

C: As we refer to it here, yeah.

K: Yeah. I'm looking for a word to describe this kind of . . .

C: Well, I think that's as good as any. Overpoliteness maybe would be more correct.

K: Let's call it *overpoliteness* then, you and I.

What Kelly is attempting to do is to assist Cal in *articulating* his preverbal construction, in finding an appropriate verbal symbol to represent the otherwise tacit dimension of meaning. Once articulated in a more communicable verbal medium, the preverbal construct may be more amenable to therapeutic reconstruction and experimentation (Kelly, 1955, p. 465). Having assigned the provisional label of "overpoliteness" to Cal's construct, Kelly goes on to investigate the interpersonal incidents that it was originally designed to construe.

> *K:* Yeah, I see, overpoliteness. Yeah. Now this brings us to the next part that I wish you'd so some exploring on. And I'll help you as much as I can with the experience, but we've got to work on it together, you know. Have people been overpolite to you, in certain crucial ways?
>
> *C:* I think the answer is yes. I don't think I can pinpoint any particular, isolated incident.
>
> *K:* Let's work on it. Let's elaborate and see what we can get out of this, this kind of question.

In citing situations that exemplified his construction (e.g., his father's willingness to continue supporting him financially), Cal began to question the earlier designation of such behavior in terms of "overpoliteness." Kelly, sensitive to the difficulty of finding an appropriate verbal symbol, observes:

> *K:* Well . . . we've got to the level of indulgence now, haven't we? We're talking about a kind of indulgence of you. Is this what you're talking about now?
>
> *C:* Mmmm . . . would you express it again?
>
> *K:* A while ago we talked about overpoliteness.
>
> *C:* Umm-hmm.
>
> *K:* Then we moved in, asking about if you may get this sense of something like overpoliteness—maybe that's not the term—in your relations with your past. And you say, "yes and no"; you don't see this as anything that your father intends or that it is essentially inherent in his intent or his behavior. But you say it is a *sense* of overpoliteness . . .
>
> *C:* Well, I really define overpoliteness as sweet, syrupy politeness. I don't think that's exactly what you can say.
>
> *K:* Yeah. There's another term we ought to have now, for what we're thinking of. I tried "indulgence," in the sense of being indulged? Being patted on the head as a child? Being treated too tenderly?
>
> *C:* I don't think any of those terms define the situation.
>
> *K:* Yeah. Let's find something, so we can deal with it.
>
> *C:* "Indulged" may be the closest.

Having formulated a second, perhaps more adequate designation of Cal's preverbal discrimination, Kelly is prepared to change tacks. He moves Cal into the investigation of his problematic role relationships to others—both in the microcosm of therapy and the macrocosm of his familial and social world—with an eye to the operation of the client's tacit construction in these areas.

ANXIETY AND HOSTILITY

Kelly begins this exploration by focusing upon the character of the therapeutic relationship.

K: . . . you've said, both by implication and explicitly, you've said so often in here, "I don't want to get too close." There's something in the relationship that turns soft or something that does not enable us to get on with our job.

C: Now, may I throw something in there? When you meet an individual—and I think this goes for anybody—you mentally develop a picture of them . . .

K: Yes.

C: And then you build upon this picture, embroider it, put sweet roses and lilacs and so on around it. (Laughs.) In getting close to that person, you might tear this down. You might find out that your mental picture of beauty and so on is not entirely correct. The roses have thorns.

K: Yeah, you know before, you put it another way. You didn't want to get close because you didn't want that person to lose his objectivity. You wanted to always be prepared to, . . . for the surgeon's knife. That you might become . . .

C: Yeah.

K: . . .protective of yourself. Now let's turn this a little bit differently. You're saying essentially you start with a rosy picture, but behind these roses you have a sense there may be thorns. And so by keeping at a distance, you can see him as a rosy person.

This line of inquiry is clearly an important one for Cal, and he spontaneously documents "a situation in which an individual doesn't seem to fit the pattern" in which he put him. He refers to an incident that occurred when he was quite young.

C: The time [was] up at Centerville where I was pushed into the goldfish pond.

K: Yes.

C: Now I'd say I'd pictured Tom, the fellow that pushed me in, in a certain way.

K: Mm-hm.

C: Well, he pushed me in . . . it's a perfectly natural reaction. I mean, there are times when you do it just for the heck of it. But this might not have fitted into that picture.

K: So there almost . . .

C: So there goes my picture.

K: So there almost, in a literal and perfectly physical sense, you got close enough to him to get pushed into a pond (both laugh), and suddenly your picture of Tom had to be revised.

C: And I think the anger which exploded in me was not an anger directed at Tom alone.

K: But at the loss of your picture.

C: But at the loss of my picture. And it was a, what, radiating anger just booming out in all directions at anything and everything that comes in its path . . . it's not an anger that . . .

K: It was barely that, being pushed in the fishpond, but the destruction of this beautiful picture you had drawn of Tom.

C: That follows.

Both Cal and Kelly recognize that this incident from the remote past remains significant, not because Tom had mischievously pushed Cal in the pond, but because, in so doing, he *invalidated* the "rosy" constructions Cal had used to anticipate the behavior of a friend. The client's experience of intense *anger* is particularly noteworthy here, since anger, in construct theory terms, can be conceptualized as "the awareness of invalidation of constructs leading to hostility" (McCoy, 1977, p. 121). Indeed, Cal shows remarkable perspicacity in recognizing that his rage is a reaction to the "loss of his picture" and not merely a response to Tom's literal behavior. To grasp the full implications of this scenario, however, one also must appreciate Kelly's unique definition of *hostility:* "The continued effort to extort validational evidence in favor of a type of social prediction which has already proved itself a failure" (1955, p. 510). By defining hostility in terms of the phenomenology of the hostile person rather than in terms of his or her impact upon others, Kelly draws attention to its psychological function: it forces the social "facts" to fit a failing hypothesis, to buttress a shaky construction which might otherwise crumble under the weight of the evidence. Examining the scenario in this light, it is Cal, rather than Tom, who may be the hostile party. Rather than revising his "embroidered" conception of interpersonal relations in the face of invalidation, he continues to interpose sufficient distance between himself and other persons that the accuracy of his procrustean framework need not be called into question. The ramifications of this childhood incident continue to unfold in the therapeutic dialogue.

K: . . . This spreading anger, spurting anger, was not so much directed at Tom but at something about having the whole situation fall apart on you . . .

C: Yeah. I would say yes. I would say that since he was the instigator of the collapse of the house of cards, the anger fell on his shoulders first.

K: Yeah.

C: But now, I'm trying to find something here. As I remember, I think my mother came to cajole me out of my anger. And I reacted in the same anger, that is, the same feeling of anger, against her.

Kelly suspects the reemergence of Cal's earlier preverbal construction relating to overpoliteness or indulgence at this point, and so remarks:

K: So you didn't want comfort then. The kind of comfort, or cajoling, or manipulation . . .

C: Evidently not.

K: Was she being "overly polite" at the time or something? Soft-soaping?

C: Soft-soaping? A word people like not to fit.

K: Okay. "Soft-soaping" now comes; maybe it's a better expression for the moment. We may find better ones later.

C: U.-hm, um-hm.

K: In other words, here you were in an emergency, your house of cards having collapsed . . .

C: Um-hm.

K: . . . and she came out with soft soap. We've got a double problem here, haven't we? Not only in relation to Tom . . .

C: I'm trying to figure it out, trying to see it here. Would it be that she approached it—now "adult" is the word I see, but it isn't, doesn't quite fit—from the adult point of view. I mean, she was witnessing it all the time, and, I don't know . . .

K: Superficial and alien, and *other* . . .

C: But that isn't the way I saw it at that particular time.

K: That wasn't your problem . . .

C: No. My problem was that I was soaking wet! (Both laugh.)

Cal's remark that these new and very apropos interpretations of the childhood incident weren't the way he saw them at that particular time is worthy of mention. It reflects his growing appreciation of the "constructive alternativism" that Kelly is trying to inculcate in him, the sense that even the most "obvious" meanings attributed to past events are subject to liberating reinterpretations in the present. Such a philosophy implies, as Kelly states, that "man can enslave himself with his own ideas and then win his freedom by reconstruing his life" (1955, p. 21). This is, in large part, the goal of personal construct therapy.

Kelly first tests his understanding of Cal's experience before elaborating it further.

K: Now let me see if I've got it. You said not only was the house of cards fallen that involved a pictured relationship between you and your friend, between you and Tom . . . but when someone came to deal with it, it was kind of an outsider who did not understand; it was dealt with superficially by soft-soaping, without any appreciation for what the real issue was based on . . .

C: Yeah—and yet looking at it, you can hardly say it was any other way; I mean you could hardly see it any other way if you were the other person.

K: Okay, of course. But we're talking about how it seemed to *you* at that moment.

C: Yeah.

K: And to come up to you and pat you on the head or try to hug you or something like this (made) you even more angry.

C: Um-hm.

K: You didn't want to be close to your mother at that time. It wasn't closeness, in that sort of soft-soaping, comforting way. You had yourself a problem.

C: Yeah.

K: And you're saying the same to me. "Don't cajole me out of my problems. Let's stand off here at arm's length . . ."

C: Yeah.

K: ". . . and make sure we understand this thing, something other than just . . . soft-soaping."

Cal then spontaneously begins to take Tom's perspective on the incident.

C: Tom, of course, had no intention of causing this to happen. Now, I don't mean pushing me in the pool (laughs), I mean my house of cards coming down . . . Tom . . . has always had a group to play in whereas I have not. So he understands, understood, a different relationship between boys.

K: Yeah.

C: Whereas I understood the essentially . . . *adult* relationship between myself and my parents.

K: So it was unthinkable to have . . . as unthinkable to have that other human being push you into the pond as it was to have your father push your mother into a pond, or push you into a pond.

C: Yeah—at that particular time it would have been unthinkable.

K: At that particular time.

C: Yeah.

K: So you perceived Tom in terms of a . . . a set of images of people in the world which were adult images.

C: Yeah.

K: Tom had behaved like . . . like children behave. He . . . it did not mean for him what it would have meant for you, or what it did mean for you. And, thus, this was *completely incoherent* behavior.

C: Um-hm.

K: Thus the structure of your social world was invalidated right at that moment. This was the falling of the house of cards.

Kelly then begins to draw together the separate but related themes woven through the dialogue.

K: You see, what I'm wondering is, you lost your framework within which you could perceive people.

C: Yeah.

K: I'm wondering if you lost an important friend at the same time.

C: In that, perhaps, at that particular time *any* friend was an important friend.

K: That makes sense.

C: Yes. That makes sense.

K: My goodness, we've got this thing falling down now in three ways. You lost the validity of a framework within which you see social relations . . .

C: Yeah.

K: . . . completely irrational behavior on his part. Two, you lost *him,* since you didn't have too many "Toms" in your life.

C: Yeah.

K: And finally, you got treated by the soft-soap method . . .

C: Yeah.

K: Which pulls together quite a number of things here.

Cal clarifies Kelly's second point, maintaining that he "did not lose Tom as a physical being, as a person, but as a house of cards." Kelly acknowledges this and continues.

K: Well, that's the part that you've made pretty clear, I think. That's a point that would be easy to overlook, 'cause you could look at it merely in terms of losing Tom. But as you point out, that was not the key. It was perhaps a more important loss than the loss of any one person.

C: Yeah.

K: The loss of Tom you could stand. You might have regretted it for a few days, but this was a specific loss. The loss of your framework within which to see interpersonal relationships is a devastating loss. Throws you right back at the beginning again, got to start all over, learning about people.

C: Um-hm, um-hm.

K: And you ain't never quite felt that you caught up, huh?

C: (Sighs.) I'd say you're correct.

Cal takes the next step, relating this original incident to his present interpersonal aloofness.

C: Uh, in rebuilding, having once had—I don't think this comes entirely from one event—but having once had this beautiful, false-fronted building knocked into kindling wood, in rebuilding, there's a (sigh), what, sense of fear? That someone's going to come along and kick it down again. And perhaps each time someone—well, I guess I'm getting fantastic in the description—someone hauls off to swing his foot at it, you pull it down yourself, or duck, or dodge, something like that. That follows anyway.

K: Here's my framework for looking at people, but don't you folks come too
close to it because I don't want you to kick it over.

By this point Cal seems to have established a revised, more communicable
construction of the character of his role relationships which appears *permeable,*
applicable to new as well as old experiences. Kelly tests the range of convenience of
the new structure by assessing its ability to subsume a specific problematic situation
from the recent past: Cal's intense, seemingly inexplicable anger at pledging a
college fraternity and then being told he would have to go through an initiation
period.

K: Now when the fraternity situation came up this fall and it looked as if . . .
They decided you should go through an initiation . . . This was like being
pushed into the fishpond? Adult relationships you would expect, and suddenly
it turns out to be kid stuff?

C: That might have been . . .

K: You had a house of cards for your fraternity?

C: I wouldn't limit it to that.

K: Even broader than that, huh?

C: I would say—now this is supposition, I don't know—but following this on
through, my statement would be that it was not my house of cards for the
fraternity, but the house of cards for my entire life.

K: I suppose the moral of this is to stay away from fishponds and fraternities
(Both laugh). I think it's a very pointed issue.

Having recognized Cal's past and present hostility in forcing persons into his
inflexible, if insubstantial, perceptual categories, and having dealt with the anxiety
into which he was precipitated whenever his "house of cards" fell apart, Kelly and
his client conclude by reflecting upon the therapeutic partnership which they seem
to have formed.

K: Well, we've been hitting it pretty hard and heavy here for an hour. You've
. . . come to grips with this thing, I think, as well as I've ever seen you, if not
better. I have a feeling of your . . . your helping me more, I mean working
together as a team.

C: Uh, the feeling that I've come to grips with it better, thinking over the past
session, would the way to describe it be that it's like facing, uh, let's say,
going swimming? Until you get into it, that water's awfully cold. But once
you're in there for a minute or two, it's okay. You get along fine.

K: Uh-hm. You have a feeling yet that you're in over your ears? Or at least up
to your neck?

C: I don't know.

K: Yeah, that's a little hard to answer.

C: But very definitely there for a while I was having trouble keeping the thoughts together. And yet, what, the past minute or so I've been doing pretty good. I've been clicking right along.

K: We've been wrapping up a little bit, too.

C: Um-hm.

K: We had so many things kind of coming in at us there for a while, it was hard to keep together. It is for me, too. But if we work at it as a kind of team combination, I think between the two of us we can probably make a lot of sense that neither of us could make alone.

C: Um-hm.

K: Provided, of course, you help me.

C: Vice versa.

K: Yes.

CONCLUSION

In writing this chapter, I have sought to illustrate the interpenetration of theoretical concepts (e.g., anxiety, constructive alternativism) and technical procedures (e.g., tightening, self-description) that characterize personal construct therapy by citing the clinical work of George Kelly. In so doing, I have not intended to suggest that Kelly's approach is, or should be, paradigmatic for others engaged in the process of helping people change. Nor am I implying that the working concepts and principles treated here are definitional of the therapy that follows from Kelly's theoretical outlook. In part, this is so because the brevity of this chapter precludes the explication of many strategies that were central to Kelly's therapeutic efforts (e.g., the interpretation of transference, the use of behavioral experiments). More important, however, the material discussed here is incomplete because it fails to encompass the *frontiers* of construct theory as a discipline, the significant recent contributions to the theory, some of which are contained in the present volume. Both Kelly's original theory and therapy are enjoying a period of rapid elaboration. Personal construct psychotherapy, like the persons with whom it deals, must be defined less by what it has been than by what it is becoming.

REFERENCES

Bannister, D. Personal construct theory psychotherapy. In D. Bannister (Ed.), *Issues and Approaches in the Psychological Therapies*. New York: Wiley, 1975.

Bannister, D. The logic of passion. In D. Bannister (Ed.), *New Perspectives in Personal Construct Theory*. New York: Academic, 1977.

Epting, F. R. *Personal Construct Theory Psychotherapy*. London: Wiley, in press.

Fransella, F. *Personal Change and Reconstruction*. New York: Academic, 1972.

Fransella, F., & Bannister, D. *A Manual for Repertory Grid Technique*. New York: Academic, 1977.

Landfield, A. W. *Personal Construct Systems in Psychotherapy*. Chicago: Rand-McNally, 1971.

McCoy, M. M. A reconstruction of emotion. In D. Bannister (Ed.), *New Perspectives in Personal Construct Theory*. New York: Academic, 1977.

Neimeyer, G. J., & Neimeyer, R. A. Personal construct perspectives on cognitive assessment. In T. V. Merluzzi, C. R. Glass, and M. Genest (Eds.), *Cognitive Assessment*. New York: Guilford, in press.

CHAPTER 6

Personal Construct Treatment of a Severely Disturbed Woman: The Case of Sue

L. M. Leitner

Kelly (1955) stated that a central focus of convenience (application) of Personal Construct Theory is psychotherapy. In spite of this, clinicians sometimes react to presentations of Personal Construct Theory with statements like: "That is very nice but how do I *use* it in a clinical setting?" This chapter attempts to answer that question by systematically using the theory to conceptualize and treat a seriously disturbed woman.

Before presenting the case, two points should be made. First, it is assumed the reader has some knowledge of Personal Construct Theory. Approaching this material with no prior knowledge of the theory would be a very difficult task. If the reader feels he does not understand the theory, he should study Chapter 1 of this volume before tackling this chapter.

Further, it should be pointed out that, to protect the identity of the patient, a fictitious name has been used and certain nonessential aspects of Sue's life have been deliberately falsified.

The presentation of the case will be in three parts. First, some basic clinical material of the intake interview will be presented. This will allow the reader to conceptualize the case within his preferred theoretical orientation. This will be followed by a conceptualization of the case within Personal Construct Theory. The presentation will conclude with a systematic analysis of the treatment.

THE CASE

Sue was a 24-year-old white female with whom I worked during my internship at the Oklahoma University Health Sciences Center. She was married and had two children. At the time of the intake, she was complaining of experiencing many "peculiar things." For instance, she could not shake the impression that "pieces of colored yarn are like friends." She was preoccupied with this thought when knitting. She also reported a decrease in "decisiveness," an increase in "dependency,'' and an increase in her "temper" since her marriage. She stated that on her wedding day her husband (John) went with his father to a "whorehouse." Furthermore, John was only interested in "sex or making me suffer." Whenever Sue had made any attempts to change the marital situation in any way, John had reacted violently, on occasion destroying the furniture in their house. Sue often feared for the safety of herself and her children. She stated that she wanted to divorce John, but that she "can't live with him and can't live without him." She reported constant and serious sleep and appetite disturbances since the marriage.

The marital couple had been in psychotherapy previously with unsatisfactory results. In one instance, Sue reported that the "therapist gave up on us." According to Sue, the therapist "told us we were hopeless" and stated that Sue faced a "life in mental hospitals."

By way of medical background, Sue reported having "died" several times before age five. These "deaths" involved her "passing out" with a marked decrease in vital signs. There were no physiological reasons found for these episodes. She reported a long history of "accident proneness," involving—among other things—broken fingers, stepping on nails, and being bitten and scratched by animals. Other "physiological" problems included her having a history of "false pregnancies" and an extremely irregular menstrual cycle. These were treated with birth control pills during adolescence. After she left home at age 17, several accidents resulted in her returning to the care of her mother. For example, when she was 18, a fall resulted in a concussion (no loss of consciousness) and a back injury. She returned home and was bedridden for 6 weeks. At the end of that period, she reported being "kicked out" of the house. The next day, she was involved in an auto accident which resulted in "whiplash." She consequently returned to the care of her parents. She also had many negative attitudes toward doctors. She elaborated many instances of being misdiagnosed and misunderstood by the medical profession. Sue was also plagued with chest pains so severe that she had to cease all activities during their occurrence. No physiological reasons were found for these pains.

Although Sue denied having any delusions or hallucinations, she did report many upsetting experiences. For example, she reported amnesia with regard to four innings of the 1977 World Series while "wide awake" and "not daydreaming." (This occurred shortly before entering treatment.) She also reported having difficulty in driving a car. When she did drive, she had to continually fight the impulse to drive the car "between the wheels of oncoming semitrucks." She also was frightened of repeated dreams of being decapitated by John. In these dreams, John "cut me in half" and "used me for a sandwich." Sue also reported many dreams of decapitating her son.

Sue's background was also quite revealing. She stated that her mother constantly told her that she would "go crazy" and called her "retarded." (Her intelligence was estimated by the intake interviewer to be at least average.) She described many instances of her mother "throwing butcher knives" at her. When placed on birth control pills at age 13 (due to the false pregnancies and menstrual difficulties) her mother "told the whole neighborhood I was a slut." She reported that her mother "was always talking about what a horrible, ugly child I was." Reportedly, Sue was compared to an older sister who could do no wrong. According to Sue, only her grandmother was "good" to her. She recalled always "acting nice" for her grandmother because she felt "loved by Granny" and she "wanted Granny to be pleased with me." This contrasted with her willingly acting up around her mother because "she wouldn't love me anyway."

At the beginning of therapy, Sue's life revolved around John and the two children. She did not work and, except for visits to her family of origin, she did not associate with other people. Her days were spent at home with the children. At night, she and John watched television.

During the beginning of therapy, Sue smiled as she discussed many of these issues. Her elaborations, which were not at all spontaneous, were often interrupted by nervous and inappropriate laughter. She seemed to want to convince me of the hopelessness of her situation. Her voice had a "whiney" quality to it. When listening to her voice on tape, one had the impression she was crying. (She was not.) Often, when attempting to express herself, Sue's eyes would drop and her eyelids would briefly close.

This behavior changed significantly when Sue discussed her children. Spontaneous elaboration occurred and her voice was much "richer" in tone. Further, the nervous laughter and the eyelid dropping decreased markedly.

As part of the normal supervisory process of the internship, this case was presented to a case conference of clinicians. The clinicians engaged in a spirited debate over whether Sue was "hysteric," "borderline," or "schizophrenic." Related to this debate was the issue of whether Sue could tolerate "reconstructive" psychotherapy. Reconstructive therapy implied having the ability to withstand high levels of anxiety associated with a basic reorganization of the personality. Many clinicians felt that a more reconstructive therapeutic strategy would be very detrimental to this person due to the "borderline" nature of her pathology. There was a fear she might "act out" and severely injure herself or someone else. The existence of these fears was supported by the fact that Sue carried a gun. Sue stated that, given the opportunity of doing so without getting caught, she might kill some of the individuals who had "wronged" her. This case conference will be referred to again later since I felt that my wish to do reconstructive therapy did not have the approval of some of the participants.

PERSONAL CONSTRUCT CONCEPTUALIZATION

Before conceptualizing the case, a slight detour is necessary. Many therapists would be concerned with whether these life events in general, and the medical-psychological events in particular, "really happened." The Personal Construct Therapist is not as interested in the "truth" of these events as other therapists. Of more importance for the Personal Construct Therapist are the actual constructions in use, not the "truth" of the matter. Further, the "right" Diagnostic and Statistical Manual (DSM II) diagnosis is not relevant to the Personal Construct Therapist. For the construct therapist, diagnosis is a formal attempt at conceptualizing the person's construing of the world. It is based upon understanding the internal person, not external symptoms. In this section, this will be done by showing some of the inferences a Personal Construct Therapist can make from the data just presented. In particular, three major personal construct diagnostic axes will be emphasized: looseness-tightness of construction, threat, and constriction-dilation of the perceptual field.

Looseness-Tightness of Construction

The dimension of *looseness versus tightness* of construction was, for Kelly, a most important diagnostic axis. A loose construct is defined as one that leads to varying predictions but still maintains its identity. When a construct is loose, elements are sometimes subsumed under one pole; sometimes under the contrast pole. Loosened construction can be seen most clearly in dreams. The dream may seem both conforting and frightening. Things that could not possibly happen in reality are commonplace in dreams. If the dreamer attempted to understand his dream with tight, literal constructions, he would wind up feeling frustrated and confused. By way of contrast, a tight construct leads to unvarying predictions.

As can be inferred from this discussion, if one's superordinate constructions are quite loose, the person will be subject to peculiar experiences due to the inability to adequately understand these experiences in a consistent way. Within this diagnostic axis, Sue gave many indications of an alarming loosening within the more superordinate aspects of her personal construct system. At the same time, there were encouraging indications of her potential to tighten these dimensions of experience.

For example, Sue's first complaint had to do with thinking that pieces of colored yarn were her friends. The range of convenience of the construct of which "friend" is one pole had been stretched to the point that the meaning of the construct was not very clear (colored yarn was included in the range of convenience). Extending the range of convenience of a construct is one way in which loosening can occur. This complaint did not tell us *why* loosening had occurred on this dimension. However, a likely hypothesis is that the stretching was an attempt to find an area where Sue could apply her interpersonal constructions of friendship.

It is also important to note that Sue labeled this experience of stretching the meaning of "friend" as "peculiar." In the context of perceiving peculiarity, she had tightened and put to an experimental test her construction of friend. The ability to loosen and tighten constructs was, for Kelly, the hallmark of creativity. Further, Kelly envisioned good reconstructive psychotherapy as weaving between loosened and tightened construction. Therefore, this potential for tightening might enable Sue to be reached by a more reconstructive therapeutic strategy. In other words, there was still some potential creativity in her interpersonal experiments.

Being married lent further support to the hypothesis that Sue could still elaborate role relationships. However, Sue also dated her problems to the onset of the marriage. The role constructs governing the marriage were thus being invalidated. Her symbol for this invalidation was John "visiting the whorehouse." Within

Personal Construct Therory, invalidation can lead to a loosening of the conceptual system. The loosening prevents the system from being overwhelmed with invalidating evidence. The system can thus remain somewhat intact. The invalidation that Sue was experiencing in the marriage could be associated with the loosening in her construct system.

Sue's sleep and appetite disturbances could also be taken as evidence of loosening within the construct system. In this case, the core constructs (those governing her maintenance processes) were loose. Kelly stated, "In a healthy person, the core structures tend to be tight. He has regular habits with respect to such matters as eating, sleeping, and so on" (1955, p. 484). Sue's inconsistent and irregular habits in these areas indicated that her core structures were markedly loose. Since Sue dated this loosening as beginning with her marriage, this suggested that the superordinate role constructs governing her marriage had been invalidated to the point that, to prevent further invalidation, Sue's core constructs had been loosened. Thus, she did not have to clearly confront the nature of the marital relationship.

Sue gave further evidence of looseness in her superordinate structures, shown by amnesia in regard to four innings of the World Series, fantasies and impulses to drive between the wheels of semi trucks, and dream experiences of herself and her son being decapitated. These experiences were loose in the sense that they had a dreamlike, unreal quality to them. The reality of the dreams is of little concern to the Personal Construct Therapist. If they were not dreams, her experience was "dreamlike" enough for her to construe them as dreams. The "dreamlike" quality is the hallmark of loosened construction irrespective of the state of consciousness of the experiencer.

The fantasy about driving between the wheels of oncoming semi trucks, as well as the decapitation dreams, contained some suicidal ideation. Within construct therory, suicide can be viewed as an attempt to protect one's most superordinate constructions from invalidation (Kelly, 1961; Landfield, 1976). Death is preferable to life without these important constructs. The suicidal fantasy thus showed the desperateness with which Sue was struggling to maintain a viable structure. It also showed the potential implications of continued invalidation. On the positive side of the ledger, Sue had some constructs which were so meaningful that she considered dying for them. Since the suicidal ideation was still in the fantasy stage, these constructs might not have been invalidated to the point that a decision was imminent in this area. Her system might still be operating in some areas of interpersonal relationships. These areas had to be discovered and closely monitored. If the constructs in these areas were to be invalidated, the possibility of suicide would become quite real. A similar line of reasoning could be applied to the homocidal ideation—that is, taking the lives of invalidating others protects one's system.

Further indications of looseness of construction can be inferred from Sue's inappropriate laughter at the beginning of therapy. Sometimes Sue laughed as she discussed these serious matters. Within Personal Construct Theory, humor can be viewed as the awareness of contrast. Sue's paradoxical smiling and laughing thus became an indication of conflicting feelings. Even as she defined herself (and others) on one pole in the construct system, she became aware of the potential for defining herself (and others) on the contrast pole.

Sue's dropping of her eyes was also very much associated with her smiling during therapy, and could be interpreted as her awareness of contrast. The shifting of elements between the poles of a construct is another hallmark of loosened construction.

Finally, the potential for tightening could be seen by Sue's "temper." She was frustrated. She became angry. McCoy defined anger as the "awareness of invalidation of constructs leading to hostility" (1977, p. 121). For the person to be aware of invalidation, the constructs must have been tested. For the constructs to have been tested, they must have been tightened. Further, it is important to note that, for invalidation to lead to hostility (as McCoy's definition implies), there must be threatening implications around the struggle to reinterpret basic aspects of oneself. We now turn to a systematic discussion of Sue's experience of threat.

Threat

Threat, or the awareness of an imminent, comprehensive invalidation of core structures, was very much a part of Sue's daily experience. Before discussing the many ways in which she revealed threat, it would be most helpful to discuss the underlying dimensions responsible for the experience of threat. These dimensions can be seen most clearly in Sue's discussion of her parents and "Granny."

When Sue discussed her mother, it was apparent that certain fundamental constructions of herself were being considered. Within Sue's system, the only meaningful manner of relating to her parents was to define herself as "crazy," "retarded," "ugly," and "dumb" as opposed to her more positive conceptualizations of her parents.

However, when Sue spoke of "Granny," she spoke of the contrasts to the poles mentioned above. These contrasts involved notions of herself as "normal," "good," "trustworthy," and "lovable." When discussing "Granny," Sue told us that she could (and sometimes did) place herself on these poles as opposed to the more negative poles given above. These value-laden dimensions will be discussed throughout this chapter as they played a major part in Sue's therapy. For the purposes of conciseness and clarity, I will construe Sue's construct as a dimension involving "good self," or "self in relation to 'Granny,' " versus "bad self," or "self in relation to parents." Henceforth, my construction will be used when referring to this dimension.

The reader will note that the shifting of the self from one pole to the other showed the looseness of this superordinate structure. It was quite threatening for Sue to tighten this dimension. Tightening would lead to experimentation and the subsequent clear defining of herself on the *good self vs. bad self* construct. If this experimenting caused Sue to define herself on the *bad self* pole, she would be left with little other than the role of a "wretched" person. If she defined herself on the *good self* pole, core notions of what mothers are all about ("good," "kind," "loving," etc.) would be invalidated. Although Sue experienced angry feelings toward her mother, she still was ambivalent about her.

Sue prevented a massive potential invalidation along the *good-self vs. bad self* dimension by keeping this structure loose. If she became the *good self* she gave up the "good mother." If she became the *bad self,* she had to live with her badness. Since this looseness resulted in Sue's inability to define herself, her placement of the self on the *good self vs. bad self* dimension was governed more by how others reacted to her than by any conception of herself. Her willingness to pay this price attested to the amount of potential threat involved in her decision making. In other words, she was remaining open to alternative notions of selfhood without having a clear notion of who she was as a person.

The potential invalidation along the *good self-bad self* construct was so real that Sue could not elaborate these notions in therapy without feeling threatened. Whenever this dimension came up for discussion, it was a crucial point in therapy. When these notions were discussed, it implied that a shift had already occurred within the construct system. For her to discuss the *good self vs. bad self* dimension in therapy, the threatening implications to the system would have to have been reduced. This would most likely occur if (1) Sue felt that therapy had few or no immediate implications for her life, (2) this dimension was so isolated from other constructs that defining herself on it did not lead to the devastation of the entire system implied earlier, and/or (3) a more stabilizing superordinate structure could be brought to bear on this part of the system. Given the critical nature of these issues, the wise therapist would not push into these areas prematurely.

Threat and the C-P-C Cycle

Sue's inability to define herself on the *"good self* vs. *bad self'* dimension was indicative of difficulty in the control phase of the C-P-C (circumspection, preemption, control) cycle. Sue gave other indications of problems in the control phase of this cycle. For example, as mentioned earlier, Sue stated that she wanted to divorce John but that she "can't live with him and can't live without him." Here she was stating that neither pole of this construct (live with him—live without him) defined, extended, or elaborated her self-role (see the choice corollary). If she stayed with John, she would be forced to define herself on the "ugly," "retarded," "crazy" poles of her Superordinate structure. If she left him, constructs governing what a "good" wife is in marriage would become invalidated. Consequently, in her organization of her experience of the world, she made sense—she couldn't live with him and she couldn't live without him.

One of Sue's primary complaints was of a decrease in "decisiveness" since her marriage. By this she meant that she could no longer make up her mind and stay in charge of things. Indecisiveness is one manifestation of difficulty in the C-P-C cycle. Once she reached the control phase of this cycle, she was unable to follow through by defining herself on a dimension.

Within Personal Construct Theory, impulsivity is a shortening of the circumspection stage with the remainder of the C-P-C cycle proceeding normally. Given Sue's problems in the control phase of this cycle, the likelihood of her impulsively acting out at the time of intake was lessened. Therefore, there was one positive aspect to this C-P-C cycle disruption due to the threat of change in core structure.

Threat and Dependency

With the loosening of her more superordinate role constructs due to threat, what constructs were governing Sue's interpersonal world? One answer was given in Sue's discussion of "dependency." Immediately after discussing her decrease in decisiveness (a C-P-C difficulty), Sue discussed an increase in dependency. Kelly defined dependency constructs as "the constructs by which certain persons are construed by the child in relation to his own survival" (1955, p. 669). An example of dependency could be clearly seen in Sue's description of the impact others had on her self-conception: "If even one person feels like I'm bad, I just feel terrible about myself."

In this context of dependency, Sue's descriptions of her accidents on leaving home were most enlightening. In these descriptions, she implied a relationship between her "accidents" and "illnesses" and dependency constructs. The invalidation of more mature role constructs had left Sue with little other than dependency constructs to govern her interpersonal relations. She returned home. When these dependency constructs had been tested (i.e., by "moving home" to her parents), they were not validated (i.e., being "kicked out" of the home).

The relationship between Sue's "physiological" symptoms and dependency constructs was an interesting one. Sue's success in elaborating and validating new role constructions could be monitored through the fluctuations in her "physiological" problems. If the new role constructs were being validated, there would be less need for using dependency constructions. With the dependency constructs decreasing, Sue would have less need for "physiological" problems. Thus, one can see a positive implication in the linkage of physiological symptoms (constructs) and dependency constructs.

Threat and the Transference

Sue gave many indications that the transference relationship during therapy would be highly threatening. Doctors would "let you down when you need them most." Psychologists would "give up on you" and "hospitalize you"—thus validating her mother's words. Since I would be construed as both a psychologist and a doctor, I might also be placed in many difficult positions. Given Sue's heightened dependency, I expected that the transference relationship would be extremely important quite early in treatment. Sue would be extremely sensitive to any indications that I would "give up on her" or "let her down." I expected that she would go out of her way to test the sincerity of my wish to help her.

Clinical Indications of High Threat

Sue showed several important clinical indications of high threat. First, she was quite passive (unwilling to test her constructions of the world). Given what Sue had at stake, her passivity was understandable. Any active testing (aggression) risked the tightening of the *good self vs. bad self* construct. Once tightened, Sue would have to define herself on it and large changes could follow. As Kelly said, change can be threatening.

Along a similar vein, Sue's hostility was understandable. She wanted appease-ment, not reality. Her voice was whiney. She attempted to convince me that her situation was hopeless. In the face of the comprehensive invalidation discussed earlier, she maintained the loose *good self vs. bad self* construct. If she were not hostile, she would have to face the possible invalidating evidence for her core structure. The resulting disorganization would be overwhelming. Thus, both Sue's hostility and passivity were attempts to maintain superordinate structures. If a decrease in passivity and hostility was seen, it would indicate the presence of new superordinate constructions. Therefore, when the passivity and hostility decreased, significant growth would have already occurred.

The lack of spontaneous elaboration also revealed high threat. Sue was not yet ready to elaborate and discuss her constructs. She consequently responded only minimally to questions and refused to deal with these issues on her own accord. The wise therapist would not push too hard in these areas until Sue's level of spontaneous elaboration indicated that she felt she could tolerate the stress.

Threat and Her Children

All of the clinical indications of threat decreased when Sue discussed her children. This was a very important point. Here was an area of Sue's interpersonal world where the system worked. There was less likelihood of a sudden disruption and change in the system. With her children, there was not the imminence of change and loss of core structure.

It was important to understand the constructs governing her relations with her children since the range of convenience of these constructs might be extended to other areas of Sue's interpersonal world. However, there were other important implications here. First, her relationship with her children could be used very profitably in making emotional contact with Sue. This would help her feel at ease in therapy. Furthermore, this relationship could be used to touch upon Sue's sense of integrity as a person. Finally, this relationship with her children could be used as a "safe haven" for the therapist to return to when Sue's elaborations in other areas became "too hot to handle."

It is now understandable *why* Sue was entering therapy at that time. It was her attempt to prevent the invalidation of role constructs in this last area of application (her children). If this invalidation were to continue, Sue was faced with limited options: (1) loosening into "psychosis," (2) the abandonment of all role constructs leaving her with only dependency constructs to govern her world, (3) becoming hostile to the point that she might actually physically harm others to protect the integrity of her system, or (4) suicide—the ultimate constriction of her perceptual field; a final act of dignity within Personal Construct Psychology.

Constriction-Dilation of the Perceptual Field

Sue's response to this threat of core role invalidation had been to constrict her perceptual field. There was very little in her life other than her children, her husband, and her family of origin. Of these three, she was much more involved with her children than with her husband or parents. Thus her "subjective," psychological constriction was even greater than her "objective," environmental context. Although she wanted to leave John, she could not take the children and leave him. First, making a decision on the *live with him–live without him* construct was highly threatening. "Living without him" implied the invalidation of constructs governing her role as a good wife with implications for the *good self vs. bad self* construct. Furthermore, to decide to leave John, Sue's subjective, psychological field would have to dilate. Maintaining a more dilated approach to life greatly increased the likelihood of having her tenuous superordinate structure invalidated. Thus, Sue's constriction to her children was an attempt (in a small area of relationship) to develop a better functioning system. However, things were not going well in this constricted field, given how she described her days and evenings.

Sue's constriction gave me the opportunity to determine how well her system was working. Within construct theory, the choice corollary and the principle of the elaborative choice state that a person always chooses in the direction of furthering the elaboration of the system. Thus, Sue's constriction offered her the best opportunity of elaborating her system. Since a more dilated field resulted in chaos, she constricted. Progress in her interpersonal construct system could be monitored by looking for signs of dilation. Once the potential threat to the *good self vs. bad self* dimension was lessened, Sue would be able to dilate her perceptual field. It was hoped that this important sign of growth would be seen.

THE THERAPY PROCESS

Therapy was initially defined to Sue as a place to come and "just think about life." She would not be forced to act upon the issues discussed in therapy. It was a "safe haven" away from the ravages of the rest of the world. Therapy was defined in this way in order to decrease Sue's experience of threat due to the central nature of the constructs with which she was working. If therapy became a "special place" within her personal construct system, Sue might be able to tighten and test notions (in therapy) without her whole psychological world collapsing. In more technical terms, it was hoped that, by reducing any immediate and sweeping possibilities of change (threat) outside therapy, the C-P-C and creativity cycles could be freed for use in forming new constructions of herself and others. The new constructs formed would initially have a very limited range of convenience (the therapy room). The range of convenience of these new constructs could then be gradually extended until the older constructions became unnecessary.

Sue's therapy began with my wanting to know more about her and her children. This was done for the reasons discussed earlier (establishing emotional contact, exploring the area of role relationships where the system was working, etc.). Sue described how easy it was for her to love her children and how they meant everything to her. Essentially, Sue utilized many of the *good self vs. bad self* constructions in this area. The freedom and spontaneity observed in this area argued that Sue felt safe in applying her constructs more tightly within the mother-child relationship. She felt that her children would love and accept her, "no matter what," just as she loved and accepted them.

However, extending this good mutual relationship to the therapy would be another matter. Sue defined love and acceptance in terms of "no matter what." The task of relating to her in therapy would be a tenuous one. The testing of the therapy relationship would be quite strenuous for both of us.

This testing of my caring allowed for two opportunities to work with Sue. First, if I survived the testing, Sue would elaborate her system. Further, I had the chance to work with the construct governing another's caring since it would be brought into the therapeutic relationship. I discovered later that Sue's label for this construct of caring was understanding people as "saints" as opposed to "sadists." Thus, for Sue, any "nonsaintly" behaviors on the part of others (or herself) would lead to the construction of the person as a "sadist." The sadist would attempt to make Sue "crazy," "retarded," "ugly," and so on. It was hoped that the *saint vs. sadist* dimension could be replaced by less extreme, more useful understandings of her interpersonal world.

After the initial sessions, Sue began applying the constructs concerning doctors and psychologists in the therapy room. These dimensions were elaborated in the context of deciding how much to trust me. I was a psychologist and "all you psychologists think alike." This was handled through the use of tightening techniques. I first had Sue elaborate exactly *how* we psychologists think. I then had her compare my words and reactions to her predictions. As with all tightening techniques, these maneuvers hastened Sue's testing and determining the validity of the constructs being tightened.

Further, Sue spent time elaborating what it would mean to her if I were (and if I were not) like other psychologists. This is what Kelly (1955) termed *controlled elaboration*. Controlled elaboration helps the client and therapist check the internal consistency of the system. This allows the system to become more clearly delineated. The superordinate structures may thus be tightened.

For Sue, this elaboration led to an interesting predicament. If I were like other psychologists and doctors (expecting hopelessness), Sue's existing way of understanding her world would be validated. She would not have to risk the confusion, anxiety, and threat of exposing her very vulnerable superordinate structures. However, if I were not like other psychologists, Sue would face the threatening implications of invalidation of her more superordinate role constructs.

The potential threat involved on both sides of the construct *(like other psychologists—not like other psychologists)* resulted in Sue's refusing to take a stand on this issue early in therapy. The following small exerpt from one of the therapy sessions is quite illustrative in this regard.

CLINICAL VIGNETTE 1. *Sue:*   You don't act like other psychologists. (Silence.) But it could be that you're just smarter than they were. (Silence.) You may be more subtle.

Larry: More subtle?

Sue: Yeah.

Larry: What would it be like if I were more subtle?

Sue: I might trust you.

Larry: And if you trusted me?

Sue: You might get me. Better than any of them.

There are many interesting points to this vignette. First, Sue's experience of threat was revealed by the lack of spontaneous elaboration. She did not say more than three sentences at any one point. These three sentences were interrupted by long silences. No elaboration followed my reflection of the last sentence (''more subtle'').

Further, it should be noted that Sue did not want to place me on either pole of the *like other psychologists vs. not like other psychologists* construct. Once again, this shows Sue's problem in the control stage of the C-P-C cycle. The construct had been chosen but Sue refused to definitively place me on one of the poles. Further, within Sue's personal construct system, trust was associated with a devastating betrayal. The implications of this betrayal would be the validation of her mother's words. By hospitalizing her, I could prove that she was ''crazy'' and ''retarded.''

A few sessions later, Sue began to take stands on my identity. However, these stands were quite fleeting. She would place me on the *like other psychologists vs. not like other psychologists* dimension but would quickly back away. This prevented any potential invalidation from occurring. Generally, these stands were in the direction of not trusting me (i.e., I was ''like other psychologists''). However, the taking of these stands showed a movement in the construct system toward an increase in trust. She was beginning to trust me enough to consider actively experimenting with me on the implications of not trusting me. Therapy was becoming a place to experiment.

In conjunction with this shift, Sue began to discuss events outside of the therapeutic relationship. As with the brief stands she was taking in the therapeutic relationship, these outside elaborations were fleeting, often along the lines of the trust issue. In this regard, Sue discussed various individuals who had ''stabbed me in the back.''

A few sessions later, Sue began to experiment with both poles of the *trust vs. not trust* dimension. For example, after discussing ''not trusting'' me, she would talk about events in her current life. She no longer introduced the ''not trust'' pole followed by a retreat into indecisiveness. This showed a further increase in her trust in therapy. I was now trusted enough to discuss issues other than the trust one. However, it should be noted that this increase in trust only occurred when the threatening implications of invalidation had been reduced. As long as trusting me had the threatening implications to the *good self vs. bad self* dimension, Sue would not trust me. Her lack of trust protected the integrity of the system. She did not have to risk placing herself on the *good self vs. bad self* construct.

My stance throughout this work on the *trust vs. not trust* construct was to continually attempt to understand Sue's experience. I never became angry or defensive over Sue's lack of trust. My clinical impression was that Sue would use any sign of irritation from me as an excuse to not trust me. This was her way of testing me to determine if I would "love and accept her, no matter what." Sue would assume that any irritation showed a lack of acceptance.

As an example of Sue's experimentation with the *trust vs. not trust* issue, consider the following vignette.

CLINICAL VIGNETTE 2. Sue alluded to having done terrible things but could not tell me about them. I sat silently. Sue then implied that these terrible things might be illegal. I decided against asking why she could not tell me these things since it implied defensiveness. Instead, I asked her to fantasize about what I might do if she told me. This led into fantasies of my betraying her trust. I might turn her over to the police or have her hospitalized. I decided against reassuring Sue on the confidentiality of the therapeutic relationship. Sue knew quite well that our relationship was confidential. Reassuring her about what she already knew could be seen as my protesting too much. I therefore commented that she might be predicting that I would act like her mother. I asked her to elaborate on the similarities and differences between her mother and myself. We sat silently. Sue then stated that she really could not see how I was like her mother. However, she was afraid of being hurt if she trusted me—particularly with this information. We sat silently. She really did not know how she would come to trust me. Once again, silence. She felt that this was not making very much sense. At this point I intervened. I commented that it must be frustrating to feel so lonely and yet be unable to trust others. We sat silently as she struggled with intense feelings. Sue began talking of how her doctor had failed to be present for her deliveries. Her babies were attended by a resident. At this point I interrupted her. I said, "You're really afraid I'll let you down." Sue began to cry. She then stated that she had smoked marijuana. Further, she carried a gun without a license. We sat silently. She then spoke of hoping to meet a certain man again. This person had tried to rape her. She would like to kill him. I asked, "What would killing him be like?" Sue talked about how pleasant killing him would be, then stated that she could not kill him. The police would arrest her and she would no longer be able to care for her kids. This led into a discussion of how a person could feel like doing something but then choose not to do it.

Within this interaction, it became apparent that Sue was struggling with the *trust vs. not trust* dimension. She initially construed me as someone she could "not trust." My "hanging in there" and attempting to understand this allowed her to decide to elaborate the "trust" side of the construct. This was clinically evidenced when Sue showed her pain through tears. She had resolved never to cry again after one of her mother's assaults on her. Her reason for this decision was that she should never allow another person to know how weak she felt. If others knew, they could attempt to destroy her, as she felt her mother had. At this point, the critical experiment began. Sue discussed acts, fears, and feelings about which she felt very guilty. My responses to this sharing were used by Sue as validation or invalidation for the *trust vs. not trust* dimension. Since I did not hospitalize her or call the police, I became someone she could trust. Moreover, since I did not moralize with her, I did not see her as a bad person.

Further, our subsequent discussion of the differences between feelings and behaviors was beneficial. Sue did not have to fear that she would do something simply because she felt the impulse to do it. This reduced the threat she experienced as a result of her angry feelings—angry feelings could not dictate her behavior. This discussion allowed Sue to place herself more on the "trust" pole of the *trust vs. not trust* construct by helping her differentiate between feelings and actions.

At this point, some very interesting things began to happen. Sue started the next session by announcing that she had taken a job as a waitress in the evenings. Although John did not like it, she felt she needed to get out of the house more. What might be related to this change?

Returning now to our earlier discussion of Sue's constriction of her perceptual field due to threat, it was predicted that Sue would dilate her field when the threat to the superordinate *good self vs. bad self* structure had been reduced. With the threat reduced, she would be able to open her world to new experiences. Following the critical session discussed in Clinical Vignette 2, Sue apparently made the choice of trust. She then dilated on her own accord, as the principle of the elaborative choice would suggest.

Sue began to experiment with trust outside the therapy relationship. This involved sharing some things with a waiter at her place of employment. She was quite excited about the results of this experiment and began contemplating having an affair. However, this notion was upsetting to Sue because of her belief that a wife should remain faithful to her husband. Further, the notion that he was attracted to her forced Sue to struggle with the conflict over being "ugly" and "retarded." She was consequently experiencing both threat (the potential tightening of the *good self vs. bad self* dimension) and guilt (the possibility of acting against her values as a wife).

Then I made a serious error. Even though I knew Sue was not yet ready to seriously attempt any tightening of the *good self vs. bad self* construct, I ventured aggressively into this area. When I reflected on this later, I decided that my reasons for doing so might be tied to my hostility (in the Kellian sense) about the case conference presentation mentioned earlier. Because of my own insecurities and a feeling that my professional competence was attacked during the debate over Sue's ability to tolerate a more reconstructive therapeutic strategy, I impulsively and perhaps hostilely tried to prove that Sue could be reached with a more reconstructive therapy. Remember that Kelly defined impulsivity as a shortening of the circumspection stage of the C-P-C cycle. Thus, at this time, I was not as thoughtful about my patient as I could have been.

In response to my probing in this area of high threat, Sue's spontaneous elaboration decreased to nothing. Her attempts to answer questions were very brief. She raised the issue of the therapy going too fast. However, my desire to prove myself right was so strong that I did not listen as sensitively to my patient as I had done previously. By forcing Sue to look at the *good self vs. bad self* dimension, I caused construct tightening. She had kept this dimension loose because there was the potential threat of seeing herself as a "bad self." Thus, in Sue's organization of the world, I was making her face the possibility that she might be "ugly," "retarded," or "crazy." Sue thus felt a lack of acceptance in the therapeutic relationship. This error caused Sue to experience much pain and misery. It also came close to destroying our therapeutic relationship.

The afternoon of the next appointment, Sue called the clinic secretary and stated that she was terminating therapy. She then hung up before the confused and frightened secretary could utter a word. I called Sue and urged a final session before terminating. She agreed. In this session, Sue shared having a "terrible fight" with John. She cancelled the previous appointment when he implied that she and I were in an alliance against him. Sue had decided that she could not help herself. She would just live with John as best she could. While she was furious with the world, she felt incapable of doing anything about it. She felt regret over leaving therapy because she felt I was genuinely concerned about her. However, she refused to reconsider her decision. I informed her that I would be in town through August and that, if she wished, she could call me.

This is a clear example of the hazards of premature tightening. When the clear confrontation of the *good self vs. bad self* dimension resulted in a tightening process, Sue had to define herself on this dimension. Her experiences with "Granny," the waiter, and me argued for the "good self" pole of this dimension. However, her experiences with her family of origin and her marriage argued for the "bad self" pole. This premature tightening caused Sue to terminate therapy, to get into more difficulty at home, and to have an affair, resulting in a subsequent pregnancy.

On the positive side, there had been a marked decrease in her presenting symptomatology. The dreams and fantasies were not as bothersome. Her physiological concerns had decreased somewhat. However, the basic issues had yet to be resolved.

Approximately two months later, Sue's life was at a serious crisis point. She had had the affair, thought she was pregnant, and felt rejected by her lover. She called and asked to start therapy again. Much the wiser for my blunder, I agreed.

To avoid premature tightening in the *good self vs. bad self* area, I focused my efforts on the elaboration of constructs only with regard to the therapy relationship as opposed to her total world. However, even while doing this, no session passed without having Sue speculate on the implications of these constructs for her problems in the world. Tightening the *good self vs. bad self* construct in the therapeutic relationship was less threatening to Sue than tightening it in all areas of her life. At this point, the therapy focused extensively on the transference. I will not detail the specifics of these interactions as the principles of handling the transference have been discussed in detail elsewhere (Kelly, 1955). However, therapists who are psychoanalytically oriented would find much in common with the Personal Construct Theory treatment of the transference. "Much of what we have to say regarding the use of transference, as indeed much of what we have already said about therapeutic technique, has been said by those who approach therapy from the standpoint of psychoanalysis" (Kelly, 1955, pp. 662–663).

With this focusing, Sue quickly regained lost ground. The *trust vs. not trust* issue had to be worked through again. Once this occurred, Sue became more introspective, less hostile, and more propositional (or orthogonal) in her construing. We then began dealing with the *good self vs. bad self* dimension in the transference. Sue was thus confronted with this dimension, and subsequent tightening occurred in the very constricted field of the therapeutic relationship. One specific example of this will be discussed in Clinical Vignette 3.

At this point in the therapy, Sue decided to rent an apartment. She stayed with her children during the day. At night, she worked and returned to her apartment to sleep. This move was more than another dilation of her perceptual field. Sue was experimenting with a new life but was not burning the bridges to her past. As the *good self vs. bad self* construct was tightened in the more constricted field of the therapeutic relationship, Sue was beginning to make moves outside therapy without pressure from me.

These moves caused Sue to "declare my independence to everybody." She was going to "be my own person." By this statement, Sue meant she was going to do as she wanted without being paralyzed by what others might think. This was an interesting experiment with her role constructs. It signified a shift toward trusting her own experience as opposed to depending on others for her view of herself. She was experimenting with tightening her superordinate structures outside of therapy.

In other words, as Sue gained predictive accuracy with these constructs in the more constricted field of the therapeutic relationship, she was willing to dilate (once again following the principle of the elaborative choice). Within this more dilated field, Sue decided to experiment with tightening and placing herself on the "good self" side of the *good self vs. bad self* construct. In addition, there was a new construct at play—the notion of "being your own person." With this tightening of the structure, Sue's physical symptoms and frightening dreams (which had returned after the termination) decreased markedly.

In subsequent sessions, Sue became anxious as she dealt with the implications of tightening the structure. People began to like her, told her she was attractive, and wanted to do things with her. When Sue explored the implications of these experiences, she could not understand the things her mother had said and done to her. The inability to understand part of the world is central to Kelly's (1955) concept of anxiety. Sue's struggle with this anxiety over both "good" and "bad" selves can be seen in the following vignette.

CLINICAL VIGNETTE 3. Sue could not understand how men could like her and see her as an attractive woman. As we dealt with this issue, she began discussing her mother and her older sister. Her mother always talked about how lovely Ellen was. She spent hours working on Ellen's hair. In marked constrast, Sue was told she was ugly. She was also told there was "no use messing with" her hair as nothing could be done for it. Sue consequently became a "tomboy." She then spoke of how difficult it was to relate to men as a woman. She had related to them as "one of the guys" throughout her life.

Sue then returned to her mother. How could Mom be wrong? She spoke of her mother throwing butcher knives at her. I intervened and asked whether she felt her mother hated her and wanted to kill her. Sue replied that she did indeed feel that way. A long silence ensued as Sue struggled with painful feelings. Sue then wondered what her mother would think of her affair, pregnancy, and abortion. All she had ever wanted was for her mother to love her. Her mother compared her so poorly to Ellen. Sue was the one who was able to make money, buy her own car, and leave home. Sue's chest hurt. It felt like someone was "cutting my heart out." I pointed out the possible relationship between the chest pains and her desire for her mother's love. The session ended with Sue fantasizing as to how her life would have been different if her mother had loved her.

Sue followed this session by focusing on my feelings for her. In her perception of the world, I fluctuated between four roles—the mechanic, Mom, Granny, and the doctor. As the mechanic, I could read everything in her mind and fix or destroy her at will. In relation to the mechanic, Sue was a car—a nonperson. When Mom, I was hateful and vindictive and would do anything to hurt her. In relation to Mom, Sue was a hated person. While Granny, I was a kind, forgiving, loving parent. Sue was a little child who desperately soaked up love. In the role of the doctor, I would not give Sue the time of day. Any question she might ask only irritated me. I resented her occupying my time. In relation to the doctor, Sue was a total nothing—not even a car. I pointed out that, as long as I was understood in those terms, she did not have to struggle with the possibility of my genuinely liking her. Openly considering my genuinely liking her implied the possibility of her being a worthwhile person (i.e., a "good self").

We worked on this issue in many ways. For example, Sue role-played interactions between herself and the various therapists. When Sue discussed an issue, I did not respond to it. Rather, I had her respond as she believed the mechanic, Mom, Granny, and the doctor would. This, as with most role-playing techniques, resulted in her clearly defining her understanding of these dimensions (a tightening procedure). I also encouraged her to fantasize as to what it would be like if I liked (and did not like) her. Although it pained her, she felt more comfortable with my disliking her. How could anyone like someone who had totally "botched" her life. In future sessions, I often asked, "Who am I today?" or, "Who was I today?"

In the next session, as Sue was elaborating her worthlessness, she mentioned her children. I commented on her love for her children. How did she reconcile that love with her being a worthless person? After a long silence, Sue stated that all mothers love their children. It was only natural. I asked about those mothers who did not love their kids. After another silence, Sue said that was impossible. She paused for a few moments and said, "They must be pretty rotten people to not love their kids." I asked about her mother. A long silence ensued. Sue stated, "Maybe I did something to deserve being hated. Even a loving mother would hate me." I asked how that felt. Sue stated, "It hurts. She may hate me because of who I am." I then shared my confusion. Sue was describing her perfect mother as hating her, but mothers who hate their children are rotten. How did she explain this discrepancy? The session continued in this manner.

Sue's ability to struggle openly with these important issues signified a shift within her personal construct system. The system had changed because of the addition of a new superordinate construct (being your own person vs. being controlled by others). This construct allowed her to work on these critical issues without her whole psychological world collapsing. She was more concerned with understanding herself on this dimension than on the *good self vs. bad self* construct. Thus, although the conflicts were just as "objectively" serious as earlier, Sue was not as threatened with the possibility of sudden change in core structure since she had construed herself as "being her own person." She was then able to experience the anxiety of not understanding certain events in her life. Her temporary reconstruing of her mother as "rotten" in Clinical Vignette 3 was the result of the addition of this new superordinate construct *(being your own person vs. being controlled by others)*. With this construct at play, Sue was then free to reconstrue her mother, since there was not so much of herself on the line.

Subsequent to Clinical Vignette 3, Sue developed another new superordinate construction of herself. She began to feel that she was a "person who has made mistakes but has done the best she could" as opposed to simply a "rotten person." When she looked at her mother as being a similar type of person, interesting things began to happen. First, the decapitation dreams disappeared. Further, she experienced physiological problems (chest pains) only when actually interacting with her mother, not when just thinking of her. Finally, she began to construe me in different terms. I no longer fluctuated between the mechanic, Mom, Granny, and the doctor. As Sue stated: "Today you're just Larry."

The work with Sue's differing conceptions of me (in Clinical Vignette 3) exemplified Kelly's (1955) notion of secondary transference. When a client is construing a therapist in this manner, the constructs that are "tried on for size" are permeable to figures outside of therapy. With a secondary transference construct "validation or invalidation has significance for the manner in which the client will approach, not only the therapist, but other persons outside the conference room. The therapist can use the transference as a basis for reorienting the client's constructions of other persons" (Kelly, 1955, p. 674). Kelly felt that secondary transference was much more productive in therapy than the highly impermeable dependencies involved in a primary transference. Since the primary transference constructions are so impermeable, they do not generalize to figures outside the therapy room. "Therapeutic movement may appear to take place within the therapy room, but no really new approaches appear to be tried outside the therapy room" (Kelly, 1955, p. 675). With the exception of my technical and personal error, I consistently cared for my patient without burdening her with other aspects of my personal life. This allowed Sue to develop a secondary transference relationship which was most helpful in working out her problems. This is my conception of Kelly's statements regarding the anonymity of the psychotherapist.

Shortly after the addition of these superordinate constructs, termination became an active issue as my internship year was ending. When I introduced termination, Sue stated that she knew it was coming and felt some sadness about it. However, as will be illustrated in Clinical Vignette 4, Sue had some feelings about termination that she was not putting into words.

CLINICAL VIGNETTE 4. Sue started the next session by stating that she was angry. Her employer was not treating her with respect. He was putting her down. She had a good mind to quit. After all, he would probably fire her. As a matter of fact, she had a good mind to just not show up anymore. That would teach him. "After all, Larry—I mean Mike—is not a nice person." At this point I intervened and said, "I'll teach that bastard Larry for stopping therapy. I'll leave him before he leaves me." Sue responded with a laugh. She then said, "Well, it seemed like a good idea at the time."

In this example, because Sue was angry with me for terminating therapy, she considered terminating therapy first. However, rather than state this in so many words, Sue communicated this construct by way of her feelings toward her employer. The good therapist has to listen sensitively for such communications from the patient. By promptly interpreting this to Sue (a tightening procedure), I enabled her to discard quickly the construct as applied to me.

Our last sessions were spent working on the termination issue. As can be inferred from Clinical Vignette 4, Sue associated termination with my not respecting and caring for her. When she felt that way, her chest pains increased in intensity. I pointed this out to her as support for the hypothesized relationship between the chest pains and feelings of not being loved.

In these final sessions, Sue shared many fantasies about continuing to see me. Each time these fantasies were tightened and discarded, Sue experienced openly the pain of termination. In the final session, I shared my impression that her progress had been substantial. I then "verbalized" (for the first and only time) my feelings toward her. I told her that I cared for her as a person. I also stated that I respected the courage and integrity which enabled her to engage in the 10-month struggle we had shared. Upon hearing this, Sue stated that her chest no longer hurt. She handled our parting maturely.

POSTSCRIPT: 10 MONTHS LATER. While finishing this chapter, I called Sue to obtain some information regarding her current life situation. Sue reported that she has decided to divorce John. She elaborated this by discussing it in terms of a growing feeling of "independence." She stated that she and John were "good friends" but "were not meant to live together."

Related to this growing sense of independence, Sue is now attending college. She has set her sights on a career in nursing. She has an "A" average, and is on the President's Honor Roll. She is justifiably proud of these accomplishments. Her financial support is a combination of scholarship, welfare support, and child support from John.

Sue reported an upsurge in chest pains immediately after my departure. However, these rapidly disappeared and have not returned. The terrifying dreams and fantasies are no more. Sue reported experiencing a "sadness" one day when she felt her dreams and fantasies were gone forever. When her mother became condemning about the impending divorce (even calling her a "slut"), Sue confronted her. Sue told her that she "should know better than to say things like that." A noticeable improvement in their relationship occurred following this confrontation. Sue even took some responsibility for contributing to their problems.

As Sue talked to me, the notions of "taking responsibility for myself" and "being human" appeared to be very meaningful to her. This latter notion allows her to forgive herself and others for mistakes and shortcomings. Consequently, her resentments over her past are gone.

Perhaps the best way of concluding the story of Sue is to quote her view of herself and her therapy.

I've grown up at long last thanks mainly to our visits. I went from a shaky kid ready to kill myself and take my kids with me, to an adult willing to take responsibility for my life. As I look back on it, I don't see how we came so far in so short a time. My basic self hasn't changed like I was afraid it would. Just my outlook has. I really can't describe it. . . . I'm still the same person only I'm totally different.

REFERENCES

Kelly, G. A. *The Psychology of Personal Constructs:* Vols. 1 and 2., New York: Norton, 1955.

Kelly, G. A. Suicide: The personal construct point of view. In N. L. Farberow & E. S. Schneidman (Eds.), *The Cry for Help*. New York: McGraw-Hill, 1961.

Landfield, A. W. A personal construct approach to suicidal behavior. In P. Slater (Ed.), *Explorations of Intrapersonal Space*. London and New York: Wiley, 1976.

McCoy, M. M. A reconstruction of emotion. In D. Bannister (Ed.), *New Perspectives in Personal Construct Theory*. London and New York: Academic, 1977.

CHAPTER 7

Personal Construct Psychotherapy: A Personal Construction

A. W. Landfield

This chapter describes a view of psychological treatment within Personal Construct Theory (Kelly, 1955). However, this view is not a description of how George A. Kelly would have necessarily pursued his role as psychotherapist. Instead, the author of this chapter, reflecting on his own constructions, tries to show how he has pursued some of the implications of construct theory. Rather than emphasizing formal statements of the theory, implications will more often be expressed in the author's own language.

The reader, even though following the beat of a different theoretical drummer, may feel that the construct approach described in this chapter bears a resemblance to his own. Such feelings of similarity can be anticipated (Fiedler, 1953). After all, the experienced therapist not only listens carefully for the personal meanings of his clients, but also communicates with them in relevant ways—by employing their words and symbols. Assuming that experienced therapists function within the construction systems of their clients, the material that follows will not be entirely new. At the same time, certain points of theoretical and systematic emphasis will distinguish the Personal Construct Therapist from other professionals.

THE COMPLAINT

Any consideration of psychotherapy begins with a person and his complaint. A person shares his negative evaluation of certain experiences.

Complaints may be defined as feelings of personal distress which are generated by the capacity of the human being to differentiate between his experience of what is or seems to be and his alternative experience of what could be, should be, or must be. This capacity to differentiate and to experience alternative viewpoints directs our attention to man's dialectical nature, a quality of human feeling and thought that encourages the cry of distress as well as man's foremost creative effort. Paradoxically, it is possible that the same dialectical process which leads the person to his most debilitating experience may also be utilized in resolving his distress. Psychotherapy may be viewed as one way in which the person attempts to confront the dialectic of pain with a more hopeful dialectic of new directions in feeling, thought, and behavior.

Since distress may be experienced in relation to either physically defined or psychologically construed causes, there is a tendency to speak of psychological complaints and physical or medical complaints. Although at some levels of discourse this differentiation can be useful, . . . it is important to note that complaints, even as they relate to organic or bodily pathology, can be defined as psychological phenomena. The attribution of a physical cause to an experience or the employment of a physical treatment in relation to it does not exclude the importance of also describing the experience psychologically. Experience, no matter what objective cause is attributed to it, remains a personal and psychological construction for the human being. Moreover, a personal construction of stressful experience is the starting point for the psychological complaint which eventually may be externalized, exhibited, or shared in some form with a friend, casual acquaintance, physician, or psychotherapist. (Landfield, 1975, p. 3)

These experiences which make up the initial complaint do not necessarily represent all of the person's complaint or even the most important aspects of the complaint. As a way of beginning a conversation about his trouble, the client's first verbalizations may really be more of a statement of distress than a definition of the problem. The therapist, in response to this complaint, does not immediately determine its nature. At the same time, he does not reject the client's initial statement and at points of crisis may work closely within the context of this complaint. For example, one does not "play about" with statements of suicidal intent. They are taken seriously and in a manner that communicates the therapist's concern and caring for another human being. The therapist, at the point of crisis, does not worry about whether he is being manipulated or whether the complaint is real. He does what most caring people would do—the client's statements are accepted at their face value. Later, such statements may be placed within other contexts of interpretation.

The initial complaint, comprehended by the therapist as a statement of distress, must be explored, extended, clarified, and elaborated if the client and his therapist are to know the full import of its meaning. It is even possible that the initial complaint will be discarded as the client—through his experimentation with the relationship—feels comfortable enough to share what has really been on his mind all along. Thus, the defining of a complaint must involve the developing therapy relationship. Facilitating "good" feelings in a relationship are just as important as the technical employment of such elaborating techniques as listening, reflecting, questioning, relaxing, imagining, experimenting, dreaming, free associating, and thinking about similarities and differences. In other words, one uses his professional techniques in ways that support the development of mutuality in a "working" relationship.

Since the complaint is what brings the person into therapy in the first place, complaints do become a focal point for determining the effectiveness of therapy. However, since the complaint, as initially given, may take on new meanings and even be replaced by other complaints, a more abstract view of the complaint must be taken if it is to be used as a criterion of change. It may be helpful to employ the more general term "the person with complaints." Not only should the original complaint be reduced, but, just as importantly, the client at the close of treatment should be seen as one who complains less. Certainly, a client who ends his treatment with more complaints should not be construed as improved. Likewise, positive feelings about the treatment do not necessarily point to improvement. For example, statements of mutual enjoyment by the therapist and his client, although highly regarded, should not mask the complaint, either as initially stated or later revised. On the other hand, one should not dismiss feelings of personal growth that may seem unrelated to the complaint. Feelings of growth can point to the emergence of an exploring and experimental attitude toward one's life, a common denominator of all successful Personal Construct Therapy.

Although it has been stated that complaints should be reduced at the end of therapy, how does one judge the end of therapy? In this regard, the following statements are enlightening. They were given by a female client several years after therapy termination:

I think it takes me quite a while to get any perspective . . . , in November everything literally tumbled together for me. . . . Throughout this year I've been thinking about our talks and experiences I had in the group. Once I played a word game with myself similar to the one we played using realist, idealist, true, and false. It was fun and enlightening. . . . I've read Fromm's *Chains of Illusion* and Storr's *Aggression* and seen myself as another person. Really, I am another person. I'm not scared of being with men. I can't believe I ever was. I remember how panic stricken I was in group therapy when one of the guys reached out and held my hand. Held my hand! That's really fantastic. . . . Sometimes I get scared of what people are thinking of me but that doesn't happen often. My stomach hardly ever acts up now. I don't plan what I'm going to say or how I'm going to say it. I disagree with the people at work. I even tell them to shut up and go to hell—I'm not mad, though, and they don't get mad either. . . . I want to have meaningful relationships and not play roles. I realize now that I used to play roles. I see people around behaving just like I did and I have a real feeling of salvation. I'm not so confused or concerned about myself. That's peace, I think. . . . At first I needed just one person—you—sort of a reassurance of worth. Then I got to know (others) who were nearer my age but still had the attitude you had and I found out I didn't have to change.

This quotation suggests that the end of therapy should not be linked in a literal manner with the termination of a professional relationship. A personal construct approach, one that encourages an "experimental attitude" and the feeling that "I have a right to my own life," can have a later and profound influence on the change or reduction of complaints.

Defining and Elaborating the Complaint

Experienced therapists listen carefully to the emotional and logical themes of their clients. However, in this process of careful listening, the construct therapist may behave somewhat differently from other professionals. He is more likely to ask questions and respond in ways that emphasize *contrast in meaning*. This emphasis on contrast in meaning is related to the definition of a personal construct as a bipolar dimension of awareness.

Since statements of the complaint can be construed as personal construction, the therapist will want to understand what the client contrasts with the experiencing of various facets of his complaint. For example, "How would you experience your life without the problem? Do you know anyone who has a strong feeling of well being? Imagine that you have *actually* failed; what will happen? What would Jill be doing if she had your problem? How might you feel if you were free of your headaches?" If the response to this latter question is "Kind of scared" or "I wouldn't know" rather than "I would feel just great," the therapist could hypothesize several possibilities. He might anticipate that the first and second responses point to a "way of life" headache. The headache is purposive and well organized within the personal construct system. The headache is a problem solution and one's life is well structured around it. The third response suggests a greater willingness to lose the headache. Perhaps this headache is primarily an expression of distress in relation to some underlying conflict.

That contrasts in meaning can offer a clue to the nature of a problem is vividly shown by the following illustration: A young man was apprehended for trying to fraudently acquire transcripts of medical school graduates. In an interview with a psychologist, the imposter differentiated between persons as being "saintly good" or "boyishly mischievous." This contrast in which he seemed to dimensionalize a moral value, helps one understand the nature of his "bad" behavior as mischief and further explains why he did not become markedly upset when apprehended. His primary upsetness related to a disbelief that people would become so up-tight over the forging of three signatures. That his feeling of perplexity could be quite genuine is supported by his atypical social background. He was a foundling raised by a group of isolated, contemplative priests, a background which certainly suggests how he might have developed his strange moral conception of *saintly goodness* versus *boyish mischief*. One can imagine these priests communicating their sense of comic relief as they experienced the boyish antics of this foundling.

The complaints in this case were both internal and external. This young man was in trouble with the law because of a complaint about his bad behavior. His own complaint was that people were viewing his behavior too seriously. Although this latter self-complaint could have brought him into therapy, it did not. Assuming that this person had been open to therapeutic help, how might the construct therapist have worked with him?

Approaching this question in a most general way, the therapist would assist his client in playing a more profound social role. Kelly defined social role as one's behavior which occurs in relation to how one understands the points of view of the other person. Employing this idea that social role should encompass one's view of how the other person feels and thinks, the therapist must also learn to play a relevant social role in relation to his client. Learning to play a relevant social role demands that the therapist listen carefully to the self-description and social language of his client. This careful listening will be integrated with questions and checks on how well he is understanding his client. "Is this what you mean?" is a familiar question in the context of Personal Construct Therapy. In some instances, formal procedures (Fransella & Bannister, 1977) might also be used to assess the content and organization of the client's personal construct system.

Having developed a sensitivity to his client's system through listening to the contrasts and definitions of his personal world of people, the therapist might then be able to assist him in an exploration of how other people think, feel, and value. Rephrasing this point, the therapist should learn the dimensional language of the other person's experience and be able to talk with him in this language. When new feelings and ideas are introduced to the client, it would be done in ways that the client might comprehend. In this regard, a study by Isaacson and Landfield (1965) is most interesting. It was found that persons more readily assign to "most like me" personal construct poles derived from acquaintance description than construct poles provided by the investigator. Even negative description could be applied to oneself when couched in one's own language. The fact that even negative description could be applied to "most like me" when stated within one's own construct system has interesting implications for psychotherapy. If one must confront a client with negative interpretation, it is best done within the personal language framework of the client.

SOCIAL ROLE AND THE CONSTRUCT THERAPIST

Assuming that an accurate appreciation of how one's client feels, thinks, and values will lead to a more useful elaboration of and working with the complaint, how does one get around the problem of low client-therapist congruency? Landfield (1971) showed that a lower degree of overlap in the content of client-therapist social language is related to greater premature termination in psychotherapy. This finding, based on middle-class clients and therapists, suggests that some attempt should be made to match clients and therapists in relation to their personal construct systems. When such matching cannot be accomplished, the therapist may need to bridge wide gaps in construct communication between himself and his client, even those clients with socioeconomic backgrounds similar to his own. Of course, the closing of such gaps would be facilitated by a therapist who is widely experienced in his culture. Such a person would have some idea about a variety of life-styles, values, and modes of adjustment. However, in the absence of this wider experience, a therapist can struggle to locate a bit of shared experience as a basis for an expanding relationship. He can also listen carefully and make sensitive inquiries about how his client dimensionalizes and organizes his experience.

Using the language of personal constructs, the therapist utilizes the superordinate construction of careful listening and exploratory questioning. That this superordinate questioning and listening can bridge the communication gap is supported by Poser's study (1966) in which young, untrained, female therapists were as effective as the older, highly trained professionals. Perhaps it can be hypothesized that in the absence of professional experience and dogma, one may both question and listen more openly—even objectively. This constricting effect of some professional experience and training is certainly supported by Rosenhan's study (1973) of mental hospital patients. In the context of this study in which pseudo-patients became fixed within superficial diagnostic statements, one can only speculate how persons trained in construct psychology might have interacted with the normal, but hospitalized, patients. Personal Construct Psychology, an open system (Von Bertalanffy, 1967) approach to human beings, encourages the psychologist to take a fresh approach to each client. This implies that the other person's behavior should not be forced into concrete preconceptions of the meaning a bit of behavior should have for all persons.

The idea that one should listen carefully and somewhat uncritically to the client is hardly a new idea (Fielder, 1953). However, the construct therapist brings to his listening a less elaborate system of "ready-made" hypotheses and interpretations about the meaning of specific bits of behavior and the true nature of complaints. In this respect, Kelly and Rogers bear a resemblance. At the same time, the construct therapist will be more active than the *traditional* nondirective professional. He will make greater use of questions about how his client perceives self and others. He will inquire more extensively about the contrasting nature of his client's experiences. He will also provide more structuring for experiments in living which may constructively challenge his client in the direction of new experience. Although one expects more activity from the construct therapist, one also expects him to show more variety in his behavior. His role should encompass the classical passive listening as well as the more active use of such techniques as reversed role playing,—that is, where the therapist and client act out interpersonal situations, then switch roles. Interpretation, a hypothesis about relationships, will also be employed. However, interpretation will be phrased as a question—not as an assumption or a God-given insight.

Earlier, it was stated that the therapist should play a relevant social role in relation to his client. The therapist also assists his client in playing a more effective social role in relation to his acquaintances. Furthermore, the construct therapist will actively question his client about contrasts in his feeling, valuing, and behaving. At this point, one could ask how a therapist can be sensitive to his client, which implies respect for his difficulties in communicating or working through his problem, and remain an active therapist. Activity, of course, can serve the purpose of aggressively directing, structuring, and forcing the client into a predetermined mold. Therapist activity can also mean that one guides and orients his client into new channels of self-exploration and interpersonal experimentation. It is this latter activity that identifies the Personal Construct Therapist.

Some therapists have confronted the issue of directiveness and the importance of allowing the client to struggle for his own life by taking a "low-key" approach marked by little interpretive lead or structuring. Unfortunately, this nondirective response, although good for some clients as a total therapy, tends to restrict unduly the role of the therapist. Even as the construct therapist will employ the nondirective response, he will understand that certain clients—because of their values and personality styles, based upon their personal construct systems—both want and need a more vigorous interaction with the therapist. Moreover, there are times when the same client will vary as to his openness for greater and lesser degrees of therapy structure and interpretive lead. As a consequence, the most appropriate social role for the construct therapist will vary somewhat from client to client as well as from time to time with the same client. All of this seems consistent with Kelly's idea of playing a social role.

The foregoing discussion suggests the need for therapist flexibility which may be difficult to attain. Although training and experience will help in the attainment of such flexibility, it is an ideal that will not be reached. However, there are some persons who come to therapy training with greater potential for developing therapy skills. If we could understand more about these persons, it might be possible to better select our students.

Understanding the factors which contribute to the greater potentiality of certain students for growth as therapists is not easy. However, a personal construct researcher might relate greater potential to the ways in which students describe their acquaintances on a Rep Test. Essentially, a Rep Test involves asking subjects to describe their acquaintances or situations in various combinations of similarities and differences. Starting with this procedure, it is hypothesized that students who eventually do better as therapists will employ certain descriptive dimensions, one pole of which will suggest some interest in or concern about (1) openness to experience, (2) sociality and warmth of interaction, (3) independence, (4) ethical values, (5) emotionality, and (6) energy or forcefulness of expression and activity. Furthermore, still employing the Rep Test dimensions along which all acquaintances are rated, one may hypothesize about how students with potential as therapists will organize their interpersonal conceptions. Using measures employed by Landfield and Barr (1976), one would expect a social construct system that is both complex in its variety of content and integrated by higher-order or more superordinate conceptions. In regard to this integration, the degree of relationship among one's different descriptive dimensions would not be tight. For example, one's constructs of friendship and honesty might be highly related, but not to the point of equivalence. In other words, a friendly person would *not always* be honest. To take another example, one's notion of integrity would *not always* point to a particular type of behavior. Rephrasing this, there would be exceptions to many relationships, suggesting that the person functions more with hypotheses than assumptions.

AN EXPECTANCY FORMULATION OF RELATIONSHIP

The idea that anticipation or expectancy will play a critical role in human relationships is built into the fundamental postulate of Personal Construct Psychology: "A person's processes are psychologically channelized by the ways in which (the person) anticipates events." Although expectancy is a primary conception within construct theory, other investigators of psychotherapy have related the client-therapist relationship to aspects of anticipation (Stone et al., 1964; Levitt, 1966; Doster, 1971, 1972). In the following sections, both client and therapist anticipations will be considered within the clinical setting.

Client expectancies and uncertainties. The person seeking assistance from a psychotherapist feels anxious and upset in relation to his problem. He also experiences other kinds of anxieties—those which are related to his anticipations and uncertainties about the nature of the therapist, the treatment, and what will happen when he relates the details of his complaint. It is the latter kind of anxiety which may complicate the task of defining the nature of the complaint at the first interview.

Although persons who have previously experienced the therapy encounter and those who are overwhelmed with the urgency of their dilemmas may talk more freely about their complaints, most persons seeking help from a professional therapist for the first time, even those who are more sophisticated in their understandings of treatment procedures, are concerned about how they will feel about talking to a particular therapist and how he will react to their problems. The following comments are commonly heard by psychotherapists: "I know you will think I'm just a kook, but . . ." "I realize that you must have heard this problem a hundred times . . ." "Maybe I shouldn't be here. Other people are able to solve their problems." "Well, here goes." "I guess I've talked too much." "You must think of me as a terrible person." "I feel very silly now that I have told you." "I guess you are trained to react that way." "Do you want me to come back?" "Tell me something about yourself, Doctor!"

Focusing now on more specific problems of expectancy, it is not uncommon for a client to expect that his problem will be minimized by the clinician. After all, friends and relatives have told him many times that he ought to quit complaining so much. Thus, in the context of this expectancy, he may exhibit a "worthy" complaint by exaggerating his situation and his feelings about it. He may even fabricate a complaint. Experienced therapists expect that complaints sometimes will be exaggerated. They also expect that some improved clients, at the point of termination, will revive old complaints which have been "laid to rest."

The fear that one will be stigmatized by seeking professional counsel is another expectancy affecting when and how a complaint will be stated. Moreover, it is a fear which the professional may overlook because he is accustomed to the idea of pathology. In spite of the efforts of mental health organizations, there is evidence that having an emotional problem tends to lessen one's status in the eyes of other people (Farina et al., 1966, 1968). It seems reasonable that a society which defines the good life as personal achievement and an ability to independently cope with the problems of one's life would not reward the complaints of the maladjusted.

Another expectancy which could markedly affect, positively or negatively, the elaboration of a complaint is the client's anticipation that the clinician will be a kindly, understanding, and helpful sort of person. Hopefully, this expectancy will be validated by the clinician. However, if this positive anticipation of therapy is challenged by a detached professional who quizzes and confronts him diagnostically, the client may become sullen and uncooperative. When the clinician becomes patronizing in relation to his client's sullenness, and the client feels that he is being treated like a child, the interview assuredly will deteriorate quickly. The clinician, failing to comprehend the nature of his relationship with his client, may focus on the client's uncooperative attitude which is recorded as an "objective" trait, one which later is associated with mental disease.

In contrast to the previous expectancy is the client's anticipation that the professional will assume a disinterested or even rejecting attitude. Such an expectancy would severely reduce possibilities for a constructive communication between a client and his therapist. Sometimes this expectancy may be construed by the therapist as an aspect of his client's problem, a dissatisfaction with people which is "acted out" directly in relation to his therapist. Although an expectancy of rejection is more frequently encountered in state hospital situations where treatment is forced on the patient and where life values of lower class patients are in sharp contrast to those held by the professional, it is a problem with which the private therapist also must contend. Being misunderstood is a common complaint among those who suffer from personal and social maladjustments.

Finally, there is the client who expects his therapist to assume full responsibility for his cure. This type of client tends to be impatient, demanding, and hypercritical at the one extreme and passive at the other. In the passive role, the client may quietly and steadfastly share his feelings of complete helplessness. In the aggressive role, the client may demand that the therapist ask him questions or insist that he should be told exactly how to behave, although reserving for himself the right not to follow any prescription. He also may be most unwilling to elaborate the context of his well formulated complaint. Then again, he may insist that he can be cured only if the therapist changes certain people who are thwarting or frustrating him. In response to such expectancies, the therapist may point out that he and his client have joint responsibility to work on the client's problem. Furthermore, without denying the influence of other people, the therapist may encourage his client to consider how his own attitudes and behavior may influence the ways in which others treat him. In certain instances, the therapist may try to influence both his client and those whom his client complains about by playing the role of family therapist or community consultant. Sometimes the clinician may threaten his client with treatment termination if he continues to insist that his therapist assume all the responsibility.

A psychotherapist who wishes to convince people that each person must bear some responsibility for his problems as well as his cure works against heavy odds. His underprivileged patients learn early that life has limitations. They also learn that treatment for them is largely custodial and medical. His more privileged clients do learn that professionals will talk with them about their problems. However, they also learn from pamphlets circulated by associations for mental health that an emotional problem is sickness (Beisser, 1965) for which the person often is not responsible. A corollary to this type of logic suggests that if one is not responsible for his problem, then he assuredly cannot be held responsible for his own cure. To further complicate the therapist's task of encouraging his clients to assume more responsibility for their lives, the ''body'' theorists attribute the cause of behavior to genetics and spleen, while the ''environmentalists'' attribute cause to external circumstances. The psychotherapist, not wishing to be caught up in the expectancies of environmental laws or organic truths, may resort to theories about how man actively experiences his world, a position that neither denies the realities of one's culture or the impact of organic structure.

Therapist expectancies and uncertainties. Just as client expectations influence how complaints are stated, therapist expectations also affect the ways in which complaints are initially presented and elaborated. Beginning with the therapist's preferred theory or model of man, a client's behavior will be guided to some degree by the therapist's theoretically based questions and the differential interest he shows in relation to certain of his client's statements. If the therapist has strong preconceived ideas about the nature of his client's complaint and how his client should respond, he may seek only those kinds of information which validate his preconceived notions about the complaint. If his client fails to provide him with validational support, he may become upset. And, it is conceivable that a therapist might communicate this anxiety to the client by accusing him of being defensive or uncooperative, a strategy which often retards the client's elaboration of *his* complaint.

The experienced therapist, more tolerant of ambiguity, also may feel uneasy about his therapy role since he realizes that many facets of the initial interview cannot be quickly or easily comprehended. It is not uncommon for an experienced therapist to leave a first interview with some feelings of perplexity, that there are many loose ends that he does not understand, loose ends which include the ''not so remote'' possibility that he will experience difficulties in understanding and communicating with his client.

Occasionally, we find a therapist who feels quite secure in relation to any client or patient. Perhaps he is an ''activity secure'' therapist who does not attend to the relationship between himself and his client. This type of therapist defines his role as the "doing" of therapy. In this role context, any difficulties experienced in the first interview can be attributed to the client. After all, the client is the one who has the problem. In contrast to the "activity secure" therapist is one whose generalized therapy role has emerged through being sensitive and responsive to the ongoing interpersonal process; a therapist whose "doing" role is integrated with an empathic understanding of how his client feels and thinks.

The therapist who can integrate "feeling with his client" and "doing for his client" is likely to continue in his role of psychotherapist. The therapist who develops his therapy style with little interpersonal awareness may depart from the therapy enterprise and employ his energies in more rigorous and scientific ways. He may even specialize in psychological diagnosis (Landfield, 1975, pp. 10—13.).

ILLUSTRATIONS FROM PERSONAL RESEARCH AND CLINICAL EXPERIENCE

A first experience in facilitating behavioral change can be rewarding. Then again, it can have mixed implications. My first experience as a catalyst for constructive change was of the latter kind. This near-disastrous experience began with a father seeking help with his 10-year-old son, a conscientious truant who disappeared from home at the slightest provocation. The father stated that he had tried all manner of alternatives with his son, which translated into more and better whippings. Even though the father readily admitted that increased whippings were accompanied by increased truancy, he perceived no functional relation between the two events.

Very early in the first interview, I developed a strong impression that the man cared for his son. He stated his position vigorously and I believed him at the pit of my stomach, an indicator that might not appeal to a logician. Thus, beginning with my construct of *"out-front"* versus *"hidden agenda,"* I construed the father as "out-front" and "caring" for his son. Then, not fully understanding the importance of being sure of one's clinical ground prior to taking definitive action, I did the following: First, I elicited the statement from the father that whipping is the best way of correcting troublesome behavior. Next, I asked the father how his own father had treated him. The father immediately replied, "My father whipped the hell out of me and it was good for me." Then, I followed his response with my own "show stopper." I asked him how he felt about his own father, a question that precipitated a nerve-shattering quietness. The silence was finally broken with an anguished, "I hated my father!" This was followed by, "Oh, my God, is that how my son feels about me?" And, back in the hidden recording room, my supervisor, who was not George Kelly, but might have been, turned beet red at my impulsive intervention.

What could be learned from this? My supervisor focused on one lesson—be cautious. "You made a serious mistake." Now if he had been a Personal Construct Psychologist, he could have urged me to wait for more information concerning the father's personal construct system. He might also have noted that my intervention did lead to a constructive modification in the father's behavior, something that intrigued me much later, after I had overcome my feelings of guilt. After all, I had been dislodged from a core role. In retrospect, I realize that some of my later therapy encounters bear a resemblance to this first one, but in the context of greater elaborations of the person's construct system, an increased sensitivity to what may happen as a consequence of definitive action, and greater confidence in coping with the unexpected.

In this first experience, there is a theme of questioning which leads the client to juxtapose certain experiences in ways which create a new conflict. In the process of experiencing the new conflict, the person broadens and reorganizes the original context of problem dilemma—a reorganization which allows the person to take new perspectives on his problem. In our illustration, the father was encouraged to juxtapose two constructions of experience within the context of "really caring" for his son. Father was asked to lay side-by-side his feeling about proper parental discipline with his awareness of how the recipient of such discipline might feel. He was asked to do this in a most personal way by thinking about it in relation to his own father. Fortunately, my client was able to rise to the occasion, take perspective on his situation, and consider new approaches to his son. Caring for his son was a more important value for this father than a particular mode of discipline, even though the father's rigid behavior might suggest otherwise.

Further analysis of this illustration points to the idea that the father was functioning at a concrete, assumptive level of experience when he knew that punishment would work. There could be no exception to the direct relationship between punishment and behavior, an assumptive stance that can be contrasted with two other levels of functioning. First, there is the level of hypothesis in which feelings of relationship lead to further exploration. There is also the level of fragmentation in which feelings, thoughts, and behavior are experienced in confusing and unrelated ways which fail in providing guides to the future (Landfield, 1977).

The father in our illustration assumed that punishment would eventually stop his son's truancy. Even the father's awareness that punishment was not stopping his son's truancy did not invalidate his idea about punishment. It had to work. He was going to make it work by doing more of it. Here we have a beautiful example of Kellian *hostility*—the extortion of validational evidence. Of course, the father's assumptive stance can be readily understood because his own father stopped his son's bad behavior. Only when the father examined punishment in the context of "feelings in relation" to his own father did he begin to question the efficacy of punishment. Because his construct of "caring and feeling cared for" was superordinate and more important than his construct of behavioral control through punishment, he was able to change. If his concept of control had been his primary construction, the outcome of this story might have been different. Therapy directed his attention to his more superordinate construction—the relationship with his son. Further, the therapy presumably encouraged a more hypothetical and child-centered (child's constructs) view of punishment.

The Personal Construct System

The construct psychologist makes inferences about the person's construct system. One aspect of the system is definable by the particular dimensions along which the person makes sense of his life. In the next illustration, the therapist is confronted with a client who presents a make-believe but positively valued social history, one that contrasts sharply with the social values of his actual family.

Several years ago a professional athlete was referred for psychotherapy. His complaint was a persistently sore shoulder which did not respond to medical treatments. In his first interview with me, this client initiated discussion of his parents and grandfather, a theme that was elaborated throughout eight sessions. Father and grandfather were described as builders of sailboats who were proud of both their manual skills and their son. They were also described as "down-to-earth, light-hearted, generous, and uneducated." Mother was the "salt-of-the-earth," ever loving and supportive of her family.

Much of our discussion focused on the client's feeling of support from his family and their acceptance of his recent athletic failures. At the end of eight sessions, the client terminated, feeling that we had talked about what was important to him. How this might relate to his sore arm was an open question. Six months later the referring agent called me and asked if I had been reading the sports pages. My client was having a fine season. In this conversation, I mentioned that the client seemed to have very supportive parents. The referral agent listened to me in disbelief. "I thought you knew about his background!" What I did not know was most enlightening. His father was a world-renowned medical specialist; his mother was a clubwoman. My client was destined to become a famous doctor, not a professional athlete. In working with his fraudulent social history, we had probably talked most helpfully about his construct system. In talking about values antithetical to those of his family, the client had focused on the critical dimensions of his problem.

Suspension of Life Events

The next client, whom we will call Sam, a law student aged 26, nicely illustrates Kelly's (1955, p. 466) position that some events may be so narrowly construed that they have little meaning. The phrase "suspension of life events from fuller interpretation" may be useful here.

Sam referred himself because of a strange feeling of not "making much of his life." He also complained of marital discord. He related the marital problem to his wife's griping about the time he was devoting to his role of fraternity counselor. In the first series of interviews, Sam focused on events that validated his success. He had been a collegiate golf champion, president of a fraternity, an excellent student, and a naval officer. His credentials were impressive. He further stated that he had traveled worldwide with his parents who had introduced him to famous people. In this context of protesting too much, I asked him what all of these events meant for him personally. A long period of silence followed this question. Finally, Sam stated that he was unable to answer the question. He also admitted to confusion. After all, these life events should have meaning for him. This session marked a transition in therapy. Sam began to actively explore with the question of meaning. During this period of exploration, he often remarked that he was a superficial fellow. Within his emerging construction of *"deep versus shallow fellow,"* he became dissatisfied with himself. Functioning from the deeper side of his construct, he began to make more of his past experience, an activity that changed his future.

At the end of the year, Sam apprenticed himself to a federal judge. Prior to this, he had expressed his future ambition as that of making a fast buck and being social. Sam summarized his primary gain in therapy as having developed a greater sense of purpose in his life. He also stated with some pride that he had quit fraternity life and was devoting more time to his wife.

Redefining a Construct

In the next illustration, a type of interpretation was employed which helped the client rearrange the coding of his experiences without seriously invalidating an underlying, or core value, dimension that contributed to his problem. In this instance, the client redefined his construct, "*manly* versus *unmanly*," by taking a more internal and independent view of it.

Frank was a late-afternoon self-referral who insisted that he be seen immediately. Redness about his eyes suggested that he had been crying and his clothes were disheveled. Frank stated that he was unhappy with his graduate work in geology. He began to weep, his body shaking convulsively. Between sobs, he said that he had bought a gun and planned suicide. The clinic was his last resort.

The crux of the problem was quickly stated. His father, a most physical man, wanted him to learn a man's job. However, Frank wanted a career in music. He documented in detail this talent in music as well as his father's serious intent of disowning him if he quit geology and entered the field of music. He wanted to please his father, yet he could not continue in graduate school.

At the practical clinical level, I was faced with the decision of hospitalization for him. I also wanted to help him through this crisis. I said to him, "I think it might take a great deal of strength, character, and sense of purpose to be able to go into music in spite of what other people might say." A long pause ensued. Frank then sat upright in his chair, looked at me squarely, and said he would return tomorrow. I made the uncomfortable decision not to talk about hospitalization with him. Frank departed. He returned the following day with his shoulders squared and a smile on his face. He had made the decision to enter a conservatory of music (Landfield & Allee, 1966).

Frank initially defined his concept of manliness by the "macho" nature of behavior as defined by his father. I assisted him in developing an inner sense of manliness which could be defined by his own sense of courage and struggle. Now this change from an external to an internal and actively constructive orientation is not a strange conception to the psychotherapist. Moreover, the statements of Personal Construct Psychology, in particular, highlight the active, reconstructive, and responsible roles which are possible for the human being.

This client also illustrates what Kelly called *controlled elaboration*. In this process the therapist helps the client work through his construct system. "The purpose is to make the system—or large sections of it, rather—internally consistent and communicable so that it may be tested out and its validity or invalidity discovered" (Kelly, 1955, p. 585).

Reversed Roles

In this illustration, a form of Kelly's reversed role procedure was successfully employed. Dr. Tom was self-referred at the instigation of his wife. She maintained that with only one drink he became a changed person—argumentative, distant, or just obnoxious. Although denying the truth of her allegations, Dr. Tom did not want his wife to divorce him. This reluctant client admitted to having drunk large quantities of alcohol during his military service. However, this was no longer the case. I asked him how he would know that he was not an alcoholic. He replied that he could quit drinking; in fact, he would quit for three months. Later, I inquired about his experiment. At first he denied any drinking. Then he admitted to having drunk a glass of wine at a dinner party. He also admitted that he took just one drink with his buddies at a professional convention. However, this wasn't really drinking! At this point, I asked him to imagine that he was the therapist and I then repeated his statements to him. At first Dr. Tom seemed perplexed, then he blurted out, "I'd say that you are a god-damned alcoholic!"

More illustrations of the personal construct approach come swiftly to mind. There is the up-tight law student who was helped through his mock trials by imagining himself in the role of Mr. Tutt, a slow-speaking legal hero of many skirmishes with fast-talking lawyers. The role of Mr. Tutt exemplified Kelly's "fixed" role therapy. There is the suicidal woman who was helped to value her own validational evidence rather than to depend solely on the views of other people. Then there is the girl who found it most difficult to state a problem, but insisted that she talk with me. For six sessions I tried to understand the nature of her problem. Finally, I gave up. I told her that she seemed like a healthy, mature person. She replied, "I was hoping that you would say that, although I was not certain what would happen." If she had given away her game plan at the first session, it would not have been a fair experiment. I was the unwitting subject in a most interesting and serious life investigation in which a client was validating her life.

Then there is Carmen, a 17-year-old girl who was brought to a university clinic by the Dean of Women. The complaint of others focused on Carmen's refusal to attend classes, avoidance of other girls in the dormitory, and an unwillingness to talk with anyone—even her roommate. She remained in her room except for eating one meal each day. Carmen, rather than explicity stating her complaints, was exhibiting her dissatisfactions through her withdrawn and uncooperative behavior. At the fourth interview, I elicited a statement of her complaint. Carmen stated that she became very upset when her roommate asked her to accompany her home for the weekend. Such a visit was not possible because Carmen would have had to reciprocate. How could she do this when her parents lived in a shack along a railroad siding? Carmen reasoned that her roommmate would reject her because of her parents. Further, the invitation also reminded Carmen of the "fact" that she could not make friends among her middle-class associates. In this fact-bound, assumptive context, Carmen became angry and depressed. Constructive change occurred when Carmen switched to an hypothesizing stance and shared her background with the roommate. Fortunately, the roommate was able to validate the primary significance of Carmen. She told Carmen that where she lived made no difference to their relationship. And she meant it! The successful therapy with Carmen points up the value of the Kellian "experimental attitude" toward one's life, in contrast to what might be called "an acceptance of the stimulus bind."

Insight

Our final illustration points up the potential uses of the Rep Test as a vehicle for therapy. The Rep Test is essentially a device for eliciting descriptions, in contrast, of situations and acquaintances. In this instance, the client, Dr. Joe, was asked to find similarities and differences among various combinations of his family, friends, and acquaintances. After the therapist had recorded 15 contrasting descriptions from the client and their application to each of 15 persons, this material was given to the client. He was instructed to think about this material for about 20 minutes prior to the next session. Dr. Joe, a rigidly proper man who suffered from stomach ulcers, found this material most challenging. At the next session, he commented with both humor and perplexity that only a very authoritarian army general *or* his own father could have given those descriptions. "And, just maybe my wife is right about me. How ridiculous!"

Research

Turning now to formal research, I will comment briefly on how several of my own construct investigations have contributed to a comprehension of psychotherapy.

In a partial replay (Landfield & Nawas, 1964), but not a replication, of a Rosenthal (1955) study of how patients identify with the values of their therapists, we discovered that improved clients tend to identify with therapist ideals when therapist ideals are plotted within the elicited construct dimensions of his client. That the movement to the therapist's ideal was not found when the improved client described himself within the elicited construct dimensions of his therapist raises an interesting question. It is conceivable that the psychoanalytically oriented value items of the Rosenthal questionnaire, relevant for his subjects, might not have been relevant in our context of treatment. If we had simply used his questionnaire, there is the possibility that we might have reported a negative finding on the hypothesis of client identification with therapist values. How often do investigators of psychotherapy lose sight of good hypotheses because they are *not* attuned to the personal constructions of their client subjects?

In a second study, Varble and Landfield (1969) found some evidence for Kelly's contention that self is more likely to change on peripheral than on core constructs in shorter-term treatment. Moreover, one can expect changes in both "present self" and "ideal self" construction. In a third set of studies (Landfield, 1971), premature termination in psychotherapy was found in two contexts; first, when there is less dyadic meaningfulness, as measured by rating scale polarization; second, when there is less congruency in the content of personal constructs within the dyad. This study, which suggests client-therapist matching, can be related to Dr. Carr's chapter (12) on the treatment relationship.

A recent development (Landfield & Rivers, 1975; Landfield, 1979) called the Interpersonal Transaction (IT) Group with Rotating Dyads shows great promise in the study of acquaintanceship and in the treatment of alcoholics and mental hospital patients. It also has been used to facilitate discussion in the classroom and community groups. The IT group, a derivation from Kelly's (1955) sociality corollary, emphasizes the constructs of listening carefully; sharing, but not to the point of great discomfort; and, questioning within the context of understanding rather than criticizing. These superordinate and process constructions are employed in a multidimensional and systematic manner in brief dyadic interactions of four to eight minutes. Interacting pairs may be given such general discussion topics as: share something you value and something you don't value; share who you are and who you are not; share something about how people may understand you both accurately and inaccurately; share one of your own personal constructs (derived from a Rep Test), and so forth. Research on the IT process, using methods of construct theory (Landfield, 1979), focuses on changes in meaningfulness of self and others; positiveness of regard measured within the person's own language of values; predictive accuracy as the person enters the construct systems of others; and, social conceptual organization as measured by construct differentiation and integration (Landfield & Barr, 1976; Landfield, 1977).

IN CONCLUSION

As the personal construct therapist tries to comprehend the complaint within its narrower and expanded contexts, he will encounter the same problems experienced by other therapists. The initial statement of the complaint may be fragmentary, peripheral, precise, diffuse, simple, complex, or even fraudulent. In response to the complaint, the construct therapist will listen carefully to the contrasting nature of the person's experience, ask questions that will define and elaborate the problem, and introduce strategies of personal exploration with a continuing appreciation of the person's dimensional system and how he uses it in organized and disorganized ways. As the therapist focuses on the person's dualities—his contrasts in feeling, valuing, and behaving—he will pay careful attention to the nature of his client's core constructions or central values. Elaborating this point, the therapist will do his work sensitively, recognizing the vulnerability of some clients to a sudden, overwhelming invalidation of primary dimensions of experience and value identification. The therapist will, of course, keep in mind that his own personal constructs, which reflect his feelings, values, and expectations, can influence how the person presents and elaborates his complaint.

Reaching out for a more integrated understanding of therapist potential, the following ideas may be stated. First of all, certain therapy students tend to believe in "instant" wisdom. These impatient students, caught up in shortening the circumspective phase of Kelly's C-P-C cycle, do not want to engage in the never-ending struggle for wisdom. They seek out "proper" training from experts who really know the "truth." Sometimes these students become obsessed with a technique. In sharp contrast to these impatient students, one finds those who become lost within the circumspective phase, unable to make and test out even momentary commitments.

The second conception involves three statements (Landfield, 1977): (a) The person searches for unity in a changing and contrasting world of experience. (b) The mature person must develop a conception of "self in the world" which gives him definition, clarity, and stability. (c) The person, particularly the psychotherapist, must develop a self-conception which gives him a sense of personal meaning which does not close him to experience. His unities will not close him to change in himself and others. His unities will not close him to an appreciation of variation within and across persons.

It should be remembered that the construct therapist does not have fixed conceptions about the meaning of a bit of behavior. Moreover, there are no rules within Personal Construct Theory about how all people symbolize their lives or their complaints. Also, behavior is seen as an experiment and a tool for exploring the unknown. Psychotherapy is a context for exploring the unknown—a statement that should become true for both members of the therapy pair (Kelly, 1970, 1977).

Finally, any description of the construct therapist should touch on the concept of defense. Although the construct therapist may well perceive his client as defensive, he will be most careful not to overuse such terminology. First of all, defensiveness can be in the eye of the beholder. The term can too readily substitute for the therapist's struggle to comprehend his client's system of personal meanings. Thus, to some degree, the defensiveness of a client could also be construed as the insensitivity of the therapist to what his client is communicating.

Rather than viewing the client as constantly warding off attacks of an internal or external nature, it might be more useful to perceive both therapist and client as searching for structures of stable meaning. The diagnostic and often critical term, defensive, is replaced by a more constructive process of understanding. In this context, both client and therapist, in their struggles to comprehend, will hang onto islands of stable meaning rather than risk an exploration of the unknown. The therapist will clutch his formal theory and favorite insights. His client will cling to the patterned truths of his personal experience. At the same time, the therapy *pair* will slowly experiment with the unknown. The results of this experimentation and pursuit of new perspectives will be known in duality: the continuing growth and maturing of a therapist and the "cure" of his client's complaint.

REFERENCES

Beisser, A. R. The paradox of public belief and psychotherapy. *Psychotherapy: Theory, Research, and Practice,* 1965, **2,** 92–96.

Doster, J. A., & Strickland, B. R. Disclosing of verbal material as a function of information requested, information about the interview, and interviewee differences. *Journal of Consulting and Clinical Psychology,* 1971, **37,** 187–194.

Doster, J. A. Effects of instructions, modeling, and role rehearsal on interview verbal behavior. *Journal of Consulting and Clinical Psychology,* 1972, **39,** 202–209.

Farina, A., Holland, C. H., & King, K. Role of stigma and set in interpersonal interaction. *Journal of Abnormal Psychology*, 1966, **71**, 421–428.

Farina, A., Allen, J. G., & Saul, B. B. The roie of the stigmatized person in affecting several relationships. *Journal of Personality*, 1968, **36**, 169–182.

Fiedler, F. Quantitative studies of the role of therapist feelings toward their patients. In O. H. Mowrer (Ed.), *Psychotherapy: Theory and Research*. New York: Ronald, 1953, pp. 296–315.

Fransella, F., & Bannister, D. *A Manual for Repertory Grid Technique*. London: Academic, 1977.

Isaacson, G. I., & Landfield, A. W. The meaningfulness of personal and common constructs. *Journal of Individual Psychology*, 1965, **21**, 160–166.

Kelly, G. A. *The Psychology of Personal Constructs:* Vols. 1 and 2. New York: Norton, 1955.

Kelly, G. A. Behavior as an experiment. In D. Bannister (Ed.), *Perspectives in Personal Construct Theory*. London: Academic, 1970, pp. 255–269.

Kelly, G. A. The psychology of the unknown. In D. Bannister (Ed.), *New Perspectives in Personal Construct Theory*. London: Academic, 1977, pp. 1–19.

Landfield, A. W. *Personal Construct Systems in Psychotherapy*. Chicago: Rand McNally, 1971.

Landfield, A. W. The complaint: A confrontation of personal urgency and professional construction. In D. Bannister (Ed.), *Issues and Approaches in Psychological Therapies*. London: Wiley, 1975, pp. 3–25.

Landfield, A. W. Interpretive man: The enlarged self-image. In A. Landfield (Vol. Ed.), *The Nebraska Symposium on Motivation, 1976, Personal Construct Psychology*. Lincoln/London: University of Nebraska Press, 1977, pp. 127–177.

Landfield, A. W. Exploring socialization through the interpersonal transaction group. In P. Stringer and D. Bannister (Eds.), *Constructs of Sociality and Individuality*, London: Academic, 1979, pp. 133–151.

Landfield, A. W., & Allee, R. A. Twelve case reports examined in terms of Shaw's reconciliation theory. *Psychotherapy: Theory, Research and Practice*, 1966, **3**, 125–134.

Landfield, A. W., & Barr, M. A. Ordination: A New Measure of Concept Organization. Unpublished manuscript, University of Nebraska, 1976.

Landfield, A. W., & Nawas, M. M. Psychotherapeutic improvement as a function of communication and adoption of therapist's values. *Journal of Counseling Psychology*, 1964, **11**, 336–341.

Landfield, A. W., & Rivers, P. C. Interpersonal attraction and rotating dyads. *Psychotherapy: Theory, Research and Practice*, 1975, **12**, 366–374.

Levitt, E. E. Psychotherapy research and the expectation-reality discrepancy. *Psychotherapy: Theory, Research, and Practice*, 1966, **3**, 163.

Poser, E. The effect of therapeutic training on group therapeutic outcome. *Journal of Consulting Psychology*, 1966, **30**, 283–289.

Rosenhan, D. L. On being sane in insane places. *Science*, 1973, **179**, 250–258.

Rosenthal, D. Changes in some moral values following psychotherapy. *Journal of Consulting Psychology,* 1955, **19,** 431–436.

Stone, A. R., Frank, J. D., Hoehn-Saric, R., Imber, S. D., & Nash, E. H. Some situational factors associated with response to psychotherapy. *American Journal of Orthopsychiatry,* 1964, **34,** 682–687.

Varble, D., & Landfield, A. W. Validity of the self-ideal discrepancy as a criterion measure of successful psychotherapy—a replication. *Journal of Counseling Psychology,* 1969, **16,** 150–156.

Von Bertalanffy, L. Robots, men and minds. New York: George Braziller, 1967.

CHAPTER 8

Culture-Shocked Marriages

Mildred McCoy

Three themes are intertwined in this discussion: *Culture Shock,* which signifies a sequence of adjustment challenges in working and living in a foreign setting; *Intercultural Marriages,*[1] long recognized as riskier, if possible, than the more typical unions of people from the same cultural background; and *Personal Construct Psychology* (Kelly, 1955), an approach that illuminates the culture-shock experience and, through an allied technique, the Repertory Grid (Rep Grid), provides empirical evidence of the unique problems of certain intercultural marriages. The purpose is an exploration of some particularly beleagured couples' plights as they are caught in "culture-shocked marriages." While each theme must be discussed separately for conceptual clarity, rather than irreparably shred their interaction, a selection and shaping for relevance (as opposed to comprehensiveness) will reflect this entwining.

Culture-shocked marriages form a particular group within the larger class of intercultural marriages. They originate as couples who meet and marry while the man is a temporary resident in the woman's homeland. Their relationship and life-style developed in the setting which first fostered it. This, incidentally, is the typical pattern for international marriages which are generally between minority-group males and majority-group females. While initial adjustments in intercultural marriages may be somewhat greater than the average, usually the need for accommodation has been anticipated and few drastic demands arise unexpectedly. If this couple leaves their original setting to relocate in the homeland of the male, not only does their union become a relative rarity as an intercultural marriage of a minority-group female and majority-group male, but unexpected demands arise in the cultural adaptations required of each party. This is when an intercultural marriage may become a culture-shocked one. The change of residency in this particular manner signals a potential crisis. Its depth and intensity are certain to be a surprise to the couple; its results are often life-shattering.

The following account has been developed from experiences in counseling such

---

[1] "Intercultural" is used here, rather than the more common "interracial," because many interracial marriages require no crossing of cultural boundaries, while members of the same racial group may belong to quite different cultures. The cultural differences between a third-generation American Asian and a third-generation American European are less than those between the American Asian and an Asian born and traditionally raised in Tokyo or Beijing. It is the difference in outlook, expectations and approach to problems, which is highlighted in the term "intercultural" marriage.

couples who sought help with their distress. As patterns became apparent in working with intercultural marriages, and similarity with some of the processes of culture adaptation for other expatriates were noted, the culture-shocked marriage hypothesis emerged. Its usefulness has been established in counseling, and an attempt has been made to find examples of similar intercultural marriages which have not developed pathological disorders in order to understand the limitations of the model—the exceptions that prove the rule. These exceptions are as illuminating for understanding the culture-shock phenomenon as they are potentially helpful in guiding couples in intercultural marriages who contemplate relocation. A major limitation of the approach is that it has been derived from experience in Hong Kong only. Its generalizability has not yet been tested, although the culture-shock phenomenon from which it is derived has been demonstrated to occur widely and the process appears to be related to a much larger class of similar adjustment experiences. Because of its origin, this account will use illustrations from marriages involving a Chinese male and a non-Chinese female who met when the man lived abroad, usually during a period of professional education.

Several problems in teminology arise. First, *Chinese* is a nonspecific cultural designation for Hong Kong people and barely useful ethnically. It will be used here broadly and interpreted with varying degrees of specificity and sophistication by readers with varying degrees of knowledge of contemporary Hong Kong and the differences in Chinese identification. Second, the contrast term will be *Western,* to designate the non-Chinese. Other Asian but non-Chinese instances are not included in either term. These terms, Chinese and Western, stress that the significant differences are not racial but stem from cultural traditions. *European* is a term often used for this purpose in Hong Kong, but that designation would be misunderstood in both Europe and North America.

When a couple, a Western wife and a Chinese husband, move to Hong Kong after having begun married life elsewhere, each must make a different adjustment and will have different experiences. These different individual experiences will interact and impinge on the marriage relationship as well. The husband, who probably was raised in a Hong Kong Chinese family, presents a special case of reentry adjustment after his stay abroad and separation from cultural roots and family system. The reentry process, identified by Gullahorn and Gullahorn (1963) for example, is attracting an increasing amount of academic interest but has not yet been integrated into a sufficiently helpful theoretical approach, so the description here is necessarily atheoretical and rather specific. The wife's experience can be characterized straightforwardly as the culture-shock phenomenon but this is not a single-path process through a transition. The marriage relationship, with established patterns of communication and problem solving, will be jarred if either or both parties' experience brings about changes in those areas. With so much agitation in the individual components, the stress within the closed system is likely to be critically disruptive.

The Husband's Reentry

Hong Kong is a predominantly Chinese community, perhaps somewhat advanced in adopting Western technology and associated values, but doing so in a Chinese manner. Holland (1977) reminds us that there is evaluation and attenuation in the process of borrowing from another culture. Transplanted ideas and values are never quite the same in another medium; so the appearance of Westernization, skyscrapers, jeans, golden arch hamburgers, and so on, is deceptive. The fact that more than 98% of the population is ethnically Chinese and most families have come from the mainland since 1950 is more useful in designating the nature of Hong Kong culture. Despite being an international business center and becoming progressively more Western, Hong Kong has a solidly Chinese core in its culture.

The returning Chinese husband regards Hong Kong as home and believes his reentry should feel good and natural, offering an external support and security which he has long missed. He consciously identifies himself with his native culture and easily lapses into the use of his first language, the predominant Cantonese dialect. Amid an initial euphoria and the joy of reunion, a few jarring confrontations remind him of how much he has changed during the past years away, operating not only separately, but independently.

The pervasiveness of the family's control of details of life, the multitude of extended family obligations and the reestablishment of his responsibilities to his parents as a "filial" son are irritating, but accepted as inevitable. However, they regularly remind him of how much he has changed and the changes are seen as non-Chinese foreign ways, habits, and viewpoints. A version of an identity crisis ensues, which this husband probably resolves by repudiating his recently Westernized self and trying to be properly Chinese again. It appears impossible to him to accommodate the life-long duties enjoined by filial piety with functional independence, which is a component of Western conceptions of adulthood. Needless to say, his Chinese behavior and rejection of Western values and practices are jagged and often exaggerated with the strained, false quality associated with reaction formation. Consistent with the traditional Chinese conception of self, which seems more socially derived and integrated than the individualistic and Western views (Hsu, 1971); this process probably proceeds at a relatively low level of awareness, thus minimizing conscious recognition of attendant emotions such as guilt and hostility.

The Wife's Culture Shock

In the meantime, the Western wife must make all the adjustments to Hong Kong of any recently arrived expatriate. These include dealing with severed family relations, the loss of identity which had been provided by employment or participation in her former community, the lack of support of a friendship network, communication difficulties, a failing sense of independence and mastery, and above all, lack of knowledge of how her role as a wife and daughter-in-law and sister-in-law should be managed. The culture-shock model (Adler, 1975) proposes a view of the transitional experience precipitated by exposure to a second culture. While it does not take into account the interactions of the couple and an external cultural environment in an intercultural marriage, it clarifies a significant portion of the experience of the Western woman in the situation we are considering. The model forsees movement or growth from a state of low self- and cultural awareness to a state of high self- and cultural awareness, a journey into self which permits a person to transcend the boundaries of ego, culture, and chauvinistic thinking. If the model is valid and the experience evolves completely, then having endured the painful transition through to greater personal development, one is well prepared for any new cultural experience, including the lately discovered reentry difficulties. The model also holds out great promise for successful intercultural marriages and offers a clue to the fantastic richness which those who find them happy have claimed they provide.

The version of the model presented here follows Adler (1975) closely in his description of the behavior and emotions associated with each of five stages. Personal Construct Theory (PCT) is called upon to provide the theoretical foundation which accounts for the sequence and relates the emotional and behavioral manifestations to the internal, cognitive structure changes which comprise the personal transition. The essential features of PCT that are employed are:

1. Its view is of construing as the fundamental human process, thus the construct system is the functional equivalent of personality (Kelly, 1969, p. 56).
2. Kelly's idea is that construct system change is the basis of personal growth (1955, p. 73).
3. The various effects of awareness of the construct system's adequacy or inadequacy, and the need to change it underlie the experiences commonly called emotions (McCoy, 1977).
4. Constructs are organized in hierarchical systems but incompatibility between parts of the organization can be tolerated (Kelly, 1955, p. 88).

Stage models, whether of culture shock or any other development, create a false impression of a rigid succession of clearly distinguished events. This overly sharp separation does not reflect human experience, which is more typically marked by uneven progress on different fronts as well as some vacillation between progress and regression. Thus it should be kept in mind that the stages which are described represent broad or general descriptions of a process sequence. Likewise, there are individual and circumstantial differences which govern the duration of time when a stage is predominating.

THE CULTURE-SHOCK MODEL

1. Contact

This stage encompasses the experiences of the tourist, a short-term visitor, as well as those of a resident at the beginning of a longer or permanent stay in a foreign country. It is a period in which one is functionally integrated only into one's own culture; the second culture tends to be viewed superficially and mainly in terms of its similarity to previous experiences and life-style. Most newly arrived visitors are more attuned to similarities than differences between their own and the new culture, but even those who embark on a determined search for the exotic reflect this rootedness in the already known. By definition, the exotic is what is strange or bizarre only in terms of the familiar; not where it belongs.

The contact stage is a period of excitement and enthusiasm. The buoyancy of this stage comes from self-confidence, which itself indicates a reaffirmation of identity in successful construing of the familiar (McCoy, 1977). Required adjustments are perceived as minimal and manageable. This may not be based on a realistic estimate of what is actually involved in adaptation and living within the new culture, but as yet, no sense of a pervasive difference in values and organization of life-style has been compiled. In PCT terms, the new visitor's construct network that was developed within the former culture serves as a template through which reality is perceived and evaluated. New constructs may soon be developed, but for the present only the old ones are available, so only those discriminations of which the system is already capable can be made. Since the system has not yet been shaped by experiences with the reality of the new setting, the second culture cannot be construed with definition and complexity. However, the visitor has not been transported to some science fiction environment completely alien to human life and existence as it is known. There remain the commonalities across cultures to provide many opportunities for successful construing within the existing system. When the validations deal with relatively peripheral aspects, for example, recognition of familiar brand names, it is likely that this becomes significant through links in the construct system's hierarchy with the core constructs by which identity is maintained. The more central constructs of status and role often are carefully validated by the travel industry with its capacity for varying degrees of obsequiousness. The happiness and satisfaction of travel are indications of this characteristic validation of the contact stage.

2. Disintegration

The second stage in Adler's model is a function of the invalidating experiences of the new culture. Differences are increasingly noted over a wide range of experiences, differences in the realms of public order and private transactions. While some culture-shock theorists focus on the loss of familiar cues by which we orient ourselves to the situations of daily life (Oberg, 1972), PCT would identify the cause of this stage as an awareness of the inadequacy of the construct system in the face of new and unconstrued cues, as well as awareness of the deficiencies of predictions from the old construct system. Not only do experiences fail to "make sense" but expectations do not materialize.

Many of the negative emotions which indicate awareness of an inadequacy of the construct system, or that change is required, can be identified in expatriates in Stage 2. These include the master negative emotion, anxiety, which indicates an awareness that the events which confront one lie outside the range of convenience of the construct system. Threat and fear are also typical. They signal imminent changes in core structures of the construct system, while doubt and bewilderment indicate awareness of imminent change in noncore structures. Attempts to make the construct system more useful can be expected to ensue. Loosening is one such response. It may be manifest as a loss of purposiveness, or experienced as generalized confusion and difficulty in carrying out tasks. Alternatively, or in alternation, tightening can also occur. It leads to withdrawal and/or compulsive behavior.

In this stage so aptly named, disintegration, one feels very much outside of all, yet surrounded and overwhelmed by an alien world. The familiar symptoms of this stage include mild to moderate depression, loneliness, and a sense of alienation. But the expression varies a great deal, as does the intensity. Awareness of the need to develop the construct system arises as the differences of the new culture are distinguished. This heralds the growth envisaged in the culture-shock model, although growth is not inevitable simply through immersion in a second culture. One can be preserved from much of the discomfort of this stage by mechanisms which assist in suppressing awareness of the need for new constructions to process differences, thus avoiding the occasions of growth.

3. Reintegration

In choosing this descriptive title, Adler identifies Stage 3 as the process of reconsolidation of the construct system after initial efforts to construe the new experiences have produced considerable awareness of its inadequacies. Given the fundamental human need to construe, and to order and make sense of reality, a prolonged state of Stage 2 disintegration would signal a considerable pathology. This is not common. Quite typical is a period when the new culture is construed, as well differentiated from one's own culture. There appear to be parallel construct subsystems for construing the two cultures. The constructs of each subsystem are relatively impermeable in this early stage of the system's development in order that they can be tested without invalidating each other. In this stage, awareness of one's own culture emerges out of the growing awareness of the contrasts which are now construed, a process described by Hall (1959) as one of the advantages of cross-cultural experiences.

Behavior associated with this stage makes it the most unpleasant step in the sequence. In Stage 3, thinking about cultures is stereotyped and judgmental and there tends to be a rejection of the second culture. This unattractive phase signals a new and essential sensitivity to cultural differences and their pervasiveness, hence there is a personal relevance in cultural contrasts which was not present earlier. Personal relevance coupled with the rejection of a potential self-construction is the recipe for threat (Landfield, 1954)—that is, awareness of imminent comprehensive change in one's core structures.

Threat and hostility are the major emotional states of Stage 3. The hostility often takes the form of critical griping and an ugly chauvinism (unfounded sense of superiority over the "natives"), with personal difficulties projected onto the second culture. This is a crisis point. The individual may proceed from this growing cultural awareness to resolution of the difficulties and frustrations being encountered, the growth envisaged as an acceptance of and capability within the new culture. Regression to the superficial behavior of earlier stages is the alternative, usually accomplished by efforts to minimize interaction with the new culture through retreat into enclaves of like-minded complainers. Returning home with bitter tales of the experience abroad may also be an alternative. The choice between growth or regression depends upon the urgency of the threat, which in turn is a function of the permeability of the core structures and perhaps the amount, centrality, and initial incompatibility of the portions of the construct system which must be integrated. Despite the high risks of this stage and its general unattractiveness, within Adler's view of culture shock as a producer of growth through increased self- and cultural awareness, Stage 3 is a necessary and predictable, albeit perilous, section of the developmental journey.

4. Autonomy

The fourth stage is based on an understanding of the new culture, of its integrity and adequacy, and an appreciation of its values. The person who reaches this level of development through the culture-shock journey has mastered the skills necessary to be recognized as sensitive to the local viewpoint and ways, and is comfortable in communication. There is a freedom from defensiveness as the differences perceived between the two cultures are no longer threatening. Interactions with the members of the second culture are relaxed and flexible, based on confidence in a personal ability to cope. The two separate construct subsystems which have been evolving have been integrated into the core structures and are no longer incompatible. Identity has been extended to include both sets of dimensions and self is not construed preemptively, or as functionally identical with either culture. Although depth of understanding of the new culture may not yet be as deep as the individual believes, the key to further development lies in a genuine acceptance of an alternative point of view—that is, understanding, valuing, and respecting the integrality of another culture. Specific objects of former criticism are seen as the other side of valued aspects, both construed along some new dimension probably not salient in the former culture. A person in this stage often feels like an expert on the second culture and, in a newfound enthusiasm, expounds on or interprets cultural manifestations for other expatriates when the opportunity arises. Adler notes, "The stage of autonomy is especially marked by the growth of personal flexibility and by development of appropriate coping skills for the second culture" (1975, p. 17). The growth attained in this stage is probably among the much touted "benefits of travel," whereas halting the developmental process at earlier stages would appear to add to the rigidity and stereotyped thinking about other cultures.

5. Independence

In the final stage of the culture-shock transition, the individual is able to view self and others as human beings shaped by culture and can value cultural differences. This is knowledge of an experiential sort which recognizes the pervasive influence of culture in shaping attitudes and behavior as well as the prospects of one culture being an alternative for another, the way one might change lenses on a camera. To a certain extent an acceptance of all cultures as "born equal" leads to cultural relativism; but if so, the stage is still free of the simplistic judgments which characterize those who have not reached this stage of development, as well as those who idealize equality from inside only one cultural experience.

Whereas in Stage 4 the construct system had integrated dimensions relevant to two cultures into the core structure, this stage signifies the development of a superordinate system of permeable constructs dealing with culture and human nature. This system expansion enables an individual to continue development of the construct system, incorporating new explorations of human diversity in freedom from the constrictions imposed as one defends oneself against the changes required by interaction with another culture.

The PCT interpretation of Adler's culture-shock model has focused on internal changes in the transition process to the neglect of variations in the external circumstances which are responsible for requiring the changes. This narrowing of perspective has been necessary to provide a general scheme, but does not imply that the reality of the external world and individual differences play little or no role. Both are under continuing investigation with regard to culture-shocked marriages and the culture-shock model itself. Some are illustrated in the account that follows.

CULTURE-SHOCKED MARRIAGES

With the culture-shock model in mind, let us look at the special problem of the marriages of Western women and Chinese men when couples move to Hong Kong from a Western cultural environment. We start with a little reflection on the difficulties of the male in this move.

The husband, whose early socialization has stressed a "filial" son identity, may be in a fair amount of conflict with his family for having taken a non-Chinese wife. It is a likely guess that this was against the expressed wishes of his family, but with eventual, if grudging, consent. He is very exposed, and he would like to have his decision validated. His confidence that he and his wife can fit into Hong Kong's polycultural, volatile milieu and make a good life while he, at the same time, fulfills his obligations of filial piety, is more a case of youthful optimism than a hardheaded appraisal of reality.

This young man left Hong Kong for reasons of higher education and has been away for many years. His associates of secondary school days have scattered, perhaps formed new associations, and he no longer has a nonfamily social network of any sort. This amplifies his dependence on his family, while its authoritarian style of control is exceptionally irritating after the freedom of years of living on his own and making decisions for himself. The more irritating this becomes, the more he must disguise it from himself, for it is additional evidence of what he already suspects, that he is not a good "filial" son. If you add to this inner conflict the likely problems of housing (of necessity the couple may end up sharing his parents' quarters or living with other relatives), the shock of inflation, and how skimpy his salary seems now compared with his memory of its value, he himself may be very disillusioned about his decision to return. But the more he thinks he made a poor choice, the less likely it becomes that he will admit it, since the alternative would be an even worse blow to his self-image, now being only precariously maintained. This is the typical model for precipitating compulsive behavior, and the husband is likely to become very compulsive about his decision to stay in Hong Kong. Let us leave his sad state for a while to look at his wife.

She, too, has some decisions to validate in having chosen to marry a "foreigner." She was making a statement about her own liberality and her trust in a concept that love conquers all difficulties. Consistent with the first stage of Adler's (1975) culture-shock model, when she arrives in Hong Kong, she is probably optimistic and confident of her own and the couple's ability to make a good life anywhere. Her initial impressions of Hong Kong are probably not negative, unless she was already apprehensive about the decision to move there. But far more than any typical expatriate, this young wife is plunged totally into the Hong Kong culture and is without alternative support systems. When the second stage, alienation, arrives on the heels of her inability to communicate with her husband's omnipresent relatives, the intensity of her sense of isolation in the midst of so much bustle and so many bodies is enhanced. She attributes her depression to loss of family and friends or to the loss of some other accustomed role, such as employment or being the mistress of her own dwelling. Depending on her coping style and resilience, she soon reaches the third stage of culture shock. She is hostile and strongly rejects Hong Kong and Chinese culture. While this stage is normal, even necessary for the development of a genuine second culture adjustment, unfortunately, her complaints about difficulties in Hong Kong can be taken as criticisms of her husband, his decision to return to Hong Kong, his culture, his family, and a failure to appreciate his obligations. Normal outlets for this hostility are less available to her. Rather than bouncing harmlessly off a sympathetic ear, virulent complaints are suppressed until they explode, or if voiced, are quite naturally, taken personally.

The husband looks to his own difficulties in her country and expects his wife to accept her suffering without complaint because he survived a similar painful adjustment relatively successfully. His own difficulties in coping with demands from the modern Hong Kong Chinese culture are more urgent than anticipated and he may have no reserve of compassion to provide the acceptance she needs in this stage of hostility and alienation.

Their marital relationship becomes a source of stress itself. Soon he recognizes a nagging wish that he had married his purely imaginary Chinese bride who would be compliant and would smooth out his problems instead of adding to them—a bride who would know the proper relationship with his family and particularly with his mother. The joys of life as a traditional husband beckon, and Chinese values are once more attractive to him. His former view of marriage may change from a fairly Western self-fulfillment model to the more traditional social/economic role viewpoint. This may not even be typical of his social class. There appear to be very rapid changes under way which have yet to be documented. Patterns of communication, which might have developed to meet the tensions of a Western marriage, are not allowed in the face of traditional suppression of conflict and the lack of privacy for fighting constructively. Only angry feelings seem to pop out from time to time, triggered by her nagging to talk about the things that are going wrong in their marriage. He sputters that she should get along better with his mother and, with some appreciation of the vast changes in status that she has undergone, may suggest that they have a baby or that she find a job. She feels he is siding with others, particularly his mother, against her and that he is rejecting her, pushing away a nuisance. Her first attempts to learn Cantonese do not really help enough. She feels her husband is no longer the sympathetic, "modern" man she married, and she sees the only hope for their union's survival in a rapid flight from Hong Kong back to her homeland, where their relationship once flourished.

The scenario from this point on is no longer so uniform. Many culture-shocked marriages flounder, although there are variations. Usually things are held together until the birth of the first child. At this point the wife is less mobile and the husband's family has a greater stake in the marriage surviving, particularly if the baby is a boy. If certain external things have improved, and it is impressive to see how great can be the real accommodation of the Chinese family, it may be possible to reduce the overall stress level. Housing, language, income, and outside-the-family social network problems yield to persistent attack. Time seems to reduce acute discomfort to a tolerable, chronic level.

The pressures that hold the marriage together also determine which value scheme will dominate in it. If these pressures come primarily from the husband's family, he may negotiate for more autonomy and a less restrictive definition of his duties toward it. This enables him to act more like his wife's ideal husband in a Western marriage and give priority to their relationship and consideration of her views. If it is lack of options for the wife (because of financial dependence or lack of support from her family) that exerts the binding pressure, she may shift her view of marriage closer to the traditional social/economic scheme and opt for personal fulfillment either through her mother role or outside the home in social life. (Her prospects for involvement in a career are complicated and this solution is relatively uncommon.) Despite the survival of the marriage arrangement in response to such pressures, a resolution in which everyone lives happily ever after happens only in fairy tales and not in these culture-shocked marriages. They remain vulnerable to upsets in their precarious psychological balance.

Maria and H.[2]

The account of culture-shocked marriages has been a composite one, garnered from case records and 10 years of counseling experience in Hong Kong. A particular case, that of Maria and her husband H., has been chosen to provide a specific example. She completed Repertory Grids on two occasions, the first during a course of marriage counseling and the second two years later.

Maria was the child of an immigrant family who had moved to Canada when she was young, but there were still psychological ties to the family's eastern European origins. It had been a struggle to be economically successful in the new country, but the frugality of the mother and her strong business sense had effectively provided economic security, a major goal.

[2]All names have been changed and revealing personal details altered. The subjects have agreed to participate in psychological research and to the publication of disguised case records and other data for legitimate purposes.

The mother offered a model of success and upward social mobility in her self-discipline, frugality, and nagging or pushing of her husband which had been necessary to reach it. However, Maria saw her as too bound by religion and thought that her disposition wasn't particularly good.

Maria and H. married while he was still completing his medical training. She worked as a librarian, but without permanent professional qualifications. They had lived together for about a year prior to the wedding and believed they had carefully considered the difficulties of an intercultural marriage. They returned to Hong Kong under a contract with the Government Health Service after completion of his minimum training, although he still needed to pass more examinations to become a specialist as he desired. He found a general practice onerous; however, he couldn't quite get down to studying for the specialist examinations. The early days of his working career brought a series of disappointments ranging from a misunderstanding that they would be supplied with housing to trouble living on his salary in the grand manner he thought he deserved. There were family problems as well. They originally moved into his father's home, but the father was just taking a third wife, a woman of very low class and reportedly foul manners, whom the entire family rejected. H. was the eldest son of the family born of the "legitimate" wife and he was particularly upset with his father's behavior, coming at a time when the father was receiving public recognition. This woman accompanied the father to official functions and since she was unskilled in social graces she was an embarrassment. She remains a source of contention today, although the father shows no signs that he appreciates the entire family's dismay and rejection of his "wife." Family gatherings, even to celebrate his momentous birthdays, are either impossible or terribly strained by her presence and the inability of any of his children to be even civil to her.

Apart from the financial disappointments in H.'s occupational setting, the need to sit for examinations was looming and he was procrastinating. Maria was unhappy and came to believe all their troubles, including financial ones, would be solved if her husband would just move back to Canada. In order to ensure his professional flexibility (so he could return to Canada in style) he had to pass not only a first set of examinations to permit him to practice, but two further ones in the specialty that he had chosen. But he couldn't get down to studying. It took the combined nagging of his wife and pressure from his father, whom he still respected despite the third-wife problem, to get him off to a special cram course and eventually through the first examinations.

Maria and H. moved out of the father's home and into their own apartment supplied by the government as soon as he qualified. An elder sister, her husband, and children moved in with them to what was seen by the relatives as overly spacious accommodations. H. seemed to agree that this was in the family's financial interest and did not consider resisting the intrusion. Maria and H. soon were laden with all the household tasks, a great deal of interference with and criticism of their life-style, and partisan ganging up for one or the other when they had a quarrel. Maria suffered the added burden of feeling displaced in what she thought was her own home. She sat through endless dinners and gatherings with other family members not understanding Cantonese (although she was taking language lessons) when everyone present was capable of speaking English. By now Maria was pregnant.

Her pregnancy was difficult, and an unsatisfactory job which she had secured as a diversion, as well as for the income, did not contribute toward a greater appreciation of Hong Kong. Following the pattern she had learned from her mother and which H. had appreciated in the past, she began to complain vocally and vigorously, and to nag. Her aim was to return to Canada. Although H. was dissastisfied in Hong Kong, a return to Canada was too threatening to entertain even momentarily.

Following the birth of their daughter, H.'s rejection of Maria seemed almost total. This included his loss of interest in sexual relations. She was in the third stage of the culture shock in which hostility was very high; everything Chinese and Hong Kong was rejected. H. was identified as having changed from the man she married into the epitome of the culture she now detested at first hand.

She managed to escape from Hong Kong with borrowed money and returned to her parents' home. They rejected her, and on the basis of their religious convictions insisted that she go back to her husband. The shock of her departure from Hong Kong communicated her desperation to H.'s family. They mobilized, putting pressure on him to do whatever was necessary to save his marriage, although he had already given up in despair. There followed long-distance negotiations about conditions for her return to Hong Kong which enabled her to come back with some hope. These included that H. at least admit that the marriage was in trouble, which he had denied until then. Upon return to Hong Kong, the hope was short-lived. A pattern was reestablished. She nagged, either to return to Canada or for him to get down to the necessary study for the examinations which she saw as a prerequisite to that, and a way to use the sojourn in Hong Kong to advantage. He escaped from her nagging. This took the form of passive withdrawal or extravagant spending on entertaining his acquaintances, thus reducing her careful budget to shambles and eliminating the funds she was accumulating for their eventual move back to Canada.

It was at this time that Maria completed two Repertory Grids which were analyzed both impressionistically and with a principal components analysis (Slater, 1972). One grid was based on personally elicited constructs and the other on a set of supplied constructs (Irwin et al., 1967). Both used the same set of elements, 15 significant people nominated from a personalized role title list.

The outstanding feature of the elicited construct grid was the content of the first component and the overwhelming domination of her construct system which it exercised. This component distinguished people who had a *modern Canadian viewpoint* from those representing *traditional Chinese culture* and it accounted for 70% of the grid variance. This is extremely high for any normal, intelligent adult but was not evidence of cognitive simplicity, a habitual cognitive style. (Maria was capable of construing people with normal complexity because the first component of her *supplied* construct grid, completed on the same occasion, accounted for a more typical 49% of the grid variance.) Rather, the overwhelming domination of the first component was a sign of the tightening of her system in response to the threat of Stage 3 culture shock. This could be observed only through analysis of her own *personal* constructs which were more relevant and in daily use to make sense of her world.

The salience of the culture variable and marriage values in her personal system is obvious from the content of the component as derived from the constructs loading most heavily on it. Of 12 elicited personal constructs, 10 loaded heavily on the first component and only one had a negligible loading. Table 1 lists her constructs in order of the size of their loading on the first component. It also identifies them by number. Constructs 4 and 6 did not load highly on the first component. Particularly orthogonal was no. 4, *content vs. satisfied*. This construct was least bound up with culture and thus it offered promise as a dimension area which could be developed, through counseling, to eventually supplant the more judgmental dimensions of her stereotype.

There were two clusters of functionally identical constructs. Very heavily loaded on the first component was a group including constructs 2, 3, 5, 9, 11, and 12. In this cluster Maria equates *being westernized* with *seeing marriage as sharing* rather than *seeing marriage as a role*. The latter is *old-fashioned*. This confluence and contrast seemed to emerge from her own immigrant experience and her analysis of her immigrant parents' views and struggles in their new Canadian homeland, but it now is particularly salient in the context of Chinese culture. Her use of stereotyped thinking typical of Stage 3 was also shown by the similarity in use patterns of constructs 8 and 10. *Hong Kong people* are viewed as having *superficial relationships* as opposed to the *sincere relationships* of *others*. For Maria, sorting elements as Hong Kong people comes to the same thing as sorting them on the superficiality of their relationships.

An even more dramatic illustration of the compartmentalization of Chinese people in contrast to others is shown by globe graphs of the elements in the principle components' space. A major feature of this graphing is the segregation of the

Table 1. Maria's Elicited Constructs (First Occasion) in order of Their Loading Size on the First Principal Component[a]

Construct Number	Constructs		
9	Sees marriage as role	vs.	Sees marriage as sharing
11	Self centered	vs.	Giving
12	Culture bound	vs.	Open to other cultures
3	Victim	vs.	Personally responsible
2	Old-fashioned	vs.	Modern Canadian
1	Authorities (older generation)	vs.	Equals (my generation)
8	Hong Kong people	vs.	Others
5	Chauvinistic	vs.	Free
10	Having superficial relationships	vs.	Having sincere relationships
7	Unfeeling	vs.	Warm of heart
6	Have sexual problems[b]	vs.	No sexual problems
4	Content with own life[b]	vs.	Dissatisfied

[a] The poles have been reversed when loadings were negative, for easier alignment of functional similarity.

[b] Constructs 6 and 4 load less significantly on the first principal component than do all the others. The loading of #4 approaches zero.

elements into hemispheres which represent the poles of the first component. In Maria's graphs (Fig. 1), one globe represents the ''modern Canadian'' culture pole (the positive pole) and the other globe the ''traditional Chinese'' culture pole (the negative pole). Of particular interest is Maria's construction of H. As the element X6, Husband-before-moving-to-Hong Kong, he appears in the modern Canadian hemisphere; as element X5, Husband-now, he is sorted with the traditional culture elements. (This is an illustration of slot change in PCT terminology.) The positive hemisphere contains five of the seven non-Chinese elements and other than Husband-before-moving-to Hong Kong, Father-in-law is the only Chinese person sorted on this pole. In the negative hemisphere, six of eight elements are Chinese and only Maria's own Father and an Ex-boyfriend appear there from the non-Chinese group. The slight discrepancy from a completely clear-cut discrimination on the basis of race supports the interpretation of the first component as a psychological, rather than concrete, dimension. Nevertheless, it is functioning in such a way as to demonstrate a positive versus negative cultural stereotype.

The globe graphs also vividly demonstrate Maria's loneliness. She had been asked as a separate task to rank order the elements from liked to disliked. That rank ordering and the rank order derived from the element loadings on the first component correlated 0.89 (p < 0.01) indicating that the first component was functioning as an evaluative dimension. It follows that the hemisphere graphs separate the elements into potentially likable and dislikable groups, whether or not they were being so construed. H.'s family apart, such elements as X9, Important co-worker, and X13, Local friend, also are in the disliked hemisphere. Everyone physically near Maria, except Father-in-law, was seen with the potentially dislikable group. When queried about the incongruity of her local friend being potentially dislikable, Maria said, ''Oh, I use her and she uses me''—a pitiful commentary on the poverty of her social life and support system.

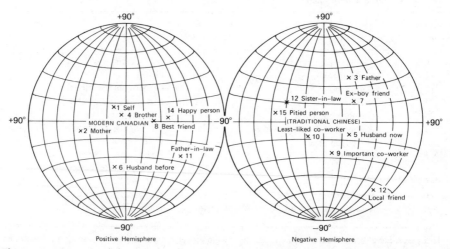

Figure 1.   Maria's globe graphs showing elements in the space of first three principal components.

Two years later Maria completed another set of Repertory Grids. By this time, culture shock had abated. Although she was not happy, her circumstances being far from her own ideals for the marriage and living conditions, she was no longer in need of professional support. She had initiated a limited revival of the counseling relationship to explore the impact of an extramarital romantic encounter. Consequently, the role title list on the second occasion was slightly different from the prior version and 15 rather than 12 constructs were elicited. A major change had occurred in the character of the constructs she supplied. Missing were any which specifically derived from construing cultural variables. Likewise, constructs referring to marriage values were gone. The tightening that had been apparent on the previous occasion in the domination of the first component had also vanished. In the second principal components analysis, the first component accounted for only 46% of the grid variance, in contrast with 70% earlier. A sizable second and third component emerged as well. Table 2 lists the highest loading constructs on each of the first three components which were the basis for deriving their names as used in the interpretation.

The first component, while appearing to be culture-free and overtly sorting people on a dimension of *warm and friendly vs. cold and unexpressive,* still effectively sorts the Chinese people from the non-Chinese. All eight elements but X6, Husband-before-moving-to-Hong Kong, loading at the *warm and friendly* pole are non-Chinese. The remaining six Chinese elements are located among the seven

Table 2. Maria (Second Occasion)—The Highest Loading Constructs on the First Three Principal Components[a]

Component I:	Warm and friendly	vs.	Cold and unexpressive
8	Demonstrative	vs.	Not demonstrative
11	Values close relations	vs.	Superficial
4	Deep feelings	vs.	Mechanical responses
10	Vivacious (open)	vs.	Bland (inscrutable)
2	Expressive	vs.	Inhibits positive feeling
Component II:	**Generous and tractable**	vs.	**Domineering and self-promoting**
5	Spends money freely	vs.	Money grasping
12	Considers others	vs.	Takes care of self first
13	Conservative	vs.	Goes to excesses
14	Does the work	vs.	Seeks glory
6	Subject to influence	vs.	Courage of convictions
Component III:	**Felicitous**	vs.	**Manipulative**
1	Accepting	vs.	Wants to change people
15	Concern for self-growth	vs.	Concern for appearances
9	Considerate	vs.	Spoiled
13	Goes to excesses	vs.	Conservative

[a] The poles have been matched according to the positive or negative value of the loadings on the components for easier alignment of functional similarity.

loading at the *cold and unexpressive* pole. While Maria may have recovered from culture shock to the extent that she no longer construed cultures preemptively, she still construed people in a stereotyped manner related to either a racial or cultural discrimination. The dimension she uses is a classical Western discrimination (i.e., "the inscrutable Oriental"), although one which does not usually endure with a better knowledge of nonverbal cues and deeper interactions. Nevertheless, this construction represents some development from the excessively tight and relatively concrete construing of the earlier period. Also, the addition of more significant discriminations represents progress.

The second component accounted for 17% of the grid variance and was the basis for distinguishing people who are seen as *generous and tractable* from those who are *domineering and self-promoting*. Examination of the loading of the elements turned up no discernable stereotyping such as sex role or culture patterns. The third component, accounting for 14% of the grid variance, distinguished *manipulative* from *felicitious* people. Here, the appearance of many of her relatives (mother and father, her older brother and husband both before- and after-the-move-to-Hong Kong) nearer the manipulative pole while her friends are seen as felicitous, indicates the emergence of a new dimension of awareness. The lack of satisfaction in being dependent on family and husband is probably the seedbed of this construing. It accompanies a greater self-reliance and movement toward personal (rather than marital) satisfactions, which she judged her friends to facilitate. Maria does not appear to have reached Stage 4 or 5 of the culture-shock model. There was no evidence of the development of autonomy in operating within the Chinese culture and no independence with regard to cultures even after four years in Hong Kong. While she has moved through the crisis of Stage 3, it was so devastating that she attempted to escape entirely by returning home. When that didn't work out for her and she was forced to return to Hong Kong, the accommodation she made was necessarily one of small steps out of a well defended, antitraditional (Chinese) promodern (Canadian) viewpoint.

At the time the second Rep Grid was completed, the marriage relationship was stable. Maria had agreed to cease pressing for an immediate relocation and H., in turn, was consulting her more about his career decisions which affected her, and where her considerable business acumen was advantageous. Their life-style provided occasional satisfactions for each, but major areas of disagreement remained where the values and viewpoints of their respective cultures differ most widely. Specifically, these areas were the relative predominance of extended family versus wife, overt versus covert approaches to relationship problem solving, and conventions of influence and domination within the marital relationship. For example, Maria refuses to learn to play Mah-Jongg, a popular and traditional gambling game which is the focal point of nearly every Hong Kong social occasion, from birthday parties and weddings to simple gatherings after the evening meal. This would enable her to participate in H.'s family's social life. For her, Mah-Jongg is symbolic of many Chinese attributes that she still finds threatening, and her refusal is thus symbolic of her rigidity and lack of acceptance of Hong Kong culture. She is still disappointed that their marriage is not characterized by sharing as a way to reach the goals she envisaged; H.'s goals seem peripheral to the marriage and he looks elsewhere for the help he needs to attain them. Maria has retreated into a circle of friends who also have marital problems, many with intercultural marriages. This circle offers mutual support to its members in shared understanding and exchange of helpful tips. Social life as a couple seems to involve other culture-shocked couples and follows a Western pattern. H. maintains a more traditional pattern with his work associates and family.

In many ways, Maria and H. illustrate the culture-shocked marriage hypothesis. In this, they are typical of certain other Hong Kong couples—a local male who married a non-Chinese female while studying in her homeland, and who then relocated in Hong Kong. Mercifully, the number who return is a small proportion of such marriages, for the tradition has been for Hong Kong people to relocate elsewhere whenever possible, often at great sacrifice. Hong Kong has been viewed by its Chinese residents as a temporary refuge, but this is changing. An identification with Hong Kong is emerging and more of the educated young people are staying or returning after education abroad. The number of culture-shocked marriages is bound to increase.

Families established in Hong Kong with family businesses offering attractive job prospects for their foreign-educated sons have long advised them that their marriages to foreign women are doomed if they move back to Hong Kong. The explanation offered lies in a conviction that the wife will be unable to adjust to life in the Orient. In view of the illustration, the case of Maria and H., the advice appears to be sound, although it fails to recognize the naturalness and inevitability of the culture-shock experience for anyone, not just wives. That wives should be seen as particularly vulnerable tallies with the hypothesis that it is the hostility of Stage 3 directed at the husband, which is both too devastatingly intimate a threat for the growth to autonomy of the next stage to emerge and too shattering for their relationship, which must support some extra dependency demands in its new setting. Recognition of the culture-shock process can help to defuse its potential for damage. It provides distancing, which allows for humor in blackest moments; reassurance, which reduces guilt; and the hope that a grim stage will be only temporary and is the price to be paid for better things to come. Support, whether from friends or professional counseling, is particularly useful. The hypothesis that some intercultural marriages will experience the progression described has been of assistance to marriage counselors in Hong Kong, while friends—who have themselves survived—knew intuitively about the process. Extrapolation to other settings seems feasible but has not yet been attempted.

EXCEPTIONS AND LIMITS

Following the development and early use of the culture-shocked marriage hypothesis with counseling clients, the first test of its limits has been to seek out similar intercultural marriages in Hong Kong which seem to be reasonably happy and successful and therefore not congruent with its predictions. Why do some unions escape the predicted ravages? Whereas the disturbed marriages appeared among counseling clients, it was necessary to seek out the successful ones. Securing cooperation was exceptionally touchy, because the wives had accepted the Chinese value of privacy for family matters and they were reluctant to take unnecessary risks. The women stressed a need for confidentiality and discussed participation in the research with their husbands, securing consent before agreeing to participate. Each indicated at the end of the first interview session that this was the first time she had ever discussed many of her experiences or revealed things which she believed might be seen as criticism of her husband's family. This containment, in itself, is evidence of accommodation to Chinese cultural values and also of the wife's ability to live within the prescribed limits of the Chinese family. Despite the difficult circumstances, it was possible to establish rapport. Perhaps because it was so uncomfortable to verbalize things long held privately, the subjects made an extra effort to be candid. At any rate, each completed a Rep Grid, either at the conclusion of the first interview or at a second session. The grid was analyzed and then discussed in a subsequent meeting. Subjects reported satisfaction. Their appreciation for what they viewed as an opportunity for some personal exploration was expressed in many ways, small gifts, thank-you notes and so on. Kelly's views on a professional relationship emphasize the mutuality of the enterprise. Communication of this approach rather than one where subjects are exploited for the benefit of the research, was undoubtedly helpful.

Although the sample of exceptions is still very small, each case appears to offer a different example of why culture shock did not prove overly damaging. Some cases also supply evidence on factors effecting an attenuation of culture shock itself. The general rule appears to be that anything which modifies the expected pattern reduces the intensity of the experience to a more manageable level.

Gudrun and W.

One example of this is the case of Gudrun, a German woman who married a Hong Kong Chinese man, W. There are several variations in the pattern of their relationship and marriage which have lessened the potentially disastrous effects of culture shock. They met in a third country, England, in which both were foreigners, rather than on her home territory. Although they lived together there, they did not marry, retaining a sense of freedom from any excessive demands of their relationship during a period of the extra adjustment requirements. W. returned to Hong Kong to work for a British firm. Of his family, only his mother remained, so although she was a significant responsibility, his filial obligations were minimized and well defined. Work in the Western environment reinforced his Western identity and minimized pressure to disavow it and precipitously reidentify with the Chinese culture.

Gudrun came to Hong Kong without making a commitment to W. or requiring one. She was exploring career prospects while seeing how their relationship developed. She was able to work through much of the negative phase of culture shock before they decided to marry. At any rate, it seems likely that she may have achieved some of Stage 4 and 5 development during her prior lengthy stay in England, which may have made the adjustment to another new culture and setting in Hong Kong somewhat easier. Living arrangements have also been helpful in not creating additional difficulties. With two good incomes and a subsidy from W.'s employer, they have taken an apartment in a luxurious building occupied by a mixture of very Westernized Chinese and expatriates. This reduces the intensity of exposure to the Chinese life-style which has often proven to be overwhelming. Although W.'s mother lives with them, she regards him as the natural head of the family, so he can moderate her demands on her daughter-in-law and mediate when tensions arise, such as over child care practices. Gudrun has mastered Cantonese to the extent necessary to communicate with her mother-in-law but leaves all difficult conversations to W. To Gudrun, their marriage is one that requires accommodation to a person rather than to a culture, although in 12 years in Hong Kong she has come to value her contacts with Chinese people and appreciates the opportunity to live among them.

Gudrun's Rep Grid sheds further light on the construct system of a person who can make a success of such a difficult enterprise as an intercultural marriage. She has a strong sense of identity, with the element Self loading heavily on the first component which is a discrimination between *cheerfully forthright and active* people as opposed to *closed, secretive and introverted* ones. This discrimination is most useful in understanding her mother, who has proven to be a negative model for Gudrun. Her husband, W., and a mixture of Chinese and non-Chinese elements, are located at the positive pole of this most important construct. Her second component defines good marriages for her. Her husband, as well as a favorite sister and a male Chinese friend, exemplify the valued pole of this dimension which is *committed to family by choice (not strangled) vs. hemmed in by marriage (struggling against its restrictions)*. Gudrun also sees *herself* as committed to the family by her own free choice and thereby not strangled by it. This second component has arisen as a discrimination between her own marriage and that of her best friend. None of her elicited constructs were either overtly cultural or reminiscent of typical stereotypes. There is no evidence that culture is a significant basis of discrimination among people for Gudrun, while there is evidence of considerable complexity in her views of people regardless of culture.

Alison and K.

Another example of a successful intercultural marriage in Hong Kong is that of a British-born Australian woman, Alison, and K., a Chinese man. There were several factors that lessened the likelihood of their marriage becoming culture shocked. Their three-year courtship had been stormy, with many of the typical cultural issues resolved, rather than repressed, before marriage. His mother, who is particularly domineering, decided to move in with her son in Australia and proceeded to control his life to such an extent that Alison precipitated a crisis over his loyalty to her. This was settled in Alison's favor and was the occasion from which they learned to deal with differences by talking about them. Alison appreciated that this was not K.'s accustomed manner, but she was able to insist on it as a relationship prerequisite. It appears to have served them well.

K. is a Malaysian Chinese, so he has not been identified with the culture-shock hostility that Alison directs at the Cantonese Hong Kong residents, and since his family lives in Singapore they do not present any additional demands. Also, Hong Kong is not their first residence abroad. Before moving to Hong Kong they lived in a third country where he regularly dealt with a Chinese population in the course of his work. This enabled her to begin developing an understanding of Chinese culture without being engulfed by it at the outset. Also, it provided an opportunity for the emergence of necessary relationship skills in an unsupportive foreign setting. Possibly this period helped them both through initial culture-shock experiences, lessening the hazards of moving to Hong Kong. However, when interviewed, Alison was still fairly negative about the Cantonese whom she distinguished from the Singaporean or Malaysian Chinese as "rude and clannish." This probably represents Stage 2 awareness of differences and a sense of isolation. External stresses were fairly severe as they had only moderate financial security, difficult housing arrangements, and her social life was at the beck and call of her children and their need for transportation. Despite some negative feelings about life in Hong Kong, the marriage is seen as a source of strength. She described it, as they neared their eighth wedding anniversary, as a "happy marriage still getting better."

Jane and L.

Both of the preceding cases (Gudrun and W., Alison and K.) illustrating exceptions to the culture-shocked marriage hypothesis have had external circumstances which set them somewhat apart from the typical Chinese male and Western female couple in Hong Kong. In contrast, the next case, Jane and L., would appear to be more like those which had developed such severe difficulties that counseling was sought. Nevertheless, Jane and L. are satisfied with their marriage and are enjoying most aspects of their life in Hong Kong.

Jane is British; L. is the second son of a wealthy and worldly Chinese family with several other members also married to non-Chinese. L.'s mother died when he was a young boy, and when the father remarried, L. and his brothers were sent to boarding school in England. They rarely returned to Hong Kong even for visits, so L.'s Cantonese, both spoken and written, is very weak. Jane and L. met as students in England. His father worried about L.'s relationship with a non-Chinese woman, but conveyed his reservations about it through another party, so that when the decision to marry was announced he could graciously give his blessing as well as institute an equal allowance for her in addition to the one he gave his son.

Jane and L. had been married about six years when they moved back to Hong Kong, after two visits and an extended negotiation about the job L. would perform in the family business, which is managed by several elder members of his father's family. There were difficulties about his insistence upon the major benefits usually granted to expatriates, but compromises prevailed. However, from the first, his adjustment to Hong Kong was troubled. He found the working environment oppressive and unresponsive to his suggestions for modern management techniques. Not only was his language inadequate, but he did not have the least idea about many important Chinese customs. Jane was able to appeal for help on those matters to other female members of the family who were flattered by her concern to do things properly. They enjoyed having the opportunity to teach an interested pupil. In assuming the role of the family member who was responsible for participation in Chinese culture, she was expressing an understanding of L.'s misery. He was having a more serious version of culture shock than she. This was a continuation of a role that she had always filled and found satisfying—that is, being available when he needed her for listening, sympathy, and advice. He frequently availed himself of her sounding-board services. L.'s struggle upon his return did not seem to be with his identity, which is fairly securely Western, but rather with adjusting to the Chinese way of doing business and its associated demands.

Jane also experienced culture shock and reported feeling "penned-in . . . claustrophobic" in the early days of her stay in Hong Kong. This was despite living in a luxurious neighborhood, in a very large apartment with a garden. A confined feeling is a common manifestation of Stage 2 of the culture-shock model. Several episodes which she recounted indicated a period of high hostility. She resorted to some fairly dramatic gestures, which can only be described as aggressive, to attract L.'s attention when she felt the giving in the marriage was too one-sided. Apparently they were successful.

An unusual feature of Jane and L.'s adaptation to Hong Kong was the unexpected moving of their circle of friends from London to Hong Kong just about the time they were settling in to the negative stages of culture shock. Unconnected with their own relocation, several friends, both Chinese and English and intercultural couples, moved as they had. This social circle was very helpful. It reduced dependency on L.'s family and provided Jane with her best friend with whom to share gripes and a social network which was still in effect four years later.

Also unusual is Jane's very secure relationship with L.'s family. She is clearly loved and finds the family helpful. In turn, the family has not demanded anything of her as she is a "foreigner," and each of her successes in mastering Chinese culture has pleased them. Her difficulties are anticipated and she is gently guided toward the proper course of action. She has been used to communicate the family's wishes to her husband, but was respected when she refused to try to influence his decisions.

Analysis of Jane's Rep Grid indicated that she has been operating with a great deal of self-abnegation. Her first component (40% of the grid variance) was useful for distinguishing other people but not herself. It is a construction of *caring, giving, trustworthy* people as opposed to *remote, egocentric, and unreliable* ones. The elements Self, her Mother, a Person she admires, and her Best friend in Hong Kong all had near-zero loadings on this dimension. When the construct was described to her she responded quickly in agreement to a suggestion that it represented a dependency dimension, identifying the elements at one pole as "You can't be emotionally dependent upon them." The second component (25% of the grid variance) was defined by contrasts between her husband and herself on the basis of his ability to be a *good manager* while she saw herself as *scatterbrained, insecure, and dreamy*.

Although this was a feedback interview, not a counseling session, it required very little reconstruing to alternatively identify the pole at which she sorted herself as *open and flexible*. This had a more positive connotation for her, one that she could relate to the role she has chosen to fill in her family life. She later reported discussing this with her husband with a new found confidence that she wished to resist demands from all quarters that she do something visibly more important than ''be available when needed'' as her first priority. She reaffirmed that other activities and uses of her talents would be subservient to that objective, which she can now verbalize and value positively. The third component appears to be a remnant of earlier cultural discriminations although it no longer is overtly that. It distinguishes a *Chinese masculine* set of qualities from *busybody and feminine* ones. Father-in-law defines the Chinese masculine pole and the four elements loading most heavily on it are also Chinese. Her own Mother and a Person-who-has-had-trouble are located at the other pole. The elements at this pole are all females. This may reflect sex and culture stereotypes and raises the question, ''Is the Chinese culture a male culture?'' in Jane's construing of it. The third component is another major dimension (11% of the grid variance) which is not useful for thinking about herself, as the loading of the Self element is near zero.

The low level of self-awareness and absence of positive self-evaluation which Jane displayed in her Rep Grid has probably made her adjustment to Hong Kong less painful and enables her to fill the flexible, openly available role she has chosen. At the same time, it is very similar to patterns frequently found in Chinese Rep Grids. On the other hand, she is conscious of how much she treasures Chinese values, particularly with regard to the family, and how aware she is of the Chinese way of doing things. She wants to remain in Hong Kong. It is not possible, coming on the scene so late, to be certain, but Jane may be a person whose construct system was always fairly congruent with Chinese cultural values and therefore the changes required by her move to Hong Kong may have been relatively peripheral, dealing mainly with management of the environment and acquiring new skills to manifest familiar values.

There are several unique features in the case of Jane and L. which appear to have modified her experience of culture shock, thus reducing its virulent impact on their marriage relationship. These include a minimum threat to her identity which is primarily that of a supportive wife. This role was actually enhanced since she perceived L. as especially needing her in his own crisis with Chinese culture. She had reported some threats in the realm of her mother identity. They included the family's disapproval of her breast-feeding her eldest son for what they viewed as on overly extended time. Other instances are more difficult to assess as there are cultural differences with regard to intense mother-child ties versus a more diffuse family-child relationship. However, Jane was not deeply perturbed for long, as most of the problem was experienced during the early, brief visits to Hong Kong. Her ability to escape back to London eased any crisis until more mutuality of approach was achieved. A second son, born in Hong Kong, has been raised harmoniously in the Chinese family setting and Jane has not felt threatened. Other areas of threat did not materialize since the family had already developed a mode of interacting with non-Chinese members, and their own son, L., was perceived as very Westernized yet still loyally Chinese when it was important. Since L. did not reject Western values, either as part of his identity or in the marital relationship, this eliminated one of the most difficult hurdles in many culture-shocked marriages.

Another significant feature in this case is the unusual amount of support Jane and L. garnered from his family and a transplanted social network. The latter was particularly timely. It arrived just as the negative phases of culture shock were emerging. This diffused the intensity of social interactions with the family and at the same time reaffirmed aspects of self which were being shaken by experiences with the new culture.

Finally, the lack of demands upon Jane to be proficient in expressions of Chinese values and customs coupled with the pleasure exhibited at her efforts to conform in this regard provided the smoothest possible setting for learning the externals of a culture. The practice of ritual roles, regardless of motivation, operates in the manner of Kelly's fixed role therapy to promote reconstruing of the values inherent in the practices.

The review of three cases of intercultural marriages which superficially matched those in the culture-shocked marriage sample has indicated some of the circumstances which modify the culture-shock experience. From consideration of general research on culture shock, duration and intensity of interaction with the host culture appear as obvious factors affecting the onset of culture shock and the pace of proceeding through the stages. Not so obvious are factors such as degree of difference between the host and home culture and the amount of change required in dimensions held to be particularly valuable in the home culture (Spradley and Phillips, 1972). Similarly, personality variables are significant. Greater sensitivity to the uniqueness and pervasiveness of differences in the host culture engenders a greater reaction. Rigidity staves off culture shock (Ruben & Kealey, 1977).

The cases of Gudrun and Alison illustrate exceptions to the culture-shocked marriage hypothesis. In so far as there were external diversions, the hostility and negative emotions inherent in culture learning were not directed at their husbands. At the same time, the husbands were not struggling through an identity crisis of their own with a resulting rejection of Western marriage values and modes of resolving differences. Thus, the hazards to the transplanted intercultural marriages did not exceed those of any other more typical transplanted marriage. Jane illustrates a different type of resolution. She seems to have had a light case of culture shock and the negative feelings it generated were sublimated in her concern for her husband's similar, but more serious difficulties. The sublimation was made easier to maintain because she was not required to make any major personal changes, she had the added support of a familiar social network, an undemanding, helpful in-law family and few of the typical environmental stresses such as crowded housing and language difficulties.

A review of exceptions to the culture-shocked marriage hypothesis highlights the psychological mechanisms underlying the special problems of this group of intercultural marriages. The emphasis has been on the culture-shock transition as effecting identity revision or reconfirmation through an exploration of personal and situational factors which alleviate or exacerbate the inherent dangers. In addition to the specific points already noted in the discussion, several prescriptions have emerged.

1. The negative phases of the culture-shock transition become easier to accept if they are perceived as normal and as precursors of the growth and future joys of the Autonomy and Independence Stages of Adler's model.

2. It is helpful to recognize that the anxiety of culture shock derives from an awareness of the need to improve construing of a "new" reality and that threat is inevitable as the need to change core role structures becomes apparent. This not only enhances the understanding of helping professionals but provides a basis for constructive intervention if necessary. In that, the PCT interpretation illuminates the therapy venture and suggests several avenues of approach. For example, the case of Jane and L. demonstrates two types of assistance toward alternative construing as examples of that PCT objective. (These were, in the first instance, the reconstruing of constructs subordinate to a negatively valued pole, *scatterbrained, insecure, and dreamy* under a positively valued superordinate construct pole, *open and flexible*. Secondly, playing the role of a Chinese woman,—that is, fulfilling ritual family and social obligations and teaching children good Chinese manners, enabled new constructs to be tried in a nonthreatening manner which permits them to be more smoothly incorporated into core role structures.)

3. Support for the management of high levels of stress inherent in the culture-shock transitions is also indicated. In response to the extreme stress and distress of Stages 2 and 3, support (Brammer & Shostrom, 1977, p. 174—178) is likely to prove more valuable than detrimental. Damping down anxiety permits construct system change to proceed at a tolerable pace. Also, it prevents abortive solutions to the crisis, such as suicide or a departure and enduring bitterness towards the spouse's original culture.

On the other hand, there is little evidence that the full development envisaged in the culture-shock model is regularly attained in culture-shocked marriages. It may be that transplanting an already at-risk union to a new cultural setting so seriously stunts the potential for growth that full recovery has been delayed beyond the period observed in my sample. (The maximum has been five years.) The growth associated with culture learning does not seem to have these limits. The complexities of another culture offer a limitless challenge. Their mastery is a progressively unfolding source of human discovery and joy.

REFERENCES

Adler, P. S. The transitional experience: An alternative view of culture shock. *Journal of Humanistic Psychology,* 1975, **15,** 13—23.

Brammer, L. M., & Shostrom, E. L. *Therapeutic Psychology* (3rd ed.). Englewood Cliffs, N.J.: Prentice-Hall, 1977.

Gullahorn, J. T., & Gullahorn, J. E. An extension of the U-curve hypothesis. *Journal of Social Issues,* 1963, **19**, 33–47.

Hall, E. T. *The Silent Language.* Garden City: Doubleday, 1959.

Holland, R. *Self & Social Context.* London and Basingstoke: Macmillan, 1977.

Hsu, F. L. K. Psychological homeostasis and jen: Conceptual tools for advancing psychological anthropology. *American Anthropologist,* 1971, **73**, 23–43.

Irwin, M., Tripodi, T., & Bieri, J. Affective stimulus value and cognitive complexity. *Journal of Personality and Social Psychology,* 1967, **4**, 444–448.

Kelly, G. A. *The Psychology of Personal Constructs:* Vols. 1 and 2. New York: Norton, 1955.

Kelly, G. A. Personal construct theory and the psychotherapeutic interview, 1958. In Maher, B. (Ed.), *Clinical Psychology and Personality.* New York: Wiley, 1969.

Landfield, A. W. A movement interpretation of threat. *Journal of Abnormal and Social Psychology,* 1954, **49**, 529–532.

McCoy, M. M. A reconstruction of emotion. In Bannister, D. (Ed.), *New Perspectives in Personal Construct Theory.* London: Academic, 1977.

Oberg, K. Culture shock and the problem of adjustment to new cultural environments. An edited talk originally presented in 1958, reprinted in Hoppes, D. S. (Ed.), *Readings in Intercultural Communication,* Vol. 2. Pittsburgh, PA: University of Pittsburgh, Regional Council for International Education, 1972.

Ruben, B. D., & Kealey, D. J. Behavioral assessment and the prediction of cross-cultural shock, adjustment and effectiveness. Paper presented at the 3rd Annual Conference of the Society for Intercultural Education, Training and Research, Chicago, February 1977.

Slater, P. *Notes on Ingrid 72.* Mimeo from author at Academic Department of Psychiatry, Clare House, St. George's Hospital, Blackshaw Road, Tooting, London, S.W. 17.

Spradley, J. P., & Phillips, M. Culture and stress: A quantitative analysis. *American Anthropologist,* 1972, **74**, 518–519.

CHAPTER 9

The Relationship Between Personal Construct Theory and Psychotherapeutic Techniques[1]

Thomas O. Karst

Psychotherapists, while generally rejecting a purely functional and naive eclectic approach (Eron & Callahan, 1969), do experiment with treatment techniques to an extent that might not be inferred from their theoretical positions. This variety needs to be taken into account. The purpose of this chapter is to show how one may understand and integrate a diversity of therapeutic techniques through the use of Personal Construct Psychology.

CONSTRUING THEORETICAL AND TECHNICAL CONNECTIONS

As psychological theory matures, differentiation becomes possible between technique and rationale (Karst, 1978). Several commentators have noted the contemporary trend to move toward "flexibly applying the methods of diverse approaches" (Schaefer & Millman, 1978, p. 3; see also Haley, 1967, pp. 530–535). These authors, as well as others (Chambless & Goldstein, 1979; Dimond & Havens, 1975; Dimond et al., 1978), point to the fact that theories are available or can be created that can be rationally systematic and yet can incorporate "technical eclecticism."[2]

While Kelly (1955) derived a relatively specific treatment technique called fixed role therapy from his Personal Construct Theory (PCT),[3] the theory's implications

---

[1]An initial sketch of some of these ideas was presented in a paper read at the Second International Congress on Personal Construct Theory, Christ Church, Oxford University, England, July, 1977 (Karst, 1978). I would like to thank Ronald Diehl for reading an initial draft of this chapter and offering comments from his perspective. Barbara Karst typed more than one draft and gave other help in many ways. Professor Landfield, the editor of this volume, generously critiqued the manuscript and for this I am also grateful.

[2]It is unfortunate that the term *prescriptive* (e.g., Dimond, Havens, & Jones, 1978) has been used to describe attempts to creatively adapt treatment methods to particular problems, persons, and situations, since this term also denotes a directive and authoritarian style.

[3]The general audience of psychologists is probably better acquainted with this technique, as well as the theoretically derived assessment procedure, the Rep Test, than with the more general theoretical position. Fixed role therapy is generally misconstrued by this larger audience, however, as a behavioral technique, as simple role playing, or as role rehearsal.

for psychotherapy go beyond any single technique. In what follows, I hope, through a discussion of theoretical structure and clinical example, to explore some of the technical variety that PCT can generate and incorporate. It is my opinion that PCT is one of a small set of theories which can afford to be technically eclectic, is technically fertile, and still remains rationally integrated.

Concepts and Operations

Some systems of psychotherapy, including psychoanalysis and nondirective counseling, commenced with treatment methods and later devised theories to explain etiology and change. Both Freud and Rogers were aware that technical innovation was possible. Rogers (1957), for example, attempted to state the "necessary and sufficient conditions of therapeutic change" in fairly general terms indicating that even an analyst's interpretations might serve as a ". . . channel for communicating the essential conditions which have been formulated" (p. 102). That is, analytic interpretations may communicate *empathic understanding, unconditional positive regard,* or the state of *therapist congruence* and thereby have a therapeutic effect. Systems that grow out of a given treatment method, however, tend to become rather technique-bound and orthodox.[4]

There are other theories, PCT among them, that do not attempt to prescribe or dictate treatment methods (e.g., Adler, 1964; Beck, 1976; Frank, 1973; Rotter, 1970; Sullivan, 1940). In an article, not, I think, very well known, Carl Jung (1971) indicated that if a patient's own view of the world corresponds to Adlerian psychology and another's world-view corresponds to Freud's psychology then:

It would be an unpardonable error to overlook the element of truth in both Freudian and Adlerian viewpoints. . . . Both truths correspond to psychic realities. There are in fact some cases which by and large can best be described and explained by the one theory, and some by the other. (p. 76)

Jung, like Kelly, seemed to be attempting to formulate a personality theory abstract enough to incorporate a variety of "psychic realities" (personal construct systems?), each of which has some "element of truth."

Karst (1978) has characterized such "open" theories (Vetter & Smith, 1971, p. 656) as logically more differentiated. They are able to generate a set of abstract propositions regarding the goals of treatment somewhat independently from a set of statements regarding the means (techniques) to reach these goals. Parenthetically, behavioral approaches may gain a similar advantage by a somewhat different strategy. Treatment goals may be stated in terms of concrete, directly observable behavioral changes. Questions as to the efficacy of treatment methods may be left to the outcome of experimentation and empirical test (Chambless & Goldstein, 1979).

The interplay between theory and treatment technique is easily construed as the interplay between the general and specific, the abstract and the concrete, or between concepts and empirical referents. Piotrowski (1971) points out that such relation-

---

[4]One advantage of orthodoxy, however, is that students of a system can believe that there is a right way to do things and that their task, simply, is to learn that right way.

ships have a "nonrational" (not irrational) quality about them; and this is specifically acknowledged in PCT as the creative aspect of "inventing" therapeutic techniques: "Every case a psychotherapist handles requires him to devise techniques and formulate constructs he has never used before" (Kelly, 1955, p. 600).

This nonrational aspect is true in the general field of therapeutics whether treatment techniques are devised within psychological or biological frameworks. Consider the abstract etiological statement *"Spirochaeta pallida are bacteria which can cause syphilis."* One can deduce principles of treatment from this generalization, two of which might be (1) to prevent syphilis, prevent *Spirochaeta pallida* from invading the body and (2), if *Spirochaeta pallida* does invade the body, to get rid of them in some way will help control and possibly eliminate the process and outcome of the disease. Note first of all that more than just a single principle can be deduced. But also note that such deductions are themselves generalizations which are open to many or at least several concrete and specific treatment strategies.

How does one get rid of *Spirochaeta pallida?* In the history of this disease (Cartwright, 1972), many things have been tried. The patient has been infected with malaria to kill the bacteria with the heat of the resulting fever, since these organisms were found to tolerate a narrow range of temperature. Broad-spectrum antibiotics are now used, with some decreasing success. But who is to say that a more specific spiroceticide won't be discovered or some other more effective treatment method found? There is, as yet, no known inoculation or vaccination, but, in the case of syphilis, it is known that various other types of prevention are well worth more than pounds of cure. Thus, no matter how elegant the theory of etiology, finding rational and specific treatment methods is still a creative process. Second, the same etiological theory supports more than a single treatment method. Third, evaluation of therapeutic "inventions" depends not only on the rational connection between theory and treatment but also on questions of economy of time, space, and money; ethics and values; even esthetics—if two treatments are equal in every other way, wouldn't one choose the more esthetically pleasing?[5]

PCT propositions regarding psychological change procedures are generalizations which take into account some of this complexity; for example, "The therapist helps design and implement experiments" (Kelly, 1955, p. 592). This general statement can be operationalized in an infinite variety of ways. Although the theory does not dictate or prescribe treatment, it does help point us in general and useful directions.

Propositions Relevant to Change

A useful psychological theory should be capable of generating sets of propositions relevant to the antecedents, maintenance, and change of a given psychological process (cf. Dimond et al., 1978). PCT is capable of this level of differentiation. Buchwald and Young (1969) have discussed the difference between etiology and change while noting that the ways processes are changed need not parallel the ways

---

[5]Is it possible that in applying an esthetic criterion we might be able to judge more critically such techniques as primal screaming?

in which they were established. The causes of and treatments for broken bones are certainly not the same. Whether one's tonsillitis is treated with surgery or medicine is a function of several variables, perhaps not the least of which is the specialty training one's doctor has completed. Further, demonstrating that a given technique leads to an expected, therapeutic change does not necessarily validate etiological propositions. Such demonstrations do, however, help validate treatment or change propositions.[6]

PCT generates propositions specifically focused on changing psychological processes. In his two volumes, Kelly (1955) explicates several generalizations regarding change which are theoretically connected. In fact, the entire second volume is mainly addressed to this task, along with giving concrete examples and putting these concepts into operation. In a later article (Kelly, 1969a), these principles have been abstracted and summarized in convenient form.[7] "I have summarized what goes on in therapy under eight headings. More might have been used" (p. 231). Such a statement indicates the fertility of the theory in providing propositions regarding change. Psychological change does not occur in only one way; it can come about in several different ways. Second, Kelly's statement indicates that the clinician is free to construe the principles themselves in different ways at different times. For example, the same list could be reorganized and renumbered yielding either fewer, more abstract propositions (Paine, 1970) or a larger number of more specific statements. Finally, the list of change statements generated so far is not exhaustive. If the theory is useful, future clinicians will generate others. In fact, every clinician working in the intimate role relationship of psychotherapy will create others that seem to be useful at a particular time for a particular person.

Personal Construct Psychotherapy is a way of getting on with the human enterprise and it may embody and mobilize all of the techniques for doing this that man has yet devised. . . . The techniques employed are the techniques for living and the task of the skillful psychotherapist is the proper orchestration of all these varieties of techniques. Hence one may find a Personal Construct Psychotherapist employing a huge variety of procedures—not helter-skelter, but always as part of a plan for helping himself and his client get on with the job of human exploration and checking out the appropriateness of the constructions they have devised for placing upon the world around them. (Kelly, 1969b, pp. 221–222)

TECHNICAL VARIETY

In this section, I will take the propositions that Kelly has summarized (1969a, p. 231) and illustrate each general statement with concrete, clinical examples. This will be done through clinical vignettes drawn from my own practice or, in some cases, from the general literature. The latter illustrations will suggest that techniques from other systems, sometimes with just slight modifications, can be reconstrued and incorporated within PCT psychotherapy.

[6]See Rychlak's (1973) discussion of personality theories organized under the headings of *theory of illness, theory of cure,* and *therapeutic techniques.*
[7]Bannister and Salmon (1975) discuss educational techniques based on this same summary.

Before proceeding, however, it should be noted that Kelly viewed psychotherapy, like any other human enterprise, as a complex, interactive, and ongoing process. Basic to this process is the client-therapist relationship, technically their role relationship or *Sociality* (Karst & Groutt, 1977, pp. 87–90). The ultimate goal of PCT is not that the client accept any given alternative interpretation of an experience or set of experiences. In fact, Kelly points out (Landfield & Leitner, this volume, Chapter 1) that even rather dramatic changes brought about by fixed role therapy can be transitory unless the client adopts the interpretative attitude itself—that is, becomes open and amenable to reconstruction and experimentation in one's total life. The clinical examples that follow, therefore, should be considered only for what they are—one or two instances or interchanges construed in PCT terms out of innumerable such experiences that would constitute a more complete psychotherapy.

Reversing Positions on a Reference Axis—"Slot Rattling"

In another paper (Karst, 1978), I described an early therapy case which I considered a failure.[8] The essence of that illustration was that as a neophyte therapist I was using psychodynamic theory and interpretations in a manner that could be construed as "hostile" (see Kelly, 1955, p. 533). I was forcing my own understanding onto my client. My client's construction of his difficulties was that he was physically sick and needed to get well *(sick vs. well)*. This man was ultimately helped when the clinic physician prescribed medication and began seeing him in 10-minute supportive treatment once per month. The latter interventions were helpful in moving him toward the other side of his own reference axis with observable changes in his behavior, level of adaptation, and feelings about himself. He was able to return to work and the frequency of his anxiety attacks diminished.

In working with children, many clinicians have had the experience of helping parents understand and guide their children. Some of that counseling can be construed as directly encouraging slot rattling. I worked with the parents of a severely delayed, autistic child. He was a little over two years old and was not walking, although he had begun to take a few tentative steps when he was willing to allow someone to hold his hands in the process. In offering guidance to these parents, many issues were salient and they needed a great deal of information. However, one of the most important interventions is pertinent to this discussion. The child's mother was quite concerned about her son's reactions to some initial attempts at toilet training. Mother construed him on the "ready" end of the *ready vs. not ready* construct—after all, he was over two years old and was almost walking. With some gentle urging, empathy, and education, she was able to move back to a "not ready" position and thereby avoid a great deal of unhappy interaction with this very special child. The parents, then, were able to focus on helping their child with some much more important and appropriate developmental tasks such as establishing regular and predictable eye contact.

---

[8]Jung (1971, p. 77) has indicated ". . . failures are priceless experiences because they not only open the way to a better truth but force us to modify our views and methods."

Applying a Construct from the Client's Current Repertory

In a case I supervised, a psychiatric resident was seeing a graduate student who consistently applied a *work vs. fun* construction on large portions of her life. As a consequence, she was unable to enjoy anything construed as work, and writing assignments were consistently viewed as work. Having managed to accrue several grades of incomplete, she was now facing the task of writing a major paper upon which the continuance of her course of study depended. She had made several halting attempts to try to turn writing into something fun (slot rattling) with little success.

We then explored other possible constructions with her. She recalled that in some previously successful attempts to write (elaboration of construct system) the *work-play* dichotomy was not so salient. This seemed generally true when she felt that she was critiquing other's ideas, showing people how wrong they were, or in other ways "giving them a piece of my mind." The major assignment facing her was fairly readily conceptualized in this context, and she was able to begin. She took a construct readily available to her and applied it usefully to the current situation. This was a relatively superficial change. Although this "trick" got her started, the possibility of failing (construed as "wasting money"), and beginning to see finishing the paper in more economic terms (making good use of money already invested) seemed to provide for a more effective channel, and she finished the paper.

Making Preverbal Constructs More Explicit

Kelly (1969a, p. 231) points out that while he does not find it particularly useful to ". . . think of this as dredging the unconscious," this type of "interpretive" maneuver can be therapeutically useful. Children sometimes express their feelings behaviorally because they do not have a verbal label for their experiences or because they are attempting to deny an appropriate verbal label. For example, a child in our Day Treatment Program consistently provoked rather violent fights with other children and even the staff. We began to understand his behavior as a result of an unverbalized construct of himself as frightened and inadequate. Acting upon this, the staff began assuring the child that we would protect him and not allow others to hurt him. We wanted to teach him how to swim, hit a baseball, and be more competent as a student. His provocative behavior became less frequent.

Interpretations do not necessarily have to be "deep" or Freudian.[9] Adler (1963) points out how useful it is to make explicit interpretations regarding aims, goals, anticipations, and purposes. He discusses the case (pp. 1−8) of a young girl who was demanding, irritable, "nervous," and dependent. She upset her whole family as they tried to get her ready to go to school in the morning. Adler directly interpreted

---

[9]Within psychoanalytic theory, however, there is a literature on the concept of "reconstruction" (e.g., Rees, 1978). On one side of a debate is a view quite compatible with PCT represented by Kennedy (1971, p. 400), who indicates that "reconstruction in child analysis functions primarily as a means of providing a conceptual framework [construct system] to the child whereby he can understand his present dilemmas. . . ." rather than an attempt to provide insight into what has truly happened in the past.

to this child that her unrealized purpose seemed to be to get her family angry and make them uncomfortable. He suggested that she write a big sign above her bed saying, "Every morning I am going to make my family terribly upset." In the face of such awareness, Adler believed, she would no longer be able to continue her behavior with such excuses as not feeling good or not having the right clothes to wear. He also believed that the child would find her own ways of changing her behavior.

In PCT terms, this child's behavior might be construed as channeled by a series of experimental tests of the unverbalized hypothesis—"If I behave in certain ways, certain things that I want, need, or should have will follow." By interpreting this, or making the experiment more verbally explicit, the child has the opportunity to decide whether indeed this construction of things is generally or in the long run useful. She may begin to reconstrue the experience of getting up and off to school as a more useful test of pleasing her family or herself rather than simply harassing those around her.

In the same vein, interpretations suggested by Rational Emotive Theory can be useful (Ellis, 1962; Mosher, 1966). Clients can be asked to consider the possibility that their fear of public speaking, for example, may be a result of believing that they must do a perfect job or other "irrational" ideas (Karst & Trexler, 1970; Trexler & Karst, 1972). Such an interpretation checks on the possibility that an unverbalized (unconscious) construction is the channel for a given, but unwanted, experience.

In a PCT frame of reference, however, interpretations like these are offered in the hypothetical or conditional mode. A question such as, "Would it make any difference to you if you understood your experience while speaking in front of groups as a result of your fear of being rejected by people in your audience?" certainly is in a different style and has a different objective than a typical dogmatic, Ellisonian interpretation. A PCT therapist is not interested in convincing his or her client of the "truth" only in suggesting alternative and perhaps more useful constructions.

Elaborating the Construct System; Testing for Internal Consistency and Predictive Validity

The next illustration is from a therapeutic relationship with a young man, 17 years old, which lasted almost two years. I am convinced that the following incident was crucial to the generally successful outcome of the treatment.

A central issue for Joe was his relationship with his parents and particularly with his mother. He construed her as hypercritical, punitive, intrusive, and nagging. He had developed a style of relating to her that he felt minimized the effects of her actions. He was quite secretive and unrevealing with her, and he arranged his life (school, work, and extracurricular activities) in such a way as to minimize the chances of interacting with her. During her own treatment, Joe's mother had gained some insight into which of her actions and strategies (e.g., cleaning his bedroom when he wasn't around) helped maintain her son's constructions and had indeed changed some of these in a very appropriate way. In addition, she began to view her son as getting older and becoming more mature, and she was ready to give him more personal freedom and responsibility. Joe, on the other hand, did not readily perceive these changes in his mother.

Generally, Joe drove to his appointments on his own, a quasi-fixed-role arrangement tending to foster independence and personal responsibility. It also led to his placing more value on our sessions. Several months after beginning treatment, on an icy day, he had a slight accident on his way to our meeting. When he arrived, Joe was quite upset and anticipated much criticism, personal embarrassment, and punishment (elaborating current construction) from his family. His plan was to not reveal this accident until absolutely necessary, because he was convinced that he would lose out on several planned activities, including losing the privilege of driving, as soon as the accident was discovered.

In discussing how he would prefer his parents to react to his news (elaborating an alternative construction), Joe indicated he wished they would understand that the accident was not totally his fault. He also wished that they might know how bad he felt. He even wondered why they could not be proud of him, since he had done all the appropriate things—notify the police, exchange names, addresses, and names of insurance companies.

I pointed out that this might be a time when he could test which of these constructions might prove more predictive. To test this hypothesis I suggested that he immediately inform his parents about the accident. He declined the offer to use my phone, however, and we went on to other things.

Later in the day my secretary gave me a handwritten note that said the following: "Dr. Karst, after I left your office I phoned my mother about the accident, and guess what? Not only was she totally rational in her reaction, but she even sympathized with me. What a relief!" We were over a hump.

Increasing the Range of Convenience of Constructs

A client may have a generally helpful conception of himself or herself but use it too narrowly. A somewhat sexually inhibited couple began to lose some of their inhibitions when they began reading about variations in sexual experience. As it happened, the woman considered herself a gourmet cook. The suggestion that she might begin seeing herself as creative in the bedroom as well as in the kitchen brought a laugh but was meaningful enough to keep the process going.

Adams (1973) described a constricted, perfectionistic, and obsessive child who needed to be urged to try the new experience of riding a bicycle. The child construed this as frightening and refused to try. Instead of suggesting that the child reverse positions on the *afraid vs. not afraid* dimension, the therapist took advantage of the fact that his patient had not yet defined "perfection" relative to bicycle riding. "His wish for perfection was used therapeutically by defining perfection on a bike as getting where one wants to go" (Schaefer & Millman, 1978, p. 29). The fact that he could ride the bike and meet this criterion of perfection allowed him to take the risk of learning the new skill.

One of my patients had multiple phobias, among them a strong fear of static electricity. During the winter a humidifier in the house was seen as absolutely necessary to lessen the chance of being shocked. In the spring, the patient always became quite anxious to have the humidifier put into storage. This was taken as a signal that he had less to worry about. It seemed to me that this concern was evidence that he was construing the humidifier narrowly as only a way of dealing with his fear. I suggested this and also that he might broaden his construction of the humidifier—for example, the humidifier might be retained during the summer to make it more comfortable, say, on those few dry summer days. My patient indicated that indeed he had not thought of things this way before and that seeing the wider use of the humidifier lessened his anxiety about the decision as to when to remove it.

Decreasing the Range of Convenience of Constructs

Again, from the area of child guidance, certain common techniques illustrate this principle. Ginott (1965), Gordon (1970), and others have suggested that people who work with children, especially teachers and parents, should evaluate the things a child does, not the whole child: "I was pleased that you did the dishes" or "Stealing cookies was wrong" is much better, in the appropriate situation, than "You are a good boy!" or "You are a bad girl!"

Certain analytic interpretations also can serve to decrease the range of convenience of certain constructs. The woman who seems to be continually relating to her husband as if he were her father would, perhaps, do well by encapsulating her construct of "father" and not applying it where it gets in the way. The analyst, by pointing out this possibility through interpretations, may aid that process.

Also in psychoanalysis, transference interpretations have as their ultimate aim encapsulating or decreasing the range of convenience of the patient's construal of the therapist. As a transference neurosis is operating, the patient is construing the analyst as mother, father, or other people with whom the patient has been neurotically enmeshed. Through interpretations the patient comes to realize this. As transference is resolved (parental constructs narrowed) the patient can begin to relate to the analyst more objectively, and in that process the patient is helped.

Altering the Meaning of Certain Constructs: Rotating Reference Axes

This proposition might be illustrated by the homosexual person who basically devalues his or her sexual orientation. Homosexuality for this person may be tied up with other constructs such as "bad," "deviate," or "unlovable." Altering the meaning of the construct "homosexuality" is to begin dissociating these related constructs. The construct "homosexual" might be left as a purely descriptive term without any other positive or negative constructions associated with it (decreasing the range of convenience). Other more useful and predictive constructs might be found to associate with the homosexual construct. One client began seeing that his homosexual relationships were not just a source of sexual release. He began valuing the more general aspects of these relationships—the human contact, the exchange of ideas, giving someone else pleasure—and this proved more useful to him.

One aspect of altering the meaning of constructs is to help people find superordinate constructions that can incorporate heretofore incompatible ideas or ways of viewing themselves. Harter (1977) describes how important this is with children, especially since, from a cognitive-developmental point of view, this is particularly difficult for the preoperational child. In a very sensitive article she describes the process through which she helped a young girl, K., begin to deal with seeing herself as *both* good and bad, sad and happy, dumb and smart. As treatment progressed, K., even though not always able to verbalize her ambivalent feelings and ideas about herself, showed evidence—through her drawings and her improved behavior and achievement in school—that she was achieving a more differentiated and, thus, different and more meaningful view of herself.

Finally, in a funny short story, Hooker (1971) describes an airline pilot who developed a strong fear of flying. The pilot began to see flying as increasing his chances of dying before he reached old age. He was also frightened that if he died, his large family would not be provided for. A veterinarian friend whom he consulted about this pointed out to the pilot that if he took out large insurance policies every time he flew he could then begin seeing the possibility of dying as not a bad thing at all. It could be seen as a way to make his family rich! This seemed to provide the cure.

Erecting New Reference Axes

A rather clear example of a technique based on this principle from the contemporary literature is assertiveness training. Typically, people who enter into such training tend to construe their own interpersonal relations along a dimension of *submissive* on the one end and *aggressive* on the other. This dimension is evidenced by such comments as, "Sure I hit him in the mouth, what did you want me to do, sit there and take it?" A new reference axis is erected in the course of such training. The person learns that he or she doesn't have to choose between the poles of being aggressive or being submissive but that a new possibility, assertiveness, is possible.

With PCT, however, assertiveness training is better construed as a fixed role therapy technique rather than simply as training (Horvath, 1977; 1979). Skill-learning is undoubtedly a part of such an experience. However, the real changes being sought are on a construct level (Bonarius, 1970, p. 218). No one could ever hope to learn all the assertive responses, one by one, that might be needed and appropriate to the varied situations and role relationships that people are apt to find themselves in. Deep-structure rather than surface-structure (Grinder & Bandler, 1976)[10] changes are needed—a construction of assertiveness—so that new and

---

[10]Apparently uninfluenced by Kelly or PCT, these authors explicate a "Meta-model for therapy" based on transformational linguistics which, in large measure, overlaps and is in agreement with PCT (cf. Pepinsky & Karst, 1964).

never before performed assertive actions can be generated as appropriate. This involves reconstruing situations and social interactions, not just the learning of a few simple skills. Ultimately, it depends on being able to reconstrue the self.[11]

Most of the examples in this section are not very unlike the attempts any psychotherapist might make to help those troubled people who come for consultation. One doesn't have to be a Personal Construct Theorist to see some clinical value in the strategies described. On the other hand, viewing the variety in PCT terms allows us to see the wide range of convenience of the theory, at least insofar as treatment techniques are concerned. The direct implication of this is that Personal Construct Theory, combined with clinical accumen, sensitivity, and above all creativity, will prove a very useful therapeutic tool even though, or perhaps because, it does not tell the therapist exactly what to do.

RECONSTRUING HYPNOTIC AND OPERANT TECHNIQUES

In the preceding section of this chapter, the issue of the relationship between theory and technique was explored by looking at some theoretical propositions regarding change derived from PCT. This was supplemented by providing examples from clinical experience and the general therapeutic literature. In what follows I am reversing that process to look at two technical areas—hypnosis and operant learning—in an attempt to try to find PCT meaning in these procedures. The techniques themselves are not described in any detail, but the question is asked: Could such techniques be incorporated and used in a theoretically consistent way by a PCT psychotherapist?

Hypnosis

Erik Erikson once stated that one of the greatest technical advances that Freud made was to give up his use of hypnosis and to begin looking for other methods of treatment. His apparent rationale for stating this was that hypnosis treats the patient as an object; free association and analysis of the patient's unconscious brought the patient back into the treatment process as a more cooperative partner.

PCT also values a therapeutic relationship with shared responsibility, and if hypnosis is construed as a manipulative or even a coercive treatment, what is a respectable PCT theorist doing even considering it? The answer lies, of course, in the fact that hypnosis, like any other experience, can be reconstrued—and indeed this has been done by hypnotists themselves, independent of any PCT influence. Many modern discussions of hypnosis (Frankel, 1978; Spiegel & Spiegel, 1978) conceptualize the endeavor as a cooperative, interpersonal venture. The hypnotist is, in effect, a consultant to the person experiencing hypnosis. The crucial factors lie

---

[11]Kelly (1969c, p. 59) has stated, however, that "the key to therapy might be in getting the client to get on with a new way of life without waiting to acquire 'insight' ", and assertiveness training is also an example of such a strategy.

in what the subject does and experiences: "It seems to be an essentially subjective experience. . . . Hypnosis per se [hypnotic procedures or what the hypnotist does] might or might not be the factor of primary importance in these changes" (Frankel, 1978, p. 664). Such factors as the person's ability to tolerate logical inconsistencies, his or her imagination skills (loosening), and willingness to participate are the elements that are focused on, rather than any magic words, formulas, or rituals that the hypnotist performs.

Kidder (1972), a social psychologist, has presented a sensitive participant-observer study of the hypnotic training experience. Though not a Personal Construct Theorist, her results and interpretations of the experience are congruent with PCT; learning about hypnosis and hypnotic procedures basically involves an attitude change—a reconstruction of the experience.

Having undergone this type of training procedure myself, and, in the process, changing from a relatively "poor" to a relatively "good" hypnotic subject, I agree with Kidder that this involved primarily a reconstruction. The trainers themselves offer alternative constructions—"exercise in imagination," a "cooperative enterprise between subject and operator"; a "pleasurable, relaxing, growth-enhancing experience"—all as alternatives to the construction of hypnosis as having to do with giving up control of self, losing consciousness, or sleep. Participants, then, can adopt a construction or reconstrue the experience in a way that makes sense to them. In this way, individual reactions to the experience are not only allowed (Sheehan et al., 1978), they are encouraged and utilized.

I personally suspended construing the hypnotic experience as having anything to do with who is in control. I was able to begin understanding it as an experience that depended on my ability to imagine creatively and to contribute personally and actively. An example is found in one of the training exercises. One student is the "operator," the other is the "subject." I was the subject in an arm levitation exercise. My operator used the standard patter given to us: "I'll touch your left hand and it will be like I'm attaching a string to it, connected to a sky hook that is slowly raising your arm and hand." My hand and arm did not rise, and I initially found myself using various constructions—"I'm looking ridiculous; I'm still in control; I'm going to stay in control." Suppressing these constructs was a first step. I then said to myself, "This image is not working. What I need to do is to find a better image." I ignored what the operator was saying, but, at the same time, I became cooperative instead of contending. I began to construe a balloon under my hand which was slowly filling with air and in the process pushing my hand up. The actual experience of my hand rising then felt very natural and consistent with the image. Periodically I would change constructions back to *control vs. not having control*. In these instances, I always construed myself as having control. Then I switched back to the balloon image. Basically I felt I had accomplished something rather than giving up control. Overall, I felt very much in control and I went on to find other images and constructions that fostered other hypnotic experiences, such as hand anesthesia and arm rigidity.

Thus the hypnotic experience can be construed in PCT terms. What about its use therapeutically? Several points might be made. First of all, the hypnotic experience—or for that matter, simple relaxation training—might be seen as a procedure that could help ready the client for PCT psychotherapy. Hypnosis is not indexed in Kelly's two volumes. However, in a discussion of criteria for assessing the client's readiness for treatment (1955, pp. 1104ff.), Kelly mentions several parameters such as relaxation, spontaneity, and ability to loosen construction. The hypnotic experience may accelerate the process of attaining readiness, especially if it is construed as a relaxation or loosening procedure.[12]

The hypnotic experience might also be seen as an experiment in changing constructions, particularly if this is how the experience is explained or presented to the client. Related to this, most hypnotists feel that a major aspect of hypnotherapy is to teach the person self-hypnosis. The client takes from treatment a new problem-solving strategy that he or she may find useful in the future and may no longer need a therapist or hypnotist. Kelly has frequently described psychotherapy as a process in which the client ideally "becomes his own psychologist" (1969a, p. 264).

Finally, the Spiegels' (1978) conceptualization of hypnotherapy has some considerable congruency with PCT. These authors separate the trance experience from treatment. That is, having a hypnotic experience is not in itself seen as necessarily therapeutic but rather as a method that can enhance and, perhaps, accelerate therapy. It elicits the cooperation of the patient, helps focus attention, and eliminates extraneous material. More important, they see the hypnotic experience as aiding the person in suspending time constructs and some concrete notions of cause-effect relationships (loosening). Treatment itself, then, focuses on enhancing personal control through the use of self-hypnosis. And "the fundamental conception [of treatment] is the goal of helping the patient to develop a new frame of reference which includes his old and problematic behavior, but in a different perspective" (p. 190). In other words, treatment consists of a reconstruction of experience.

Operant Learning

Like hypnosis, operant learning seems at first glance to be a system diametrically opposed to the principles upon which PCT is based. At the level of philosophical foundations and basic assumptions, this is undoubtedly true. Kelly, as discussed by Holland (1970), could never resist ". . . attacking behaviorism." But at the technical level of finding PCT meaning in operant treatment procedures, these sharp distinctions fade. What, for example, could be more in the experimental spirit of PCT than asking parents to test their construal of their child as "completely incorrigible"? This might be done, first of all, by having them define their term "incorrigible" as specifically as possible (narrowing the range of convenience). Keeping track during the week as to just how often and in what situations the child behaves in ways that are construed as incorrigible could be a second step. Most clinicians who have worked with children and families have, on occasion, seen the effects of such an exercise on parents. It can be a "corrective emotional experience" in and of

---

[12]See Karst and Groutt (1977, pp. 79–80) for a short discussion of mind-altering drugs and their relationship to the loosening process.

itself and not just the first steps to setting up an operant treatment program. For example, the parents may come in the next week and say ''I found that my child's not completely incorrigible at all! He was only insolent and defiant when we tried to discipline him for teasing and bullying his little sister.'' The problem has been redefined and perhaps more easily solved.

In pursuing a possible solution, why not suggest another experiment to the parents? For example, that instead of reacting to their son's incorrigibility in their customary way with anger, criticism, and punishment, they instead attempt to communicate to their son that they understand his feelings toward his sister, and moreover, that he needs to find a different way of expressing them. He might write them down or talk to his parents about them instead of having to bully and tease. If this ''experiment'' doesn't work after a fair trial, another can be proposed.

Asking clients to keep track of their own reactions, an operant technique, can lead to significant change. Such changes may be difficult to explain simply in operant terms. When reconstrued as changes in the construct system they begin to make sense.[13] For example, as part of a school consultation, a teacher complained that one of his students continually disrupted the class each morning as seat work was being distributed. The teacher was a good observer and had, indeed, construed a reliable relationship between certain classroom events and this child's behavior. The teacher was asked, however, to keep a log of his own reactions to this set of circumstances for a two-week period. When the consultant returned, the teacher indicated that the problem had been solved.

What had occurred was not simple. First of all, the suggested procedure had the effect of changing the teacher's construction of events. Before the consultation, the child's behavior was construed as a set of ''upsetting events.'' With the suggestion that further observation was needed, the same events were now reconstrued as ''needing more attention.'' Second, the teacher quickly saw that his own reaction—becoming upset and angry, disrupting normal procedure, and attending to the child's concerns as to how much work had to be done, how to get started, and so on—was probably adding to the problem rather than helping. The teacher indicated that on the third day after consultation he simply made sure that the ''problem child'' was the last to receive the work handed out. A little extra time was devoted to explaining the work, helping the child plan his time, and making sure the child understood how to get the first paper started.

Similarly, a college student whose general anxiety was manifest in many ways was able to stop nail biting after a period of self-observation disclosed that the habitual behavior seemed to occur most frequently when he was reading. He thus anticipated the occurrence of the behavior and arranged conditions that decreased the likelihood of biting his nails. His ability to change in this rather small way also encouraged him to continue working on more major reconstructions in treatment.

Finally, Martin (1975) reports a case of chronic thumb sucking in a four-year-old girl, Mindee, who was helped with an operant program largely designed by the

---

[13]Operant therapists refer to this phenomenon as a ''reactive measurement procedure,'' and operant theory per se accounts for such change only with some clumsiness (see, e.g., Kazdin, 1974).

child's six-year-old sister! Various mechanical means (gloves, Band-Aids, etc.) had been tried with little success. The parents had limited the thumb sucking to bedtime by giving her a blanket and sending her to bed whenever she put a thumb in her mouth. The program, of course, made use of operant learning paraphernalia—charts and rewards taped to the refrigerator door. Of most interest, however, was the fact that when the experiment was about to begin Mindee made the remark, "The blanket makes me do it"; that is, she construed her own behavior as related to holding her security blanket. As the program started, Mindee and her mother intelligently arranged to remove the blanket. Also of interest is the fact that Mindee did not suck her thumb either on the first or the second night of the experiment. She did on the third and fourth nights and on three other nights of the month-long program. Such a quick "cure" is not generally expected using operant techniques. The fact that her parents took advantage of Mindee's spontaneously offered construction of the problem seems to help explain the process.

These brief illustrations are meant to show that certain procedures and techniques taken from operant approaches to behavioral change might be useful when reconstrued by the Personal Construct Therapist. A last example, however, will help emphasize that the therapist should never allow technical matters to interfere with the main therapeutic task of conceptualizing the case and construing the constructions of the patient or client.

Some years ago I was supervising a clinical team of graduate psychology practicum students. We had begun the assessment of a bright, six-year-old boy brought to the clinic by his single mother because she and her son were both concerned about his general unhappiness and his school performance. The child was also enuretic.

The clinic team was rather anxious to experiment with operant techniques. Among other treatment recommendations, the initial plans were to include operant procedures in the attempt to help with the enuresis. During one of the last assessment interviews and prior to implementing the learning program, one of the students was exploring with the child his own perception of the problem with enuresis. The young boy explained that he always went to bed worried that he would not wake up in time to make the bus for school. The child felt that this could have something to do with wetting the bed. (Mother worked nights and had, indeed, failed to get him up on time on a few occasions.) Sensitively, the student-clinician pursued this further by asking the child what he thought might help with this problem. The boy responded that if he had his own alarm clock he might be less worried. Upon hearing this, his mother indicated she thought that was an excellent idea. They stopped on the way home to buy an alarm clock. Although the team worked with this child and mother about six months on several problems, from the day that the child got his alarm clock his bed was dry.

CONCLUSION

When the controlled and behaviorally oriented studies of psychotherapeutic treatment began to flourish in the early 1960s, there was a flush of hope that experimental analysis would ultimately ferret out the real and operative variables in the therapeutic process. For example, Marks and Gelder (1965) argued that the several claims of highly successful treatment of phobias, using different types of therapies, were a direct indication that many variables were active in the process that were not yet identified. They assumed, however, that with diligent and careful study, experimental psychologists would soon separate the wheat from the chaff.

Here at the dawn of the 1980s this has not happened. In fact, as I think George Kelly might have predicted, experimental study itself, rather than isolating the essence of psychotherapy, seems to generate new treatment methods for psychological problems. He has indicated for example (Kelly, 1970, p. 267) that generally he found nothing wrong with the descriptive accounts of operant treatment methods, desensitization, and behavior therapy. However, the descriptions confuse roles and fail to assign the role of "principal investigator" to the person who does the work and does the most changing—the client. This all suggests, at least to me, that we may be in a different stage of intellectual development than we think we are.

A simple, elegant, and true idea can generate, through divergent processes, infinite operational variety. To be concrete, the physical truth that heat applied to objects will cause objects to expand is an accepted, known, and deceptively simple proposition. Think for a moment how many thousands of ways this principle can be applied, tested, and observed. The relationship does not just hold in the laboratory, it is true in real life; it is taken into account when expansion joints are left in a sidewalk, bridge, or highway, or when instruments are designed for space vehicles. Heat can come from many sources, it can be applied to a myriad of objects in diverse ways, and expansion can be observed in many ways; and, the generalization holds, herein lies its power.

Is it too bold to suggest that we are in some ways in an analogous situation in the field of psychotherapeutics? That is, we have a simple, useful, and perhaps even true idea of a singificant, general relationship. This idea has been stated elegantly and inelegantly by different people. Kelly, who has been one of the few to attempt a full elaboration of its implications, chose these terms: "A person's processes are psychologically channelized by the ways in which he anticipates events." In addition to Kelly, several other authors have put the idea into useful form for understanding psychopathology and psychotherapy. One of the more recent psychologists to do this is Raimy (1975), who also has provided a short history of the idea along with a potpourri of treatment techniques. In the conclusion of his book, Raimy points out that this generalization is most useful to the practicing therapist in ". . . that it frees him from the tyranny of technique" (p. 199). I think that is exactly what George Kelly wanted to do, and I hope this paper has illustrated some of that freedom.

REFERENCES

Adams, P. L. Psychotherapy with obsessive children. *International Journal of Child Psycotherapy*, 1973, **2**, 471–491.

Adler, A. *The Problem Child*. New York: Capricorn, 1963.

Adler, A. *Social Interest*. New York: Capricorn, 1964.

Bannister, D., & Salmon, P. A personal construct theory view of education. *New York University of Education Quarterly*, 1975, **6**, 28–31.

Beck, A. T. *Cognitive Therapy and the Emotional Disorders*. New York: International Universities Press, 1976.

Bonarius, J. C. J. Fixed role therapy: A double paradox. *British Journal of Medical Psychology*, 1970, **43**, 213–219.

Buchwald, A. M., & Young, R. D. Some comments on the foundations of behavior therapy. In C. M. Franks (Ed.), *Behavior Therapy: Appraisal and Status*. New York: McGraw-Hill, 1969.

Cartwright, F. F. *Disease and History*. New York: Thomas Y. Crowell, 1972.

Chambless, D. L., & Goldstein, A. J. Behavioral psychotherapy. In R. J. Corsini (Ed.), *Current Psychotherapies* (2nd ed.). Itasca, IL: Peacock, 1979.

Dimond, R. E., & Havens, R. A. Restructuring psychotherapy: Toward a prescriptive eclecticism. *Professional Psychology*, 1975, **6**, 193–200.

Dimond, R. E., Havens, R. A., & Jones, A. C. A conceptual framework for the practice of prescriptive eclecticism in psychotherapy. *American Psychologist*, 1978, **33**, 239–248.

Ellis, A. *Reason and Emotion in Psychotherapy*. New York: Lyle Stuart, 1962.

Eron, L. D., & Callahan, R. *The Relation of Theory to Practice in Psychotherapy*. Chicago: Aldine, 1969.

Frank, J. D. *Persuasion and Healing*. Baltimore: Johns Hopkins University Press, 1973.

Frankel, F. H. Hypnosis and related behavior. *American Journal of Psychiatry*, 1978, **135**, 664–668.

Ginott, H. G. *Between Parent and Child*. New York: Macmillan, 1965.

Gordon, T. *Parent Effectiveness Training*. New York: Peter H. Wyden, 1970.

Grinder, J., & Bandler, R. *The Structure of Magic I*. Palo Alto, CA: Science of Behavior Books, 1976.

Haley, J. *Advanced Techniques of Hypnosis and Therapy*. New York: Grune and Stratton, 1967.

Harter, S. A cognitive-developmental approach to children's expression of conflicting feelings and a technique to facilitate such expressions in play therapy. *Journal of Consulting and Clinical Psychology*, 1977, **45**, 417–432.

Holland, R. George Kelly: Constructive innocent and reluctant existentialist. In D. Bannister (Ed.), *Perspectives in Personal Construct Theory*. London: Academic, 1970.

Hooker, R. Sex comes to thief island. *Playboy*, 1971, **18**, (Dec.), 131ff.

Horvath, P. University of Ottawa, Psychological Services. Personal communication, Dec. 1, 1977.

Horvath, P. *The effects of demand characteristics referring to the self in covert treatments*. Unpublished doctoral dissertation, University of Ottawa, 1979.

Jung, C. G. The aims of psychotherapy. In H. J. Vetter & B. D. Smith (Eds.), *Personality Theory: A Source Book*. New York: Appleton-Century-Crofts, 1971.

Karst, T. O. Technique-free and non-prescriptive theories of psychotherapy. In F. Fransella (Ed.), *Personal Construct Psychology: 1977*. London: Academic, 1978, 250–251. (Abstract)

Karst, T. O. & Groutt, J. W. Inside mystical heads: Shared and personal constructs in a commune with some implications for a personal construct theory social psychology. In D. Bannister (Ed.), *New Perspectives in Personal Construct Theory*. London: Academic, 1977.

Karst, T. O., & Trexler, L. D. Initial study using fixed-role and rational-emotive therapy in treating public-speaking anxiety. *Journal of Consulting and Clinical Psychology*, 1970, **34**, 360−366.

Kazdin, A. E. Self-monitoring and behavior change. In M. J. Mahoney & C. E. Thoresen (Eds.), *Self-Control: Power to the Person*. Monterey, CA: Brooks-Cole, 1974.

Kelly, G. A. *The Psychology of Personal Constructs:* Vols. 1 and 2. New York: Norton, 1955.

Kelly, G. A. Personal construct theory and the psychotherapeutic interiew. In B. Maher (Ed.), *Clinical Psychology and Personality*. New York: Wiley, 1969a.

Kelly, G. A. The psychotherapeutic relationship. In B. Maher (Ed.), *Clinical Psychology and Personality,* New York: Wiley, 1969b.

Kelly, G. A. The autobiography of a theory. In B. Maher (Ed.), *Clinical Psychology and Personality*. New York: Wiley, 1969c.

Kelly, G. A. Behavior is an experiment. In D. Bannister (Ed.), *Perspectives in Personal Construct Theory*. London: Academic, 1970.

Kennedy, H. Problems in reconstruction in child analysis. *The Psycholanalytic Study of the Child,* 1971, **26**, 386−402.

Kidder, L. H. On becoming hypnotized: How skeptics become convinced: A case of attitude change? *Journal of Abnormal Psychology,* 1972, **80**, 317−322.

Landfield, A. W., & Leitner, L. M. *Personal construct psychology*. This volume.

Marks, I., & Gelder, M. A controlled retrospective study of behavior therapy in phobic patients. *British Journal of Psychiatry,* 1965, **111**, 561−574.

Martin, D. A six-year-old "Behaviorist" solves her sibling's chronic thumbsucking problem. *Corrective and Social Psychiatry and Journal of Behavior Technology Methods and Therapy,* 1975, **21**, 19−21.

Mosher, D. L. Are neurotics victims of their emotions? *Etc.: A Review of General Semantics,* 1966, **23**, 225−234.

Paine, C. *Reconstruction and personality change within personal construct theory*. Unpublished doctoral dissertation, University of Missouri, 1970.

Pepinsky, H. B., & Karst, T. O. Convergence: A phenomenon in counseling and psychotherapy. *American Psychologist,* 1964, **19**, 333−339.

Piotrowski, Z. A. Basic system of all sciences. In H. J. Vetter & B. D. Smith (Eds.), *Personality Theory: A Source Book*. New York: Appleton-Century-Crofts, 1971.

Raimy, V. *Misunderstandings of the Self*. San Francisco: Jossey-Bass, 1975.

Rees, K. The child's understanding of his past: Cognitive factors in reconstruction with children. *The Psychoanalytic Study of the Child,* 1978, **33**, 237−259.

Rogers, C. R. The necessary and sufficient conditions of therapeutic personality change. *Journal of Consulting Psychology,* 1957, **21**, 95−103.

Rotter, J. B. Some implications of a social learning theory for the practice of psychotherapy. In D. J. Levis (Ed.), *Learning Approaches to Therapeutic Behavior Change*. Chicago: Aldine, 1970.

Rychlak, J. F. *Introduction to Personality and Psychotherapy*. Boston: Houghton Mifflin, 1973.

Schaefer, C. E., & Millman, H. L. *Therapies for Children*. San Francisco: Jossey-Bass, 1978.

Sheehan, P. W., McConkey, K. M., & Cross, D. Experimental analysis of hypnosis: Some new observations on hypnotic phenomena. *Journal of Abnormal Psychology,* 1978, **87,** 570–573.

Spiegel, H., & Spiegel, D. *Trance and Treatment*. New York: Basic Books, 1978.

Sullivan, H. S. *Conceptions of Modern Psychiatry*. New York: Norton, 1940.

Trexler, L. D., & Karst, T. O. Rational-emotive therapy, placebo, and no-treatment effects on public-speaking anxiety. *Journal of Abnormal Psychology,* 1972, **79,** 60–67.

Vetter, H. J., & Smith, B. D. (Eds.), *Personality Theory: A Source Book*. New York: Appleton-Century-Crofts, 1971.

CHAPTER 10

Teaching Personal Construct Psychotherapy

Fay Fransella

If all behavior is an experiment, as George Kelly saw it to be, then what 12 of us undertook in October 1978 was a vast experiment indeed. We sought to find out how, or rather if, it might be possible to show to experienced professional clinicians what the Psychology of Personal Constructs means when it is applied to helping others solve problems. Thus, two of us who profess to have some clear and some misty ideas about what Kelly is driving at, met up with 10 others for three hours once a week for 22 weeks. This chapter is the story of these meetings. It appears in this volume because A. W. Landfield thought some readers might find the outline of hopes, fears, and achievements of use when about to undertake similar ventures.

BACKGROUND

Ever since I first came across Kelly's psychology in 1963, during my postgraduate clinical training, I have become increasingly engrossed with the unrestrictive nature of its philosophy, the enormous complexity of its theoretical statements, its fantastic range of convenience—in fact, with "it." I now find that I live "it" to the point that it is a mental effort to think in other ways. Without the constant need to teach the theories and philosophies of other psychologists, my struggle against having a solely Kellian view of life would have failed.

This constant threat of leading a "blinkered" life may, in part, have been responsible for the resistance I put up to pressures for teaching in a new area—that of Personal Construct Psychotherapy. I had become aware of an increasing demand for something beyond lectures and general tutorials on the subject. People were beginning to say that theoretical knowledge was fine, but also to ask where they could gain practial experience, so that they could use the approach in their clinical work. For a time I showed hostility and persuaded myself either that the need was not there, or else that it was not my job to meet it—I did not have the time, for one thing. But eventually, the evidence could not be ignored. So I pondered the predicament. Assuming the need of others was truly present and not a figment of my imagination, then it seemed that I could well be a person to meet this need—both my job and my location in central London made me an obvious choice—and one can always find time.

But it still was not possible to go ahead with an easy mind. For I came face to face with another problem. How could I teach something for which I had had no teaching myself? In any case, I did not know enough about Kelly's approach to psychotherapy to make me a competent teacher. This latter argument grew stronger and stronger but I could no longer ignore the fact that others teach psychotherapy without specific training—psychiatrists, for instance, not to mention Kelly himself. And there was certainly something I could pass on to others since I presumably knew more than the people asking for assistance.

But even now I was not totally convinced. All very well to talk about knowing something that can be taught to others, but what exactly was it that I could impart? I became very concrete in my personal arguments. I tried to specify the minute details of what I thought I really knew.

Constricting the problem to the analysis of specific details suddenly enabled me to verbalize an enormous threat hanging over my head (or over my core role structure). I have no real problem introducing graduate clinical psychology students to the mysteries of Kelly as applied to therapy—I know full well that I have more experience in therapy than they have. Also, the problems encountered in group supervision of students is well described in books such as *Dialogues for Therapists* by Rioch and colleagues (1976). But what sort of people were these who were now pressing for enlightenment? They were people who were already immersed in the whole therapeutic endeavor. They would come to a course with ready-made, alternative sets of constructs. More important still, they could well be much more experienced therapists than myself—and could well be better therapists than myself! Thus my commitment to offering an introductory course in Personal Construct Psychotherapy would mean risking real exposure, risking real core role clobbering. No wonder, looking back on it all now, that I vacillated!

This autobiographical preamble has a purpose. First, it is possible that others are facing personal threats when contemplating extending Personal Construct Psychotherapy teaching beyond the relatively safe context of graduate students to experienced therapists. But, more important, the reflexivity of the framework makes it important to know something of the construing of the teacher to give an insight into what happens when teacher and students face each other at that first encounter. For, certainly in this first course, we were all learners. And we were all facing personal threats.

CRITERIA FOR GROUP MEMBERSHIP

One of the constraints on the course was that participants could have no involvement with clients at the hospital where it was to be held. This meant that all participants would need to have ongoing therapeutic commitments elsewhere. This was thought necessary since their experience with these clients would form the basis of therapeutic discussions. Even this seemingly simple criterion met with problems. It was forcibly argued by one mature student who had just graduated that it seemed impossible to get any psychotherapeutic training unless one were involved in psychotherapy oneself, and one could not do psychotherapy without training. This seemed a valid argument, so there was one exception to the criterion that members should have some ongoing "helping" commitment.

To plunge into Kelly's Volume 2 without a knowledge of Volume 1 seemed logically impossible. A second criterion therefore was that each member should have some knowledge of construct theory and its language. There were no exceptions to this, but differences in level of knowledge proved to be a major problem.

Knowledge without personal meaning is sterile. Therefore a third criterion was that all should find Kelly's approach both exciting and interesting. There is no doubt that this criterion was most fully met.

Because 10 seemed a maximum number for a group of this type, it was important that those selected should be prepared, as far as they were able, to commit themselves to attending regularly, one afternoon a week for 20 weeks, with a 2-week break after the first 10 weeks. This, therefore, became the fourth criterion for membership.

THE APPLICANTS

My first inclination was to offer the course to clinical psychologists only. The advertising in 1977 was therefore limited to that group. Although there had always appeared to be a demand from clinical psychologists for more psychotherapeutic training, as it turned out there were not enough applicants to form a group. I breathed a mental sigh of relief and shelved my "threats" for another year. At the end of that time, I took them off the shelf, dusted them down, and placed advertisements in several journals of the "helping" professions—counseling, occupational therapy, and speech therapy, as well as clinical psychology. There were now 20 applicants to whom the selection criteria had to be applied.

THE GROUP

My former training as an occupational therapist has meant I am often called on to talk about Kelly's psychology to nonpsychologists. It could have been this that led to my original awareness of the need for some organized course on its psychotherapeutic applications. Whether this is the reason or not, the group members formed a motley crew in terms of background experience.

Those finally selected were four clinical psychologists (one working as a student counselor), two counselors, one social worker who was working toward a degree in psychology (previously an engineer), one speech therapist, one probation officer, and one newly graduated student. These, together with myself, made 11. But, in view of my qualms about the possibility of illness or unavoidable absence, plus a growing belief in having more than one group leader to show different slants on the same problem, I invited a clinical psychologist to join me as co-leader. Any success the group achieved was as much because of the skill and personal involvement of my co-leader, Maureen Sheehan, as anything else. The total group consisted of 12 people, 8 women and 4 men.

At the first meeting, the postgraduate student who had successfully argued her case for inclusion said that she had been accepted for a group psychotherapy course and so would not be taking up her place with us. So we were effectively 11 people from the start.

THE COURSE CONTENT

It had been difficult enough to come to the decision to form a group to meet one afternoon a week for 20 weeks, to have 10 participants and two leaders, and to meet on a certain day; to decide on the content in advance seemed—and proved to be—impossible. Having no personal difficulty in tolerating a fairly high degree of looseness in my construing, I was happy to operate on the basis of a few superordinate constructions. It was a blessing that Maureen was willing to go along with this idea. We agreed to determine the content session by session, within the general rules that each session should have some academic and some practical activity; that the course was definitely an introduction and not a training in psychotherapy; and that learning should come mainly from "doing" and not from teaching. These criteria were discussed with the group at the first meeting, but the members were far too apprehensive and themselves suffering a variety of personal threats to want to disagree with anything at that stage.

WHAT ACTUALLY HAPPENED

Many important questions arose concerning the present and, it is to be hoped, subsequent courses, during the group meetings. These, and any other relevant matters, will be discussed as and when they arose during the course. What follows is a summary of what took place, taken from the notes made after each session, and quotes from the "thoughts" on the course each person was asked to write after it had ended.

SESSION 1. We followed the usual format of allowing all participants to introduce themselves to each other and to outline their knowledge of and interest in Kelly's work, and their psychotherapeutic/counseling experience.

In order not to force the pace of "getting to know you," each person wrote a self-characterization (as described in Kelly, 1955, pp. 322–326) and then discussed these as the first step in understanding the client. With agreement that no one would be required to discuss personal details, we launched into a general discussion of the types of information we saw emerging. As is so often the case, several people found that something personally meaningful and interesting had emerged as well.

Apart from learning, in this first session, of personal threats and anxieties that were almost tangible, it became apparent that the two and a half hours allotted for the meeting were a grossly inadequate amount of time. This highlighted the need for "homework." Volunteers were asked to do some reading and to prepare notes for discussion at the second session. Since we had launched into self-characterization, Tony and Margaret volunteered to read Chapter 7 in Volume 1 of Kelly's work (pp. 319–359) on the types of information to be gained from the analysis of the self-characterization. I also suggested that it might be interesting to study ourselves as a group in relation to the stages Kelly describes as occurring during group psycho-therapy. So Peter and Sheila agreed to read that section in Volume 2 (pp. 1155–1178).

Over and above the anxieties, there were clear feelings of excitement and expec-tation at this first meeting. During the tea break in the middle of the afternoon (we made tea for ourselves in the same room), the level of general conversation was high.

SESSION 2. Margaret and Tony had contacted each other during the week to discuss the best way to organize their presentation on self-characterization analysis. They agreed to each present written notes on the sections they had read and to have copies of these to distribute to the others. This started a pattern that was adhered to throughout the course. Several participants commented on this in their "thoughts." One said "the thoroughness of people's presentations of the material and the con-vention which developed for presenting typed sheets was truly remarkable—a mea-sure of people's commitment to the course." Another remarked, "I look back at my collection of summaries with pleasure, because I know that it is easily accessible and that I can at any time recall some of our better group discussions and some of the issues I never thought about before."

Margaret also brought along a self-characterization she had obtained from a client. Time was short (a horribly recurrent theme), so she agreed to leave the discussion of this to another occasion. Margaret also mentioned her anxiety about the group. She had taken on the "homework" as a challenge, but during the week had felt so anxious that she thought she might have to opt out. The group as a whole gave clear evidence of its support for her.

Sonia and Peter chose to delay discussion on stages in group process until later because "it is too early, better to look at the group objectively during its progress." We then went on to practical work, which was the traditional elicitation of con-structs, working in pairs. For homework, Mary and Sheila agreed to take sections on the nature of constructs in Volume 1 (pp. 105–183), and Tony and Margaret to follow up their work on the analysis of self-characterizations by both reading pages 984–993 on the subject in Volume 2.

SESSION 3. Maureen led this afternoon and reports finding the academic part of the session hard going. Over tea Mike commented that it was "all very academic" and asked when the end of the term was and whether it was going on like this for the whole 6 months. It was now clear that the participants had not realized just how much theory there was to learn before it could be applied, particularly those who had more enthusiasm for, than knowledge of, Kellian language.

The practical work consisted of laddering constructs (Hinkle, 1965) elicited the previous week, working in the same pairs. Penelope wanted to read Hinkle's thesis, particularly the part to do with laddering, for homework; Arthur and Peter offered to read Landfield's pyramid, or "laddering down," technique (1971).

SESSION 4. We now clearly had to balance between burdening the group with too much academic work, while preventing it from evolving into a watered-down encounter group—which many of the participants would have welcomed!

Maureen started the general discussion by asking whether anyone had tried laddering during the week. Several people had and a very lively spontaneous discussion occurred. Mike did not join in. Margaret reported how a client had gotten angry with her, torn up the pieces of paper, and said he was not going to play games any longer. She told him to go away and think out what he wanted from therapy. We then discussed how a client-centered therapist (Margaret's style) would not be accustomed to provoking people in that way and so could well be disconcerted by it. This led, for the first time, to a brief discussion on different therapeutic styles and how these lead to different client behaviors.

Penelope gave a very thoughtful account of Hinkle's ideas, but it was clear that several of the group were not understanding her. Her already good grasp of construct theory enabled her to see the full significance of Hinkle's ideas and she was clearly very excited by them. It was at this point that I realized how important it was going to be to keep enough control of the discussions so that no one felt too ignorant to participate, while at the same time giving the group the freedom to develop its own ideas in its own way. Peter followed Penelope with a very simple and good account of the pyramid technique.

We then watched a videotape of me laddering a client. We again ran short of time and had very little left for discussion. (This was the first occasion on which we did not finish at the appointed time.) One issue raised was the skill needed to decide whether or not to allow a long silence to continue; another concerned the difficulty of suppressing old ways of thinking—for instance, Sonia's background of Kleinian analysis meant she kept wanting to interpret, to discuss the client's sex life, and so forth. It was very apparent that the participants were all impatient to get on to discussions of more practical therapeutic issues. So we agreed that we had covered enough of the theory to enable us to take specific aspects of it and relate these to client needs.

The only area that had not been covered at all was Kelly's grid technique, and homework therefore consisted of Sonia and Sheila reading the first chapter of the *Manual for Repertory Grid Technique* (Fransella & Bannister 1977).

By now, Maureen and I were both concerned about Mike, who continued to be very quiet. He was the only one who had not volunteered to do any homework reading. At the end of this session he came up to me and commented that I looked very tired—that my eyes were tired (I had been suffering from an infected throat for a week or so). It was as if he wanted to make contact with Maureen and me, but did not want to interact with the others.

SESSION 5. We were already getting behind with our discussions of what people had prepared the week before, or had wanted to cover. So we decided to try to catch up. Both Margaret and Tony had brought along self-characterizations of clients that they wished to discuss, and we agreed to do this now. Arthur said he felt unwell but had forced himself to come along, as otherwise he would "lose touch and might miss something."

Margaret took over the session by asking each of us to discuss aspects of her client's self-characterization in terms of the criteria previously detailed by Tony in written notes (Session 2). All thought this a good idea and I felt it would be worth letting the group "have its head" for this session. When we were happily engrossed in our paired discussions of the self-characterization, Mike came in and, since we were an odd number, had no partner. Since Tony and Margaret were in charge of the group at that point, neither Maureen nor I made a move to welcome Mike—nor did the others. He therefore did not know what was happening and just sat reading the copy of the client's self-characterization which someone gave him.

The ensuing discussion was very lively and took all the time up to the tea break. There was then a discussion of whether the time should be increased from two and a half to three hours. All thought that it should. The group by this time was very well integrated—except for Mike. They were full of ideas. Peter wanted the group to discuss his personal self-characterization sometime, and he and Sonia wanted to book time to discuss Kelly's ideas about groups.

After tea, I read a self-characterization of the client whose laddering they had seen on the videotape. This raised a number of useful points. All wanted more video sessions and were outspoken in their concern over not having time to discuss all the questions raised by the previous session. But no concrete suggestions were made of how to deal with the problem of lack of time.

After five meetings, enthusiasm had, if anything, increased. Arthur may have felt ill when he arrived, but by the time he left he commented that he hardly felt ill at all. Margaret said how much she looked forward to the group each week. In her "thoughts" she calls it "a weekly high" and continues, "My main reaction to the six months was every Monday afternoon had been, and will continue to be, a major contribution to my life." I made the note at the end of this session: "Maureen and I feel all is going too well—where are the snags?"

SESSION 6. No snags apparent; just a group getting well into its stride with members beginning to strike the occasional spark off one another. The sparks were usually occasioned by one or another of the group threats coming into focus. For example, in a discussion on aggression, one member demonstrated a very clear knowledge about what it meant for Kelly, thus apparently making some others feel ignorant. This lead to some verbal aggression (in the lay sense) indicated by such remarks as "Well, clearly I just haven't understood. . . ." with a quiet glare at the accused.

But a new area of threat emerged in this session during a discussion of the first chapter in the grid manual. The threat was related to anxiety over statistics in particular, and measurement in general. There were some members who had a real liking for grids, others who had never confronted one and just felt ignorant, and a few who had a nearly phobic reaction to them.

After some 15 minutes of very detailed discussion among the "informed," Margaret asked in a despairing voice if it were possible to be a construct therapist and not use a grid. She also pointed out that the group seemed to be very much divided into the "scientists" and "nonscientists." Tony, one of the grid-lovers, was particularly supportive toward her. He dwelt on this aspect of the course in part of his "thoughts." He wrote:

It has always been something of a paradox to me that in psychology and closely related fields, a branch of the social sciences which relies on empiricism as one of its most important foundation stones, that amongst students there is a widespread phobic reaction to anything that vaguely smacks of statistics. . . .

He saw this as a major hurdle for course members and continued:

They began to enthuse over this new and refreshing approach to their work, when experimenting with self-characterizations, laddering, etc. However, some seemed to be almost at the point of giving up in despair when the strange things called grids eventually reared their threatening heads. I share your concern that the construct theory approach should be taught in such a way as to stress that there is a lot more to Kelly than the grid, but feel that its relatively late introduction to the course resulted in a development of a kind of awesome mystique surrounding this ominous unknown quantity, often alluded to or seen lurking in the shadows, the nature of the beast not fully being appreciated until it finally makes its appearance, almost like the shark in *Jaws*.

By now, members were often carrying out tasks with clients which were not part of homework. Husbands were being laddered and clients being confronted with requests for self-characterizations. Arthur brought a small grid to this session which he had carried out with his stepdaughter and which he was eager to discuss.

At the end, when loose ends were being tidied up, Margaret came back to the threat of measurement, commenting that she had perhaps "boggled" at any suggestion of figures and formulas, but would no doubt come to terms with them. "It doesn't alter my feelings about this group—I wouldn't miss a session for anything." She had raised again the issue of the wide disparity of basic knowledge and experience within the group.

Homework was the same for everyone this week—reading Kelly's essay on the psychotherapeutic relationship (1969a).

SESSION 7. Margaret had done a grid with a client! She had even done an eyeball analysis and grouped the constructs into clusters. I thought this Kellian aggression should be given every encouragement, so, after calling her an "intuitive statistician," I offered to have the grid analyzed by computer for her. Her reaction to this was mentioned in her "thoughts." She said, "I was enormously glad, for example, when Fay did a grid run for me to allow me to reconstrue my fear of using them—I'm not 'cured,' but my anxiety about it is much less acute and the awareness that my anxieties were picked up gently at the opportune moment and given back to me for reappraisal was marvelous."

Tony discussed his paper on self-characterizations until tea time. It was very clear that nearly all members were using some form of this assessment in their work, and were finding it very useful.

For the practical session I offered to do some "covert laddering" with anyone who would like to volunteer a personal difficulty. By this term I mean laddering in conversation rather than in the standard manner. Sheila offered the fact that she gets very anxious and fussed when buying Christmas presents. It went something like this: "Yes, I get much more anxious than most people when buying only one present—it is important that the recipient like it—they may think I don't care if they don't like it—they will think I'm unreliable."

It was clear at this point that she was gaining some insight into her problem, in the sense of being aware of an aspect of her construing which was new to her. I therefore stopped any further exploration and instead talked with her about the logic of her construing. Did she *really* think that if someone did not like her present they would think her unreliable? She thought probably not. She said she would like to meditate about it and would tell the group whether it had made any difference to her at a future meeting. Maureen now calls this procedure "instant solutions to problems."

It was then suggested that someone else might like to do a similar interview. Mike asked if a phobia was any good. Although I realized it was a difficult subject, I thought it was worth someone seeing what they could do with it. There then followed a very long pause—unknown in this group before; no one volunteered to be interviewer. I asked if the group would like to look at itself and find out the reason for this reluctance. Arthur thought the problem was the prospect of being judged by the others. Eventually Penelope offered to be interviewer, but made little progress in increasing our understanding of Mike's phobia. Not surprising with a difficult topic and all sorts of anxieties floating around the group.

On the positive side, the two interviews enabled me to make the point that they all wanted to discuss "the problem" rather than the style of interviewing. It was evident that this style was different for them all. Arthur commented that the group was feeling very threatened, as shown by the fact that it had never discussed itself. Sonia thought everyone was still being very competitive and that this was something that could be looked at when she and Peter discussed Kelly's views on the group process.

At the end of this session—again we had gone into extra time—Sonia remarked that there was a lot of "unfinished business" around, especially with Sheila and her present-buying problem. We worked on this one for a few minutes and raised an interesting point. For Maureen and me, Sheila had some "personal homework" to take away with her; but for Sonia the problem remained as one in which the only way to solve it was between the therapist and client. All seemed to find it unusual to contemplate a psychotherapy which places its main emphasis on what goes on *between* sessions, instead of within those golden 50 minutes when therapist and client have their weekly meetings.

The official homework was for Arthur and Sheila to read and report on the first two chapters in Kelly's Volume 2. All members were also asked to read Kelly's paper on the psychotherapeutic interview (1969b).

SESSION 8. Arthur and Sheila presented their notes and views on the role of the psychotherapist and the psychotherapeutic approach.

In spite of the anxiety raised last week by the interviewing, we chose role playing for the practical part of the session. Peter was the client with the problem of whether to allow his 19-year-old daughter to bring boyfriends home to sleep at the weekend, and Mary was the therapist. This worked well and the group disquiet seemed to be greatly reduced.

Because of the build-up of homework that had not been discussed, it was agreed that people should try to catch up on the reading they had not managed to do so far.

SESSION 9. Free from the constraints imposed by the presentation of some reading task, the session was started by Peter. He asked us to pair up and to do a ''Landfield'' pyramid. First though, he asked someone to come and be a client so that the procedure could be demonstrated publically. Tony volunteered and all went very well. Everyone was then free to choose the person with whom he or she would like to work, with Tony's instructions that ''Fay and Maureen are to be regarded as part of the group.'' With Mary absent, there was an even number. Tony chose me to ''pyramid'' him. Everyone seemed to enjoy this exercise and to find it personally illuminating.

The group then decided to move on to enactment. Margaret and Arthur volunteered. Margaret went out of the room and Arthur told us how he had been to a party and, on the way home in his car, knocked over a child. The enactment concerned his going to the boy's home and telling the parents that their son was in the hospital. What followed was most interesting and both role-played their parts very well indeed. The discussion afterward centered mainly on why it was that Arthur had refused to tell Margaret whether or not it was actually he who had knocked the boy down.

Peter then asked for volunteers to repeat the enactment. Silence of fairly deafening proportions followed. It must be remembered that this was the first time that the group had done anything so personally involving. I decided that it was important to show that I regarded myself as a member of the group, and so said I would play the role of the car driver. Mike said he would be the father. He took me by surprise by attacking me as driver rather than showing concern over the fate of his son. Both enactments were particularly useful in producing further group cohesiveness and demonstrating how personally involved the role players become.

This then led to a discussion about the group itself. Peter asked if we (the role players) had felt supported by the group during the enactment and in the discussion afterward. The general feeling was ''no'' and that the group was still defensive. It was pointed out, for instance, that no one had asked Margaret about her feelings when she described how she had had a row with her son before the accident and had even ''wished he were dead earlier in the day.'' Mike followed this by expressing his disappointment with the group because it was not looking at personal problems.

This focused on an underlying and important conflict in conducting a group such as this. To what extent should it be allowed to become a therapy group and to what extent should it be directed to providing an academic-cum-group-learning situation?

We worked through this and concluded that, as therapists, we were there to learn about a new way of viewing clients and of trying to help them. It was therefore more important to discuss problems in the context of learning to use professional constructs, as Kelly calls them, rather than to get involved in sorting out personal problems and so "wasting valuable group learning time," as one member put it.

Peter then mentioned his realization of the importance of support that Kelly emphasized. He felt the group had not yet moved on to the second stage of group process after 9 weeks. Sonia commented on my "openness" in letting people see myself engaged in therapy on a videotape and felt others should be more open as well. The lack of movement in group process was considered to be partly, if not wholly, the result of the dual role each is playing—that of a therapist learning new skills, and also as a member of a group risking psychological exposure. It was the most personally involving session we had had.

After the group closed, Sonia asked me if she could come to me for therapy supervision when the group meeting had finished. Even though she was finding it very difficult indeed to take off her Kleinian lenses, she found something very important in Kelly's approach and knew she wanted to adopt it in its entirety. The approach made her feel much more "professional" in that she felt it gave the therapist the total responsibility for what happened. There was no massive structure of doctrine to fall back on, only one's own ability to understand how another is viewing things. Needless to say, the thought of supervising such a very experienced therapist rekindled my earlier threats and so I promised her I would think about it!

Homework was for Arthur and Tony to report the following week on "the clinician's conceptualization of his role" and "basic approaches to the revision of constructs" from Volume 2 (pp. 589–595).

Session 10. Arthur and Tony presented their pieces and this led to a discussion about therapists' abilities to suspend their own value system, particularly centering on the notion that "acceptance" does not necessarily imply "approval." We then got on to some of the "unfinished business" of the previous week—the conflict between group learning as therapists, and dealing with personal problems. Peter said that, in his experience, encounter groups are never successful with colleagues. This was useful as it gave us the opportunity to feel we were not alone in finding this a problem. I emphasized the difficulty a person experiences in being involved in a situation and, at the same time, subsuming that experience with a set of superordinate constructions—probably an impossible task.

During the discussion about the content of the next 10 weeks after the Christmas break, there arose a request for an extra session before Christmas, since "there was still so much to be done." Maureen and I fully agreed about the enormous amount still to be gotten through and so an extra session was decided on.

For the practical part of this session we all wrote our own obituaries, occurring at the end of our natural lives. This was designed to point to paths along which we each saw ourselves as moving, tasks already accomplished, and so forth. One person noted in "thoughts" that this was "a splendid exercise."

Homework was for Sheila to report on the section in Volume 2 on "therapist's skills'' (pp. 595—605), and they were all to read Kelly's paper, "Psychotherapy and the Nature of Man'' (1969c).

SESSION 11. This extra session consisted of Sheila leading a discussion on therapeutic skills, and the playing of an audio tape in which Kelly talks about his views on the nature of man. I had thought that the group might like to follow up the obituary "at the end of a natural life'' with one on "if I die tonight.'' But, whether it was the Christmas spirit, or good old-fashioned threat, there was almost unanimous agreement that this was *not* a good idea.

We ended the session with a discussion of what each individual would most like to cover in the meetings after Christmas. These were a) individual case presentations, b) more video playbacks, c) discussion on exactly what validation means, d) discussion on emotions and the part they play in Kellian therapy, e) the use of implications grids in therapy, f) more practical exercises; and g) discussion of problems in the theory.

Penelope decided to read Mildred McCoy's chapter (Bannister, 1977) on emotion for homework.

SESSION 12. I was not present at this meeting, but Maureen reports that it went very well, although all were concerned by the absence of Sonia, who had had an accident on a pedestrian crossing; she was not hurt but was resting.

Maureen played them more of my psychotherapy video tape, giving an example of the role of threat in therapy and its effects on a client. They had the freedom to discuss this in my absence.

For homework, Peter and Mary read the sections in Volume 2 on transference (pp. 662—686). Margaret and Tony prepared the introduction to Disorders of Construction and the sections on dilation (pp. 830—847) and tightening and loosening (pp. 847—868) for discussion 2 weeks hence.

SESSION 13. At the start of the group meeting I read a letter I had had from Mike, saying he no longer wished to attend the group meetings. He disliked the over-lengthy discussions of theory and felt there was too little place for personal involvement. The tone of the letter was seen by the group to be hostile in its demand for more leadership from Maureen and me, and in the implication that other members should have wanted things differently, as he did.

This had a profound effect on the group. For the first time, members talked at length of their own anxieties, aggressive feelings, and threats. These largely focused on issues already partially raised. Two were threatened by others who knew more of the theory than they did; these theoreticians, in turn, felt threatened by those with more therapeutic experience than they themselves had. Some mentioned feelings of anger and annoyance last term at not being able to express these concerns.

Much of the annoyance seemed to focus on the lengthy discussions of prepared work. Mike had pointed out that most people had made comprehensive notes, distributed copies of these to each person, and then proceeded to read these out. Many referred to this session and to the teaching style in their "thoughts.'' The following extracts from these may help clarify their concerns.

The style of teaching . . . has been very effective. At first I found myself fairly frightened, feeling unread, unacademic, maybe out of my depth. I THINK this was partly a personal response, and partly the effect of experiencing the client role and the effort involved in using Kellian spectacles to make an attempt to use other people's construct systems. Mike, I think it was, expressed his dissatisfaction with the "boring" recital of seminar papers by the "non-experts" and the lack of formal leadership in the teaching approach. His verbalizing of that feeling in his letter of withdrawal from the group pinpointed a change for me and I became very aware of how much I had already learned from the struggle to put across difficult ideas in terms others, varied in their talents, might construe similarly. These struggles could not have occurred if the teaching had been central from the "experts"—Fay and Maureen. My use of quotation marks around "experts" is because I feel that in Personal Construct Theory experts don't really exist, only the more or less learned members of group. "Man-the-scientist" can't learn by rote, can he?

I think that the "homework" system went a long way to meeting people's need to tackle the subject on differing levels. When I started the course nothing was further from my mind than reading Kelly. . . . In fact, when I got down to reading and studying, this turned out to be one of the most positive aspects of the course for me. For some time I had been flicking through psychology books, perhaps starting them but never really getting into anything. Suddenly I was reading, I was absorbed, and things were opening up which is very exciting. Coupled with this was a very strong regret of having shelved Personal Construct Theory for three years when all the time I had known it was an approach that suited me. . . . I did find Kelly quite frustrating to read at times mainly because sections frequently didn't contain what their subtitles lead one to expect. I tended to go over and over the text looking for a connection with the title and sometimes I think came up with quite bizarre connections. It was invariably much simpler than I had thought. Now that I know his style a bit better I find him easier to read. In fact, looking at Vol. 1 in the last week or so it seems much smaller!

The necessity to "learn the language" of Kelly seems of prime importance, bearing in mind that most people coming to this work will need to "unlearn" much of their previous perspectives in counseling/therapy. The seminar method which we have been using seems most appropriate and the amount of time spent during the two terms is about right. I liked the "student presentation" method—it left the tutors free to comment over and above the student work—which was often considerable—and also gave us students the task of really grappling with Kelly in the raw. Hard work but worth it.

So much for some of the comments written "after the event." Maureen and I are in no doubt that it is impossible to talk about Personal Construct Psychotherapy without a very clear idea of the theory. I am glad to say that there seems to be no doubt in the minds of nearly all the participants that such is the case. Where a fault may lie is in our not paying enough attention to their differing expectations and their coming to terms with that fact.

This letter of Mike's worked as a catalyst in enabling others to express their own feelings and was therefore extremely useful, although it was unfortunate that it took the departure of a group member to achieve it. As this discussion had taken up a fair proportion of the session, we turned to the presentations of views on transference occurring between the client and myself seen on the video tape. The session finished with a case report given by Tony. It was suggested that in future the distribution of notes to all members should continue but that the presentation should be limited to 10 minutes and should center on basic issues.

SESSION 14. For some reason both Arthur and Peter were absent at this session, and so was I. This was the only time that so many people were not present at a meeting. The fact that no explanations were received from Arthur and Peter for their absence was due to the fact that the hospital telephone switchboard operators were on a one-day strike.

It was Margaret's turn to present her work on Disorders of Dilation, and it provided the context in which she felt secure enough to talk about personal details of her life. What occurred is best presented as stated in her ''thoughts.'' She was discussing the value of the balance between learning about the theory and practical experience.

Another time when for me personally the approach was especially valuable was in early January when I presented the section on dilation. The preparation of the chapter had been especially difficult for me as it touched so closely on my personal struggles of the last year or two—areas still fairly sensitive and vulnerable. Like Fay's patient, I suffered from vomiting the night before presenting the paper. I felt incapable of doing it. But the group picked my fear up and Maureen cleverly loosened the session so much that I was able to share much of the anxiety and to feel that *I* had contributed to the group's understanding of the theme by doing so. It was a revelation for me and I could even say that I had some ''love'' for dilation as a result!

Sheila followed this up with a case presentation of a stutterer. There was no time for Tony to discuss tightening and loosening and so this was held over for the coming week, together with Mary's account of core constructs. Mary also asked to present a case.

SESSION 15. Everyone was very excited by the news that Don Bannister had agreed to come and meet with the group in 2 week's time. Since we wanted to go through the chapter on Disorders of Transition, it was decided to ask Don to come and talk with us about aggression and hostility. Peter agreed to prepare that part of the chapter and to lead the discussion (pp. 874–894).

Tony gave a very thoughtful account of the processes of tightening and loosening and it was generally agreed, once again, how useful it was to have copies of the notes to take away so that anything not understood could be gone over again. Interestingly, reading the notes aloud was still the order of the day. There was no time left for Mary to deal with core constructs, so she agreed to do this next week. But she did give a well-prepared, concise case presentation. Arthur said he wanted to present one of his cases the next week.

SESSION 16. We started out with Mary presenting Kelly's views on core constructs. It had not occurred to me before how little he actually had to say on the topic. We all thought that we needed to do more thinking about this and that we would discuss it with Don Bannister if there were time.

I then presented a case in which I had used an implications grid. It seemed to me that it had produced most interesting results and threw new light on the person's problems. However, the ground onto which the words fell was stony and there was hardly any discussion at all. It is possible that this was the ''phobic'' reaction to grid measurement, or that I had presented it badly. I like to believe it was the former, especially as we had had no previous discussion about that particular form of grid.

Arthur then presented a case which evoked a far more animated response.

SESSION 17. Don Bannister could not reach our meeting place until after we had started, so Peter began giving his views of the chapter on aggression and hostility. I continued with a style started some weeks ago, which was to give as many practical examples as I could as the presentation proceeded. It had become apparent that Kelly's style is one that is easily understandable once one has a clear idea of the basic language, but for those who are still learning, there are often too few examples in the text for adequate comprehension.

Don fitted easily into the group and discussed issues along with the rest until Peter had finished his presentation. We kept to the topic of aggression and hostility, with Don talking about his observations of hostile and aggressive behavior in himself during therapy. For instance, he pointed out that one can be aggressive in therapy, as in a group, by not having everything planned. (This group had ample evidence of this!) Also, it is possible to show hostility by keeping a client in therapy too long in order to prove one is the sort of therapist who "cures" people, or until such time as there is ample evidence that the client thinks one is a "good" person. Don telephoned later in the week and said how much he had enjoyed the group. He felt, however, that he had talked too much, but that the group kept "triggering things off" in him.

SESSION 18. Sonia had prepared a section on anxiety, constriction, and guilt and presented this (pp. 894−913). She had found the part on weeping very relevant and important, and discussed this in a way she had not considered before. The members were now bringing to the group problems to do with particular clients and were able to discuss these in construct theory terms—more or less, at least. For instance, Margaret was describing some personal concern over a meeting she was going to have later that week with a client's father. The father seemed to be behaving in a particularly hostile manner toward his daughter, and the group members were very keen to tell her how to deal with this situation. So it was pointed out to them that a construct theory approach to such hostility might be to ask oneself why it was necessary for the father to seek validation for constructs that had already proved themselves to be failures—that is, to find out what was "at risk" for the father.

The following week, Margaret said she had indeed focused on the father's construing rather than on his behavior, and the interview had gone off very well. It is applying the knowledge and adopting the personal construct frame of mind that is most difficult for the group. Maureen and I had come only slowly to realize just how different the approach is from all others, and just how difficult it is for others to adopt it after working for some time within another framework—even though they are really keen to do so.

At this session I announced that I was willing to take on a small number for group supervision when these sessions ended and that they should come to me or telephone me after the session ended if they were interested. It was important that no one should feel any coercion.

SESSION 19. Sonia continued with her presentation, this time on constriction and guilt. This was followed by Arthur on dependency. Mary presented her work with a client.

The question of having an extra meeting in this term was brought up, making the number 22, in all. I could see no reason why this should not be so and it was clear that several people were feeling considerable anxiety about the cessation of the meetings. Five had by now expressed a wish to continue in a supervision group.

SESSION 20. The last few meetings had taken on a very standard pattern of academic presentation, discussion, and client presentation. Now it was Sheila's turn to present a section on interpretation, movement, and rapport (pp. 1088—1110) and Sonia's to talk about one of her student clients. Just to make sure that we had not gotten into a rut, I suggested that we write another self-characterization and compare it with the one written 20 weeks ago. We then discussed any changes people could see between the two.

It was also at this session that I mentioned Al Landfield's suggestion that I write this chapter. They agreed to supply me with their "thoughts" and to my using any that seemed appropriate.

SESSION 21. Margaret had prepared "Control of anxiety and movement" (pp. 1110—1123) and was followed by Tony, who discussed one of his clients who was on probation.

SESSION 22. For this last meeting we arranged for each person to come with some food so that we could meet early and have lunch. Maureen and I brought some wine. In a truly party mood, we played a game suggested by Maureen, in which we each had a description pinned on our backs. For example, "the life and soul of the party," "the odd man out on a jury," and so forth. The rest of the group was required to respond to one "as if" they were like the description carried on their back. It was a great success. Several people said they found they were actually responding to the title (although it was unknown to them); in other words, the reactions of others were determining their own behavior.

Arthur then led a discussion on a problem he faced with the whole approach. Was it possible ever to approach an event without construing (prejudging) it? He felt sure that it was and that it was wrong to think that it was impossible. It was an excellent discussion and everyone joined in. It was after this (which had ended by his suddenly going quiet and saying "that's OK then"), that he came and asked to join the supervision group. This may, of course, have been coincidence. His problems with aspects of the theory can be seen from the end of his "thoughts":

I am aware that any criticisms that I may have had of Kelly from time to time are very vastly outweighed by the enormity of the magnitude of this highly original theory—well, as original as any theory ever is!—it is a very welcome change from some of the psychoanalytic nonproductive brouhaha that is still around. I suppose that what I like best about Kelly is the pragmatic down-to-earth approach of "what is here and now" for the client.

The end of the experiment had come. All were expansive in stating what a great group it had been and we implicitly agreed to indulge in "encounter" behavior by all hugging each other.

THE GROUP COMMENTS ON THE COURSE

Much of what the group thought of itself has already been shown by excerpts from the various "thoughts." I will now allow the group members to speak further for themselves on various issues and problems of the course.

The Group on the Group

I think the most memorable personal experience has been meeting people who were skilled therapists from a completely different background and yet could open themselves so readily and totally to such a different way of seeing things. It made me realize how full of prejudice and "tight bits" I am. . . . On thinking about it I can't decide whether people were very open or were actually much more threatened by Kelly than seemed to be the case but, in wanting to be supportive, didn't give any impression of it.

We seemed to cease being self-conscious and preoccupied with examining ourselves as a group. Though in retrospect I feel a bit worried about the fact that we never returned to Kelly's stages in group work; maybe one has to feel safe in dyads before one ventures any further? Working as a group has not been easy for me and it has made me very conscious of thinking in a different way from other people. This is something I avoided in all my past group therapy experiences, where I have been submerged in working out "group constructs" rather than my own. It also made me think quite a lot about "conceptual maps" and 3-D Models, i.e., how people construe construct systems. This links with all the sculptures I make in my head and the realization that not giving them tangible form often obscures the flaws. This is a bit like a self-characterization; it has a beginning but no end. . . .

What has been interesting is how the group has been so self-supporting in terms of shared work, shared notes, shared preparation, shared case studies. I thought at first this might not occur but it seems to reflect the accuracy of Kelly's view of group experience. There was an enormous excitement generated among us, and our varied work contexts were I think an asset in providing how PCP can be applied in lots of different ways.

Working on the course with others with far wider experience in therapy than my own, has, in itself, been very valuable. They have provided a vast range of sources of reference as various aspects of the theory were discussed. And without their vivid examples, the ideas would have been far harder for me to grasp. Practical comparisons with other psychotherapeutic approaches, about which I have only read, have also, incidentally, shed light on them, as well as clarifying the philosophy that is Kelly's alone. Each of them brought to the course not only experience but an ability to construe this experience in new ways.

I am left with many questions and a sense of the shortness of time: This is a pretty dramatic effect I think and one Kelly might have wished for!

The Course: An Introduction to What?

It was emphasized from the beginning that this was only a "starter" and not the main meal. For many, this left feelings of incompleteness, and hence the desire for more. But we felt it essential that no one would be under the mistaken impression that they were going to receive training in a therapeutic skill.

It is with some trepidation I set out to summarize my impressions about the course, having made several previous attempts mainly while driving or brushing my teeth or being otherwise safely occupied. The main difficulty is that I have not yet come to terms with the course ending and it seems impossible to try to get it into perspective while I still feel so much in the middle of it. I don't know if my feeling of incompleteness is in the usual "the party is over" sense or whether it is healthy anxiety about being left with a head buzzing like a beehive with unanswered questions after what turned out to be a massive dilatory experience. . . . The course set out to be an introduction and this accounts for feelings of just beginning to integrate theory and praxis and "what the hell do I do now" feeling. I have kept in touch with developments in PCT since 1972, but always as something peripheral, a bit too precious for everyday use and I have also found it very difficult to come to terms with the "objective" and "scientistic" measuring side as opposed to actual involvement and doing and the course seemed to offer an opportunity to look at some bridging superordinate constructs to this. So I suppose I really came to see whether I should once and for all "set aside these childish things" and return to the folds of mainstream psychology or analytic training. I am left feeling rather irritable—there was no easy dance routine and I am left if anything with more questions than I set out with (an excellent state of affairs in a Kellian sense). So on one level I wish I had not started on this weekly dose of PCT since it turned out to be no placebo and on the other hand I keep catching myself sneaking back to unfinished puzzles to see if a bit would fit.

I feel that the course has given new perspectives as well as a great deal of very valuable information which I can use in a practical way with clients. My only criticism would be to say that another term, especially one with a more practical slant, would have been invaluable. However, I realize that there are limitations to all things and that the "ideal" situation probably never exists!

Different Levels of Theoretical Knowledge

This very important aspect of a group such as this has already been discussed at some length. That it can lead to serious discontent can be seen in the following:

One of the problems inherent in groups such as ours is that members start with a very varied degree of background knowledge of the subject. I feel that over all we managed to steer a reasonably good compromise path which met the need and pace of most people. However, there were times when I felt a little frustrated. After the first three or four weeks, I began to despair that we would ever get beyond very basic principles, and did consider at that stage dropping out of the group.

The weekly homework undertaken by a few group members at a time dealt with the varying levels of knowledge to some extent. It may, however, be better to ask all members to do the specified reading. This would mean really hard work for those less well versed in the theory and would necessitate a large enough supply of books for all to read. To test this, it is intended that each person on the next course shall be given a copy of Volume 2 to keep for the course period. This will enable the more informed to move ahead at their own speed.

Learning Through Doing

A number of comments on the teaching style, with its focus on homework and active participation, have already been cited. Maureen and I have no doubt that this was the preferable approach, but were not fully aware of the amount of anxiety it raised.

It seems to me wholly right that PCP should be best learned through PCP methods. I often wanted just to sit back and receive, to learn by ''magic wand'' methods as I'm sure most clients do. I am so glad that I felt I had permission to do this only when my level of anxiety obviously reached a point where some dependency on the group was appropriate for a while.

For the first term at least I was frustrated and irritated by the lack of disagreement and what I saw as an excessively ''adoring'' attitude to Kelly which prevailed. If anyone did disagree with another member, then the first would modify what he or she said and it would be all smoothed over. I am not sure why this irritated me as much as it did. Perhaps it is my wanting a directive leader who gives lots of feedback and clear messages, compared to a group which I saw as being very positive and supportive and encouraging members to find out for themselves. I acknowledge that the latter is more likely to lead to learning and change—but it's so uncomfortable! This has important implications for me as a therapist in that I can see that sometimes I take the former role rather than leave someone with the anxiety which would be more productive in the long run.

The theory really lives when we apply it to a situation/person and it's obviously very important to do this, which would be the purpose of practical work. There is an argument for not spending a lot of time doing this during the session as people can do it between sessions. Given the time limitations I would have liked a bit more practical work, especially at the beginning, because I think it not only gets one using the theory more quickly but also helps the group to ''gel'' initially.

The Threats of Measurement

Not all found grids a threat; some even found themselves reluctantly seduced by them.

I came with a firm feeling of giving up on grids and now I have a whole shopping list with extremely awkward questions such as—When is a construct a construct and not just a verbal label? How to differentiate between super and subordinate constructs in a grid? (A bit like a Smirnoff ad: ''I didn't know what life was like until I discovered Hinkle.'')

It had already been suggested that an introduction to grid technique might come much earlier in the course, and we will certainly do this next time. But some suggest that more than this is needed.

I'm still conscious that I don't quite see how to translate the grids into significant results (partly not having access to or much experience of using computers) and I think at least five of us felt the need to do some real basic study on grids. I would like a short course on JUST grids in fact—perhaps an active use of the Manual for Repertory Grid Technique? I think a group grid would have been fascinating.

I feel that in a future course, it may well be advisable to build in some kind of desensitization to defuse the panic reaction sometimes elicited by the sudden emergence of high-powered statistical analysis. I am not sure whether the idea of doing a group grid together fairly early on would be a good one, as I feel that this exercise might detract from the work task, causing the group to become somewhat introspective, and the consideration of group behavior an end in itself.

While I agree that the actual use of grids depends very much on the individual therapist, also that it may be by no means essential, I think that it would have been helpful to have had a few sessions more on grid work.

These references to a "group grid" stem from a suggestion of mine early on that we might study the group process by each of us doing a grid using each other as elements (see Fransella, 1970; Watson, 1970). When the various anxieties within the group became apparent, the idea was not followed through on the assumption that it would be threatening and possibility disruptive.

Group Members as Therapists or Persons?

This problem has been touched upon a number of times in this chapter and was referred to in passing by a number of people in their "thoughts." Of all the issues raised, this seems to be the most difficult and the one least well tackled. Clearly, several participants were expecting that there would be experiential sessions in which personal issues would be discussed. All but one came to see that this was not compatible with learning a new, theory-intensive approach to therapy.

It is just not possible to focus on personal growth and the learning of therapeutic skills at one and the same time. This is not to say that most members of the group did not learn something about themselves during the course. Far from it, as several of the "thoughts" demonstrate. We found that we had to concentrate on *either* personal growth *or* learning about personal construct theory and its application.

It might well be more helpful if this aspect of the course were to be spelled out early on. Yet, this might preempt the issue and cause the dreaded "hardening of the categories," leading to the conclusion that the approach is not about feelings, emotions, and experiences, but about theories and cognitions.

One way around this problem might be to focus on the essential reflexivity in Kelly's approach, making it clear that the professional constructs about the client are equally as applicable to the construing of the therapist. In the next course, we plan to use more interviewing in the practical sessions. In this context one participant may learn something about himself or herself and the interviewer something of the nature of the therapeutic relationship as a mutual endeavor in the exploration of personal problems of the client.

Its Application

The object of the course was to enable people to approach their clients in a Kellian way. Its success can, in part, be judged by the extent to which members found themselves able to reconstrue, both in relation to themselves and their clients.

The most important part for me has been the link between theory and therapy. The client tapes and the linked discussions made me see several things in a completely new light and the difference between actually observing and following nonverbal cues as compared to reading transcripts and edited case histories seen through the writer's construct system, a translation of a translation became very clear. The focus on anxiety and threat (and other "professional constructs" or "emotions") is a "just beginning" area for me and I still need to nudge myself when working with patients. It seems as if we just started to look at individual styles with our own case histories and the end here seems particularly abrupt—I don't think we could have done it any earlier because of the threat involved and maybe lack of sufficient understanding of each other's constructs. In my job I have found the practical application of methods using PCP quite wonderful—it has given me the structure I wanted to work within. It *is* effective and I have had a really positive response from students (clients) using PCP. They LIKE to be active participants in the changing of their lives and the approach feels right. There are always alternatives, not many cul-de-sacs. In my personal life I have found the awareness of working in personal construct terms more and more helpful to my living of it. I too have alternatives.

I entered the group with a fair degree of knowledge about the theory and the nuts and bolts of laddering, self-characterization, grid techniques, etc., but had little idea as to how I could integrate this knowledge into a whole therapeutic style when face to face with a client. I was often able to complete the diagnostic stage within a Kellian framework, formulating an assessment of a problem in personal construct terms. However, I had little idea of where to go from there, and usually then left the Kellian standpoint and resorted to other models with which I was more familiar. I have now been able to follow through a number of cases from start to finish within the construct theory psychotherapy model, and no longer feel anxious that I will reach a point in therapy from which I do not know where to go.

I am left with a constant desire to know more, am reading more; . . . and finding "loosening and tightening" in particular creeping into pretty well every counselling session I take, alongside a constant "checking out" that I understand things in the client's terms.

At the end of this "introductory course," with so much work still to do, I nevertheless feel that I have some very clear ideas of at least some aspects of Personal Construct Theory and therapy. I can, in a sense, approach the ideas a person expresses, or only half-expresses, with a feeling of a structure behind them. And instead of being blurred by the conflict between another's constructs and my own, I find it easier, really, to listen to what he is saying and to link apparently disjointed ideas into more of a whole. In practice, I have found a number of my clients have begun to move from somewhat static positions of repeatedly going over the old ground of their "complaints" into new directions of thought and exploration. The notion of partnership in therapy, which has always been my own notion, seems to be far more possible when the work you are doing is this kind of joint experiment, where therapist and client move and reflect on movement together.

What I liked best about the whole program was the contractual nature of it—the tightening and loosening processes which were a necessary part of each session. It felt inappropriate to leave a little early, as I did once or twice, as the tightening of the formal end had not occurred. It proved to me the need for contracts in therapy and highly structured interview sessions, in a clear way which I had not had before. At least, it gave me a "method" for structuring the sessions which perhaps I had only used on a hit-or-miss basis before. I think the course stimulated me, as if in therapy, into dilation in its creative way—leading not to chaos, but to order.

CONCLUSIONS

There are none. Or, perhaps, that is too sweeping a statement. We concluded that the experiment was a success and that it should be repeated with some modifications based on the experience; that an extension of the course was necessary for some—this is taking the form of therapy supervision; that, implicit in Kelly's approach, there is much that is threatening and anxiety-provoking for established therapists; and that the course evoked excitement and reconstruction not only in the "students" but in the "teachers" as well.

REFERENCES

Fransella, F. ". . . and then there was one." In D. Bannister (Ed.), *Perspectives in Personal Construct Theory*. London: Academic, 1970.

Fransella, F., & Bannister, D. *A Manual for Repertory Grid Technique*. London: Academic, 1977.

Hinkle, D. N. The change of personal constructs from the viewpoint of a theory of implication. Unpublished Ph.D. thesis, Ohio State University, 1965.

Kelly, G. A. *The Psychology of Personal Constructs:* Vols. 1 and 2 New York: Norton, 1955.

Kelly. G. A. The psychotherapeutic relationship. In B. Maher (Ed.), *Clinical Psychology and Personality*. New York: Wiley, 1969a.

Kelly. G. A. Personal construct theory and the psychotherapeutic interview. In B. Maher (Ed.), *Clinical Psychology and Personality*. New York: Wiley, 1969b.

Kelly, G. A. Psychotherapy and the nature of man. In B. Maher (Ed.), *Clinical Psychology and Personality*. New York: Wiley, 1969c.

Landfield, A. W. *Personal Construct Systems in Psychotherapy*. Chicago: Rand McNally, 1971.

McCoy, M. M. A reconstruction of emotion. In D. Bannister (Ed.), *New Perspectives in Personal Construct Theory*. London: Academic, 1977.

Rioch, M., J. Coulter, W. R., & Weinberger, D. M. *Dialogues for Therapists*. San Francisco: Jossey-Bass, 1976.

Watson, J. P. A measure of therapist-patient understanding. *British Journal of Psychiatry*, 1970, **117**, 309–318.

PART THREE

Personality and Social Interaction

CHAPTER 11

Personal Construction and Human Interaction

Joseph A. Doster

Social role is the theme of this chapter. However, social role will not be defined in the more traditional fashion—as just a sequence of disembodied and depersonalized behaviors played out in some standard or "objectively" understood context. Instead, we accept George Kelly's (1955) thesis that social role should be construed interactively—that is, when a person's behavior in relation to another reflects the person's attempt, correct or incorrect, to comprehend the thoughts, feelings, and values of the other person. The specific aim of this chapter is to show how certain theorists and experimenters, often working outside the framework of Personal Construct Psychology, seem to have provided support for the usefulness of the Kellian interactive and personal-meaning approach to social role. In the concluding section, a statement will be made concerning what personal construct investigators are doing about processes of social role.

THE CHALLENGE OF MEANING

During the process of preparing this introduction, I recalled an earlier experience which might help to exemplify the consideration of meaning and human interaction that will be the focus of this chapter. The incident occurred within the context of a formal meeting of colleagues when a brief debate arose as to my theoretical allegiance. Heretofore, I was aware that the membership had dichotomized into traditionalists and behaviorists, though I regarded myself more or less as a citizen of a nonaligned nation. Fortunately, the label-affixing ceremony ended in deadlock when the spokespersons for each group assigned me to the other and consequently invalidated the assignment of membership to their own group. Of course, all of this was a bit amusing since my opinion went unsolicited, but there was also a sense of threat as I anticipated the rather intense demands to conform to the social expectations that composed the respective categories. I seem to have encountered the *if-then-but-not* nature of others' personal constructs conjointly held by a social unit.

Even so, as I became more intimately acquainted with a number of these associates, I discovered that their representation of self was not wholly congruent with their presentation of self. For clarification, Danziger (1976) distinguishes representation and presentation as functions of human communication wherein "the former is concerned with conveying information about the world in which the communicators live, the latter conveys something about the relationship between the communicators themselves" (p. 35).

As a member of the aforementioned social unit, I also had the opportunity to observe the behavior of other individuals who arrived each year for professional preparation. Very soon, each new group would divide along the lines defined by the larger unit they were entering. Now this posed an interesting dilemma to me as the case supervisor of small teams of clinicians, mixed with respect to professed theoretical belief. Invariably, a struggle would ensue among the membership to define what would take place during our involvement as a group and the meaning we would give to our behavior. I found it practical, for the sake of progress, to work initially within the frames of reference I encountered. Yet, my emerging role as a member of these small groups was not so much arbiter as a benign saboteur, attempting to undermine the status of meanings that had become regarded as though they were fact. Such an elevation of meaning often forecloses prematurely a fuller understanding of the subject of study and concomitantly establishes the primacy of the construers' system of meaning relative to those construed.

The tendency to foreclose ourselves to understanding others is not simply a condition that arises in informal, interpersonal relationships. Considering the context of psychotherapy, Kelly (1955) notes that clinicians too often impose their language and belief systems on their clients and regard the attainment of insight as the client's adoption of the therapist's constructs. And more recently, Landfield (1971), reflecting on the premature defection of clients from psychotherapy, implicates the interactive meaningfulness of meanings between client and therapist, or the lack thereof, as a decisive factor in the continuation of the relationship.

There has evolved a long and impressive list of technical terminology that connotes both the responsibility for and the failure of constructive communication in the therapy enterprise. Frequently, the meaning assigned to premature termination is that the client is not psychologically minded, is unmotivated for treatment, lacks counseling readiness, is resistant to the intervention of others, or is defensive, exhibits a low need for interoception, or is a poor conditioner. Apparently, clients are not permitted to seek professional help for debilitations and deficits that interfere with the process of therapy. A refreshing alternative would be the remark by the expert on understanding and motivation that, "I have yet to meaningfully know this person."

The primacy of one person's meaning over that of another also pervades the very formal context of psychological research. Considerable effort is devoted to the design of procedures by which human interaction will take place that affirms or disaffirms prearranged meanings. Restrictions on performance usually disallow creativity and an acquaintanceship with the experiencing of the person. Further, methodological dictum, theoretical interest, and social-ethical concern have evolved and imposed meaning on differing experimental contexts. We have advancing bodies of knowledge on the naive, the deceived, and the informed individual. There can be only wonderment for the meanings subjects would impose on their interactional experiences. Bakan (1967) concludes, "By the studied ignorance of the meaning of the subject's protocol language the scientist guarantees that he will not enter upon the psyche of the subject" (p. 42).

Even in the highly technical endeavors to establish classificatory systems for human behavior, there is a push to elevate inference to the status of explanatory principle. In seeming desparation to become meaningful, the behavioral sciences have ignored the need for rigorous standards by which to distinguish "inference" from "valid phenomena" (Kety, 1965), and consequently have foreclosed prematurely on an understanding of the phenomena that our systems are designed to help us understand. The appearing, disappearing, reappearing nature of disorders in the *Diagnostic and Statistical Manuals* of the American Psychiatric Association (1968) challenges meaningfulness. Likewise, progress in understanding is not advanced when the description of behavior in turn appears as an explanation of behavior. Individuals underachieve because they are underachievers, or self-stimulatory behaviors arise because they are self-stimulating. As these examples demonstrate, the imposition of meaning can impede the development of knowledge. On the other hand, the experience of meaning is an intrinsic attribute of human interaction.

PERSPECTIVES ON HUMAN BEHAVIOR

Following the intense debate of traitism and situationism during the last decade (Mischel, 1968; Bowers, 1973), there emerged strong interest in interactionism during the 70s. Although the dual emphasis on both individual and situational variables at first glance may give the appearance of compromise, the propositions of theories adhering to this school of thought clearly offer a different view on human behavior. A fundamental assumption of the interactional model is succinctly stated by Ullmann and Krasner (1975) early in their effort to formulate a sociopsychological approach to abnormal behavior. Specifically, *"human behavior is always interactive"* (p. 36). Although this assertion is a radical departure from orthodox learning theory, the interactive assumption has had an impressive history in man's theorizing about man.

Moving Man Versus Man as Motion

In the *Psychology of Personal Constructs*, Kelly (1955) wrestles the traditional preconceptions of man as a static entity, as well as the propositions of push sources (stimuli) and pull sources (needs) to explain the activity of the organism. In contrasting fashion, he resolves the dilemma of moving the person by assuming that the person is "a form of motion" and that the subject of psychology is the person's processes. By taking this step, Kelly concludes:

Thus the whole controversy as to what prods an inert organism into action becomes a dead issue. Instead, the organism is delivered fresh into the psychological world alive and struggling. (p. 37)

Others, deliberating man within this same time frame, also seem untaken with a mechanistic view, perhaps the consequence of self-reflexive endeavors. Whatever the circumstance, it is probably important to observe that the assertion of the interactive nature of man is put forth in their writings at the very outset. For example, Ruesch and Bateson (1951) identify communication as ''. . . the matrix in which all human activities are embedded . . .'' and the process that ''. . . links object to person and person to person . . .'' (p. 13). Hall (1959) sorts human activity into 10 Primary Message Systems, but only the first,—that is, interaction— underlies all of man's involvements. Indeed, the interval by which he defines the living organism is a function of interaction, or lack thereof, with the environment. In similar fashion, Rotter (1954) states as the first postulate for his Social Learning Theory, *''The unit of investigation for the study of personality is the interaction of the individual and his meaningful environment''* (p. 85).

An intriguing variation on the interactional theme, one ascribed to Sullivan, is that ''man is literally always in some form of situation, 'having commerce' with one or more 'others'. . .'' (Rychlak, 1973, p. 245). Sullivan appears to have taken into account several facets of human behavior on reaching this conclusion. One is the inclination to impose human attributes on persons, lower organisms, and objects; and another is that participants of interaction may be real or fantasized persons. The situation then of man's involvement becomes an interpersonal situation. Although there are detractors of such an extreme position, nevertheless it is a novel alternative to an impersonal view of human interaction.

It is reasonable to suspect that movement toward the interactional alternative was no small struggle for these theorists when we consider that their formulations of man's nature ran counter to contemporaneous and prevailing views. For perhaps too long a time, the concept of movable man pervaded the literature of psychology and eclipsed the psychological assumption of man in motion. Today, there is increasing interest in and exploration of implications that follow from the latter perspective. With a fervor that does not appear to be faddish, professional colleagues are turning their attention to the classic writings of forebears of interactionism, or in independent fashion are elaborating the implications of their own personal beliefs or experiences. A good while ago, as I began to read in the Bandler and Grinder series (1975) on the *Structure of Magic,* I was both amazed and delighted by the goodness of fit between the perspectives they take on man and those of George Kelly, even at the level of corollaries.

Persons Invalidating Persons

I am probably well past the juncture of having risked belaboring a point. Nevertheless, although the concept of interactionism is widely endorsed today, contradiction often is observable in what takes place within human interaction. This process occurs in one of several ways.

1. One person impersonalizes or objectizes another person. Removing the person attributes from persons transforms them to static states needful of a mechanism to restore motion. Obviously, immobilized, immovable, or immutable patients are likely candidates for the restorative maneuvers of therapists. Once, as I listened to a therapist present his treatment strategy with a client, I began to fantasize his getting behind the wheel, igniting the engine, and driving his client to mental health!

2. One person denies the existence of another person. The effect of institutionalization on the individual—that is, depersonalization—is an often cited (Rosenhan, 1973) example of this process. Medical and psychiatric patients, as well as social welfare clients, on reexistence give vivid accountings of this experience along the lines of "conversations were held, my condition discussed, plans were made, and all of this occurred as though my feelings did not matter or I were not there."

3. One person atomizes another person. In this process, the person as such fades into the background while a particular process emerges into the foreground of interpersonal attention. For example, we may hear that "the schizophrenia is now in remission following positive response to treatment," or that "the incidence of ticking increased with the number of assertive responses," or that "inappropriate verbalizations were eliminated through negative practice."

Embeddedness, Detachment, and Human Nature

Sometimes, in man's attempt to gain perspective on his existence, he loses perspective. I am reminded here of one of Thomas's messages (1974) in the *Lives of a Cell*. Essentially, he observes that man has so alluded himself in his efforts to "detach himself from nature" that it becomes very difficult for him to manage the growing awareness of his "embeddedness in nature." Likewise, mental health practitioners in their roles as scholars, experimenters, psychometricians, diagnosticians, and healers often surprise themselves by their recollection that the processes of understanding, anticipating, and influencing human interaction are themselves human interactive processes. Not only are professionals inclined to depersonalize their clients but often depersonalize themselves in the process. Whenever two or more persons come together, communication takes place; it is impossible not to communicate (Watzlawick et al., 1967). Silence, inactivity, "uh-huhs," and so forth, are messages that influence what takes place. Detachment is an interactive process in which one person ascribes meaningfulness to his behavior, such as observer or spectator rather than participant.

How easily this process occurs when, for example, experimenters, assessors, or therapists assume prescribed, standardized roles to minimize their influence or intrusion on the processes of the client, and then presume detachment from the interpersonal situation. Purposefully, the more depersonalized the examiner, the more justified are the attributions that explain the client's performances in terms of himself. Yet, in moving from the clinical context to other social contexts, the likelihood that others will act in the same, uninfluencing way with the client is quite low. How much more meaningful are generalizations when clinicians consider themselves in their interactions with a client and thereby the implications for others who may be with this client. For example, when I evaluate a "learning problem" child on different assessment tasks, I also try to discover what I can do to improve his performances on these tasks. I have found this useful later when consulting with the child's teacher in helping to formulate the teacher's role with the child.

The Monadic-Dyadic Distinction

Perusal of case folders on clients maintained by clinicians are very revealing about therapists' perspectives on their clients. Typically, they are the product of a solitary effort by the clinician about the client rather than the conjoint effort of the two about themselves. By the way, conjoint progress notes are an interesting way to meet a client. Reading along on these hypothetical case notes, we may gradually sense that the processes described and interpreted are exclusively intrapersonal on the part of the client. The operating assumption is that the smallest unit of analysis is the monad or the individual. A variation on this theme is the discovery of two reports per each session's process notes. One is an intrapersonal accounting of the clinician's behavior, the other is an intrapersonal accounting of the client's behavior. Though it is easy to surmise that two persons were in proximity, clearly, the smallest unit of analysis is individual A and individual B. A hint of interaction may be achieved by establishing an S-R-S-R-S-R sort of cadence. Yet, what we have are isolated components threaded together in temporal sequence. The monadic approach, as these examples help clarify, brings separate units together, but maintain their separateness. Danziger (1976) summarizes the effect quite well:

> The doctrine of an essentially atomistic, monadic view of the individual plays a special role. It has led to a marked tendency to explain phenomena of social interaction in essentially intraindividual terms like social motives, attitudes, cognitive balancing mechanisms, personality characteristics, and so on. Viewing social processes in terms of the influence that one set of intraindividual variables has on similar variables in another individual has led to a relative neglect of the process of human communication, which constitutes the ongoing interrelationship *between* individuals. (p. xiii)

The dyadic approach to social interactional analysis assumes that the smallest unit of study is the personal dyad rather than the individual. Consequently, description and evaluation reveal the unfolding processes of personal dyads across the dimensions of time and space. The processes of personal dyads may be construed relative to their similarities or contrasts with the processes of other personal dyads, relative to variations of contextual variables, or relative to congruencies or differentiations that arise within dyads.

THE CLASSIFICATION OF HUMAN INTERACTION

Unlike many of our colleagues in other fields of science, psychologists are in the peculiar circumstance of attempting to define and explain the very phenomena in which they are engaging. Scientists devise artifical systems of classification to sort phenomena under study into mutually exclusive and jointly exhaustive classes in order to discover eventually the principles and laws that seem to explain the recurrence of phenomena. There is a set of beliefs that underlies the endeavors of scientists to learn, namely that differentiation and order exist in the universe of phenomena they study (Adams et al., 1977). By comparison, there seems to be decided disinterest in or attention to events as unique, nonrecurring, random phenomena.

In the previous section, the perspective was taken that man is a form of motion who is embedded in and intimately involved with other processes of his personal universe. Some have construed the person's initial experiencing of this universe of phenomena as an "unending," "undifferentiated," and "monotonous" flow (Kelly, 1955) and as the "raw feel" of life (Sullivan, 1953). Yet, in the fashion of his brethren scientists, the evolving person also is assumed in the dimension of time to attend to, discover, and learn about the "recurrent themes," "repetitive characters," and "cycles and rhythms" that exist within the flow of events (Kelly, 1955; Ruesch & Bateson, 1951; Hall, 1959). Further, Kelly adds that the person's differentiation of these recurrent themes is a temporal separation, imposing "beginnings and endings" on the interactional flow. Just as man is not construed as a static entity, neither is he construed as construing an involvement with a static field of circumstances.

Defining Attributes of Human Social Interaction

Human communication has been defined (Haley, 1963) by four common elements: a sender, a receiver, the messages exchanged among participants, and the social context in which the exchange takes place (time, place, circumstances). Several classificatory steps are involved in categorizing social interaction in this way. First, the type of category constructed is a conjunctive one, requiring that all of the intrinsic attribute properties or elements be present in order to designate an event as human social interaction (Bruner et al., 1965). Second, the defining attributes distinguish human social interaction from other forms of interaction such as person-object, machine-machine, person-machine, and so forth. Third, each element has served as a basis for further classificatory endeavors of an informal as well as a technical sort.

Description of Observable Properties

Persons, independent of their behavior, have been subdivided according to red, blonde, or brunette hair color; ectomorphic, mesomorphic, or endomorphic body type; beady-, bright-, or wide-eyedness; apparent or actual age; height; weight; race; complexion of skin; gender; eye color; and so on. Classification has utilized types of attributes—for example, color—and the value of attributes—for example, amount of weight. There seems to be an unending list of physical attributes along which persons vary, without regard for what they do, that have composed classificatory schemes.

Similarly, the range and definition of subcategories by which to classify message exchange seems limited only by human physiology, the viability of transmission-reception modality combinations, and perhaps the imaginativeness of human interactants. Traditionally, psychologists have given much systematic attention to the audio-acoustic channel, and more so to linguistic behavior than to paralinguistic behavior. Even so, investigators have increased their attention in recent years on other channels that simultaneously or sequentially compose human social interaction and that vary in saliency at particular moments in time (Birdwhistell, 1970; Danziger, 1976). Through different perceptual modalities, we attend to posture, interpersonal distance, odors, muscle tension, facial expression, gestures, mannerisms, or other aspects of body motion. We may perceive visually the eye gaze, eye movement, pupil constriction and dilation of another, or the body perspiration of another. Yet, it is quite a different experience to perceive tactually changes in the surface temperature of another, or to feel the sweaty palms or clammy hands of another. Indeed, an undercover intelligence agent who fails to sweat during the rigors of interrogation may disaffirm the intensity of stress applied, but nevertheless betray a denial of occupation to his interrogators.

Other nonlinguistic behaviors also expand the range of interpersonal message exchange to be observed and classified, for example, touching, crying, physical assault, withdrawal, and so forth. Shapiro, Krauss, and Truax (1969) have proposed that nonverbal acts may be as self-disclosing of a person as verbal behavior, even though the latter has been the modality by which self-disclosure typically is defined. Madison Avenue norm setters may exhort the public to "say it" with flowers, chocolates, a new car, wines, *ad infinitum*. An exchange of messages may be observed when members of a family line one wall of a clinic waiting room and the problematic adolescent son sits alone across the way, or when a "delinquent" youngster sets fire to a smoking lounge that services a heretofore placating, institutional staff, or when a psychiatric patient routinely defecates at the door of the nursing station some time after the administration of electroconvulsive shock treatments. Nonlinguistic messages may express more adequately our feelings and needs than verbal messages.

Finally, the subclassification of social contexts also is represented in the activities of man. There are purposeful aspects of situations such as recreation, occupation, education, treatment, or religion, with time and space set aside or equipped for particular sorts of interactions. There are playgrounds for leisure time, schools for school days but not for vacation times or recess times, offices and factories with work schedules and shifts, hospitals and clinics with regular hours for patient care and after hours for emergency care (usually with a separate entrance), and so on. Psychiatric diagnosis relies on aspects of situations for the category of "transient situational disturbances," and situations also figure heavily in categories of research and treatment. Much of psychological research depends on the manipulation of situational variables, for example, shock and no shock at fixed or variable intervals, and observation of human behavior may occur in laboratory settings or naturalistic settings. While psychological treatment for the most part occurs in offices set aside for this purpose (and they vary widely in description), therapy also may occur "in vivo," or in nontraditional settings such as ocean voyages, swimming pools, jogging trails, retreat camps, and many other imaginative places.

Impressively high interrater agreement is attainable if classification of persons, behaviors, and contexts is based on observable attributes and if: (1) technology for observation and measurement is reasonably advanced or adequate, (2) observers are alert and well-trained, and (3) the defining attributes and attribute values of categories are described sufficiently for the phenomena to be observed and classified. This level of classification, referred to by others as the alpha level of a taxonomy (see Bruner et al., 1965; Adams et al., 1977, for further elaboration), is considered the data base of a science and is more often regarded as a system of nomenclature than of taxonomy.

Scientists Construing Trends

Higher levels of classification, or the beta level of a taxonomy, involve categories defined by the relationship among attributes rather than simply the presence of the observable attributes themselves. Some examples from everyday life can help clarify the relational category. A client, seeking help for a problem, may enter a clinic with a sliding scale fee system. The category of fee assessment for services usually will be determined by the relationship between gross annual income and number of dependents. Another example can be observed in the actuarial tables that define "overweight," "underweight," or "appropriate weight" for persons. Categorization of status is based on the relationship between height and bone structure. In these examples, neither the designation of observable attributes nor the specification of attribute values alone determine classification. Rather, definition of categories exist on the basis of a specified relationship among attributes.

Psychiatric taxonomy assumes, with few supporting data, that syndromes are relational categories, binding symptoms together by proposing an underlying mental disease. Presumably, covarying changes occur in symptomatology when the underlying disturbance is treated. Treatments directed at psychiatric symptoms ought to manage, reduce, or control these manifestations of mental diseases. Whereas only treatment directed at mental diseases, in theory anyway, ought to stabilize the condition of the person, arrest the progress of the disease, and/or bring about remission of the disease. Quite clearly, decades of research have yet to satisfy the needs that gave rise to psychiatric classification (Landfield, 1975; Adams et al. 1977), but failure in these quests does not deter professional application.

An alternative approach to traditional diagnosis, one that quite clearly relies on relational categories, comes from the research of Wolpe (1963), who defined four classes of phobias. For example, he defined "proximation phobias" as those in which the person's anxiety increases as the distance from the particular situation decreases and "remoteness phobias" as those where the person's anxiety increases as the distance from a particular situation increases. Further, Wolpe found that the pattern or trend of progress clients show in treatment varies substantially, depending on the nature of their complaints. There are several reasons to note the importance of this classificatory step. First, classification occurs on the basis of the relationship, interaction, or trend among attributes rather than the presence of attributes. Second, Wolpe abstracts over traditional categories that specify descriptively different situational circumstances, such as hemophobia, zoophobia, and so on. Third, this sort of relational category raises important questions with respect to assessment methodology and differential diagnosis that are obfuscated by traditional classification. This is easily exemplified by the category "school phobia" which is often applied to the problems of young children. School phobias may be reclassified as proximation or remoteness phobias upon careful observation and understanding of the child's experiences at home and at school. Fourth, Wolpe has been able to relate one type of recurring pattern or trend in human interaction with another type of recurring pattern or trend in human interaction. Restated, the interactions that some individuals seem to have with specific life circumstances are alike and different from the interactions of others; and these distinct patterns relate to similarities and differences they show in their interactions within the context of therapy. In this way, vertical development of a classificatory schema occurs with the specification of a superordinate pattern or trend that relates to other patterns or trends. To summarize, then, the attributes of human interaction are observable, whereas the specification of the nature of interaction among person and situation attributes is an abstraction or meaning that we give to these observations; and, further abstraction occurs with the specification of relationships.

Persons Construing Trends

A number of years ago, a colleague shared with me his reply to the question "What do these test scores mean?" The inquirer showed a great deal of confidence that the test score would express itself if it only could, and so must have found puzzling the returned proposition that we give meaning to test scores rather than test scores give meaning to us. Likewise, in human social interaction, the observable properties are no more meaningful than the meaning given by the participants—including the spectators. Personal impressions can be formed that are very close to the observable data. For example, a police report may show that "each party was seated at the counter when an altercation ensued." Or, a psychometrician may report that "the client's high score on a test of comprehension reveals strong reasoning ability." On the other hand, personal impressions may elaborate the implications of observations. For example, the psychometrician may attempt to foresee the import of measured reasoning ability *in relation* to the client's interaction on the job, with family or friends, or in other contexts. There does seem to me to be a trend that personal impressions stay close to observation when an individual wishes to maintain distance from others or to impersonalize the interaction, or does not wish to risk responsibility of anticipating what will occur in subsequent interaction with others, or finds himself without sufficient expectational base to give meaning to interaction with others. The opposite direction of this trend relates personal impressions of a relational sort to interpersonal involvement, risk taking, and the fullness of one's expectational base.

One of the many exciting aspects of Kelly's "man-the-scientist" perspective on man (1955) is that not only does he construe man in a relational sense but he also construes man's construing in a relational sense. Yet, as Duck (1973) points out, readers at times fail to find excitement in the exemplification of personal constructs. This effect seems most pronounced when persons construe constructs in a static rather than in a relational sense. But on the relational nature of personal constructs, Kelly is quite emphatic. Personal constructs arise from the person's construing the replications of trend or movement, the person's constructs exist as constructs of trend or movement, and the person's constructs permit him to predict trend or movement among surrounding events. He states, "To have solid meaning the prediction must make a clean distinction between what will occur and what will not occur" (p. 123). As the person's construing abstracts over the properties of interaction from beginning to ending on the basis of similarities and differences, constructs acquire an *"if-then-but-not"* quality. Ruesch and Bateson (1951) seem to offer a similar view of man's construing. They state:

> The repetitive character of social events teaches people to react in stereotyped ways . . . so that a system of interaction is established in which cause and effect can no longer be isolated. Stimulus and response are thus welded into a unit; this unit we shall refer to as 'value.' Values are therefore, so to speak, simply preferred channels of communication or relatedness. Information about the values which people hold enables us to interpret their behavior. (p. 8)

And Kelly (1955) similarly notes:

> When a person communicates the construct under which he is operating, we too can see what he is doing. His behavior then makes sense to us; we understand him. (p. 127)

OBSERVING PROPERTIES AND CONSTRUING TRENDS

Whenever two or more individuals are together they face the task of defining what will and will not take place, as well as the task of establishing who will control the definition of the relationship (Haley, 1963). Throughout their interaction, the messages they exchange define, affirm, reject, and redefine the direction or movement of their interaction. What is and is not to take place during human social interaction is inextricably tied to the personal construct systems of the participants. One person plays a "role" in relation to others when he construes "another person as a construer," and to the extent that he construes "the construction processes of another" (Kelly, 1955). Interaction may proceed in which each person understands the constructs under which the other is operating, and each can play a role in a social process with the other. Or understanding may be unidirectional, such that one person understands the constructs of another and can engage in a role with the other but without a reciprocity of roles with the other. This does not mean that one person's behavior is not a factor in a social process with another when there is an absence of understanding for the other, but only that one person will not know how to behave toward the other without some understanding of the other person's constructs. The person's constructs that are operating in social interaction define what is and is not to occur (if-then-but-not) in an anticipatory sense to the extent that his constructs are subsumed by another. To the extent that the operating constructs are subsumed (accepted or affirmed rather than rejected) by another the operating constructs control the direction of movement in the interaction. Or as Kelly has pointed out, ". . . constructs are the controls that one places upon life—the life within him as well as the life which is external to him" (p. 126). In this sense, personal constructs channel or provide guidelines or rules that govern the flow of interpersonal interaction.

Essentially, then, the person's communication of the constructs under which he is operating not only makes him known to another but also attempts to influence or control the nature of their relationship. These two aspects of communication have received various labels in the theoretical literature, including distinctions between the semantic versus the pragmatic (Morris, 1955), the representational versus the presentational (Danziger, 1976), the denotative versus the connotative (Kiesler & Bernstein, 1974), the informational versus the integrational (Birdwhistell, 1970), and the report versus the command (Ruesch & Bateson, 1951) aspects of messages. It is most fair to point out that there is considerable variation among these concepts and the differences in definition are worthy of further deliberation with respect to their implications. Yet, a thread of commonality also appears to be the attribution of information and elicitation aspects of messages exchanged. Personal constructs in an informational or representational sense are abstractions of, but are not identical with, the factual or observable properties of events in one's life (Kelly, 1955). Personal constructs in a relational or elicitational sense effect prediction and control for events in one's life. In the remaining sections, the intricacies of properties and trends of human social interaction in different social contexts will be explored in greater depth.

Diagnosing Trends and Trends in Diagnosis

Psychiatric diagnosis has given little aid to the specification of trends in human social interaction and yet is distinctly a part of a social process that can be construed as a stable pattern or trend. In a similar vein, Landfield (1975) has inquired, "Does a nomenclature of mental disease and deviancy suggest ways of interacting beneficially with the individual patient?" Of course, the answer is no. Although some diseases are communicable, as yet we lack strong evidence that mental diseases communicate. Now it is entirely possible to anthropomorphize about disease and perhaps interact beneficially on that basis. Indeed, there is some interesting work under way of this sort. On the other hand, a very different sort of nomenclature seems needed to benefit human relationships and problems arising therein. Diseases are not people, nor are people their diseases. Yet, an outsider eavesdropping on conversations among mental health workers quickly may conclude the opposite. Almost always, psychiatric patients are referred to as their disease, and only rarely, for example, for diabetics, is this the case with medical patients. On this point, Adams, Doster, and Calhoun (1977) add:

This slippage in referring to the person by his disease seems to occur more often when the disorder is chronic, persistent, incurable, and/or requires long-term monitoring and changes in the person's life style. Under these conditions and with time, it may very well seem to others that the person is his disease. (p. 49)

Although traditional psychiatric nomenclature fails to suggest trends in human social interaction, other factors appear to be salient in predicting movement. Recently, Ullmann and Krasner (1975) identified six trends in human social interaction that are likely to end with a person's behavior being labeled as abnormal: (1) others view the behavior as "the wrong thing, the wrong time, the wrong setting, the wrong way, or inferentially, done for the wrong reasons"; (2) the behavior is "unpleasant enough or disturbing enough for someone to want to change it"; (3) the consequence of labeling the behavior "helps solve the problem raised by the aversive behavior"; (4) others construe the behavior as "senseless, self-defeating, or without favorable consequences for the individual"; (5) the person labeling the behavior "has some power over the person to be labeled"; and (6) the "availability" of the label (pp. 33–34).

Indeed, research strongly indicates that the presence or absence of mental disease has little relevance to labeling and decision-making processes. Mendel and Rapport (1969) found that history of prior hospitalization, time of day, day of the week, and whether the intake was done by a social worker were more predictive of decisions to hospitalize psychiatric patients than severity of psychopathology. Similarly, Wenger and Fletcher (1969) found that the presence or absence of a legal counselor at commitment hearings were stronger predictors of the decision than the patient's behavior. Clearly, attributes of human social interaction rather than attributes of mental disease are important to the process of persons becoming patients and formal decisions about these persons.

A collection of studies by Rosenhan (1973) helps to further illuminate the process of social decisions about persons. The most controversial of these involved his attempt to determine whether psychiatric nomenclature would distinguish "sane" from "insane" persons. He had eight "sane" persons gain admission to 12 different hospitals by complaining that they heard voices. Except for the voices, they showed no other unusual behavior. On admission, all but one of the pseudopatients were labeled as having "schizophrenia," and on discharge were diagnosed as having "schizophrenia in remission." Remarkably, the pseudopatients ceased their complaint about voices following admission, but their normal behaviors on the ward were overlooked or misinterpreted by the hospital staff. Only the other patients suspected that the pseudopatients were not real patients. Perhaps the most distressing study of this collection involved hospital staff reciprocation during interactions initiated by the pseudopatients. The presumption under investigation was that the meaningfulness of the initiator to the staff would be reflected by the duration of the interaction. In an overwhelming number of attempts to initiate interaction, staff kept moving on with their heads averted from the pseudopatient. Yet a third study of this series shows that the effect of labeling on interactional trend can occur in much more subtle ways. This study involved a young woman armed with six questions who approached individual physicians in a university medical center. With a subsample of these physicians she interjected at the end of the first question, "I'm looking for an internist" or "I'm looking for a psychiatrist." Although the cooperation she received from these staff members was much greater than the cooperation the pseudopatients received in the psychiatric hospitals, nevertheless, the woman experienced less cooperation once she disclosed she was "looking for a psychiatrist."

In a study of a different sort, Matloff (1977) had undergraduate females attending a large university involved with an experimental assistant in discussions of controversial topics such as the legislation on marijuana or the liberalization of laws on sex among consenting adults. After five minutes of interaction, the assistant interjected into the conversation that she had spent her summer at a nearby psychiatric hospital and saw the problems people had with drugs (or sex). And, five minutes later, the assistant interjected that she came to know the problems people have with drugs (sex) while she worked at the psychiatric hospital as a nurse's aide. A follow-up interview revealed that all but one of 40 students had concluded after the first interjection that their partner during the interaction was a former mental patient. Yet, students somehow missed the second interjection and were surprised during the interview when they were reminded that their partner had been a nurse's aide.

In advance of the study, the students had replied to a questionnaire designed to assess their degree of bias in a negative sense toward former mental patients. Interestingly, during the conversation phase of the study, students who showed low bias toward mental patients significantly increased their rate of interruption of their partner upon construing their partner as an ex-mental patient. Conversely, those who had expressed a high degree of bias toward former mental patients significantly reduced their rate of interruption in the conversation upon construing their partner as an ex-mental patient. Obviously, the stigmatizing effects of the mental illness label are easily induced and very resistant to change. In addition, how we relate to others changes with our reconstruing them.

Earlier in the chapter, the point was made that an assumption of the diseases-in-man model is that an underlying mental disease gives rise to and maintains psychopathological behavior. From this point of view, society is not likely to hold the patient responsible for his symptomatology nor the interpersonal consequences of his "sick" behavior. Likewise, neither would we expect psychopathological behavior to vary as part of an interpersonal process. Even so, research suggests otherwise. Considerable pioneering in this area was accomplished by the Braginskys and their colleagues. In one particular study (1967), they found that hospitalized psychiatric patients successfully manipulated the impressions of interviewers in predictable ways to connote levels of disturbance and need for a protective environment. When they analyzed the verbal content of patients during the interview, they found that professional impressions varied with the frequency of negative self-statements. Likewise, Zarlock (1966) found immense variation in the frequency of symptomatic behavior among schizophrenic patients depending on whether they were observed in a medical, recreational, occupational, or social context. And Sommer (1969) increased the affiliative behaviors of elderly psychiatric inpatients by rearranging the furniture on the ward.

Another avenue of investigation is that of Shimkunas (1972) and associates who have proposed that psychotic symptomatology serves as covert communication that prevents the development of intimacy with others. In other words, the bizarre language and beliefs communicated cannot be subsumed easily by another and the person's behavior is viewed as out of control. Generally, results from a number of studies (Shimkunas, 1972; Doster et al., 1975; Ritchie, 1976; Cogan, 1976) indicate that schizophrenic patients show higher levels of the psychopathological behaviors characteristic of their problems in increasingly more intimate, interpersonal circumstances. Even so, across studies, schizophrenic patients fare better in superficial or impersonal situations, showing lower levels of pathology and reciprocal levels of self-disclosure. Doster et al. also examined the relationship of intimacy and symptom manifestation among depressed patients. They found these patients showing higher levels of psychopathological behaviors in superficial rather than intimate circumstances. And Ritchie also related decisions about remaining on an open ward or readiness for discharge to levels of symptom expression, and decisions on hospital status attenuated the effect of intimacy demand. These findings further emphasize the need to consider "disordered behavior" within a social context rather than an exclusively intraindividual context. As a final note, the level of intimacy offered in these studies was defined by the level of self-disclosure modeled. Behavior therapy programs designed for social skills development use modeling on a frequent basis to train self-disclosure skills but do not typically consider the effects of intimacy (Doster & Nesbitt, 1979).

In the previous series of studies, the point is raised that the psychological symptoms of some patients may well be outside the range of understanding of other persons and may prevent the enactment of reciprocal roles and the development of interpersonal intimacy. A corollary of the intimacy-avoidance hypothesis, one that pertains to the psychopathological behaviors of nonpsychotic patients (Shimkunas, 1972), has received far less attention from researchers (Doster et al., 1975). Specifically, the psychological symptoms of nonpsychotic patients are presumed to be within the range of understanding of other persons and permit the enactment of reciprocal roles. Others become involved in a role with the patient in terms of his "sickness" or mental disease. Yet, interpersonal intimacy also is avoided since responsibility for what takes place is attributed to disease symptomatology rather than the patient's endeavor to influence or direct the course of interpersonal events.

By example, consider the case of a large family in which the father was diagnosed for an insidious and terminal disease. Following extensive diagnostic tests, the wife and physician kept the results of the examination a secret from her spouse and children in order to spare them mental anguish. The secret, which everyone came to know but no one would mention, controlled the affairs of this family to an incredible extent. Over a period of several years, this was the best-kept secret of the family. And within this time frame, the husband developed a drinking problem, became suspicious and demanding on the activities of family members, verbally and physically abused the wife and children, and increasingly withdrew from social contacts outside the home. For the most part, family members tempered their anger, suffered the abuse, and were placating in their behavior in the belief that "he would not act this way if he were not sick." Clearly, the family members were involved in a social process with one another, but the roles that evolved with the secret restricted openness and they avoided intimacy with one another. Indeed, the identified patient was also restricted from seeking understanding and support, especially in light of his progressively deteriorating physical condition, until the rule of secrecy was broken.

Frequently therapists, in their construing of the constructs under which their clients are operating, also encounter the dilemma of how to be influenced by their clients' "symptomatic" behavior with respect to their role enactments. In these instances, therapists may very well wish their clients to be more "motivated" for treatment by behaving differently in therapy than they do outside therapy. Yet, it is unreasonable to expect clients to have developed dual systems of personal constructs, one system for the community and another for the therapy context. More likely, therapists will construe the construing of their clients as significant others have before them and will either accept, resist, or redefine this definition of what will take place between them.

Whether the therapist accepts or resists in a role-taking sense the interactional trend proposed or presented by the client, it is unlikely that therapeutic change will take place. Understanding the if-then facet of constructs under which the client is operating and acceptance through reciprocal role enactment maintains the status quo of the client's personal constructs and probably ensures the longevity of the client-therapist relationship. Consider, for example, a middle-aged patient, Mr. C., who enters each therapy session with a shopping list of favors to request of the therapist. After each session, the therapist enthusiastically sets about to fulfill the favors requested. Very soon, though, the therapist's motivation for therapy decreases as the client's motivation for therapy increases (judged by the expanding list of requests). Many sessions later, the therapist began to resist the influencing of the client by placing favor-fulfilling activities outside the responsibility of the therapist. Subsequently, however, the client's attendance of therapy sessions became sporadic. Neither acceptance nor resistance of the client's construal of the relationship permitted change to take place.

The case of another client also helps to exemplify the dilemma for therapy. In the first session, John W. reported to his therapist his knowledge concerning a massive conspiracy under way to bring about racial integration of the population. He also disclosed how he had come to distinguish the "nonconspirators" from the "conspirators," depending on whether or not persons dressed in one or a mixture of colors. Wanting to be sorted into the otherwise small but proper group, the therapist invested in an all-blue outfit and religiously wore blue on Tuesdays when the client was scheduled for his sessions. Essentially, the therapist, through his nonverbal behavior, confirmed the patient's view of the world, while verbally attempting to modify his construing. On the other hand, this client had prematurely terminated therapy with therapists whom he had identified as conspirators.

Often, by the time clients reach psychotherapy, significant others have become annoyed with and resist or avoid the influence of clients' symptomatic behavior on their role enactments. They abandon their efforts to cheer those who are persistently depressed, or to assure those who disesteem themselves, or to encourage those who self-doubt their coping abilities, or to become close to those who feel alienated. Likewise, this pattern may become a recurring trend of client-therapist interaction wherein client symptomatology quantifiably increases with the therapist's resistance to influence. Tardiness, cancellations or missed sessions, and premature termination may represent the client's resistance of the therapist's resistances or his further attempt to impose a resisted construct on what takes place in therapy.

A paradox that arises in the relationship clients have with their therapists, family, or friends is that they often do not want control over their lives in the manner in which they have affected control over their lives. The therapy sketches that follow may help exemplify this circumstance. A young man and former soldier sought individual therapy for severe depression within months of returning to the United States following combat duty in Vietnam. A central theme of his complaints was that others were not able to understand him, what he had endured, and the effect of this experience on him. In the early sessions, the therapist quite clearly established that family members, close friends, and the fellow's wife had all tried the best they could to understand. In fact, the wife struggled so intensely to experience what her husband seemed to have experienced—"as though I had been there myself"—that she began to lose hold of her own identity. As others increased their efforts to understand, seemingly the client increasingly felt not understood. His first sense of relief came in therapy when the therapist assured him that others certainly would not be able to understand his war experience and it was unlikely that the experience ever would make sense to him. That others thought they understood sharply contrasted with the depth of the client's failing to understand a very substantial event in his life. At this turning point, both therapist and client worked successfully to redefine what would take place in their therapy relationship.

The next example is provided by a three-person family in which the parents and an adolescent son were at odds with one another on a daily basis and in their judgments on "just about anything." Of most concern to the parents, though, was that the son typically controlled the outcome of their disagreements by threatening to run away or by running away from home for several hours or a few days at a time. During these periods, the parents' worry for their son's welfare strongly competed with their anger at his leaving. The turning point in this family interactional pattern came by accident and not in therapy. One afternoon during a routine disagreement between mother and son, the latter again threatened to run away. On this occasion and quite unexpectedly, the mother went to her son's room, packed his suitcase, ushered him out of the house, and locked the door. The runaway was aborted. The son asked to be let into the house, then insisted, and later demanded to be let in, but to no avail. Hours later the husband returned home from work, at which point mother joined father and son outside in order to work out an agreeable definition of what would and would not take place in the family. The door to the house was unlocked, disagreements decreased, runaways became extinct, and over time the family began to grow closer to one another in their relationships. In the two cases that have been described, the turning point occurred when the operating construct became inoperative. Yet this point typically represents the beginning rather than the ending of therapy.

Other research has examined the social interaction of family members with one member, usually the child, as an identified patient. One very promising concept about interaction in families is that of organization within this social unit. The presumption of investigation is that as organization increases within this group, limitations on flexibility or freedom of interaction also increase. Haley (1964) looked at the patterning of "who follows whom" during interactions in family triads, with a dimension of organization ranging from low to high. To understand this measure, consider that there are six possible sequences along which interaction may flow when father (F), mother (M), and child (C) are together: F follows M, M follows F, F follows C, M follows C, C follows F, C follows M. As organization increases, some sequences become used proportionately more often than other sequences. Employing this method in his study of families, Haley found a very strong, positive relationship between organization within families and other indices of family psychopathology. The level of significance was 0.00003. In addition, Haley found that organizational patterns of families were highly stable over time.

More recently, Dammann (1969) employed the organization measure to define level of disturbance in families with an adolescent child as an identified patient. With instructions, films, and practice, she trained fathers and mothers to recognize statements that would reflect positive, negative, or ambiguous self-conceptualizations on the part of another and to use social reinforcement principles to strengthen positive self-concept statements. After parents reached criterion in analogue practice, the parents were brought together with their child in a family conversation. Parents in both high and low disturbed families showed the same high level of positive social reinforcement with respect to their children's verbal behavior. However, parents in highly organized families were also reinforcing the wrong behaviors. In summary, it would seem that families who show more freedom or fewer limitations in their interactional patterns are more likely to show better adjustment and when problems arise are more likely to profit from brief, educative therapy approaches. Conversely, higher organization in family interaction patterns relates to maladjustment in families and poor response to brief, educative therapy approaches.

Still another study, involving behavioral contracting with marital dyads, demonstrates the importance of interactional concepts for the success of treatment. Holliday (1976) worked with marital couples who came to a university psychology clinic for help with behavioral complaints in their relationship. Behavioral contracting is one of the most frequently used methods in marital behavior therapy and is generally regarded as an effective approach. Even so, Holliday was concerned with interactional factors that might moderate success or failure of this approach. She attempted to relate congruency of meanings of behaviors in the marital contract to outcome. Specifically, couples specified sources of marital dissatisfaction in behavioral terms (e.g., husband gets food on his face while we are out eating) as well as directed acts that each found enjoyable when received from the other (e.g., wife gives husband a back rub). Following the initial assessment interview, couples were given a rationale and instructions concerning the principles of contracting, and then they saw a film that exemplified the negotiating process by which couples reach explicit agreement on who will do what for whom.

During subsequent therapy sessions, couples arranged their behavioral exchanges by mutual agreement. Trained raters listened to the couples discuss the dissatisfying and satisfying behaviors in their marriage and sorted them into six categories based on the apparent meanings to the couple. The categories were those defined by Foa (1971) as resources exchanged in social interaction: love, money, goods, services, information, and status. Holliday proposed that behaviors exchanged between husband and wife for which meanings were proximal, or more alike, would lead to more successful outcomes in therapy. Conversely, therapy was expected to be less effective when couples exchanged behaviors that were more distal in meaning. Couples showed significant improvement during the course of therapy regardless of whether the contracts they followed had proximal or distal meanings. During the follow-up period after treatment, couples with proximal contracts maintained their gains in treatment. However, couples who had enacted distal contracts did not maintain their gains during the follow-up period and showed a stronger tendency toward deterioration. It would seem, then, that the meanings of behaviors for individuals involved in a change experience are at least as important as the behaviors themselves in planning treatment strategies.

After the marital couples independently coded the behaviors for the exchange according to Foa's six categories, many couples would later ask one another, "What did you put for such and such?" The self-disclosures had an interesting impact among the couples. Apparently, some were pleased by their agreement, others were puzzled or found humor in their disagreements, while still others disagreed about their disagreements.

Trends similar to these can be observed when working with couples and families in conjoint counseling. Of particular importance is how members handle differences of meanings they give to what takes place in their lives. Some persons will differentiate understanding and agreement and respect one another's individuality. Other persons will equate understanding with agreement and try to impose the "right" meaning on the other. One way that I have of trying to understand family or marital interaction is to observe their understanding of one another. Using the personal constructs of family members elicited on the Rep Test, each family member in turn is invited to say all that he or she knows about the construct of another family member. One husband who boasted he knew "all there is to know about my wife" of 14 years because "we have always communicated with each other" became indignant during the exercise when the wife, with a bit of glee, said no in response to several of his examples. Later, in a more serious frame, she revealed that she had not felt known or understood by her husband for the past several years and had doubts about whether he was still interested in her as a person. This couple had three children who, during the initial sessions, were quite out of control. One child had been officially diagnosed as "hyperactive" and the other two children had activity levels nearly as high. Soon after therapy began, observers of the family session began to systematically record the frequency of motor disruptions and verbal interruptions of each family member. The records confirmed an impression that all three children engaged in high levels of disruptive activity. Even so, a very important event had gone unnoticed—the parents verbally interrupted family members' conversations at substantially higher frequencies than their children's activities disrupted family members' conversations. Behavioral contracting quickly reduced interruptions and disruptions to acceptable levels and permitted family members the opportunity to listen, to be heard, and to begin the process of knowing one another.

Earlier in the chapter, a distinction was made between monadic and dyadic approaches to interactional analysis. A study that exemplifies this distinction quite well is one by Fruge (1976), using a rotating dyad method as a format for observing social interaction. He had several groups, with eight males in each group, and by rotation of dyads each member had an opportunity to get to know every other member of his group. He was particularly interested in the ways persons attempt to influence or control the interactions they have with one another. Toward this end, he adopted the behavioral measures used so successfully by Mishler and Waxler (1968) in their now classic analysis of interactions in normal and disturbed families. One dimension of influence is "attention-control" or behaviors that function to maintain attention on the speaker—for example, speech duration. Another dimension of influence is "person-control" or behaviors that confront the attention of another. With respect to this latter category, Mishler and Waxler distinguished direct and indirect person-control behaviors. An example of the first type is interruptions, which directly and overtly confront the attention of the other person. Questioning, an example of the second type, is much more subtle in its effect on another person. Most anyone who is asked a long series of closed questions in one sitting will soon experience a rhythm of answering, resting, and waiting for the next question. The inquirer, not the responder, is in control of what takes place.

Prior to the interactions, Fruge administered questionnaires designed to measure the assertiveness, perceived locus of control, and need for dominance of the participants. After the dyadic interaction was over, members of each group sat around and rank-ordered the other seven members on several dimensions of interpersonal impressions.

Following the monadic tradition, Fruge correlated the personality test scores of each subject with his averaged behavior across the seven dyads. The very prominent personality inventories failed to predict the behavior of these persons. He also tried to predict from the personality inventories the average impression a person made on the seven people with whom he had interacted. Again, personality measures were unrelated to the impressions others formed of how comfortable he seemed to others, how influential he appeared in the relationship, how much enjoyment he seemed to derive from the interaction, how well known he made himself, or whether others wanted to know him better. Finally, when the averaged behavior of persons in dyads was correlated with the averaged impressions others formed of one another, only one relationship was significant. Persons who, on the average, asked a lot of questions in their dyads were perceived by their partners as better known to them.

In the dyadic analysis, one dimension that Fruge looked at was the dyad as a unit relative to other dyads. For example, the verbal productivity, or total speech duration, of one dyad relative to other dyads; or the overall impressions that members of dyads had of one another—such as seeing themselves as a generally comfortable dyad or as a generally uncomfortable dyad. The second dimension he considered was role congruency-differentiation within dyads. This dimension was defined by the degree of discrepancy between the behaviors of partners in a dyad and between the impressions that partners formed of one another in each dyad. For example, if one member is a talker, then role differentiation may place the other member as a listener. Or one member may be viewed as more influential and view the other member as less influential in the interaction. Dyadic analysis of human social interaction was considerably more productive in relating interpersonal impressions to what took place in a behavioral sense in each dyad. For example, dyads whose members held highly congruent views of one another as being very uninfluential persons had the lowest level of verbal productivity and the highest rate of questioning (indirect person-control). In contrast, dyads whose members held moderately congruent, but not equivalent, views of one another (there was some role differentiation) as being influential persons had the highest level of verbal productivity, had the highest rate of interruptions (direct person-control), were more differentiated in their rate of interrupting one another, and had the lowest rate of questioning one another. Comfort and enjoyment impressions within dyads also were related to particular patterns of interaction, but space does not permit fuller exploration. In summary, individuals show a great deal of variability in the ways they relate to others with regard to what takes place, who controls the direction of interaction, and how participants construe themselves in an unfolding relationship. Causality is not inherent in dyadic interactions but is construed by participants. Two people meet for the first time and try to get to know each other. Question after question after question is exchanged between them but fails to maintain their conversation. One member of the dyad construes the other as having very little influence in maintaining the flow of their interaction. The other quietly holds a similar view of this new acquaintance. Though each may blame the other for the poor quality of their interaction, they share a mutual problem.

CONCLUSION

Among the qualities that Kelly (1955) identifies as important for therapists are "skill in observation" and "a subsuming construct system." The complexity of human social interaction, whether within the context of psychotherapy or the alternative contexts that represent the day-to-day involvements of our clients, challenges our skills in observation and understanding. It is hoped that some of the intricacies of interaction have become illuminated, if only to direct attention to potentialities and stir interest. We need to expand the range of attention with respect to what takes place in human interaction well beyond traditional verbal therapy approaches. Similarly, therapies that focus only on the actions or behaviors of clients independent of their social unit(s) will miss understanding their embeddedness in the social context. Finally, treatment strategies gain from understanding the meanings individuals give to their own behavior and that of significant others. The individualities of social units need to be understood and appreciated. Meanings are personal meanings in interpersonal relationships, and are very precious.

Although the literature surveyed for the chapter does not focus primarily on research within construct theory, the Personal Construct Psychologist is busily engaged in elaborating the concept of social role. Certainly the chapters of this volume point up this concern. Particularly, note McCoy's work with couples facing the problems of intercultural marriage; Mancuso's formal attempts to alert mothers to the construct systems of their children; and Ravenette's statement of profound understanding as he interacts with Graham. Then there is the methodology of interpersonal transaction and construct research measures introduced by Landfield and Rivers (1975) and Landfield (1979). Finally, there is the important volume by construct psychologists Stringer and Bannister (1979), *Constructs of Sociality and Individuality.*

REFERENCES

Adams, H. E., Doster, J. A., & Calhoun, K. S. A psychologically based system of response classification, In A. R. Ciminero, K. S. Calhoun, and H. E. Adams (Eds.), *Handbook of behavioral assessment.* New York: Wiley, 1977.

American Psychiatric Association. *Diagnostic and statistical manual of mental disorders* (2nd ed.). Washington D.C.: American Psychiatric Association, 1968.

Bakan, D. *On Method.* San Francisco: Jossey-Bass, 1967.

Bandler, R., & Grinder, J. *The Structure of Magic.* Palo Alto, CA: Science and Behavior Books, 1975.

Birdwhistell, R. L. *Kinesics and Context.* Philadelphia: University of Pennsylvania Press, 1970.

Bowers, K. S. Situationalism in psychology: An analysis and a critique. *Psychological Review,* 1973, **80,** 307–336.

Braginsky, B. M., & Braginsky, D. D. Schizophrenic patients in the psychiatric interview: An experimental study of their effectiveness at manipulation. *Journal of Consulting Psychology,* 1967, **31,** 543–547.

Bruner, J. W., Goodnow, J. J., & Austin, G. A. *A Study of Thinking.* New York: Science Editions, 1965.

Cogan, J. M. The effect of the presence or absence of another person on the verbalizations of schizophrenics under a demand for intimate self-disclosure. *Dissertation Abstracts International,* 1976, **36** (7-B), 3594.

Dammann, C. A. Patterns of family communication and the ability of parents to administer accurate reinforcement: A pilot study. Unpublished manuscript, Emory University, 1969.

Danziger, K. *Interpersonal Communication.* New York: Pergamon, 1976.

Doster, J. A., & Nesbitt, J. G. Self-disclosure in psychotherapy. In G. J. Chelune (Ed.), *Self-Disclosure.* San Francisco: Jossey-Bass, 1979.

Doster, J. A., Surratt, F., & Webster, T. N. Interpersonal variables affecting pathological communications of hospitalized psychiatric patients. Paper presented at the Southeastern Psychological Association, Atlanta, GA, 1975.

Duck, S. W. *Personal Relationships and Personal Constructs.* London: Wiley, 1973.

Foa, U. G. Interpersonal and economic resources. *Science,* 1971, **171,** 345–351.

Fruge, E. A multimethod investigation of influential, dominant, or assertive behavior. Unpublished doctoral dissertation, University of Georgia, 1976.

Haley, J. *Strategies of Psychotherapy.* New York: Harper & Row, 1963.

Haley, J. Research on family patterns: An instrument measure. *Family Process,* 1964, **3,** 41–65.

Hall, E. T. *The Silent Language.* New York: Fawcett World Library, 1959.

Holliday, P. B. Some implications of resource exchange theory for behavioral contracting within marital dyads. Unpublished master's thesis, University of Georgia, 1976.

Kelly, G. A. *The Psychology of Personal Constructs:* Vols. 1 and 2. New York: Norton, 1955.

Kety, S. S. Problems in psychiatric nosology from the viewpoint of the biological sciences. In M. M. Katz, J. O. Cole, & W. E. Barton (Eds.), *The Role and Methodology of Classification in Psychiatry and Psychopathology.* Chevy Chase, MD: National Institute of Mental Health, 1965.

Kiesler, D. J., & Bernstein, A. J. A communications critique of behavior therapies. Unpublished manuscript, Virginia Commonwealth University, 1974.

Landfield, A. W. *Personal Construct Systems in Psychotherapy.* Chicago: Rand McNally, 1971.

Landfield, A. W. The complaint: A confrontation of personal urgency and professional construction. In D. Bannister (Ed.), *Issues and Approaches in Psychological Therapies.* London: Wiley, 1975.

Landfield, A. W., & Rivers, P. C. Interpersonal transaction and rotating dyads. *Psychotherapy: Theory, Research and Practice,* 1975, **12,** 366–374.

Landfield, A. W. Exploring socialization through the interpersonal transaction group. In P. Stringer & D. Bannister (Eds.), *Constructs of Sociality and Individuality,* London: Academic, 1979.

Matloff, J. L. The interactional behavior of normal individuals with peers suspected of being ex-mental patients. Unpublished doctoral dissertation, University of Georgia, 1977.

Mendel, W. M., & Rapport, S. Determinants of the decision for psychiatric hospitalization. *Archives of General Psychiatry,* 1969, **20,** 321–328.

Mischel, W. *Personality and Assessment.* New York: Wiley, 1968.

Mishler, E. G., & Waxler, N. E. *Interaction in Families.* New York: Wiley, 1968.

Morris, C. *Signs, Language and Behavior.* New York: Braziller, 1955.

Ritchie, P. L. J. The effect of the interviewer's presentation on some schizophrenic symptomology. *Dissertation Abstracts International,* 1976, **36,** (10-B), 5279–5280.

Rosenhan, D. L. On being sane in insane places. *Science,* 1973, **183,** 250–257.

Rotter, J. B. *Social Learning and Clinical Psychology.* Englewood Cliffs, NJ: Prentice-Hall, 1954.

Ruesch, J., & Bateson, G. *Communication.* New York: Norton, 1951.

Rychlak, J. F. *Introduction to Personality and Psychotherapy.* Boston: Houghton Mifflin, 1973.

Shapiro, J. G., Krauss, H. H., & Truax, C. B. Therapeutic conditions and disclosure beyond the therapeutic encounter. *Journal of Counseling Psychology,* 1969, **16,** 290–294.

Shimkunas, A. Demand for intimate self-disclosure and pathological verbalizations in schizophrenia. *Journal of Abnormal Psychology,* 1972, **80,** 197–205.

Sommer, R. *Personal Space.* Englewood Cliffs, NJ: Prentice-Hall, 1969.

Stringer, P., & Bannister, D. *Constructs of Sociality and Individuality,* London: Academic, 1979.

Sullivan, H. S. *The interpersonal theory of psychiatry.* H. S. Perry & M. L. Gawel (Eds.), New York: Norton, 1953.

Thomas, L. *The Lives of a Cell.* New York: Bantam, 1974.

Ullmann, L. P., & Krasner, L. *A Psychological Approach to Abnormal Behavior* (2nd ed.). Englewood Cliffs, NJ: Prentice-Hall, 1975.

Watzlawick, P., Beavin, J. H., & Jackson, D. D. *Pragmatics of Human Communication.* New York: Norton, 1967.

Wenger, D. L., & Fletcher, C. R. The effects of legal counsel on admissions to a state hospital: A confrontation of professions. *Journal of Health and Human Behavior,* 1969, **10,** 66–72.

Wolpe, J. Quantitative relationships in the systematic desensitization of phobias. *American Journal of Psychiatry,* 1963, **119,** 1062–1068.

Zarlock, S. P. Social expectations, language, and schizophrenia. *Journal of Humanistic Psychology,* 1966, **6,** 68–74.

CHAPTER 12

Personal Construct Theory and Psychotherapy Research

John E. Carr

To the extent that one person construes the construction processes of another, he may play a role in a social process involving the other person.

While it was the final component in Kelly's theoretical system, the "sociality" corollary was clearly the most significant feature of Personal Construct Theory (PCT), since "the implications of this corollary are probably the most far reaching of any I have yet attempted to propound" (Kelly, 1970). The corollary states explicitly the fundamental psychological process underlying interpersonal relationships in general and the helping relationships in particular, but despite its implications for the whole field of psychotherapy research, it has been largely ignored by investigators in that area. Indeed, as Liebert and Spiegler (1970) pointed out, more research has probably been directed toward the Role Repertory Test than the corollaries of PCT itself. Despite this fact, a rather respectable body of unobtrusive or indirect empirical support for the sociality corollary has accumulated as a result of research efforts largely outside of PCT.

HISTORICAL PERSPECTIVE

Psychotherapy researchers have long acknowledged the important role played by the patient-therapist relationship in determining the outcome of psychotherapy. However, operational definitions of the component factors in this relationship and empirical demonstrations of the relationship of these factors to outcome were conspicuous by their absence in the literature. The concept of "therapist's understanding" emerged as a prominent feature in descriptions of the ideal therapeutic relationship in the 1950s (Fiedler, 1950). A decade later, the relationship between "understanding" and improvement in psychotherapy was well established (Lorr, 1965), but attention was turning to a more precise delineation of the psychological processes underlying this concept. In reviews of the literature on

233

the psychotherapeutic relationship, a new category of variables—therapist-patient similarity—was emerging to join the traditional categories of patient variables and technique variables (Gardner, 1964; Luborsky et al., 1971).

Not surprisingly, the majority of research effort at this time was focused on defining the characteristics of the optimal therapy patient: motivated, only moderately maladjusted, friendly, submissive, and in the middle to upper social class. Attempts to define relevant therapist and technique variables were essentially inconclusive and confounded with relationship factors. Therapist-patient similarity was, in fact, simplistically defined in terms of personality similarities, either as perceived or as measured via psychological tests. Research findings were at best ambiguous, suggesting that alternative conceptual bases for therapist-patient similarity required exploration. By the end of the 1960s, however, some notable trends were beginning to emerge.

Luborsky et al. (1971) reviewed 166 studies of predictions of outcome in individual psychotherapy with adult patients and found 14 studies that dealt with some form of similarity between patient and therapist. Nine showed positive outcome as a function of patient-therapist similarity in social class, interests, values, or compatibility of orientation to social relationships. Nonsignificant, equivocal, or negative relationships were found where similarity was defined in terms of matching on personality tests or Q-sorts. Thus, there was some suggestion that the key to the similarity factor was to be found in the area of cognitive process and not personality. Witkin et al. (1962) had already shown the significant role played by cognitive process in determining behavior. Noting that therapists respond differentially to patients of greater and lesser degrees or levels of conceptual complexity, Witkin et al. (1968) raised the question as to whether or not a study in which therapists and patients are paired based on differentiation levels might be productive in the future.

Another methodological approach to the complementarity model was provided by the development of the Fundamental Interpersonal Relations Orientation (FIRO) scales by Schutz (1958). These scales were devised as a means of operationalizing interpersonal compatibility measured in terms of (a) how the individual treats others (expressed behavior), and (b) how the individual desires to be treated (wished-for behavior) with respect to three need areas: inclusion, control, and affection. Sapolsky (1965) applied Schutz's notions to the psychotherapy relationship and found that doctor-patient compatibility as measured by the FIRO-B correlated significantly with patient improvement as assessed by therapy supervisors' ratings. Gassner (1970) attempted to expand upon Sapolsky's work by testing three hypotheses: (a) patients who are compatible with their therapists view their relationship more favorably than patients who are incompatible; (b) compatible patients show more improvement than incompatible patients; and (c) therapists' ratings of the relationship are more favorable for compatible than incompatible patients. The therapists were 24 theology students in pastoral counseling training and the patients were psychiatric patients at a large state hospital. Each therapist treated a compatible and incompatible patient (based on scores from the FIRO-B), and the performance of these two groups was compared against 24 randomly chosen no-treatment controls.

High-compatibility matched patients were more favorable toward their therapists after 3 and 11 weeks of treatment. However, therapists did not prefer relating to their high- versus low-compatibility patients. Further, there was no difference in the behavioral change found among the three groups.

While some researchers were focusing upon personality-based definitions of similarity, others were investigating the role of values and attitudes in patient-therapist matching. The study of Welkowitz et al. (1967) of the role of value system similarity and its effect upon psychotherapy outcome seemed especially promising. Thirty-eight therapists and 44 patients at two psychoanalytic training centers participated in the study. Values were measured by the "Ways to Live Scale" and the Strong Vocational Inventory. The results of the study indicated that while therapists did not share a homogeneous value system, therapists and their own patients were much closer in values than those who were randomly paired. Further, those patients who were rated as most improved by their therapists were closer to their therapists in values than patients rated least improved.

Beutler et al. (1974) attempted to predict the outcome of group psychotherapy based on an examination of seven attitudes varying in degree of centrality. At the conclusion of 3 months of therapy, it was found that among attitudes of medium centrality, initial attitude difference between the patient and the therapist was more strongly related to attitude change than were either attitude similarity or acceptability. However, initial patient-therapist similarity and acceptability of attitudes were related more to patient-rated improvement than was attitude dissimilarity.

Later, Beutler et al. (1975) examined the relative effects of attitude similarity between patient and therapist, and therapist credibility as predictors of attitude change and improvement in psychotherapy. Highly credible therapists produced higher patient outcome ratings than low-credible therapists, but initial patient-therapist attitude similarity was inversely related to the therapist's persuasive influence and unrelated to the therapist's perceived credibility. Thus, attitude similarity, in some cases, may detract from the therapist's ability to influence the patient and, therefore, may be deleterious to the outcome of the treatment.

A hybrid approach involving both personality similarity and complementarity bases for matching was taken by Dougherty (1976) in a study of patient-therapist matching for the prediction of optimal-minimal therapeutic outcomes. On the basis of 11 psychological variables, selected by a factor analytic technique, Dougherty delineated patients and therapists into three typological (personality) categories and then further differentiated the therapists into two groups with respect to a theoretical approach to therapy. Using therapist ratings of outcome as criteria, five regression equations were evolved that validly and reliably predicted outcome for various patient and therapist types. Six groups of therapeutic dyads were then formed and followed for a year in therapy. Optimal outcomes were predicted for two experimental matched groups, minimal therapist outcome ratings were predicted for two experimental mismatched groups, and each compared with two additional groups controlled for patient and therapist type.

As predicted, the matched group received higher therapist ratings of outcome than either the mismatched groups or the control groups. While the study demonstrates the potential value of matching procedures, the methodological complexity involved in providing the prediction scores makes the procedure relatively impractical from a clinical standpoint. Also, the validity of the procedure may be subject to question since it is based entirely upon therapist ratings of outcome as the prediction criterion. It has been widely demonstrated that there is often limited agreement between therapist and patient ratings of psychotherapy outcome or between therapist ratings and more objective indices of symptom reduction. Thus, one must question whether the procedure described by Dougherty optimizes a "therapeutic" effect or merely increases the probability that if one selects on the basis of therapist's criteria, one gets improved outcome, as judged by the therapist.

CONTRIBUTIONS FROM SOCIAL PSYCHOLOGY

While psychotherapy researchers were struggling to define the nature of the patient-therapist relationship and its effect upon psychotherapy outcome, two lines of research in social psychology had emerged which had significant implications for this search. In large part, this research effort was a result of the "new look in perception" which was the focus of social and cognitive psychology in the 1950s.

First, successful communication in a dyadic interaction was shown to depend on the similarity in cognitive dimensions used by each of the participants in an interaction as each attempted to communicate with the other and to independently describe environmental events (Newcomb, 1958; Runkel, 1956; Triandis, 1960). If the two individuals involved were a patient and his/her therapist, then successful treatment outcome must relate to the similarity in cognitive dimensions of the two participants. However, it remained for subsequent researchers to demonstrate that the interaction was not reciprocal. Successful outcome was specifically a function of the therapist's ability to accurately perceive and communicate within the system of cognitive dimensions which comprised the patient's conceptualization of his experience (Cartwright & Lerner, 1963; Landfield & Nawas, 1964; Rogers, 1967).

Second, social and behavioral scientists had long acknowledged that an individual's success in coping with the social environment was largely determined by the degree to which that person was able to develop a sufficiently differentiated cognitive representation of the environment (Zajonk, 1968).

Similarity in cognitive dimensions of patient and therapist could be defined not only in terms of similarity in the concepts used (i.e., the content), but also in terms of similarity in the degree to which these dimensions were differentiated. For example, a patient and therapist may share a common conceptual dimension such as *anxious vs. calm*. However, for the patient the dimension may be poorly differentiated, allowing few discriminations among persons within his/her social experience, while for the therapist it may be highly differentiated, permitting the perception of a large number of differences among persons in his/her social experience. Whether these two individuals agreed that a person was anxious or not would not necessarily depend on whether they used the same semantic label, but whether they shared a relatively common degree of differentiation in the conceptual dimension. Therefore, the functional similarity of conceptual structure could be distinguished from the semantic similarity, and operationally defined in terms of the degree to which the level of differentiation of one approached the level of differentiation of the other.

Amending the original communication hypothesis taken from social psychology, we arrived at the following *matching hypothesis:* "Optimal communication between a patient and therapist should require not only the sharing of a number of common conceptual dimensions, but a high degree of mutuality in the extent to which various stimulus objects are differentiated along these dimensions" (Carr, 1970).

THE INTERPERSONAL DISCRIMINATION TASK

If we assumed that every individual brings into any situation his own repertoire of personal dimensions, then cognizance must be taken of this variability in idiosyncratic dimensions in assessing individual behavior. It was on the basis of this fundamental concept that George Kelly evolved the Psychology of Personal Constructs, and it was on the basis of the need for a unique instrument to assess the cognitive dimensions of personality that Kelly developed the Role Construct Repertory Test (Rep Test). Regrettably, early research into the basic postulates of Kelly's system had been hampered in part by the complexity of the Rep Test, as well as the extended time required for its administration. Various attempts had been made to devise shortened and less complex alternatives to the Rep Test (e.g., Bieri, 1966), but this was done at the expense of introducing methodological modifications which appeared to deviate from or were inconsistent with Kelly's theory. Thus, the Interpersonal Discrimination Task (IDT) came into being primarily in response to a felt need to develop a simpler, less time-consuming measure of cognitive structure, yet still retain the original Kellian goal of giving the subject the opportunity to provide his own construct dimensions. Further, given one's own dimensions within which to operate, the instrument was to provide the opportunity to demonstrate the effectiveness with which the subject could discriminate among various stimulus elements (social or otherwise) in the environment. In the process, the IDT was to provide four different quantitative measures of interpersonal discrimination with which to assess S's performance. The IDT, complete with instructions to the subject, is shown in Appendix I.

While the discrimination procedure itself is moderately demanding, the instructions appear to take the subject step-by-step through the various alternatives and in the process clarify the nature of the task. We have found that, with few exceptions, practically anyone can complete the IDT, and we have successfully administered the instrument to children aged six (instructions may be delivered verbally and the discrimination task demonstrated more concretely). The exceptions include subjects who are limited intellectually and, individuals suffering severe cognitive disturbances—that is, psychotics.

SCORING

Overall Score (O-A)

The numbers of boxes into which the *S* divided his/her six conceptual dimensions are summed and divided by 6 to yield an overall discrimination-per-concept score.

Other-Other Score (O-O)

The number of persons, excluding the self (M), placed in boxes separate from Person 1 are counted on each of the six dimensions. This procedure is repeated for each of the six "other" persons. Raw scores for each "other" person on each of the concepts (36 scores) are totaled and the sum divided by 36 to yield an other-other discrimination-per-concept score.

Since the other-other score depends upon the number of boxes used and the number of people in each box (code), the score is easily obtained from Table 1, which describes all possible box-code combinations and their corresponding other-other scores. Note that the sequence of the code is unimportant. For example, in the case of the second three-box dimension, the code represents all possible three-box situations in which there are three persons in one box, one in another, and one in the third, regardless of the order of the boxes.

Self-Other Score (S-O)

The number of persons placed in boxes separate from *S* are totaled for the six dimensions and divided by 6 to yield a self-other discrimination-per-concept score.

Table 1. Box-Code Combinations and Their Corresponding Other-Other Scores

Number of Boxes	(Number of Others in Boxes)	Total O-O Score	Mean O-O Score
1	6	0	0
2	1 - 5	10	1.67
2	2 - 4	16	2.67
2	3 - 3	18	3.00
3	1 - 1 - 4	18	3.00
3	1 - 2 - 3	22	3.67
3	2 - 2 - 2	24	4.00
4	1 - 1 - 1 - 3	24	4.00
4	1 - 1 - 2 - 2	26	4.33
5	1 - 1 - 1 - 1 - 2	28	4.67
6	1 - 1 - 1 - 1 - 1	30	5.00

Self-Distinctiveness Score (S-D)

The mean number of times S places himself in a separate and distinct box is judged to be an index of self-distinctiveness. The number of self-distinctiveness ratings on differentiated concepts are summed and divided by 6.

Of the various scores, O-A is most frequently used as a general index of differentiation level. It is the simplest to compute and combines properties of all the other scores. S-O, O-O, and S-D permit the researcher to look more closely at the differentiation process as a function of who is being discriminated from whom, and to what degree. An obvious relationship exists among any subject's scores. There is reason to assume that this reflects a logical as well as a mechanical implication in the discrimination task. In comparing himself to six other persons, if an S sees himself as similar to only three of these, then he is "different" from three and can make a maximum of four discriminations among the six other persons. The relationship between O-A, S-O, O-O, and S-D is presented in Table 2. As anticipated, the scores intercorrelate highly across groups. However, we have found that the relationship may vary considerably from one individual to another, and that individual scores may vary selectively in response to certain factors, such as, the developmental level of the person or situational influences (Carr, 1965a).

Reliability

Both one day and then two months following initial administration, 25 undergraduate males were retested on the IDT. Between initial and first posttests, S's were administered a battery of psychological tests. Reliability coefficients for each measure are shown in Table 3.

Relation to Intellectual Functioning

School and College Abilities Tests (SCAT) scores were obtained from college records of 63 undergraduate males and correlated with measures of differentiation from the IDT. Correlations were generally small and nonsignificant.

In another study of 71 medical students and 61 psychiatric outpatients, the results indicated that the IDT relates negligibly or not at all to estimates of intellectual functioning in both groups.

Table 2.   Range of IDT Score Intercorrelations Reported in Four Studies

	O-O	S-O	O-A
S-O	.65 – .71		
O-A	.85 – .88	.76 – .80	
S-D	.27 – .34	.68 – .74	.61 – .68

Table 3.   Test-Retest Reliability Coefficients of Scores after One Day with an Intervening Task and after Two Months

| | r^* | |
Measure	1 Day	2 Months
Other-Other	.84	.65
Self-Other	.82	.58
Overall	.83	.63
Self-Distinctiveness	.83	.62

* All significant at 0.01 level.

Relation to Concreteness-Abstractness

Concreteness vs. abstractness (C-A) scores were obtained from 63 undergraduate males on a sentence-completion test of abstract functioning described by Schroder and Streufert (1962) and correlated with measures of differentiation from the IDT. Correlation coefficients were .34 and .32, respectively, both significant at the .01 level.

The correlations reported here suggest a low-order, though significant, relationship at best. However, C-A within any individual is highly dependent on situational demands for *abstract vs. concrete* responding, and subjects have been shown to vary widely in the degree to which they are capable of flexible response. Some S's seem more capable of shifting between concrete and abstract responses while other S's are more "closed" or consistent in responding to all situations in either a concrete or an abstract mode. Controlling for these sources of variability significantly raises the correlation. In a test of the Conceptual Systems Theory of Harvey et al. (1961), it was predicted that among "closed system" S's the most concrete (System I) would show similar low levels of S-O and O-O, and the moderately abstract (System II) would show increased levels of S-O, but no difference from System I S's in O-O. As seen in Table 4, these predictions were upheld. In addition, the relation between C-A (the measure of systems) and IDT was more strongly demonstrated.

Relation to Other Measures of Cognitive Style

An overview of unpublished as well as published research findings indicates the IDT to be unrelated to the Edwards or the Crowne-Marlowe social desirability scale,

Table 4.   Mean IDT Scores for Systems Groups

Systems	O-A	O-O	S-O	S-D
I	2.70	3.17	3.23	0.09
II	2.94	3.16	3.63	0.17
III	3.63	3.61	4.12	0.30

the Rokeach Dogmatism Scale, and the Gardner and Schoen Object Sorting Test. At the same time, the IDT has been shown to be significantly related to the following:

		Sex of Sampl
Halstead Categories Test	.46	M&F
Mednick Remote Associates Test	.36	M
Witkin Embedded Figures Test	.36	M
Schroder-Streufert Conceptual-Level Test	.34	M
Byrne Repression-Sensitization Scale	.31	M&F
Level of Aspiration-Expectancy	.51	M

Relation to Sex

Similar to reports by Witkin and his associates using related measures of cognitive differentiation, we have found small but consistent differences between U.S. males and females in IDT scores, but with males having slightly higher scores than females (whereas Witkin found females to have higher scores).

In contrast, no sex differences were obtained in a study of 125 Malaysian subjects of either Chinese, Malay, or Indian ethnic background. This suggests that the observed modest sex differences in the United States may be culturally determined, a hypothesis we shall have more to say about later.

Relation to Age in Normals and Patients

In a study of 87 normals and 92 psychiatric patients ranging in age from 16 to 44, Carr and Townes (1975) found a significant increase in self-distinctiveness in normals from the second to the third decade, with a progressive decline thereafter. By contrast, patients' scores dropped significantly below normals' from the second to the third decade, then rose significantly above normals' thereafter, although progressively decreasing in similar fashion. The results were interpreted in terms of patients' tendency to see themselves as discrepant with age-specific societal expectancies.

Relation to Repression vs. Sensitization in Patients

On the basis of previous research on the R-S scale, Carr and Post (1974) hypothesized that sensitizers are characterized by excessive negative self-other discriminations. In a study of 46 female and 22 male psychiatric patients they found that sensitizing patients endorsed more pathology (but not general traits) and discriminated themselves from others to a greater degree than normals on negative rather than positive dimensions. Results were consistent with the view that R-S is a measure of cognitive style, associated with excessive symptom endorsement, which in psychiatric patients can lead to errors in diagnosis and care management. These results were also consistent with an earlier finding (Carr, 1970) that the IDT was significantly correlated with differences in manifest behavior disorder and willingness to endorse psychopathology as measured by the MMPI.

DIFFERENTIATION MATCHING AND PSYCHOTHERAPY OUTCOME

A program of research was begun in late 1963 at the University of Washington School of Medicine to investigate the relationship between patient-therapist matching on conceptual differentiation and the outcome of psychotherapy. The IDT was used to provide a measure of differentiation, and preliminary studies in the research program were concerned with the development of this measure, determining its statistical properties and resolving several theoretical and methodological problems relevant to the concept of differentiation and psychotherapy outcome research (Carr, 1965a, 1965b, 1969, 1974; Carr & Whittenbaugh, 1968, 1969). There followed two investigations designed to test and replicate the primary hypothesis that differentiation matching of patient and therapist directly relates to the outcome of psychotherapy. In the first study (Carr, 1970), we were also concerned with the question of whether the degree of perceived success at the conclusion of therapy was related to the degree of patient-therapist matching at that time, and, as a corollary, whether or not incompatible or mismatched patient-therapist pairs will move toward increasing compatibility over the course of therapy. In addition, we were also concerned with the issue of the relationship of differentiation level to initial adjustment and diagnosis, a question raised by Witkin (1965) and the possible effect these variables might have on outcome.

The patients were 21 consecutive admissions to the psychiatric outpatient clinic at the University of Washington Hospital. The demographic characteristics were representative of the clinic population as a whole: age ranged from 17 to 46 with a ratio of female to male of 2:1, and the diagnoses were predominantly in the neurotic range. Therapists were fourth-year medical students participating in a psychiatric clerkship, thereby providing control for therapists' socioeconomic class, educational level, experience, theoretical orientation, and age. The specific contributing role of each of these factors was to be investigated systematically in later research.

The results of this first study supported the hypothesis that differentiation compatibility of the patient and therapist was essential to improved outcome as perceived by the patient and by the therapist, and as evidenced by the patient's reported symptom reduction (see Fig. 1). Further, we found that incompatible patients and therapists appeared to "seek" a more compatible level of differentiation, presumably as a basis for establishing more productive communication. Following the establishment of this level of compatibility, the matched therapists' differentiation level surprisingly increased. At the time, we speculated that this reflected the efforts of the therapist to further articulate the patient's relevant conceptual dimensions. An additional finding was that the patient's differentiation level was related to the number of symptom complaints she/he endorsed. Thus, we questioned whether differentiation change (and related symptom change) in the presence of cognitive compatibility were perceived by the patient as therapeutically derived improvement.

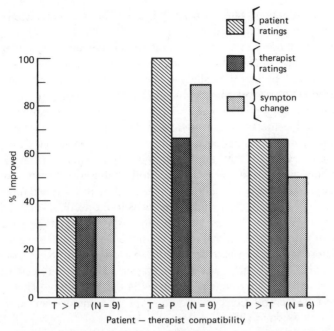

Figure 1. Percentage of patients improved in three groups differing in initial patient-therapist differentiation compatibility. (From Carr, 1970.)

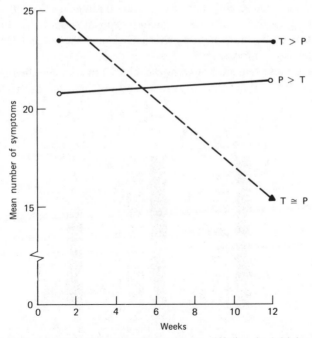

Figure 2. Patient symptom change in three groups differing in initial patient-therapist differentiation compatibility. (From Carr, 1970.)

A second investigation (Montgomery & Carr, 1971) was conducted in order to replicate the original study and to pursue two additional issues: to determine whether the compatibility in cognitive structure was perceived by either patient or therapist and, further, to determine whether or not the shifts in therapist differentiation level observed in the first study were purposeful—that is, related to the patient's differentiation level and the patient's type of disorder.

In addition to ratings of outcome, patient and therapist were asked to rate the degree to which the therapist appeared to understand the patient's problem. We found no significant differences between matched and mismatched patient-therapist groups, which suggested that the differentiation compatibility may influence outcome without patient and therapist necessarily being aware of its impact. With regard to the second question—that is, therapist shift in differentiation level, we found that in contrast to the first study, therapists in the second study reduced their differentiation level. Upon further analysis, we discovered that the patient sample was significantly different from that obtained in the first study, having higher initial differentiation scores and a preponderance of obsessive-compulsive and depressive diagnoses, as contrasted with lower differentiation scores and a greater number of psychosomatic and characterological problems in the first study. This was consistent with the observed relationship between type of pathology and differentiation level reported by Witkin (1965).

Since we had found outcome to be influenced by initial differentiation level, our original view that therapists' conceptual strategy is determined in part by the differentiation level at which the patient is operating appeared to be supported. This interpretation was consistent with an earlier finding by Zajonk (1960) that individuals modulate their conceptual structure depending upon the communication strategies demanded by the situation—that is, whether the subjects are "transmitting" or "receiving" information.

The results of these two studies were especially remarkable when one considers that we had predicted successful psychotherapy outcome on the basis of patient-

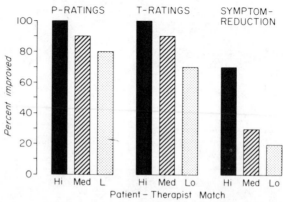

Figure 3.   Percentage of patients improved as a function of three levels of patient-therapist match.

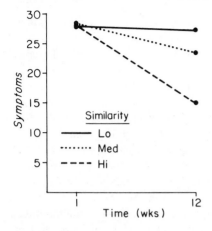

Figure 4.   Patient symptom change as a function of three levels of patient-therapist match.

therapist matching of conceptual structure, disregarding the content of their conceptual process. No better validation of Kelly's sociality corollary could have been conceived, and independent confirmation of the hypothesis began to appear in the literature.

In a study of the effects of patient-therapist similarity upon the quality and outcome of the psychotherapy relationship, Craig (1972) defined cognitive similarity as a sharing of the properties of personal language systems of the client and therapist. Operationally, the components of this definition were the level of similarity in terms of content of personal language dimensions of the therapy dyad members, the degree of meaningfulness for the client of the language dimensions of the therapist, and the degree of meaningfulness for the therapist of the language dimensions of the client.

As was predicted, the level of cognitive similarity was positively related to the assessments of therapy outcome by the client and by the therapist, to the levels of interpersonal attraction of the therapist for the clients and the clients for the therapist, and to the levels of self-disclosure by the clients. Contrary to predictions, the level of cognitive similarity was not related to the change of client self-reported symptom intensity, nor was it related to the therapist's classification of clients as premature versus nonpremature terminators. The findings were consistent with our own in that they showed a clear relationship between cognitive similarity and perceived outcome. However, the fact that cognitive similarity related to patients' perceived outcome but not to symptom change, which is based on patient self-report, was surprising.

In more substantial studies, McLachlan (1972, 1974) examined the utility of the matching hypothesis with 94 alcoholic inpatients receiving 26 hours of group therapy over a period of 3 weeks. Patients and their therapists were considered matched or mismatched based on ratings derived from Hunt's Paragraph Completion Test of Conceptual Level (Hunt, 1971). Using patients' judgments of rated improvement, McLachlan found that patients paired with therapists of matching conceptual level showed significantly greater benefit from group therapy than those patients mismatched with their therapists. The effect was found for both low conceptual level patients and high conceptual level patients, thus ruling out the possibility that it was the initial level as opposed to the matching which accounted for the change. In a follow-up study, 70% of the patients matched to their therapists in terms of conceptual level were found to have stopped drinking a year after treatment. By comparison, only 50% of the mismatched patients had stopped.

Pardes et al. (1974) investigated the role of differentiation as a factor in the treatment of hospitalized psychiatric patients. The differentiation level of 60 therapists and their patients was measured on a portable Rod and Frame Test and provided the basis for establishing three categories: high, middle, and low differentiation levels. The differentiation level of the therapist was found to be significantly correlated with the outcome of treatment, as measured by length of stay in the hospital and staff ratings of clinical improvement. A trend was manifested toward a correlation between therapist differentiation and the likelihood of readmission. In contrast, the field differentiation of the patient appeared to have little relationship to the outcome of treatment.

They also concluded that "while some tendencies were noted with regard to therapist-patient matches according to the differentiation, the numbers were too small to come to any conclusion." However, if one looks closely at the outcome rates of each of the nine groups defined by the 3 × 3 design, in each case, the highest outcome percentages obtained by therapists' groups were those groups in which patients' level of field differentiation was matched with the therapists!

DIFFERENTIATION MATCHING IN PROFESSIONAL EDUCATION

The sociality corollary is intended to have implications for social interaction other than the patient-therapist relationship. Hunt (1971) and his associates at the Ontario Institute for Studies in Education have long pursued a program of research into the impact of matching teacher, student, and educational strategy to optimize outcome in the educational setting. Our own interest in this issue derived from our concern with the training process of mental health professionals. We argued that the matching hypothesis could be invoked to support the proposal to utilize indigenous mental health workers in community mental health centers, since they purportedly share a conceptualization of the world of the target population. Our concern, however, went beyond this to the issue of whether the presence of compatibility between the indigenous worker and the mental health professional trainer would significantly determine the effectiveness of this educational effort. Thus, differentiation compatibility of the professional and the mental health worker should be as critical to the success of the community mental health movement as the compatibility of the worker and the subsequent patient.

We pursued this question (Townes & Carr, 1973) by investigating the role of teacher-student matching and teaching effectiveness in various mental health training combinations—for example, faculty/psychiatric resident, faculty/medical student, faculty/mental health worker, psychiatric resident/mental health worker, and so on. Participants in three psychiatric training seminars, providing 36 student-teacher relationships at the various levels described above, all were administered the IDT, the Object Sorting Test, and the A-B Scale. Teaching effectiveness was defined in terms of the student's rating of the teacher's performance on a 100-point scale from "least effective" to "most effective." The IDT, OST, and A-B were administered both prior to and following each course and all students rated their teachers' performances at the end of the teachers' participation.

None of the three measures (IDT, OST, or A-B) revealed a consistent significant relationship between teacher-student matching and teacher effectiveness across all possible student-teacher combinations. Rather, the differentiation level of the teacher alone seemed to account for the major portion of obtained variance. That is, the more differentiated the teacher, the higher the rating of teaching effectiveness by the student. Student-teacher matching played a secondary role only to the extent that, given the more differentiated teacher, then the more highly differentiated the student (the greater the match), the greater the likelihood of higher teacher ratings. The question was raised as to whether content area in any way affected the nature of the student-teacher relationship, or if the results were unique to training in the mental health field.

A second study was conducted using teacher-student combinations in various course content areas outside the mental health realm. The subjects were 22 faculty and 43 medical students in the first-year medical school core curriculum. Teaching was carried out within the context of courses such as Molecular and Cell Biology; Anatomy and Tissue Structure; Biostatistics and Epidemiology; Medicine, Health, and Society; and Control Systems and Mechanisms of Homeostasis. In addition to the IDT and measures of teaching effectiveness, frequency of classroom contact, defined in terms of number of hours, was also tabulated for each faculty member.

The results were essentially the same as the earlier study, with one major difference. The teacher's level of differentiation was the primary determinant of student judgments of teaching effectiveness. However, the probability of high rating of teacher effectiveness was greatest when there was a high frequency of contact with the teacher and a highly differentiated student was matched with a highly differentiated teacher. The next most optimal conditions for high teacher ratings were high frequency of contact and less differentiated teachers matched with less differentiated students. Thus, the role of differentiation matching in the teaching relationship appeared to be a far more complicated issue than was originally anticipated. The educational relationship appeared to place principal emphasis upon the complexity of the instructor's conceptual organization, and, then to a lesser degree, on the interaction between student and teacher. We presumed at the time that this reflected a demand on the part of the student for the instructor to have detailed mastery of the subject area, requiring increased conceptual differentiation in that area, and then the capability of the student to appreciate it. The findings appeared to hold for the mental health field, and for other disciplines as well, and seemed to argue most cogently against the popular mental health notion that a "meaningful" relationship can substitute for well-organized and articulated knowledge in the field.

Duehn and Proctor (1974) looked at the role of differentiation in the education of social workers by investigating the relationship between IDT scores and selected aspects of decision-making processes in social work practice. High and low scores on the IDT were compared with the amount of information transmitted about selected case summaries and the number of alternative interventions suggested. The results showed that subjects utilized more pieces of information with clients presented as similar to themselves than with dissimilar ones. However, subjects receiving low IDT scores utilized significantly fewer pieces of information with dissimilar clients than did highly differentiated subjects. Level of differentiation was significantly associated with the number of intervention activities specified, with high-scoring subjects specifying a greater number of interventions. Regardless of the degree of similarity of the clients, subjects high on the IDT suggested more interventions than did subjects who scored low.

Note that this study has features of both a psychotherapy outcome study and an educational study. Performance in a quasi-therapeutic situation is used as an outcome criterion to evaluate the effectiveness of an educational process. The results are especially fascinating since they show (1) the role of differentiation level of the "teacher" specifying intervention alternatives to the "student," and (2) the role of differentiation in the patient-therapist match in those situations requiring transmission of information by the therapist about the patient. The findings, therefore, help to underscore the nature of the differential importance of the matching hypothesis in educational versus therapeutic situations. In the formal medical school educational situation in which we conducted this research, information transmission is relatively one-way, from the instructor to the student, in the conceptual system of the instructor. In a therapeutic relationship, the information transfer is more complicated, from the patient to the therapist and back to the patient, in the conceptual system of the patient.

DIFFERENTIATION MATCHING AND COMMUNITY ACTION GROUPS

One of the most intriguing studies in our program evolved out of our concern with the implications of the matching hypothesis for the success of social interaction in a much larger context (Posthuma & Carr, 1974). The popular wisdom of the times was that prejudicial attitudes could be changed by bringing together members of disparate, estranged groups for the purpose of discussing and resolving their differences. The question we raised was whether or not this had to do simply with contact and communication or, more specifically, did conceptual matching of the participants play a role to the extent that one could predict the outcome of such interactions. We hypothesized that successful communication and task performance in action groups should be optimized when group members were matched on the basis of the level of conceptual differentiation.

An opportunity to test this hypothesis emerged when the Seattle School Board initiated plans in 1970 to establish a mandatory busing program to help ameliorate racial imbalance in the school system. To facilitate the implementation of this plan, community workshops of randomly sampled parents were organized throughout the city. On the basis of IDT scores, participants were assigned to either high-differentiation matched, medium-differentiation matched, low-differentiation matched, or mixed-differentiation groups. In addition to differentiation level of the group, groups were balanced for racial composition, and then assigned specific topic areas that were either abstract or concrete in nature (defined in terms of consensus of agreement among all workshop coordinators). It was hypothesized that matched differentiation groups would be more satisfied with the progress and outcome of the workshops than groups with mismatched memberships. Further, we predicted that the parents involved in the workshop, and particularly parents in the matched groups, would be more supportive of the busing program than parents of bused children who were not involved in the workshop.

At the completion of the workshop, participants evaluated whether the workshop had achieved its goal of increasing racial harmony and bettering the understanding of the broad range of school-related problems. A more objective behavioral criterion inadvertently became available when a court decision made the proposed mandatory plan a voluntary plan, permitting us simply to count the number of parents in the various workshop groups who voluntarily elected to bus their children versus comparable frequency rates in the population at large of parents who did not participate in the busing program.

Parents' opinions as to the success of the workshop were clearly unrelated to either differentiation level or differentiation matching, but were significantly related to the nature of the topic discussed. Of participants discussing abstract topics, 61% indicated satisfaction with the workshop, whereas among participants discussing concrete topics, only 38% indicated satisfaction.

When we looked at busing behavior, we found that matched groups, as predicted, were more likely to bus their children than mixed groups. Further, an inverse relationship appeared to exist between the differentiation level of the groups and the tendency to bus. Specifically, differentiation level among black parents primarily accounted for the group differences. More differentiated parents chose not to bus their children, while less differentiated parents evidenced the highest tendency to bus among all participants. While there was a similar trend among white parents, the group differences in busing did not attain statistical significance.

The results were not all that surprising when one took into account the political and social developments in the area at the time. Busing had come at a time when local political control of the educational system had only recently been won by the residents of the central city area. Quality school programs and local pride in education were notably on the increase. Thus, the busing proposal was viewed, by these residents especially, as a threat to their only recently hard-won local control. The tendency to oppose busing, therefore, among the more highly differentiated participants, and especially the blacks, appeared to be a product of their more articulated perception of the complexity of the issues, both social and political, involved in the busing proposal. We interpreted the results as being consistent with the notion that these individuals were better able to make the differential choices among the various contingencies based upon their knowledge of the probable consequences. By contrast, less differentiated participants and a relatively greater proportion of the white parents tended to focus more on the global workshop objectives and appeared to be either less sensitive to or less knowledgeable about the political ramifications of the proposal. Did differentiation level change as a result of the group discussion? The answer was a resounding yes, if the discussion was focused on concrete topics. High-differentiation groups decreased, medium and mixed groups increased, and low groups remained essentially unchanged, regardless of topic.

This study particularly underscored the importance of considering the role of differentiation matching in a group interaction where one might have a vested interest in the outcome of that interaction. From a pragmatic standpoint, the implications were quite clear. If the success of an encounter between estranged participants is to be measured simply in terms of verbal endorsement for public consumption, then one need only have the participants discuss relatively abstract topics (e.g., peace, brotherhood, the American way, etc.). However, if one is concerned more with demonstrating actual behavioral change, with achieving concrete resolutions to concrete problems, and effecting changes in the conceptual organization of the participants, clearly attention to the composition of the discussion groups and the relative specificity of assigned topics is required.

MODIFYING COGNITIVE STRUCTURE

Most cognitive theories postulate that cognitive structure is modifiable in response to invalidating evidence of feedback from the environment. Within Personal Construct Theory, the Experience Corollary is perhaps one of the most succinct statements of this view: "A person's construction system varies as he successively construes the replications of events" (Kelly, 1955). A few researchers (e.g., Bannister, 1963; Rehm, 1971; Schroder, 1971) had shown that certain structural characteristics of cognition could be modified by manipulating incoming information, and we had observed in our previous studies that differentiation levels appeared to change during the interaction, although we had not yet ruled out the possibility that these were merely random effects. Our next experiment (Posthuma & Carr, 1975), therefore, was an attempt to determine whether the accuracy of perceptual response and the level of differentiation in less differentiated subjects could be simultaneously increased as a result of providing relevant feedback to a subject during a perceptual task. Specifically, it was predicted that subjects receiving consensually validated feedback would increase their accuracy of perception and level of differentiation to a greater degree than subjects permitted review of their responses but without validation, and that both groups would show increases in contrast to a control group.

Thirty-six subjects with low IDT scores were assigned to one of three groups. Each group viewed films of a standardized interview of nine anonymous adults. These interviews had been prepared by Cline and Richards (1958), who also provided a "validating protocol" of extensive biographical and psychometric data on each of the interviewees. The protocol was composed of responses to four questionnaires concerning (1) behavior, (2) verbal statements, (3) physical appearance, and (4) an adjective checklist of descriptive traits.

Following each film, all subjects completed the four questionnaires. Subjects in the validating feedback group then were allowed to review the validating protocols on all questionnaires except the adjective checklist (ACL), while subjects in the nonvalidating feedback group reviewed their responses but did not have access to any validating protocols. Subjects in both groups then reviewed the films and repeated all four questionnaires. At the end of the experiment, all groups repeated the IDT. The control group neither viewed the films nor had access to any validating data.

On the ACL, the independent measure of accuracy of interpersonal perception, the validated feedback group obtained significantly higher scores following the experimental procedure than did the self-feedback group. However, we found no significant difference among any of the groups on the IDT, although the obtained differences between group means were in the predicted direction.

In retrospect, that we obtained no significant results was not surprising, for we had inadvertently corroborated what we had maintained all along—that feedback had to be *relevant,* or domain specific, to effect a modification of cognitive structure. "Provided" constructs simply do not work as well as the subject's own structural dimensions. The mistake we had made was in attempting modification training and structural change based on Cline's concepts and not the subject's.

Obviously, a reexamination of the modification hypothesis was required, but allowing for the subject's own provided constructs. In addition, we had begun to consider a design that would permit us to explore the underlying autonomic physiological correlates of cognitive change and to demonstrate their relation simultaneously to ongoing demonstrable psychometric changes.

While we had failed to demonstrate a significant shift in differentiation level in response to the training condition, a detailed analysis of the response trends obtained provided some insight into the process involved consistent with some earlier research we had conducted (Carr, 1969). Our postanalysis suggested that increased differentiation level for the structured group occurred mainly as a function of increase in differentiation among positive sources and concepts, while the self-feedback group experienced negligible positive changes, but increases among negative sources and concepts.

MODIFICATION OF DIFFERENTIATION LEVELS AND RELEVANT FEEDBACK

The use of videotape playback as a therapeutic aid had been widely advocated as a means of increasing self-awareness. Results of several studies had suggested that patients who had observed playbacks of themselves in therapy sessions had better outcome ratings (Moore et al., 1965), less extreme pathology (Boyd & Sysney, 1967), and more accurate self-concepts (Braucht, 1970) than control patients. At the same time, several investigators reported that video playback could have adverse effects on subjects (Danet, 1968), and that differential effects may be a function of criteria used, patient characteristics, or variations in treatment conditions (Braucht, 1970), although these variations had never been specified.

The videotape playback procedure appeared to provide a promising methodology for investigating the questions concerning the relevancy of feedback information and its effect on differentiation modification.

Our study specifically concerned itself with four questions.

1. Task. Is the video playback effect dependent upon meaningfulness of behavior viewed—for example, insight-inducing or self-relevant versus an irrelevant task?

2. The person viewed. Is the effect dependent upon whom the subject sees in the playback, for example, oneself versus someone else?

3. Interaction. Is the effect dependent upon an interaction between task and person viewed?

4. Autonomic functioning. Does the effect, as observed and defined behaviorally, relate to the course and pattern of ongoing autonomic nervous system functioning?

The effects of self-confrontation via a videotape playback on self-other discrimination were assessed with Leary's Interpersonal Checklist (ICL) and the IDT. Four subject groups were utilized: (1) subjects who viewed themselves in a relevant task situation (personal interview); (2) subjects viewing themselves performing an irrelevant task (counting backward from 100); (3) subjects who saw another person in the relevant task situation; and (4) subjects who saw another person in the nonrelevant task situation.

Our results indicated that for both the ICL and the IDT, only the group who saw themselves within a personally relevant task situation showed significant differences between pre- and postvideotape playback scores. The change clearly was in the direction of greater congruency between self-as-seen-by-self and self-as-seen-by-others. It was also observed that heart rate proved to be an ongoing physiological index of cognitive process, and significantly differed similarly among the groups as a function of task, and presence or absence of self-confrontation.

An additional finding of the study was that when individuals are presented with feedback information either irrelevant to themselves and/or relevant to other persons, then response variability is significantly heightened, presumably as a function of individual differences in the perceived congruity or incongruity of the incoming information as well as differences in information-processing strategies for coping with and resolving incongruity. This "congruency hypothesis" was not original, since some variant of it could be found in almost every major theory of cognitive functioning. In Personal Construct Theory, it is included within the context of the Organization Corollary, and, in discussing the implications of this corollary, Kelly aptly described the affective behavior observed in this experiment which attended the presentation of information incongruous or irrelevant to an individual's construct system.

The inclusion of autonomic nervous system measures provided ongoing indices of cognitive process during the experimental period separating the two administrations of the ICL and the IDT. Subjects who carried out the relatively simple task of counting backward had heart rates higher than subjects who were engaged in the more complex task of making judgments about themselves. The findings are consistent with the general formulation developed by Lacey and Lacey (1974) over the last 15 years—that is, relative inattention caused by simple cognitive work produces cardiac acceleration; attention to internal as well as external stimuli contributes to cardiac deceleration. When this formulation is applied to the heart rate pattern during the playback phase, it appears that one group of subjects, the people who saw themselves engaged in the interview, were significantly more cognizant (autonomically) of the video stimulus than members of any of the other groups. This was the only group of subjects who showed significant change in the pre- and post-ICL and IDT scores.

CROSS-CULTURAL RESEARCH AND THE COMMONALITY COROLLARY

Throughout Personal Construct Theory, Kelly (1955) had argued that human conceptualization is the result of attempts to construct the world in such a way as to maximize one's ability to predict and control events. From this perspective, Personal Construct Theory is clearly individualistic in nature. However, Kelly was quick to realize that individuals are social, live in groups, and manifest many basic similarities that go beyond explanations based on upbringing or environment, and he considered these issues within the context of the commonality corollary:

To the extent that one person employs a construction of experience which is similar to that employed by another, his psychological processes are similar to those of the other person.

In discussing the implications of the corollary, Kelly recognized that it was to lead him to a view of culture somewhat disparate from the highly individualistic and psychological course on which he had set out. He himself acknowledged that his interpretation of culture would be more commonly found among sociological (and anthropological) than psychological theories. His view was that culture is taken to mean similarity in what members of the group expect of each other. Thus, expectations become sources of stimuli to which individuals respond and the bases by which perceptions are influenced. Individuals within cultural groups develop unique systems of constructs for this purpose both between and among themselves. These latter public, or consensually agreed on, conceptual dimensions within a cultural group provide a basis for a shared world-view and represent that unique system of concepts out of which social and ethical values are derived for the entire group.

As Kelly indicated, not only are we interested in similarities in what people predict, ". . . but also in the similarities in their manner of arriving at their predictions. People belong to the same cultural group, not merely because they behave alike, nor because they expect the same things of others, but especially because they construe their experience in the same way'' (p. 94). Thus, in the study of cultures, we should see in bold relief a relationship between cognitive process and behavior, or to put it in the reverse, one should find relationships between those behavioral characteristics which distinguish a culture as being unique and underlying conceptual processes that are similarly distinct and unique.

The opportunity to examine further some of the cross-cultural implications of Kelly's theoretical system became available during a sabbatical year in Southeast Asia. Malaysia is a mutli-ethnic society composed of approximately 12 million Malay, Chinese, Indians, and others. In addition to this multiplicity of linguistic systems, the various ethnic groups also represent many of the world's major religious and philosophical orientations: Islam, Buddhism, Hinduism, Christianity, as well as the various sects and subgroups into which each of these is differentiated.

We were able to establish that the distribution of IDT scores from Malaysian medical students was not significantly different from that of their American colleagues. When one went beyond these global comparisons, however, some interesting distinctions began to emerge. We had noted earlier that in American samples we uniformly obtained slightly higher IDT scores from males than from females. Findings from the Malaysian sample, by contrast, were exactly the opposite. In the two ethnic groups where we had a sample size sufficient to warrant such a conclusion (Chinese and Malays), we obtained slightly higher scores for females than for males in both cases. The differences were consistent across all measures, but only significant with regard to the self-other score. Running opposite to the American trends, as they did, suggested that these differences may have more to do with culture than they do with "sex role," so we pursued this question further.

The Malaysian educational system, like its British model, is highly competitive, demanding a high degree of performance at each level before the student can be passed on to the next level. The attrition rate is such that the net result is an enormous pyramidal system beginning with universal education in the lower forms, progressively reduced to a limited number of academic and intellectual elite at the top of the pyramid. There are but two medical schools in the country and the entering classes of the two combined total no more than 200 individuals. The pressures to succeed are enormous, in order to uphold family honor and fulfill familial and ethnic expectations. The net result is that each student operates under considerable stress, which takes its toll in varied and manifest ways.

At the time we asked our students to complete the IDT, we also asked them to fill out the Cornell Medical Index. As we had observed in the American samples, significant correlations were obtained between psychiatric symptomatology and IDT scores. As we had begun to suspect with our various American samples, the relationship turned out to be curvilinear—that is, as we looked at the relationship more closely, the ordering of subject subgroups took on distinct significance (see Table 5). At the time this research data was collected, medical education at the University of Malaya Faculty of Medicine was clearly the province of the Chinese male. Chinese students outnumbered to a significant degree Malay students and certainly males outnumbered females, although to a far less degree than was

Table 5.   Psychiatric Symptoms and Conceptual Differentiation for Medical Students by Ethnic Group and Sex

Group	Symptoms C-I	Conceptual Differentiation	
		S-O	O-A
Chinese males	12.2	3.1	2.7
Malay males	12.8	4.1	2.7
Chinese females	16.5	4.4	3.0
Malay females	21.7	4.3	2.8

observed in American medical schools during that same period of time. In Table 5, four subgroups are arrayed in order of social status within the total group as perceived by this "outside observer" and confirmed by other faculty observers. Note that the Cornell Index mean scores array themselves in progressive order for the four groups suggesting that as one moves down the "status" column, the mean number of psychiatric symptoms increases. Note also that as one moves down the "status" column, the mean self-other discrimination score also increases. Taken together, these data suggest that, relative to the high-status referent group (Chinese males), Malay males, Chinese females, and Malay females, respectively, see themselves as increasingly distinct from the referent group and endorse increasing degrees of psychiatric symptomatology, presumably as an indication of the stress they are experiencing. Are we correct in presuming a causal relationship between the S-O and C-I scores? In this case, the answer appears to be yes, since the increase in S-O scores is primarily a function of increases in differentiation scores based on negative as opposed to positive self-descriptive concepts. Thus, the increasing levels of psychiatric symptomatology are correlated with an increasing tendency to see oneself as distinct from the referent group, but distinct in a self-detrimental sense.

We had hoped to design and conduct a study testing the patient-therapist matching hypothesis, but utilizing Malaysian subjects. The study proved not to be feasible for a variety of reasons. Instead, we turned to a project which we felt initially had little to do with the issues raised by Kelly's commonality corollary, but which subsequently proved to be the most intriguing project we were to conduct in this area.

PERSONAL CONSTRUCT THEORY AND THE CULTURE-BOUND SYNDROMES

Looking at a psychiatric setting in Malaysia, one cannot help but be intrigued with the phenomenon of *amok,* an acute outburst of unrestrained violence associated with homicidal attacks. Culturally indigenous to the Malay people in Southeast Asia but known throughout the world, *amok* is one of a small but intriguing class of psychiatric disorders known as the culture-bound syndromes, so named by Yap (1969) to describe those unusual forms of psychopathology that are confined to special geographic areas and are produced by "certain systems of implicit values, social structure, and obviously shared beliefs . . . ," albeit Yap construed them to be only atypical variations of generally distributed psychiatric disorders. Even in Southeast Asia the phenomena of *amok* is exceedingly rare these days, at least as officially reported, and our search for an ample number of clinical cases has been described in detail elsewhere (Carr & Tan, 1976; Tan & Carr, 1977; Carr, 1978). For our present purposes, however, I shall focus on the subsequent outcome of this research project.

In the course of doing a detailed study of a number of cases of *amok,* we turned our attention to the cultural context in which the phenomenon occurred, in the hope of identifying the characteristics of the culture which might help to explain the occurrence of the phenomenon. In our review of socialization processes, we discovered that social conduct among the rural Malay is controlled by an adherence to the following principle: All interpersonal relations imply an interaction between individuals of particular status and therefore must be accompanied by mutual respect for the status such that the status needs of the other are ideally anticipated (Wilson, 1967). Note that the Malay code expressly states what Kelly described as the cultural implication of the commonality corollary—that "personal construct theory would then understand cultural similarity, not only in terms of personal outlook rather than in terms of impingement of social stimuli, but also in terms of what the individual anticipates others will do and, in turn, what he thinks they are expecting him to do" (p. 94). We turned our attention, therefore, to the task of discovering whether or not the Malay manifested any idiosyncratic characteristics to be identified as a typically "Malay construction of the world." We began to encounter some recurrent themes. At first there were a number of anecdotal references by various authors, both Western and local, to certain unusual characteristics of the Malay view of the world. There was frequent mention of the Malay's reputed concern for propriety in form and, indeed, it was even said that form was preferred to the actual substance. The formality of social status, for example, was often regarded as far more important than the actual authority involved. We also noted that the Malay social code appeared to be remarkably differentiated and precise in defining the formal properties of social interactions—for example, what behavior or language rules are appropriate to what rank, status, interaction, setting, situation, and so on. At the same time, we began to observe that while the Malay appeared to have a propensity for precise and highly predictable behavior, at the same time he seemed capable of tolerating an almost limitless degree of ambiguity and indefiniteness in conceptualizing the substantive reasons for that behavior. Other writers had also commented on this apparent disparity between behavior and cognition and specifically on the purported vagaries of conceptual process (e.g., Mahathir, 1970; Omar, 1968; Endicott, 1970).

Taking a broadly Whorfian point of view that concepts are interdependent with language, we asked ourselves whether or not we might see reflected in the Malay language the properties of conceptual structure suggested in the value system. Specifically, we were looking for evidence of a set of broad evaluative dimensions at the higher conceptual levels simultaneous to the existence of a great degree of preciseness at the observable behavioral level and relatively less evidence of the vast array of intermediating concepts usually seen in the hierarchically organized conceptual models. Unfortunately, the testing of this hypothesis was made exceedingly difficult because of the lack of any systematic comprehensive linguistic studies of the Malay language. However, it was this scholarly neglect of one of the world's major language systems, and the reasons cited for it, which provided us with our first indirect confirmation of the hypothesis. Historically, Malay evolved as a medium of communication in a region of some 250 mutually unintelligible languages throughout Southeast Asia and, because of its intermediary role, became a highly assimilative and flexible language. It is because of this "vague characteristic of the Malay language" that it was very much neglected by linguistic experts (Hussein, 1968). A distinguished scholar proficient in Malay (Winstedt, 1923) had early noted this characteristic and commented that "the Malay language has a dozen words for fall, hit, carry, and so on, and terms for every instrument and process of agriculture, but it is destitute of words to express feelings and abstract ideas."

Setyonegoro (1970) discussed the structural correspondence between social strata and the language, and the fact that this structure determines subsequent social behavior. The language reflects a conceptualization of the world in dichotomous superordinate constructs such as *old vs. young* or *appropriate vs. inappropriate.* What constitutes such a concept as *appropriate vs. inappropriate,* however, is not defined in abstract definitions, but rather in terms of elaborate hierarchy of behavioral exemplars. Setyonegora's analysis had been confined to Javanese which is related to Malay, and we subsequently discovered a similar analysis of Malay conceptual structure that had been reported by Colson (1971) in the context of devising a typology of abnormal behavior in Malaysia. He had obtained a matrix composed of two superordinate evaluative dimensions: *usual vs. unusual* and *correct vs. incorrect (proper vs. improper).* Under these superordinate concepts were subsumed a number of discrete situations defined in terms of their tolerability by the community in degree of variation from the cultural ideal. Here we had encountered the most direct evidence of the relationship between behavior, in this case illness behavior, and Malay conceptual structure.

What we hypothesized, therefore, was a conceptual system characterized by a finite number of superordinate dimensions so broadly defined as to apply to a seemingly infinite array of behavioral exemplars depending upon the nuances of time, place, situation, person involved, and so on. We realized that what we were describing were dimensions that were at an abstract level, were central to the conceptual system, and had a wide range of convenience—that is, were related to a broad range of phenomena. Further, the concepts were highly permeable—that is, sufficiently flexible as to permit the inclusion of new elements or phenomena within their range of meaning. Among the more important of these superordinate dimensions was the evaluative concept of *appropriate vs. inappropriate* or *proper vs. improper (betul vs. tidak betul)* which appeared to be almost universally applied, but the importance of which was especially manifested in evaluations of social behavior, a focal concern among Malay values.

For over a year, the hypothesis remained essentially unconfirmed by any empirical findings until, fortuitously, an exchange of correspondence with Charles Osgood provided the necessary evidence. Professor Osgood most generously made available the semantic analysis of Malay so tediously collected and analyzed by himself and his colleagues (Osgood et al., 1975). Starting with a diverse sample of 100 culture-common translation-equivalent nouns, Osgood and his collaborators had obtained a list of descriptive qualifiers together with their opposites which was then factor-analyzed into its principal components. The first three factors obtained (Evaluation, Potency, and Activity) proved to be qualitatively the same both intra- and interculturally. When the same procedure was initiated within the specific culture without regard to cross-linguistic comparability, the results were essentially the same (i.e., the first three factors analyzed were still E, P, and A), but the indigenous concept scales which contributed to these principal factors showed interesting variations between cultures. By looking at the types of concepts which loaded on the principal factors in each language, Osgood was able to identify indigenous conceptual factors which contribute to the EPA factors.

As we had predicted in the case of Malay language, the Evaluation factor was found to be predominantly abstract in character and more so than any of the other 22 languages studied! Further, one of the two conceptual dimensions which contributed most to the evaluation factor was *betul (proper)* vs. *tidak betul (not proper)*! Further, there could be no question as to the relatively unique and central role played by this concept dimension in the language since it did not appear among the principal component concepts of any other of the 22 languages studied. Thus, Osgood's semantic analysis clearly supported the hypothesized distinctive centrality of the *appropriate vs. inappropriate* dimension to the Malays.

Subsequently, we traced the pervasive influence of this superordinate evaluative dimension, *appropriate vs. inappropriate,* from its preeminent position among Malay concepts governing social conduct to its role in defining health, illness, and specifically mental illness. Without going into the details of that analysis, which have been discussed elsewhere (Carr, 1978), we were able to show that the most severe forms of illness in the Malay conceptual system, *gila-mengamok,* are defined primarily in terms of social behavior that is considered to be inappropriate in the most extreme sense—that is, homocidal assault against the community in a culture where propriety begins with the admonition that one never confront another, let alone express aggression. The inescapable logic in such a culture is that one must be "insane" *(gila)* to run *amok.*

One wonders whether or not Kelly appreciated how the commonality corollary in its preciseness and simplicity covers a far greater range of complex cultural phenomena than is suggested in the mere five pages devoted to a discussion of its implications. Culture is not simply an organization designed for the satisfaction of sociological needs, but rather a complex system of internalized adaptation prescriptions evolved to meet the coping needs of the members of the culture. Each culture develops its own unique system of beliefs, institutions, and sanctions to enable individuals to cope with the environmental stresses that impinge upon it. Of course, not all stress is external, for the culture itself, evolved to reduce tensions, may inadvertently contribute significantly to the stress of its members. Still, the cultural system provides the means by which threatening phenomena, albeit iatrogenic, can be defined and explained, corrective measures described, and favorable outcomes anticipated. In the case of *amok,* the culture defined it, but it also provided relief from responsibility through the mechanisms of spirit possession and amnesia, thereby providing a basis for subtle social sanction under certain circumstances, especially situations associated with attacks upon self-esteem. Thus, the Malay was afforded the means by which to seek restitution from an accumulation of perceived violations of integrity and self-esteem—that is, inappropriate treatment at the hands of others. Since the perceived insults on self-esteem could be accumulated from a variety of individuals, it follows that the *pengamok* should vent his anger not against any particular antagonist, but against society in general. As Gullick (1958) has observed, the essential elements of *amok* are an intense sense of grievance and indiscriminate murderous violence against society at large. Clearly, then, *amok* is an act of social protest by an individual against his immediate social group.

Parenthetically, an unanticipated but perhaps no less valuable byproduct of this research effort is its methodological contribution to research. We attempted to show that lexical structure may reflect distinct cognitive properties which could serve the researcher by providing a means of tracing one aspect of ethnic identity through the conceptual system of the culture. The notion of a "cognitive tracer" is consistent with the comprehensive ecological adaptation model of human behavior and receives empirical support from research arising out of that model (Berry, 1977; Dawson, 1977). While our analysis was focused on illustrating utility of the cognitive tracers as a means of identifying a consistent element in the Malay construct system, we are hopeful that the approach will be useful in the analysis of other cultural-language systems.

UNRESOLVED ISSUES

A number of questions raised in our previous research have caused us to reconsider the role of race and ethnicity in patient-therapist matching. It is generally assumed that a patient from an ethnic minority will have a higher probability of successful therapy outcome if matched with a therapist with similar ethnic background. There is support of the notion that black clients have difficulties in responding to white therapists (Banks, 1972) and that white professionals fail to understand the black client from his or her own cultural perspective (Jackson, 1976). The question here is whether this difference in perspective is in fact a function of difference in conceptual system rather than simply a difference in race. Slaughter (1975) found no significant difference in counseling relationship with black clients as a function of race of therapist. Vail (1978) similarly reported neither race of therapist nor patient's attitude toward whites had a significant effect on treatment outcome of lower-class black patients. Thus the role of race per se in predicting the outcome of psychotherapy is subject to question.

Another major issue yet to be resolved in our research program concerns the facility with which some therapists modify differentiation levels, presumably in response to situational or patient demands. While the nature of our research designs tended to focus our attention on single dyadic interactions, we were aware that therapists carry on multiple therapeutic relationships simultaneously, each unique in its demands upon the therapist in terms of multiple levels of differentiation and differentiation matching. We have noted anecdotally that certain therapists have a far greater capacity for adapting their differentiation levels to those of the immediate patient and had commented upon this apparent ability to "shift" in our initial study (Carr, 1970).

From a theoretical standpoint, we would anticipate a greater degree of successful psychotherapy outcome from a therapist who is highly differentiated and also demonstrates flexibility in shifting levels of differentiation, as opposed to therapists either high or low in differentiation but demonstrating a lack of flexibility in shifting levels. We are currently exploring the methodological means for assessing "flexibility" via measures of variance from the IDT.

ADDITIONAL RESEARCH DIRECTIONS

In recent years we have undertaken a number of studies to explore the ramifications of the matching hypothesis and Personal Construct Theory in a variety of other contexts. We have developed a modification of the IDT suitable for testing hypotheses about interpersonal discrimination within group settings, essentially increasing the standard lists of liked and disliked others to encompass participants within the group itself. This measure appears to be useful in assessing changes in cognitive process related to ongoing clinical progress in studies conducted in various therapy groups as well as family and marital therapy contexts. Combining this with our interest in cross-cultural settings, we are also looking at the role of differentiation matching in communication and conflict resolution in cross-cultural or multinational marriages.

A related variant has been developed by Mezoff (1979). This modified IDT combines features of both the semantic differential and the original IDT with the result that the subject makes interpersonal discriminations along scorable dimensions as on the IDT, but the dimensions are provided by the examiner, in this case a Human Relations Workshop coordinator who is concerned with the development of members of the group along specific criteria dimensions. While Mezoff acknowledges that the differentiation measures are less "pure," since the subject's own concept dimensions are not being used, the procedure still satisfies the relevancy requirements in that specific criterial dimensions are tested. Mezoff reports that his modified IDT has been validated based on its correlation to independent self- and peer ratings on a number of specified dimensions collected over the course of several training programs. In addition, he reports correlations between his modified IDT and Witkin's Group Embedded Figures Test in two separate small groups of 0.31 and 0.47 respectively, which compares well with measures obtained in our earlier studies.

Armstrong and Williams (1977) have reported the use of a carefully developed variant called the Body Concept Differentiation Test, used to measure differentiation within the context of body image. Briefly, subjects generated a conceptual dimension by means of which they rated body parts (lungs, heart, stomach, throat, intestinal tract, skin, arm muscles, hair, fingers, and feet). The number of distinctions employed in rating the body parts in each of the five dimensions was taken as the measure of overall differentiation. Of the 10 body parts listed, 5 are internal and 5 external. By totaling the number of distinctions employed in each subgroup, measures of internal differentiation and external differentiation were also obtained.

In a study of 55 Internal Medicine and Dermatology patients, the Body Concept Differentiation Test (BCDT) was found to correlate significantly with the IDT, and internal differentiation scores correlated inversely with the barrier measure and positively with penetration scores.

Armstrong and Williams revised the BCDT, shifting to a semantic differential format. The 10 body parts were rated on each of the following five dimensions: *warm vs. cold, good vs. bad, soft vs. hard, strong vs. weak,* and *wet vs. dry.* Validity and reliability of the revised version has been established. In a sample of 60 undergraduate students, correlations obtained between the BCDT and Fisher's Sensation Questionnaire were sizable as well as significant. External Sensation correlated 0.56 with the external differentiation score, Internal Sensation correlated 0.44 with the internal differentiation score, and Total Sensation correlated 0.68 with the overall differentiation score. When the BCDT was correlated with the Cornell Medical Index, a coefficient of 0.62 was obtained.

CONCLUSION

In this chapter we have reported on a program of studies designed to investigate the hypothesis that the success of social interaction is a function of the degree to which the participants in that interaction are matched in the complexity, or level of differentiation, of their cognitive structure. Patient-therapist matching has been shown to predict the success of psychotherapy outcome. Similarly, we have found it to be an important component in the teacher-student relationship, albeit of secondary importance to the teacher's level of differentiation. These findings suggest to us that, while equally complex, therapeutic and educational relationships have unique features and researchers should not err in generalizing from one domain to the other. The need for this caution was underscored in subsequent studies of community groups where differentiation matching of the participants was found to determine outcome by differentially affecting the types of decisions, attitudes, and subsequent behaviors carried out by the group.

Given the demonstrated relevancy of differentiation matching to social interaction, we addressed ourselves to the question of whether or not such aspects of cognitive structure were modifiable in response to training. While the answer appeared to be in the affirmative, we were again impressed by the complexity of the process, especially the importance of keeping training conditions and feedback relevant to the concept dimensions in question.

Moving further along the continuum of social interaction, we considered the matching hypothesis and various corollaries of Personal Construct Theory within the context of cross-cultural research. The conceptual framework discussed here has been shown to have direct applicability to the explanation of clinical phenomena, cross-culturally demonstrating the significant potential of Personal Construct Theory and derivative methodologies in this newly emerging research area.

These findings have major implications not only for the psychotherapy relationship in particular, but for the patient management process in general. Whereas patient assignments have traditionally been made on the basis of diagnosis, availability of openings, capability of the patient to pay, the intuitive "feel" of the therapist for the patient, the training needs of the resident or intern, and so on, more attention should be devoted to the objectively based matching of patient and therapist along conceptual structure lines.

It follows that the implications for training are no less significant. It has previously been assumed that the characteristics of a "successful" therapist can be readily identified and training programs devised by which such characteristics can be acquired or augmented. An alternative approach suggested here would presume no such universal constellation of "successful therapist" traits, but rather would define success in terms of the particular degree of communicability that may exist for any given patient-therapist combination. Thus, successful communication would be dependent on the degree to which the therapist was able to readily establish a common conceptual interface. As was mentioned earlier, this implies more than the selection of mental health professionals who are in command of a body of knowledge from the behavioral sciences and who desire to "help people," or who are in the possession of such traits as "warmth" and "positive regard" and "accurate empathy." In addition, we need candidates who possess a broad repertoire of concepts in the interpersonal area, whose concepts are highly differentiated, and who possess the capacity to flexibly shift levels of differentiation in order to facilitate interpersonal contacts at various conceptual levels.

Kelly had observed that "since a theory is an ad interim construction system which is designed to give an optimal anticipation of events, its life is limited by its period of usefulness" (p. 102). He was hopeful that the theory would prove to be fertile, provide testable hypotheses, and suggest new approaches to the problems psychologists faced. He anticipated that it might eventually be replaced by a more comprehensive and explicit theory that would relegate it to history, but it is clear that no more fertile or more useful theory has emerged to replace the Psychology of Personal Constructs. It is equally clear that many of the hypotheses have yet to be "proven" primarily because they have yet to be tested. As Kelly indicated, "The establishment of real fertility . . . will depend upon what the readers of this manuscript come up with as a result of reading it" (p. 103).

I have tried to suggest here that considerable evidence exists to support many major corollaries within the personal construct theoretical system. I would assume that further research would reveal yet additional evidence in support of other corollaries. The question is whether we are to allow ourselves the ecumenical freedom to define our concepts in terms of mutually agreed upon structural and functional characteristics so that we are open to evidence from researchers working in other theoretical systems.

REFERENCES

Armstrong, H. E., Jr., & Williams, C. D. Conceptual differentiation among body parts as a measure of body image. *Psychological Reports,* 1977, **40,** 1179–1189.

Banks, W. The black client and the helping professional. In R. Jones (Ed.), *Black Psychology.* New York: Harper & Row, 1972.

Bannister, D. The genesis of schizophrenic thought disorder: A serial invalidation hypothesis. *British Journal of Psychiatry,* 1963, **109,** 680–685.

Berry, M. W. A dynamic model of relationships among ecology, culture, and behavior. In L. Adler (Ed.), *Issues in Cross-Cultural Research.* New York: New York Academy of Sciences, 1977.

Beutler, L., Jobe, A., & Elkins, D. Outcomes in group psychotherapy: Using persuasion theory to increase treatment efficacy. *Journal of Consulting and Clinical Psychology,* 1974, **42,** 547–553.

Beutler, L., Johnson, D., Neville, C., Elkins, D., & Jobe, A. Attitude similarity and therapist credibility as predictors of attitude change and improvement in psychotherapy. *Journal of Consulting and Clinical Psychology,* 1975, **43,** 90–91.

Bieri, J. Cognitive complexity and personality development. In O. J. Harvey (Ed.), *Experience, Structure and Adaptability.* New York: Springer, 1966.

Boyd, H., & Sisney, V. Immediate self-image confrontation and changes in self-concept. *Journal of Consulting Psychology,* 1967, **31,** 291–296.

Braucht, G. Immediate effects of self-confrontation on the self-concept. *Journal of Consulting and Clinical Psychology,* 1970, **35,** 95–101.

Carr, J. E. The role of conceptual organization in interpersonal discrimination. *Journal of Psychology,* 1965a, **59,** 159–176.

Carr, J. E. Cognitive complexity: Construct descriptive terms versus cognitive process. *Psychological Reports,* 1965b, **16,** 133–134.

Carr, J. E. Differentiation as a function of source characteristics and judges conceptual structure. *Journal of Personality,* 1969, **37,** 378–386.

Carr, J. E. Differentiation similarity of patient and therapist and the outcome of psychotherapy. *Journal of Abnormal Psychology,* 1970, **76,** 361–369.

Carr, J. E. Perceived therapy outcome as a function of differentiation between and within conceptual dimensions. *Journal of Clinical Psychology,* 1974, **30,** 282–285.

Carr, J. E. Ethno-behaviorism and the culture-bound syndrome: The case of amok. *Culture, Medicine and Psychiatry,* 1978, **2,** 269–293.

Carr, J. E., & Posthuma, A. The role of cognitive process in social interaction. *The International Journal of Social Psychiatry,* 1975, **21,** 157–165.

Carr, J. E., & Post, R. Repression-sensitization and self-other discrimination in psychiatric outpatients. *Journal of Personality assessment,* 1974, **38,** 48–51.

Carr, J. E., & Tan, E. K. In search of the true amok. *American Journal of Psychiatry*, 1976, **11**, 1295–1299.

Carr, J., & Townes, B. Interpersonal discrimination as a function of age and psychopathology. *Child Psychiatry and Human Development*, 1975, **5**, 209–215.

Carr, J., & Whittenbaugh, J. Volunteer and nonvolunteer characteristics in an outpatient population. *Journal of Abnormal Psychology*, 1968, **73**, 16–17.

Carr, J. E., & Whittenbaugh, J. Sources of disagreement in the perception of psychotherapy outcome. *Journal of Clinical Psychology*, 1969, **25**, 16–21.

Cartwright, R., & Lerner, B. Empathy, need to change, and improvement with psychotherapy. *Journal of Consulting Psychology*, 1963, **27**, 138–144.

Cline, V., & Richards, J. M. *Variability related to accuracy of interpersonal perception* (Ann. Rep., 1958, Group Psychology Branch, Office of Naval Research). Salt Lake City: University of Utah, Department of Psychology.

Colson, A. C. The prevention of illness in a Malay village: An analysis of concepts and behavior. *Medical Behavioral Sciences Monographs*, 1971 (Series 2, No. 1).

Craig, W. R. *The effects of cognitive similarity between client and therapist upon the quality and outcome of the psychotherapy relationship*. Unpublished doctoral dissertation, University of Missouri, Columbia, 1972.

Danet, B. N. Self-confrontation in psychotherapy reviewed: Videotape playback as a clinical and research tool. *American Journal of Psychotherapy*, 1968, **22**, 245–257.

Dawson, J. Theory and method in biosocial psychology: A new approach to cross-cultural psychology. In L. Adler (Ed.), *Issues in Cross-Cultural Research*. New York: New York Academy of Sciences, 1977.

Dougherty, F. Patient-therapist matching for prediction of optimal and minimal therapeutic outcome. *Journal of Consulting and Clinical Psychology*, 1976, **44**, 889–897.

Duehn, W. D., & Proctor, E. K. A study of cognitive complexity in the education for social work practice. *Journal of Education for Social Work*, 1974, **10**, 20–26.

Endicott, K. M. *An Analysis of Malay Magic*. Oxford: Clarendon Press, 1970.

Fiedler, F. The concept of an ideal therapeutic relationship. *Journal of Consulting Psychology*, 1950, **14**, 239–245.

Gardner, G. The psychotherapeutic relationship. *Psychological Bulletin*, 1964, **61**, 426–437.

Gassner, S. Relationship between patient-therapist compatibility and treatment effectiveness. *Journal of Consulting and Clinical Psychology*, 1970, **34**, 408–414.

Gullick, J. M. Indigenous political systems of Western Malaya. *London School of Economics Monographs on Social Anthropology*, 1958 (No. 17).

Harvey, O., Hunt, D., & Schroder, H. *Conceptual Systems and Personality Organization*. New York: Wiley, 1961.

Hunt, D. *Matching models in education*. Ontario Institute for Studies in Education, 1971 (Monograph Series No. 10).

Hussein, J. The study of traditional Malay literature. *Asian Studies*, 1968, **6**, 66–89.

Jackson, G. G. The African genesis of the black perspective in helping. *Professional Psychology*, 1976, August, 292–308.

Kelly, G. *The Psychology of Personal Constructs*. Vols. I and II. New York: Norton, 1955.

Lacey, J. I., & Lacey, B. C. On heart rate response and behavior: A reply to Elliott. *Journal of Personality and Social Psychology*, 1974, **30**, 1–18.

Landfield, A., & Nawas, M. Psychotherapeutic improvement as a function of communication and adoption of therapists' values. *Journal of Counseling Psychology,* 1964, **11,** 336–341.

Liebert, R., & Spiegler, M. *Personality: An Introduction to Theory and Research.* Homewood, IL: Dorsey Press, 1970.

Lorr, M. Client perceptions of therapists: A study of the therapeutic relation. *Journal of Consulting Psychology,* 1965, **29,** 146–149.

Luborsky, L., Chandler, M., Aurbach, A., & Cohen, J. Factors influencing the outcome of psychotherapy: A review of quantitative research. *Psychological Bulletin,* 1971, **75,** 145–185.

Mahathir, M. *The Malay Dilemma.* Singapore: Asia Pacific Press, 1970.

McLachlan, J. F. Benefit from group therapy as a function of patient-therapist match on conceptual level. *Psychotherapy: Theory, Research, and Practice,* 1972, **9,** 317–323.

McLachlan, J. F. Therapy strategies, personality orientation, and recovery from alcoholism. *Canadian Psychiatric Association Journal,* 1974, **19,** 30–35.

Mezoff, R. Personal communication, July 5, 1979.

Montgomery, F., & Carr, J. E. *Differentiation similarity and outcome of treatment: A replication.* Unpublished manuscript, University of Washington, Seattle, 1971.

Moore, F. J., Chernell, E., & West, M. J. Television as a therapeutic tool. *Archives of General Psychiatry,* 1965, **12,** 117–120.

Newcomb, T. The cognition of persons as cognizers. In R. Tagiuri & L. Petriello (Eds.), *Person Perception and Interpersonal Behavior.* Stanford, CA: Stanford University Press, 1958.

Omar, A. Interplay of structural and socio-cultural factors in the development of the Malay language. *Asian Studies,* 1968, **6,** 19–25.

Osgood, C., May, W., & Mison, M. *Cross-Cultural Universals of Affective Meaning.* Urbana: University of Illinois Press, 1975.

Pardes, H., Papernik, D., & Winston, A. Field differentiation in inpatient psychotherapy. *Archives of General Psychiatry,* 1974, **31,** 311–315.

Posthuma, A., & Carr, J. E. Differentiation matching in school desegregation workshops. *Journal of Applied Social Psychology,* 1974, **4,** 36–46.

Posthuma, A., & Carr, J. E. Differentiation matching in psychotherapy. *Canadian Psychological Review,* 1975, **16,** 35–43.

Rehm, L. P. Effects of validation on the relationship between personal constructs. *Journal of Personality and Social Psychology,* 1971, **20,** 267–270.

Rogers, C. *The therapeutic relationship and its impact.* Madison: University of Wisconsin Press, 1967.

Runkel, P. Cognitive similarity in facilitating communications. *Sociometry,* 1956, **19,** 178–191.

Sapolsky, A. Relationship between patient-doctor, compatibility, mutual perception, and outcome of treatment. *Journal of Abnormal Psychology,* 1965, **70,** 70–76.

Schroder, H. Conceptual complexity and personality organization. In H. Schroder & P. Sudfeld (Eds.), *Personality Theory and Information Processing.* New York: Ronald, 1971.

Schroder, H., & Streufert, S. *The measurement of four systems of personality structure varying in level of abstractness* (ONR Tech. Rep. 11). Princeton, NJ: Office of Naval Research, 1962.

Schutz, W. *FIRO-B: A Three Variable Theory of Interpersonal Relations*. New York: Holt, Rinehart & Winston, 1958.

Setyonegoro, R. K. Latah in Java: Mental health trends in a developing society. *Proceedings of the World Federation of Mental Health Workshop*. Singapore, 1970, 91−95.

Slaughter, G. F. Racial interaction between counselor and client as a factor in counseling outcome. *Dissertation Abstracts International*, 1975, **35**, 4260.

Tan, E. K., & Carr, J. E. Psychiatric sequelae of amok. *Culture, Medicine, and Psychiatry*, 1977, **1**, 59−67.

Townes, B., & Carr, J. E. Differentiation and teaching effectiveness in medical education. *Journal of Applied Social Psychology*, 1973, **3**, 78−83.

Triandis, H. Cognitive similarity and communication in a dyad. *Human Relations*, 1960, **13**, 175−183.

Vail, A. Factors influencing black lower-class patients remaining in treatment. *Journal of Consulting and Clinical Psychology*, 1978, **46**, 341.

Welkowitz, J., Cohen, J., & Ortmeyer, D. Value system similarity: Investigation of patient-therapist dyads. *Journal of Consulting Psychology*, 1967, **31**, 48−55.

Wilson, P. J. *A Malay Village and Malaysia: Social Values and Rural Development*. New Haven: Hraf Press, 1967.

Winstedt, R. *Malaya*. London: Constable, 1923.

Witkin, H. Psychological differentiation and forms of pathology. *Journal of Abnormal Psychology*, 1965, **70**, 317−336.

Witkin, H., Dyk, R., Faterson, H., Goodenough, D., & Karp, S. *Psychological Differentiation*. New York: Wiley, 1962.

Witkin, H., Lewis, H., & Weil, E. Affective reactions and patient-therapist interactions among more differentiated and less differentiated patients early in therapy. *Journal of Nervous and Mental Diseases*, 1968, **146**, 193−208.

Yap, P. M. The culture-bound reactive syndromes. In W. Caudill & T. Lin (Eds.), *Mental Health Research in Asia and the Pacific*. Honolulu: East-West Center Press, 1969.

Zajonk, R. B. The process of cognitive tuning in communication. *Journal of Abnormal and Social Psychology*, 1960, **61**, 159−167.

Zajonk, R. B. Cognitive theories in social psychology. In G. Lindzey & E. Aronson (Eds.), *Handbook of Social Psychology* (rev. ed.). Reading, MA: Addison-Wesley, 1968.

APPENDIX

IDT[1]

This is a survey of the various ways people can describe one another. It is not a test, and so there are no "right" or "wrong" answers. We are going to ask you to describe some people you know. As you do this, please write legibly and express yourself as clearly as possible.

On the first three lines below write the names of three persons you know and generally *like*. On the next three lines write the names of three persons you know and generally *dislike*, or like less. Please do not use relatives. List six *different* persons.

(1)

(2)

(3)

(4)

(5)

(6)

This list of names is for your convenience only. Throughout the rest of the questionnaire each person will be referred to by number only, that is, Person (1), Person (2), and so on. You may want to tear off this page in order to refer to it more easily as you complete the rest of the questionnaire. When you have finished, you may keep or destroy this page, as you wish.

Your name: _____

Your age: _____ Sex: _____

Your education: _____

Your occupation: _____

Your marital status: _____

Your race or ethnic group (optional): _____

The results of this survey are for research purposes only. All responses are confidential.

John E. Carr, Ph.D.
University of Washington
Seattle, Washington 98195

1979 edition.

Person M

Now, think about *yourself*. We shall call you Person M. In the left-hand column below write three qualities or characteristics you have which you *like*. Next, write their opposites in the right-hand column.

Quality	Opposite

1. _____   _____

2. _____   _____

3. _____   _____

Person M

Now, we want you to think of three qualities or characteristics you have which you *do not like,* or like least, and write them in the left-hand column below. Again, write their opposites in the right-hand column.

Quality	Opposite

1. _____   _____

2. _____   _____

3. _____   _____

Now, turn back to page 2 in this booklet and look at the first quality you listed for yourself. How would you compare the six people you have named and yourself on this first characteristic? We want you to show which persons are alike on this quality, if there are any alike, and which persons are different, if there are any that are different.

For example, let us say that "honesty" is the quality in question. Now, if you thought that there was really no difference among everyone, that yourself and the six others were equally "honest," then you would have one group and would represent this by merely putting everyone's number in one box:

1   5   2   4
M   6   3

Or let us say that you thought Persons 1, 3, 4, and M (yourself) were more honest, and that Persons 2, 5, and 6 were less honest. Then you would have two groups and would represent this by dividing the rectangle into two boxes:

1 3	2 5 6
4 M	

Or what if you thought that Persons 3, 5, and M (yourself) were very honest, Persons 1 and 2 were less honest, and that Persons 4 and 6 were least honest? Then you would have three groups and would represent this by dividing the rectangle into three boxes:

3 5	1 2	4 6
M		

In the same way, you could also use four, five, six, or even seven boxes, if you like, to compare everyone. As a last example, let us say that none of the six others and yourself were alike, that you were all different, that Person 2 was most honest, Person 1 next most honest, Person 5 next, then Person M (yourself), then Person 3, then Person 4, and finally Person 6 the least honest of all. You would then use seven boxes to represent this:

2	1	5	M	3	4	6

In other words, you can divide this group of seven people in any way you like by using one, two, three, four, five, six, or seven boxes. The idea is that *if people are alike, then they should be in the same box, and if they are different, they should be in different boxes.* Each box should represent *less* of the quality and more of its opposite as you move from left to right.

Now please go back and compare everyone, the six others and yourself, on each of the *six* qualities you used to describe *yourself*. Thank you.

CHAPTER 13

Training Parents to Construe
the Child's Construing[1]

James C. Mancuso and Kenneth H. Handin

Many children somehow develop behaviors that are judged to be unwanted and, therefore, changeworthy. Parents and social agencies have welcomed the efforts of behavior scientists who have tried to explain the origins and the means of altering these unwanted behaviors. Clarke-Stewart's (1978) survey of the use of child care literature led her to conclude that "parents are eager for information about children and child rearing and are actively seeking it out" (p. 368). According to data collected from a random sampling of Chicago parents, 94% claimed to have read at least one child care book or article.

Concern about the relationships between parenting approaches and children's changeworthy behaviors is further indicated by the widespread implementation of parent training programs. The growth of these programs, many of which are sponsored by funds from the federal government, also reflects the society's belief that behavior scientists can bring to bear a technology that will help parents to promote desired behavior in their children.

Mechanism in Parent Training Programs

Considering the popularity of mechanistic paradigms in American psychology, it is no surprise that the language of stimulus-response associationism has guided the major share of the formal studies of parent training. Parents are trained to understand the principles assumed to underlie operant conditioning (O'Dell et al., 1977) and are led to view the development of unwanted behaviors in terms of socially delivered positive and negative reinforcements. Parents have been taught to see relationships between their differential attention to the child and the child's undesirable behavior (Wahler, 1969). They have been trained to provide appropriate reinforcements, (Patterson et al., 1967), and to use time out from social contact

[1]The project reported in this paper was conducted with the full cooperation of and under the auspices of the administration and staff of Saint Catherine's Child Care Center, Albany, New York. The project was partially supported by New York State, Department of Social Services, Child Abuse/Neglect Prevention Funds.

(Forehand et al., 1978) to reduce changeworthy behaviors and to increase wanted behaviors.

This reliance on mechanistic principles can be attributed not only to the pervasiveness of mechanism within psychology, but also to the widespread use of mechanistic thought outside the formal discipline. People readily articulate parental corrective and reprimanding behaviors to a construct of *strong force vs. weak force*. When asked to talk about child-rearing practices, particularly about reprimand practices, people readily speak of *permissiveness vs. forcefulness* or *leniency vs. severity*. Clarke-Stewart (1978) reports that parents frequently criticized child care books with the claim that the advice promoted too much permissiveness. Mancuso and his associates (Handin & Mancuso, 1979; Mancuso & Handin, in press) found that child care workers' judgments of the effectiveness of reprimand techniques were intricately interrelated with their assessment of a *leniency vs. severity* dimension perceived to underlie different reprimands.

It follows, then, that mechanistic principles will have an immediate and appealing face validity to persons being trained in parenting techniques. The parent trainees, believing initially that application of energy forces will alter the directions of behaviors, will respond positively to programs that promise to teach them the appropriate applications of behavior-changing forces. Such constructions are well within the range of the constructs which parents have developed from everyday experiences and which they use as they regard child-rearing practices.

The Bases of an Alternative Paradigm

Despite the allegiances to and widespread use of the mechanistic principles in parent training, there has been the expected questioning of the overall value of the approaches that are generated by the paradigm's basic assumptions. One of the most crucial concerns about the use of the mechanistic paradigm is the matter of whether the principles that are assumed to be at work are, in fact, the effective principles. When a child's compliance follows a parent's applications of the reinforcement techniques that have been taught, can the compliance be attributed to the reinforcement, per se, or has another set of circumstances, concomitant to the reinforcing process, been put into effect? Another concern centers on the generality of the effects of training a parent to use reinforcement techniques. Forehand and Atkeson (1977) reviewed a large body of relevant literature and then concluded that there is not convincing evidence that parents continue to apply the mechanistic child-rearing principles they have been taught. Ironically, there has been little use of reinforcement technology to assure that the parents' behaviors are properly strengthened and generalized.

To deal with some of these concerns, investigators who had initially tried to build their procedures from mechanistic principles have begun to try to take into account the cognitive processes of both the child whose behavior is to be changed and the parent who is being taught to change the behaviors. In the past, investigators characteristically have tried to take the position expressed by Goocher (1975): "The importance of the child's 'inner world'—his covert, verbal, perceptual, and autonomic responses—is recognized, but the methods for changing the behavioral indicators of these events rests on learning principles rather than on presumed reorganization of his internal psychic structure and functions'' (p. 85). More recently, following the lead of Meichenbaum and Goodman (1971), investigators (see, for example, Bugenthal et al., 1977; and Kendall & Finch, 1978) have begun to consider seriously the place of a child's cognitions in the alterations of his behavior.

Forehand and his associates (Forehand et al., 1979; Peed et al., 1977) have made some beginning efforts to consider the cognitions of the parent trainees who have been exposed to a program intended to teach the use of reinforcement techniques to evoke compliance from their children. The investigators have not, however, included direct cognitive training procedures in their programs, as have the investigators who have discussed "cognitive behavior modification" approaches to the unwanted behaviors of children (Kendall & Finch, 1978).

Cognitive Structure, Parent-Child Interaction, and Behavior Change

Not only internal problems prompt a reconsideration of the paradigm that has guided the bulk of recent investigation into parent training. Important recent trends in the child development literature also must be taken into account in redesigning the models that guide parent training programs.

Experimental psychologists have marshaled an immense body of literature (see, for example, Neisser, 1976; Posner, 1973; Shaw & Bransford, 1977) to show that the meanings of events flow out of the constructions which a person imposes on the input generated from distal events. Additionally, several theorists (Powers, 1973, 1978; Weimer, 1977) have extended these constructivist conceptions to explain how motor behavior represents a person's efforts to arrange the environment so that sensory input becomes congruent with the constructions the person has brought to bear on the organization of that input.

As the utility of these cognitive processing conceptions has grown, developmental psychologists have steadily elaborated them and incorporated them into discussions of children's cognitive growth. Flavell (1977), for example, has written a highly useful and lucid summary of the evidence that constructivist principles explain the early psychological development of a person. This work directly ties to the large body of literature that has been generated by Piaget and his co-workers (for example, Inhelder & Piaget, 1969; Piaget, 1968, 1952, 1932) who have, over the last six decades, provided formulations that rely strongly on constructivist principles.

One major principle emerges clearly out of this mass of study and thought. The effects of any stimulation that impinges on the sensory systems of a youngster will be determined by the cognitive organizations which he has available to integrate the incoming stimulation. This principle has been applied to explain the working of infant attention (Cohen, 1976; McCall & Kagan, 1970), to discuss memory processes in young children (Paris & Lindauer, 1976), and to clarify the motive principles which define the regular growth of children's psychological processes (Ginsburg & Opper, 1979; Zeaman, 1976).

Cohen's comments, incorporated into her review of studies on infant attention, are illustrative of constructivism in developmental psychology.

New and more refined theories are beginning to appear to explain these phenomena which were once thought so simple and are now seen to be highly complex. These theories assume the infant plays a much more active role in the attention-holding process than previously believed. He is looking, abstracting certain properties of a stimulus, encoding the information in both short-and long-term memory, comparing new and old information, and terminating his fixation when the two match. (p. 232)

Describing the Motives of an Active Cognizer

The motivational implications of a conclusion like Cohen's are immediately clear. The statement incorporates the proposition that infants attend to stimuli that arouse anticipatory recognitions, yet fail to generate a cognitive model, from long-term memory, which assimilates the input. This position, which other developmental theorists (Flavell, 1977; Ginsberg & Opper, 1979) discuss as the *moderate discrepancy principle,* represents a variation of Piaget's concept of disequilibrium.

If this fundamental interaction between internal and external is taken into account, all behavior is an *assimilation* of reality to prior schemata . . . and all behavior is at the same time an accomodation of these schemata to the actual situation. The result is that developmental theory necessarily calls upon the concept of equilibrium between internal and external factors or, speaking more generally, between assimilation and accommodation. (Piaget, 1968, p. 103)

Personal Construct Psychology in Parent Training

Once an investigator has adopted a constructivist perspective with the moderate discrepancy principle as the motivational formula, he may begin to abandon the mechanistic goals characteristically set for parent training programs and to adopt the contextualist goals that take into account the constructions of the parent trainee and of the child who is the ultimate target of the training program.

When the process of parenting is discussed from a position based on constructivist principles, it is of heuristic value to note a direct relationship between Kelly's (1955) fundamental postulate and the moderate discrepancy hypothesis. "A person's processes are psychologically channelized by the ways in which he anticipates events" (p. 46). Failure to anticipate calls for either a rearrangement of the environment or a rearrangement of the schemata which are to be applied to the event under consideration. Psychological development follows from the reorganization of schemata—the accommodation of existing structure—to produce an organization that assimilates the sensory input deriving from the circumstances surrounding the event. Such reorganizations are then represented in long-term memory, and are then available to integrate those future-occurring events which can be judged to have similar attributes.

In his discussion of current motivational principles applicable to Personal Construct Psychology, Mancuso (1977) described the parent as a novelty moderator.

The parent as a novelty moderator serves several functions relative to the child's psychological development. Among other things: (1) the parent may act to arrange the environment so that there is an input that is appropriately discrepant from the cognitive organizations which the child has available to integrate information, and (2) the parent observes and monitors the child's arousal reaction, being sure to communicate to the youngster that he/she may rely on the parent as a resource which protects him/her from overarousal.

Kelly's (1955) sociality corollary is taken as a second major brace in this formulation of a parent training program. "To the extent that one person construes the construction processes of another, he may play a role in a social process involving the other person" (p. 95). The utility of the sociality corollary is highlighted by the considerable work that has been completed to show that communication processes are totally a two-way affair (Olson, 1970; Paris & Lindauer, 1976; Rommetviet, 1974). Writers and speakers cannot be studied as if they operate in a context-free environment. The reader and the listener operate in the exchange as surely as do the writer and the speaker. The text and the utterance are literally absurd if the framework of the listener's construct system is removed from the context.

This last statement is then generalized to say that the parenting person's input has no meaning outside the context that includes the youngster's construction system. In fact, referring back to Piaget's (1968) statement, any psychological development necessarily depends on "equilibrium between internal and external factors" (p. 103)—that is, between the parent-regulated input and the child's construct system. A parent's instructions and messages, whether they concern the esoteric world of numbers or the everyday world of rules that guide the conduct of social interaction, are to be understood within this framework.

These formulations have provided the basis for a series of studies (Handin & Mancuso, 1979; Mancuso, 1979; Mancuso & Allen, 1976; Mancuso and Handin, in press) on the characteristics of parental reprimand. A rule-violating event involving a child may be seen as a situation in which the child has applied constructions that are at variance with the constructions that the parent would apply. In the language of rules and morality, it is said that the child has "broken a rule." On such occasions, the parent attempts to instruct the child relative to the constructions that "should" be used in the situation. The parent delivers a reprimand. The reprimand may take many forms, and many purposes may be attributed to the reprimand. In the end, however, the primary and unequivocally basic purpose of the reprimand, whether or not this purpose is articulated by the reprimander, is to induce the arousal that attends failure to anticipate. In efforts to meet a fundamental goal of successfully anticipating events, thereby successfully maintaining an optimal level of arousal, the youngster might develop the kinds of constructions that would be associated with the behaviors that the parent hopes to observe in similar reprimand-relevant situations. A Personal Construct Psychologist would say that the transgressor is being urged to adopt the reprimander's constructions. The constructivist assumes that the reprimander's skill in construing the construction processes of the transgressor will affect the extent to which the reprimand brings about change in the transgressor's views of the rule-determined situation.

Implications for Parent Training Programs

A parent training program developed from these principles would pursue two major goals. First, the program would attempt to have parents agree that control and regulation of a child are best achieved by constant monitoring of relevant input, so that moderate and resolvable discrepancies are presented to the child. Second, the program would attempt to have parents attend fully to the child's constructions of events, taking them completely into account at any time that there is an effort to communicate with the child and to direct its growth.

A CONSTRUCTIVIST'S PARENT TRAINING PROGRAM

The foregoing propositions have guided the development of a parent training program at the Saint Catherine's Child Care Center. The Center serves children who demonstrate a large variety of developmental problems. Most frequently, these children are difficult to regulate.

From the foregoing perspective, the difficult-to-regulate children are explained by use of the following assumptions: First, difficult-to-regulate children have developed a construction system within which adults are not construed as *useful* during periods of failure to anticipate. These children have not had experiences that allow them to view adults as being a resource which aids in avoiding "epistemic strain." In fact, they see adults as forcing them into novel situations, wherein their failure to anticipate (particularly if they try to anticipate by using constructions at variance with those of the parent) leads to coercive efforts on the part of the adult. Coercive effort, of course, only introduces other self-disconfirming stimulation; and the cycle is escalated: input introduced by adult—child's effort to construe—construction invalidated—coercive reprimand, that is, self schema disconfirmation—more nonintegratable input to construe. And, of course, every input is a source of arousal.

In constant parent-child interactions of this sort, the child quickly construes every adult-initiated input at the *avoid* end of the *avoid vs. approach* construct. By the time of his entry into kindergarten, if he is well trained, he will have a repertoire of *avoid-associated* actions that would make a sailor blush. Kindergarten and nursery school teachers will refer him to agencies that conduct programs to help with such children.

Saint Catherine's Child Care Center, in Albany, New York, conducts residential and day care programs which are designed to aid parents and other agencies at those times when the child's unmanageability becomes disruptive. To supplement other programs, Saint Catherine's CCC implemented and helped to support a parent training program. Parents of children enrolled in programs are given an opportunity to decide to participate. Their continued participation depends on their own decisions to remain in the program.

The parent training program to which the parents are exposed is quite direct. The description is as follows:

1. *Therapist-child interaction* (15 minutes). The therapist will involve the child in an age-appropriate activity (putting on boots, eating a meal, drawing a picture, block building, etc.), directing the child's behavior toward a preconceived goal. The therapist will annotate the interaction for the parent, offering an interpretation of the child's ongoing psychological processing, explaining the use of behavioral management techniques, the rationale for their use relative to the child's ongoing processing, and the child's reaction to the techniques.

2. *Videotaped parent-child interaction* (15 minutes). The parent will engage the child in an activity chosen by the therapist, attempting to direct the child's behavior toward a preconceived goal. These sessions will be videotaped through a two-way mirror to minimize distraction. Tapes are to be utilized in Step 3. The videotape equipment will be run by a technician to allow the therapist's complete attention to be directed toward the parent and child.

3. *Video-tape observation and discussion* (30 minutes). Parent and therapist observe videotape presentations of the parent's interaction with the child. Comments are made by the therapist directing the parent's attention to coercive attempts. The child's differential reaction is noted. Comparisons will be viewed between the therapist's attempts at regulation and parental attempts. Alternative techniques for regulating the child are suggested.

The major task of the activity is to direct the parent to think constantly about the child's construing of the situation. For example, when the parent disrupts the child's seemingly random activity to engage it in a task, the parent is to consider, and is urged to specify, what the child's constructions of the seemingly random activity might have been. The parent is often incapable of imposing a useful construction on the child's activity. Like the teacher in Kelly's (1969) example of a teacher who is trying to interpret a child's noncompliant activity, the parent might think of the child as being "lazy" (p. 58). The child is seen as "not wanting" to engage the more "morally good," "productive" activity of working on simple puzzle solution. When the child tries to eliminate the arousal that accompanies the interruption of his ongoing, free-flowing anticipatory experiments on his world, the parent frequently sees his efforts as "willful stubbornness." Frequently this noncompliance is judged to be worthy of change, in and of itself. When the parent has developed a mechanistic implicit theory of childhood psychological development—a kind of theory that one may easily develop in our Western society—the parent may attempt to apply his version of negative reinforcement to the "willful stubbornness." The tapes made during the conduct of this program contain numerous instances of this cycle. Some of the confrontations are immensely dramatic.

Much of the commentary about the parent-child interactions recorded on the videotapes is directed toward leading the parent to construe the child's resistances as reactions to disruptions of his ongoing experiments on the world—the child's efforts to carry on continuous successful construing of events. The parent is induced to see the child's resistances as indications of his efforts to remain in or to reenter situations in which he can successfully anticipate the events around him. The parent is trained to capitalize on this basic motivation by leading the child into situations in which he can continue to anticipate successfully. When the parent can successfully moderate the input, so that the child continuously experiences successful anticipation in the parent's presence, the child will readily enter situations under the parent's regulation.

In short, the commentary about the recorded parent-child interactions is directed toward having the parent revise his implicit child-development theory toward a constructivist position. The parent should see the child as an active construer. The parent should be able to identify the child's responses to failures to anticipate. The parent should be able to plan input that will assure that the child can successfully anticipate, and so on.

More concretely, the parent might be shown how to introduce a child to new varieties of food. He would be instructed to consider the various dimensions along which the child might construe the food's stimulus properties—for example, *sweet vs. sour, bitter vs. salty,* and so on, within the taste domain; *smooth vs. coarse, fluid vs. gooey, dry vs. wet,* and so on, within the tactile domain; and *cold vs. hot* within the temperature domain. The parent would be asked to consider the novelty level of specific features of the foods and of various combinations of the features. The parent would be instructed in various ways to introduce novel features so that the child could develop means of successfully integrating the food stimulation. The parent might attempt to offer small quantities of the new food, making a game of experimenting with the new elements and helping to attach verbal labels to the constructs the child is developing. The parent could be helped to consider the widsom of avoiding superordinate constructs that would encourage rejection of novel food features—that is, a construct such as *tastes awful vs. tastes good.* In short, the family meal, like every other parent-child interaction, could be regarded as a cognitive growth experience, in that the child's construing system would be taken into account when new stimuli are introduced as elements of the child's experiments.

Evaluation of the Parent Training Program

Behavior Rating

The original plan of the study specified behavior assessment as a part of program evaluation. Segments of the parent's and the child's ongoing behavior were evaluated by judges. The behaviors were categorized in broad terms, such as *parent coercion* or *child coercion, parent cooperation* or *child cooperation, parent regulation, child noncompliance,* and so forth. The broad categories were easy to use and there was high rater agreement in the assignment of behaviors to these categories.

An analysis was carried out to compare the amount of each type of behavior shown in the first session to the amount of that type of behavior shown in the fifteenth session. The most clear-cut result was that there was a drop in the amount of verbal coercive behaviors shown by the children. On the whole, the behavior ratings did not show important changes in parent behaviors during the filmed episodes. Although there was an increase in parent effort to regulate the children and a decrease in the periods of parental nonregulation, these changes were not statistically significant. The use of behavior ratings will be discussed later.

Parent Role Repertory (ParRep) Results

Table 1 lists 14 parent role descriptors which were included in a parent role repertory (ParRep) matrix that was developed for use in evaluating the parent training program. Table 1 also lists 16 statements about child rearing and parent-child relationships. These role descriptors and statements were used to extract parents' views about relationships between child-rearing beliefs and various possible parenting roles. To collect the basic data, parents were asked to assume the role of one or another of the parents in the list. For example, a responding parent was asked to think about a father of a fifth-grade child who "breaks more rules than anybody in the fifth grade" (8. CBRAKRUL). The parent was then to deduce the position that would be taken by this father if he were judging each of the child-rearing statements. The participating parent was to tell, for example, how the father of a constantly rule-breaking child would react to the statement that a child should settle down when told to do so (C. SETLDO). The responding parents were to indicate if the parent in the assumed role would say that the statement makes complete sense (0), makes some sense (1), or makes no sense (2). After having responded to each statement as they believed that the father in that role might have responded, they then took one of the other parent roles. The final result of each of the parent responses was a 16 × 14 matrix in which each of the 224 cells contained as 0, a 1, or a 2.

Each matrix was processed through the clustering analysis and two-way permutation process designed by Rosenberg and his research group. The details of this methodology are reported by Rosenberg (1977).

The format for the parent roles and the child-rearing statements was not completed at the time when it was imperative to begin the program. Numerous revisions were necessary before the parents participating in the program could successfully respond to the task. The delay in completing a successful format made it impossible

Table 1. Parent Roles and Child-Rearing Statements Used in the Parent Role Repertory Matrix.

Parent roles

1. Frank Gable gets along beautifully with his children. Frank and his children can work out anything that might trouble them. What would Frank say about this? (GETALONG)
2. Picture Sally Smith. Sally has raised a child who really sticks to what needs to be done. If Sally's child starts to put together a puzzle, or to learn something . . . she sticks right to it. (CPERSIST)
3. What do you think about this statement? (YOU)
4. If you were the *very best* parent you could be to *your* child, what would you want to say about this statement? (UVERBEST)
5. Mary Jones is the *best* mother there could be. (BEST)
6. Three or four couples are at a little gathering; they are talking about their young children, talking about how to raise the children. If someone said this . . . would they think that this makes a lot of sense? (GROUPCON)

Table 1 *(cont.)*

7. Bob Wilson has really tried to raise his children so that they do things when they are asked to do them. What would Bob say about this statement? (CCOMPLY)

8. Jim Klinger has a fifth-grade child who can't seem to do the right thing. Jim's child breaks more rules than anybody in fifth grade. When Jim was raising his child, would he be likely to say that this statement made sense? (CBRAKRUL)

9. Ruth Kramer is a mother who knows the best thing to do when children get upset. What would she say about this statement? (KALMWELL)

10. Faye Dunn has raised a child who doesn't get along with other people outside of the family. Faye's child just has trouble getting along with other people. What would Faye say about this statement? (CNALNGWL)

11. Barbara Moore has a child who can't stand being in new situations. Barbara just hasn't helped her child to put up with anything new—new food, new places, new people. Barbara's child really fusses whenever the family tries something different or new. (CANTNOVL)

12. Sue Doyle really feels satisfied with herself as a parent. Sue feels that she does a good job. She's very happy being a mother. (SATISFYD)

13. Joe Hooker is the kind of parent who doesn't always try hard to get his children to do what they are told to do. He's kind of easy on them. (EASY)

14. John Powers is a man who is known to be very fair with his children. John's friends, and all the other kids always say, "John Powers is fair with his children." (FAIR)

Child rearing statements

A. Train a child to be afraid of his father—that way he will grow up to be a person who won't get into trouble. (FEARFA)

B. The child who has done something really bad deserves a really hard punishment, and the child who has done something that is not so bad deserves an easier punishment. (PUNFTC)

C. A child should settle down whenever he's told to settle down. (SETLDO)

D. When a child has done something that a parent doesn't like, talking to the child works better than punishing the child. (TALKNP)

E. Even though parents must teach their child to follow rules, the child can be a friend to his parents. (BFRIEN)

F. When a mother wants a child to calm down, it helps to give it a good swat on the rear. (SWATCA)

G. A 10-year-old and a 4-year-old are no different when it comes to punishment. If the 4-year-old breaks something, he gets the same punishment as the 10-year-old who breaks something. (PUNACL)

H. There are a lot of children who will turn out bad, even though the parents are really good parents. (SOMBAD)

I. It doesn't hurt to let a child disagree when a parent tries to explain something the child did wrong. (LTDISA)

J. Always try to tell a kid what is going to happen before it happens. (FOURWA)

K. Punish a child whenever he does not do what he is told to do. (DOWATO)

L. Once a parent makes a rule, a child should never be allowed to break the rule . . . no matter what. (NVBRKR)

M. If you are trying to teach a child something, such as, how to put on his shoes, let him work it out his own way. (LRNBYD)

N. A parent makes it clear to his children that they will be punished whenever they do something stupid. (PUNCLR)

O. When it's time to put a child to bed, do things in the same order each night—a bath first, then a snack, then a story—the same order each night. (RUTINE)

P. Let a child tell what he thinks when his parents ask him to do something. (LTCHLD) to obtain a preprogram assessment of the participating parents. Nine parents who had completed 15 training sessions did complete the ParRep.

Seven parents who had not yet participated in the training program also completed the ParRep grid. These parents, who had come to the Center for assistance with their difficult-to-regulate children, would participate in the next training series. Their completed grids provide some contrast to grids completed by participating parents.

Figures 1 and 2 display facsimiles of the computer printout of the permuted matrices obtained from two parents. Parent X5 is one of the parents who was judged to have profited extensively from participation in the program. Parent C1 is one of the nonparticipating parents.

The matrices are produced by permuting, in two dimensions, the parent roles and the child-rearing statements, so that the highly similar items lie adjacent to each other. The horizontal dimension shows the permutation of the clustering of the

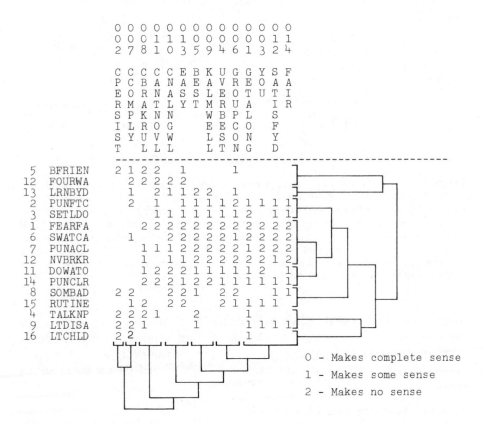

Figure 1. Plot of two-way clustering of Parent X5 Par Rep matrix. Narrative: A fair, satisfied parent gets along well with her child. Right now I feel that way, and I think that other people share my view. One must find ways not to arouse children. Good parents do this. But that doesn't necessarily mean being easy on the child. The advocating of restrictive, coercive technique is associated with children who are not able to function well. Fair, satisfied parents try to take the child's perspective and to present an orderly world to the child.

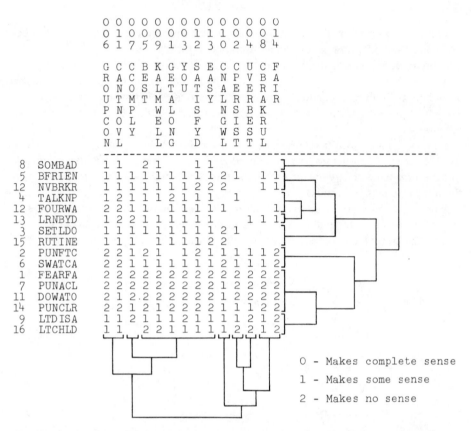

Figure 2. Plot of two-way clustering of Parent Cl Par Rep matrix. Narrative: Parents who are fair, which is what I would be at my very best, are parents who produce rule-breaking children who can't get along well with other people. Fair is a strange mixture of coercion and not attending to the child's perspectives. In fact, fair seems to represent a kind of "grand world view of fairness," which is associated with children fighting back. Easy, however, means creating a somewhat hassle-free environment, and it's then that you feel satisfied. That's the way I am right now, and that would get group validation. There seems to be a lot of confusion about what the world should be, and what it is.

parent roles. The vertical shows the permutation of the clustering of the child-rearing statements. The item and role labels are given, at the end of their respective counterparts, in Table 1. A narrative description, composed by the authors, was condensed from each matrix. The narratives from X5 and C1 are given on the figures.

Narrative Interpretations of Matrices

The permuted matrices are readily translated into narratives. For example, the matrix from Parent X5 shows a group of parent roles, clustering to the right of the display, which are easily identified as those which Parent X5 construes as *good*. The parent roles toward the left of the matrix can be identified as parent roles which Parent X5 construes as *bad*. One can identify the separation between the BEST parent and the EASY parent as the significant breaking point. To Parent X5 the easy parent (EASY) and the parent of the child who cannot get along well with others (CNALNGWL) are quite similar to each other, and are judged to have views of child-rearing practices which are quite dissimilar from those of parents in the FAIR, SATISFIED, YOU, and GETALONG roles. In terms of the numerical operations used to create the clustering patterns, the distance measures between the roles in the latter groups are relatively small. The distances between the EASY role and the parent roles which fall on the right hand side of the matrix are relatively large. One gains an overall impression of how this numerical result is obtained by observing the patterns of 0, 1, and 2 responses in the columns under the specific roles. In Parent X5's view, the FAIR parent and the SATISFYD parent would respond almost identically to the child-rearing statements. The parents in the EASY role and the CNALNGWL role also would respond almost identically to the statements. The parent in the EASY role and the parent in the FAIR role, on the other hand, are judged to hold entirely divergent views of parenting.

The parents who occupy the roles on the right side of Parent X5's matrix are judged to endorse statements that encourage parents to take into account the child's efforts to and need to construe the world (FOURWA, LRNBYD, RUTINE, LTDISA, LTCHLD) and to reject statements that call for heavyhanded applications of coercive reprimands in all situations where there has been any kind of rule violation (FEARFA, SWATCA, PUNACL, NVBRKR). In the eyes of Parent X5, the parents who occupy the roles toward the left side of the matrix are not concerned about presenting the child a world that is orderly. Parents in these roles are seen to place less value on forewarning children of impending events, on presenting them with routine, and on letting them learn by doing.

Entirely different results come from applying the same analytic process to the matrix produced from the responses of parent C1. This parent seems to think of a fair parent as one who is quite coercive and who ignores the child's perspectives. This kind of parent is quite similar to parents whose children do not get along well with others (CNALNGWL), parents whose child is stubborn (PERSIST), and parents of children who become rule violators (CBRAKRUL)—that is, the parents of children who appear to be fighting back. Yet, as the very best parent he could be (UVERBEST), Parent C1 would be quite like the fair parent. In all, Parent C1 seems to be quite convinced that regulating the child is a negative matter, and she has little idea of how to regulate other than to apply rather strong coercive measures. Thus, Parent C1 appears to believe that one should avoid regulating children, lest it produce the negative results that this parent construes to be associated with such regulation.

Comparisons of Samples

The two authors separately analyzed each of the 16 available permuted matrices. The matrices were subjectively ranked in terms of whether they appeared to reflect the kind of matrix that the authors believed should result from participation in the parent training program. The authors agreed closely on rank ordering the matrices. Four of the nine program-involved parents produced the matrices that were judged to be most ideal according to the subjective criteria. Three of the nine program-involved parents produced the least ideal matrices. All seven of the preprogram parents produced matrices that are very similar to that resulting from the responses of Parent C1 (Fig. 2). Two of the nine program-involved parents produced matrices that closely resembled that of Parent C1.

Discussion of Results of Evaluation

These first efforts to implement and to evaluate a personal-construct-oriented parent training program encourage further work in this direction. This initial work gives support to the general view that parents vary widely in their understandings of parent roles and of the interrelationships of these roles to each other and to child behaviors. The methodology of assessing these understandings, which has been extensively developed in work on implicit personality theories (Rosenberg, 1977), appears to be readily adapted to exploring the ways in which a parent construes his own role and its relationship to alternative parent-child role constructions. In short, the methods used reveal that parents are aware, to varying degrees, that there are alternative parent roles, and they believe that these different roles are associated with various views toward children and with varied child development outcomes. Further, the data indicate that these understandings can be altered by theory-based parent training programs.

The specific findings from the study show that four of the nine parents who have participated in the program produced ParRep responses that are quite compatible with the expected outcomes. The matrices resulting from the responses of these four parents reflect an awareness of the importance of (1) arranging the environment so that there is an input that is appropriately discrepant from the cognitive organizations which the child has available to integrate information, and (2) monitoring the child's arousal reaction so that the parent becomes a resource which protects the child from overarousal.

The patterns of these matrices stand in clear contrast to the patterns of the matrices resulting from the responses of the control parents. The patterns in the control parents' matrices are seen to reflect the view that there is something very positive about a "hassle-free" parent-child relationship, and that this is best achieved by avoiding regulation. This view is supported by the belief that all regulation must be coercive, and therefore unpleasant to the child. When these parents speak of the *best* parent, they seem to be thinking of a parent who allows a child to achieve what the parent believes the child to want—unrestricted freedom to follow a rather hedonistically-oriented, inner-directed life. If regulation would be imposed, they believe, it would lead to the child's counterreaction of defiance and stubbornness.

The ease with which the matrices are interpreted is particularly encouraging. The imposing of the dendrograph on the permuted clusters can be done very easily by relatively untrained persons.

Implementing Continued Program Development

These first efforts, of course, need many further developments. The most important considerations center on the actual conduct of the program. It is necessary to work constantly with the parent trainers to be sure that they are fully familiar with the practices that would emerge from a personal construct approach to parent-child interactions. This means that the trainers must continuously discuss and elaborate their own constructions of the theory. Like most people, it is very difficult for the trainers to yield their mechanistic conceptions of *leniency vs. severity,* and to refrain from using coercive efforts at those times when the child becomes particularly unmanageable.

Preprogram ParRep responses and other information will be needed to better select the participating parents. For example, the three participating parents who produced the "lowest level" ParRep matrices might better have engaged in another kind of parent training program. These three parents responded in a way that indicated that they did not differentiate the parent roles. To them, every parent would have the same view on each of the child-rearing statements. This suggests that they might have better profited from the program after they were able to show some recognition that different parents do hold different views about approaches to child rearing.

It is also clear that the evaluation procedures must be improved. The behavior ratings were useless for the evaluation of the goals developed for this program. In evaluations of future phases of the program, the category system that will be used to rate behaviors will be a system that evolves from the theory. We will look specifically, for example, for efforts to structure input so that the child can assimilate the steps that progress toward the desired outcome. We will look for the parent's efforts to de-arouse the child before presenting further stimulation, and so on.

Some of the items on the ParRep will be altered. The statement about swatting child to calm it (SWATCA) and the statement about promoting fear of the father (FEARFA) are undifferentiating. Few parents are seen to agree with these statements. The description of the parent role relative to the persisting child (CPERSIST) will be changed. Too many of the parents think that the current description defines a *stubborn* child.

The most important changes will be those related to development of techniques of comparing matrices. It will be imperative to obtain preparticipation ParRep responses which can be compared to postparticipation ParRep responses. It will be useful to obtain ParRep matrices from the responses of parents who have reared children who enjoy social participation and productive regulation. It will be necessary to apply statistical techniques that will allow all kinds of cross-comparisons of matrices. In short, the assessment techniques described above must be considered as being in the preliminary stages. The publication of this report is regarded as an invitation to collaboration.

CONCLUSION

Personal Construct Theory provides a useful guide to the development of parent training programs which take into account the cognitive systems of the parent and child. The major objective of the parent training program described above is the change in the parent's construing of the psychological processes of the child. Parents are given experiences that are intended to induce changes in the ways they construe the motivational process associated with the child's action sequences. The design and conduct of the program are based on the assumption that parents will develop alternative ways to play roles relative to the child's construing efforts. The program would be judged to have succeeded if the parent adopts the role of a novelty moderator; that is, the role of the parent who carefully assesses the child's current construing of events and then prepares input that allows the child to achieve moderate levels of failure to anticipate. In such instances the parent would continue to moderate the child's arousal by arranging input that will lead to successful resolution of discrepancy.

Ultimately, the child's construing will be affected by the parent's efforts to moderate the levels of novelty and associated arousal. It is assumed that optimum cognitive growth takes place in an environment in which the child is continuously exposed to moderately discrepant stimulation. Further, as the parent repetitively succeeds in presenting the child with opportunities to engage the cycle of discrepancy, moderate arousal, cognitive reorganization, and resolution the child would come to depend more and more on the parents as an arousal-regulating resource. The child should reduce its efforts to avoid adults, who too often had served only to introduce greater discrepancy and arousal.

As investigators turn away from the mechanistic paradigms that guide the larger part of planned parent training programs, they more and more will be able to draw on the principles that other behavior scientists have developed in their studies of cognitive processes. Personal Construct Psychology represents a systematic statement of a theory of persons which is compatible with, and can readily guide, this expected evolution toward parent training programs based on contextualist paradigms.

REFERENCES

Bugental, D. B., Whalen, C. K., & Henker, B. Causal attributions of hyperactive children and motivational assumptions of two behavior change approaches. *Child Development,* 1977, **48,** 874−884.

Clarke-Stewart, K. Alison. Popular primers for parents. *American Psychologist,* 1978, **33,** 359−369.

Cohen, L. B. Habituation of infant arousal. In T. J. Tighe and R. N. Leaton (Eds.), *Habituation.* Hillsdale, NJ: Lawrence Erlbaum, 1976, pp. 207−238.

Flavell, J. *Cognitive Development.* Englewood Cliffs, NJ: Prentice-Hall, 1977.

Forehand, R., & Atkeson, B. M. Generality of treatment effects with parents as therapists: A review of assessment and implementation procedures. *Behavior Therapy,* 1977, **8,** 575−593.

Forehand, R., Sturgis, E. T., McMahon, R. J., Aguar, D., Green, K., Wells, K. C., & Breiner, J. Parent behavioral training to modify child non-compliance. *Behavior Modification,* 1979, **3,** 3−25.

Ginsburg, H., & Opper, S. *Piaget's Theory of Intellectual Development.* Englewood Cliffs, NJ: Prentice-Hall, 1979.

Goocher, B. E. Behavioral applications of an educateur model in child care. *Child Care Quarterly,* 1975, **4,** 84−92.

Handin, K. H., & Mancuso, J. C. Perceptions of the functions of reprimand. *Journal of Social Psychology,* 1980, **110,** 43−52.

Inhelder, B., & Piaget, J. *The Early Growth of Logic in the Child.* New York: Norton, 1969.

Kelly, G. A. *The Psychology of Personal Constructs.* Vols. 1 and 2. New York: Norton, 1955.

Kelly, G. A. The autobiography of a theory. In B. Maher (Ed.), *Clinical Psychology and Personality.* New York: Wiley, 1969.

Kendall, P. C., & Finch, A. J. A cognitive-behavioral treatment for impulsivity: A group comparison study. *Journal of Consulting and Clinical Psychology,* 1978, **46,** 110−118.

Mancuso, J. C. Current motivational models in the elaboration of personal construct theory. In A. W. Landfield (Ed.), *Nebraska Symposium on Motivation: Personal Construct Psychology.* Lincoln, NE: University of Nebraska Press, 1977, pp. 43−97.

Mancuso, J. C. Reprimand: The construing of the rule violator's construct system. In P. Stringer and D. Bannister (Eds.), *Constructs of Sociality and Individuality.* New York: Academic, 1979, pp. 255−277.

Mancuso, J. C., & Allen, D. A. Children's perceptions of a transgressor's socialization as a function of type of reprimand. *Human Development,* 1976, **19,** 277−290.

Mancuso, J. C., & Handin, K. H. Comparing high- and low-rated child care workers' attributions of reprimand effectiveness. *Child Care Quarterly,* in press.

McCall, R. B., & Kagan, J. Individual differences in the infant's distribution of attention to stimulus discrepancy. *Developmental Psychology,* 1970, **2,** 90−98.

Meichenbaum, D. H., & Goodman, J. Training impulsive children to talk to themselves: A means of developing self control. *Journal of Abnormal Psychology,* 1971, **77,** 115−126.

Neisser, V. *Cognition and Reality.* San Francisco: W. H. Freeman, 1976.

O'Dell, S., Flynn, J., & Benlolo, L. A comparison of parent training techniques in child behavior modification. *Behavior Therapy and Experimental Psychiatry,* 1977, **8,** 261−268.

Olson, D. R. Language and thought: Aspects of a cognitive theory of semantics. *Psychological Review,* 1970, **77,** 257−273.

Paris, S. G., & Lindauer, B. K. Constructive processes in children's comprehension and memory. In R. V. Kail & J. W. Hagen (Eds.), *Memory in Cognitive Development.* Hillsdale, NJ: Lawrence Erlbaum, 1976.

Patterson, G. R., McNeal, N., Hawkins, N., & Phelps, R. Deprogramming the social environment. *Journal of Child Psychology and Psychiatry,* 1967, **8,** 181−195.

Peed, S., Roberts, M., & Forehand, R. Evaluation of the effectiveness of a standardized parent training program in altering the interaction of mothers and their noncompliant children. *Behavior Modification,* 1977, **1,** 323−349.

Piaget, J. *The Moral Judgment of the Child.* London: Kegan Paul, 1932. (In paperback, New York: Free Press, 1965.)

Piaget, J. *The Child's Conception of Number.* New York: Humanities, 1952. (In paperback, New York: W. W. Norton.)

Piaget, J. The role of the concept of equilibrium in psychological explanation. In D. Elkind (Ed.), *Six Psychological Studies.* New York: Vintage Books, 1968, pp. 100−115. (First published 1959.)

Posner, M. J. *Cognition: An Introduction*. Glenview, IL: Scott, Foresman, 1973.

Powers, W. T. *Behavior: The Control of Perception*. Chicago: Aldine, 1973.

Powers, W. T. Quantitative analysis of purposive systems: Some spadework at the foundations of scientific psychology. *Psychological Review*, 1978, **85**, 417–435.

Rommetviet, R. *On Message Structure*. New York: Wiley, 1974.

Rosenberg, S. New approaches to the analysis of personal constructs in person perception. In A. W. Landfield (Ed.), *Nebraska Symposium on Motivation: Personal Construct Psychology*. Lincoln, NE: University of Nebraska Press, 1977, pp. 179–242.

Shaw, R., & Bransford, J. (Eds.), *Perceiving, Activity, and Knowing*. Hillsdale, NJ: Lawrence Erlbaum, 1977.

Wahler, R. G. Setting generality: Some specific and general effects of child behavior therapy. *Journal of Applied Behavior Analysis*, 1969, **2**, 239–246.

Weimer, W. B. A conceptual framework for cognitive psychology: Motor theories of mind. In R. Shaw and J. Bransford (Eds.), *Perceiving, Acting and Knowing*. Hillsdale, NJ: Lawrence Erlbaum, 1977, pp. 267–311.

Zeaman, D. The ubiquity of novelty-familiarity (habituation?) effects. In T. J. Tighe & R. N. Leaton (Eds.), *Habituation*. Hillsdale, NJ: Lawrence Erlbaum, 1976, pp. 297–320.

CHAPTER 14

The Person as Perspectivist, Literalist, and Chaotic Fragmentalist

A. W. Landfield

This chapter represents an attempt by the author to distill from his many years of experience as a Personal Construct Psychologist certain observations and their interpretations which seem most vital for understanding how persons, including the author himself, both function and malfunction. The unifying conception of this paper is perspectivism, which is contrasted with literalism and a related idea, chaotic fragmentalism. This dimension of *perspectivism vs. literalism* will be presented in varied contexts. One context, Personal Construct Theory, will be in evidence throughout the paper.

Literalism and perspectivism, described throughout the chapter, will be defined more concisely in the final section where the threads and themes of earlier discussions will be linked together. Illustrations will be used which give special attention to the literalistic ways in which persons seem to relate their feelings, values, and behavior. Feeling, valuing, and behaving will be referred to as the "triad of knowing." It is the excessive tightness or looseness within this triad that points to literalism. It is the moderate degree of linkage within this triad that allows for the development of hierarchies of meaning and sets the stage for perspectivism. Although the relatedness of feeling, valuing, and behaving has been given special emphasis, one may also speak of literalism in the way in which a person relates his different feelings, his values, or his behavior. Again, the excessive tightness or looseness of relating points to literalism.

Perspectivism usually implies some capacity to step back from a problem and to conceptualize it more thoughtfully, complexly, and integratively. Literalism sometimes is used unfairly as an accusation of another person who stubbornly fails to see the point one is making. As it is used in this chapter, literalism refers to an absolute interpretation of an event or a relationship without the implication that it is necessarily "bad," although as we shall see, it is often associated with problems in living.

From the outset, it should be understood that the terms perspectivism and literalism do not define some new body of observation. Rather, they tend to pull together many observations of human functioning; observations that have been variously linked to such labels as abstractness, concreteness, complexity, openness, hierarchy, curiosity, flexibility, creativeness, impulsiveness, rigidity, denial, bigotry, repression, guilt, and intolerance of ambiguity. This latter term, described by Frenkel-Brunswick (1949), certainly bears a close resemblance to literalism.

If one wishes to extensively document instances of literalism, the literature is inexhaustible. A few quotations will suffice to give a bit of historical background. Beginning with Shakespeare's *King John* (Act 4, Scene 2), "How oft the sight of means to do ill deeds makes ill deeds done," we are introduced to a literal relationship between the thought and the act. A quotation from the *Book of Proverbs* (15:13) suggests a more constructive relationship between feeling and behavior: "A merry heart maketh a cheerful countenance. . . ." Freud (1929) draws our attention to the literal relationship between feeling and value: ". . . Even when a person has not actually done the bad thing but has only recognized in himself an intention to do it, he may regard himself as guilty" (p. 124).

PERSPECTIVISM

Perspectivism points to an aspect of the person which is dependent upon his capacity to construct hierarchies of meaning. A person who functions with perspective can distance himself from the immediacy of an event by utilizing higher order or more general comprehensions within his system of personal meanings.

As the person considers an event within the context of higher order construction, he can relate to the event in broader outlines than would be possible if he were to take a lower order and more limited view. Higher order construction allows the person to understand an event both within a more limited as well as within a broader framework of interpretation. In other words, higher order, encompassing, or general meanings allow the person more freedom to consider an event in different and related ways. This greater freedom through hierarchical process allows the person to be more reflective since he is not forced into one particular interpretation of an event. However, this greater freedom need not lead to hopeless confusion. The hierarchical process enables the person to differentiate along a dimension of appropriateness and meaningfulness. For example, this freedom through hierarchical process permits the perspectivist to differentiate between classes of events to which he must react with immediacy and classes of events to which he may react with greater deliberation. Whereas the literalist may force decisions on the basis of their obvious outcomes, the perspectivist, within his more elaborated and elaborating hierarchical system, tends to be more questioning about what is so obvious. The perspectivist may understand that obviousness is in the eye of the beholder and that better decisions sometimes can be made with greater thoughtfulness. Even as the hierarchical function allows the perspectivist to define certain areas of decision making as less temporally critical, he can make rapid decisions, but not with the full certainty of their rightness as experienced by the literalist.

In this discussion of the perspectivist, I have implied that the person who functions in the hierarchical style may entertain varied, alternative, or multiple interpretations of an event. This style of the perspectivist may be contrasted with that of the literalist, who reveals ways of feeling, valuing, and behaving which connote the restricted and absolute interpretation of an event or a relationship. The literalist prefers a fixity of construction and a lack of exceptions to how one understands a particular event or relationship. The chronic literalist who does not function within elaborated systems of hierarchical meaning prefers literal assumption to hypothesis and a single-minded adherence to identity while eschewing notions of contrast. Although the literalist may employ organizations of meaning, the interrelationships among his dimensions of personal meaning will be tightly bound, allowing only few or no exceptions to what he perceives as being related. These tightly bound relationships minimize openness to new experience, since he assumes certain events and relationships to be true. In the context of this literalism, ideas are not utilized as vehicles of exploration. Instead, they exist simply as facts.

Perhaps the first elaboration of perspectivism and literalism can best be done within a set of questions: First, can these contrasting styles be treated in a simple manner, casting one half of the population in the category of literalism and the other half in the category of perspectivism? Second, how does dependency relate to this dimension? Third, is the perspectivist a more cognitive and less emotional fellow than the literalist? Finally, how does the process of dialectic and argument relate to these two hypothetical styles?

CAN PERSPECTIVISM VERSUS LITERALISM BE APPLIED TO THE PERSON IN A SIMPLE MANNER?

If one were to answer this question from a literal stance, it would be easy to place all persons into one or the other pigeonhole on a permanent basis. In contrast, the perspectivist would say that, for some purposes, it might be useful to categorize in a simple way. However, the perspectivist would not feel it necessary to create pure types of literalism or perspectivism into which he could place all persons. Not only would the literal and nonliteral processes be employed to a greater or lesser degree, but it would be appropriate to examine the areas in which a person tends to play literal or perspectivist roles. For purposes of understanding and communicating about certain extreme forms of pathology, it may help to talk about the perspectivist versus the literalist; however, the pursuit of a monolithic perspectivism or literalism would not seem very useful. Nevertheless, the terms perspectivist and literalist and perspectivist and literalist styles will be employed as a way of expediting communication and this usage is appropriate for extreme cases. At the same time, it is assumed that most persons feel, value, and behave within the context of both styles.

HOW DOES PERSPECTIVISM VERSUS LITERALISM RELATE TO DEPENDENCY?

The dependent person could be defined in relation to his helplessness. He could also be defined in relation to the attitude that his fate primarily is dominated by persons or processes over which he has little or no control. The independent person would be described as more self-reliant in behavior and point of view. Using these definitions, it is possible to conceptualize the literalist as either independent or dependent. The dependency content of one's existence may vary, but the style or the way one implements independent or dependent attitudes can remain stable. For example, a husband might evaluate time that his wife devotes to other males at a party as complete rejection. At the same time, this person might refuse assistance from a colleague at work because it would mean abject dependency. At one level of discourse, in the context of dependency, this person is highly inconsistent. Yet, the absoluteness and single-mindedness of his behavior suggests literalism.

In contrast, the perspectivist's broader-based, hierarchical position would allow him to better understand the creative functions of both dependent and independent roles, recognizing that one cannot survive as a totally independent or dependent person. Able to encompass and apply both ideas to his wife as well as to himself, he might construe his wife's behavior at a party as a normal desire to relate to others, or possibly as her perception of him as inattentive or unloving. Although he might have feelings of rejection, he could also understand that she, too, might suffer rejection. Initially, the perspectivist could react angrily and, possibly, literally. However, he would then "cool down" and reflect on the situation. The literalist would continue his tirade.

Taking an extreme example of how the perspectivist may survive independently in situations over which he has little control, Frankl (1964) relates how he created a world of experience that was not completely under the domination of his captors. The guards of the concentration camp did not know his hidden thoughts, nor could they anticipate how his simple perception of a flower could generate profound experience. In using Frankl as an illustration of the perspectivist style, it is not assumed that "all good guys" are perspectivists and "all bad guys" are literalists. One must take into account the content of one's values as well as their organization. The specter of a Machiavellian perspectivist is just as appalling as the image of the literal despot.

IS THE PERSPECTIVIST A MORE COGNITIVE AND LESS EMOTIONAL FELLOW THAN THE LITERALIST?

Rephrasing this question, does the perspectivist within his more elaborated hierarchical system function more cognitively than the literalist who responds more directly to the event? Is feeling tied more closely to the grass roots of an event, suggesting that the literalist is more open to feeling, or at least is more immediately expressive of feeling?

This type of question implies that cognition occurs with a minimum of feeling and that higher order cognitions are least related to feeling. Sometimes the psychotherapist will speak about overintellectualism in his client which impedes progress in treatment. For example, Gendlin (1962) refers to clients who talk about problems without directly experiencing "felt meanings." Although illustrations from psychotherapy may seem to support a linkage between cognition and lack of feeling, it seems more likely that meaning, at whatever level of discourse, may have components of feeling, valuing, and behaving. Perhaps we could think of the perspectivist as being open to all these aspects of comprehension and meaning. It may be the literalist who is the overintellectualizer and who cannot take perspective on his momentary feelings.

HOW DOES DIALECTIC AND ARGUMENT RELATE TO PERSPECTIVISM VERSUS LITERALISM?

A first consideration in replying to this question is to differentiate between dialectic and argument within oneself and dialectic and argument with others. The literalist may be conceptualized as one who primarily argues with others. He argues with others much as one might in a sports arena. It is all a question of winning or losing. "I am right and you are wrong" is the acceptable outcome. In contrast, the perspectivist, even as he prefers to be correct, carries out his dialectic both within himself and in relation to others. His preoccupation is more with comprehension than just with being correct. Since he continually creates hierarchies, his structures of meaning become tools for further understanding, rather than monuments to his success. His style, more process than content, allows him to remain open to exceptions to his hypotheses and to question his own formulations, since his particular formulations do not primarily define him. Whereas the literalist defines himself primarily by the contents of his structures, the perspectivist defines himself essentially by the processes with which he learns and comprehends. Definition by process helps to minimize the devastating threat of meaninglessness and loss of structure when one is wrong or fails in a particular task. In summary, the perspectivist, as dialectician within himself, may avoid being trapped in ceaseless argument with others. He may also avoid the rigid overintellectualization and defensiveness of the classical neurotic. He may also avoid the rigid acting out of the person who overreacts to his momentary feelings.

Up to this point in our discussion, the contrasting focus has highlighted the dimension of *perspectivism vs. literalism*. Now there is a third idea which can be differentiated from both perspectivism and literalism, although it bears a close resemblance to literalism and would seem derived from it. The term chaotic fragmentalism seems most descriptive of this third idea.

George Kelly (1963) defined a conception which he called "accumulative fragmentalism," a term that implies that if one gathers enough facts, the sheer weight of their numbers will reveal their meaning. Kelly's conception seems to have much in common with literalism. To distinguish our use of fragmentation from that of Kelly's, the word "chaotic" is used as a modifier. Chaotic fragmentalism is most strikingly observed in the person given the label "thought-disordered schizophrenic." Not only may this person experience life in unrelated fragments, but the fragments and their patterns constantly shift. Such a person employs little hierarchical structure and reacts closely to the feeling and the stimulus. Not only does he lack hierarchical structure, but he also does not employ the tightly organizing strategies of the literalist. Perhaps one might refer to this person as chaotically literal. In summary, the chaotic fragmentalist experiences a kaleidoscopic world, one that is constantly changing. He does not link his fragments tightly into bundles, employing the horizontal linkages of the literalist. He also does not employ the hierarchical or vertical integrations of the perspectivist. The most profound anxieties can be associated with this life-style.

PERSPECTIVISM AND LITERALISM VIEWED WITHIN THE CONTEXT OF PERSONAL CONSTRUCT THEORY

Perspectivism has been defined in regard to one's capacity to employ higher order construction. This definition of perspectivism can be linked with Kelly's statements about the personal construct system. In his organization and fragmentation corollaries, Kelly (1955) writes that a construction system may embrace ordinal relationships among constructs. He also states that incompatibility can be encompassed by one's construction system. In this context of understanding order and how incompatibility can be handled within the system, he introduces the idea of superordinacy and subordinacy of constructs. It is through the integrative function of superordinate construction that man can develop ways of anticipating events that transcend contradictions. Kelly envisions the superordinate construct as one that is more abstract and encompassing of events. In the discussion of the person as perspectivist, the point was made that higher order construction allows the person to view his life within a broader based framework. In the context of this broader framework, the person may experience more freedom to be reflective, since he is not forced into one particular interpretation of an event. In other words, superordinate construing allows more freedom or greater perspective in how an event may be understood. One is not forced to accept a literal meaning of an experience. At one level, an event may be understood in a particular way. At another level of discourse, it may be understood somewhat differently. It is this difference of meaning attributable to varying levels of organization that relates importantly to one's freedom. Kelly seemed to have a clear understanding of how ordinal relationships can give man greater freedom of choice.

To transcend the obvious—this is the basic psychological problem of man. Inevitably it is a problem we must all seek to solve, whether we fancy ourselves as psychologists or not. What has already happened in our experience may seem obvious enough, now that we have been through it. But literally it is something that will never happen again. It can't, for time refuses to run around in circles . . . (p. 5).

Elaborating further, Kelly states:

"The "known realities" keep slipping out from under us. Our senses play all kinds of tricks and prove themselves to be the most unreliable informants. And our theologies, far-seeing as they appear to be, do, in time, lead to such indecent practices that sensitive men refuse any longer to take them literally. Thus we find ourselves repeatedly cut off from what once we thought we knew for sure, and we must reluctantly abandon the very faiths from which we originally launched our most fruitful enterprises. The upshot of all this is that we can no longer rest assured that human progress may proceed step by step in an orderly fashion from the unknown. Neither our senses nor our doctrines provide us with the immediate knowledge required for such a philosophy of science. What we think we know is anchored only in our assumptions, not in the bed rock of truth itself, and the world we seek to understand remains always on the horizons of our thoughts. To grasp this principle fully is to concede that everything we believe to exist appears to us the way it does because of our present constructions of it. Thus even the most obvious things in the world are wide open to reconstruction in the future. This is what we mean by the expression *constructive alternativism*. (pp. 7, 8)

Kelly contrasts this capacity for higher order reinterpretation with a philosophical view which he termed "accumulative fragmentalism" (Kelly, 1963). In discussing this conception, Kelly states that scientists sometimes assume that one must get things nailed down, "one at a time, and, using each established fact or law as a point of departure, to make further inferences and test them by experimentation. If the data confirm the hypotheses, then one will have something more to nail down, and the total job of simulating the universe will be that much nearer completion" (p. 14).

He then states that "the whole of truth lies ahead of us, rather than that some parts of it ahead and some behind. What we possess, or what we have achieved so far, are approximations of the truth, not fragments of it. Hopefully we are getting closer, in some sort of asymptotic progression, and, at some infinite point in time, science and reality may indeed converge" (p. 14).

In this distinction between the process of active reconstruction and the view that facts will announce their meanings to us, we have a very basic statement that suggests how Kelly might have understood the person as perspectivist. For him the perspectivist might have been one who actively interprets and reinterprets his life. Rather than higher order generalizations being used as capstones to one's life, or as obvious integrations of experience, they are vehicles or tools for entering the future. They are not literalisms or monuments to truth. Instead they are avenues of understanding and processes of interacting with the world. Kelly would not have confused the pyramiding of "facts" with the hierarchical constructions of the perspectivist.

The issue of *perspectivism* versus *literalism* is particularly highlighted in Kelly's own theoretical behavior. Take, for example, his treatment of threat. His definition of threat as the awareness of an imminent, comprehensive change in core structure certainly points to Kelly's capacity to construe in hierarchical ways. In stating that change of any kind, if important enough, can be threatening, Kelly rejects the primary role of a simple hedonism in explaining behavior. Not only may the person define pleasures and pains in idiosyncratic ways, but more than that, the person may experience the unstabilizing effects of change, the contents of which may be "good" or "bad." As one severely disturbed patient stated in a rare moment of candor, "I would like to be more mature and responsible; it would solve a lot of problems. But I would feel like Christopher Columbus. I might drop off the edge of the world. It's better to be what I am right now. I don't like myself, but I know who I am."

Certainly, Kelly's more abstract, process-oriented view of threat, one that is not tied to specific contents, might help to explain the resistant behavior of the well-organized depressive. When offered a message of hope and change, he beats his head against the wall even harder. Although one could interpret this behavior as masochistic pleasure, one could also view it as a sign of profound threat—the dread of moving toward an uncertain future.

Kelly's approach to threat is just one way in which he has tried to assume a less literal stance in explaining human behavior. Another of his less literal views of the person is found in his definition of guilt. He did not define guilt as "just" doing something bad. Rather, he defined it as a dislodgment of self from core role structure. In other words, one could be guilty about many things that would not be labeled as "bad behavior." His definition encompasses not only moral guilt, but other kinds of guilt as well. It is this more hierarchical stance of Kellian thinking that makes it so attractive for some professionals.

Anxiety is another interesting conception that Kelly treated at a more abstract level of interpretation. He defined anxiety as "the awareness that the events with which one is confronted lie mostly outside the range of convenience of his construct system" (1955, p. 565). For some readers, this may be a strange definition, since terms such as apprehension, nervousness, feelings of impending doom, palmar sweating, increased heart rate, and upsetness do not appear in the definition. The absence of such terms from his definition did not mean that he was uninterested in what most of us associate with the experience of anxiety. In his definition, Kelly is stating what he believes to be the general instigating context of anxiety—that is, the person's inability to comprehend aspects of life about him in a meaningful fashion. However, there was no intended implication that the anxious person would be able to freely and literally verbalize this definition of anxiety. Although the person might only experience upsetness, the psychologist could examine this upsetness within the larger context of Kelly's definition of anxiety.

In writing about anxiety at this more abstract level, Kelly has been criticized for being too cognitive. Kelly did not make a sharp distinction between what is emotional, cognitive, or behavioral. He did not state that the symbols of constructs have to be just words, nor did he state that the assignment of meaning is just unemotional. Kelly placed great emphasis on propositional construction which does not preempt meaning. In regard to his own theorizing, he preferred that professionals would not categorize his ideas as "just" cognitive, behavioral, or emotional. This point is made clear in the following quotation:

> The reader may have noted that in talking about experience I have been careful not to use either of the terms, "emotional" or "affective." I have been equally careful not to invoke the notion of "cognition." The classic distinction that separates these two constructs has, in the manner of most classic distinctions that once were useful, become a barrier to sensitive psychological inquiry. When one so divided the experience of man, it becomes difficult to make the most of the holistic aspirations that may infuse the science of psychology with new life, and may replace the classicism now implicit even in the most "behavioristic" research. This too, as I see it, is a part of "the challenge of humanistic psychology." (Kelly, 1969, p. 140)

Although Kelly tried to avoid being categorized in some literal way, he both failed and succeeded. He documented his feelings about this problem when he stated:

Personal Construct Theory has also been categorized by responsible scholars as an emotional theory, a learning theory, a psychoanalytic theory (Freudian, Adlerian, and Jungian—all three), a typically American theory, a Marxist theory, a humanistic theory, a logical positivistic theory, a Zen Buddhistic theory, a Thomistic theory, a behavioristic theory, an Apollonian theory, a pragmatistic theory, a reflexive theory, and no theory at all. It has also been classified as nonsense, which indeed, by its own admission, it will likely some day turn out to be. In each case there were some convincing arguments offered for the categorization, but I have forgotten what most of them were. I fear that no one of these categorizations will be of much help to the reader in understanding personal construct theory, but perhaps having a whole lap full of them all at once will suggest what might be done with them. (Kelly, 1970, pp. 36−37)

This quotation suggests that it has not been easy for theorists to anchor Personal Construct Theory within one single framework of interpretation, although some psychologists (e.g., Maddi, 1971) have tried it. The quotation also supports Kelly's contention that the person (psychologist) functions within his own construction system, although it could be argued, alternatively, that Kellian thought is so vague that anyone can make anything of it that he wishes. In rebuttal, it could be argued that Kelly has provided us with a genuinely creative and complex theory that must be studied carefully and within a context of trying to suspend one's own views—that is, struggling with the literalisms of one's own comprehension and attempting to transcend the obvious.

There are other conceptions within construct theory that may also be related to questions of perspectivism and literalism. Kelly introduced the idea of constriction, which he defined as the narrowing of one's perceptual field in order to minimize apparent incompatibilities. Quite obviously, this kind of narrowing of one's perceptual field could be carried to the point of literalism, exemplified by the 19-year-old boy who obsessively played with paper clips. The opposite of constriction—dilation—could also be carried to a point of literalism as the person views life only in fragments, and to the point when he declares that life has no meaning. To view life at the fingertips of fragmentary concreteness can lead to a point of constriction which is meaningless. Constant constriction and constant dilation may lead to the same singular, absolute position of hopelessness, a literal stance in either case.

Literalism can also be seen in Kelly's hostile person. Hostility is the continued effort to extort validational evidence. The person continues to force issues and outcomes that cannot be forced. His only hope is to step back or step up and take perspective on his situation. He must put his dilemmas into broader terms. For example, he might begin to define his world as including the feelings of other people as well as his own—that is, he would function within the sociality corollary.

Literalism can also be seen in relation to Kelly's ideas of preemptive and constellatory construction. In preemptive thinking, one has little appreciation for alternatives. Ideas and relationships are simple and fixed. There is little elaboration of ideas and the parameters of those ideas are fixed by the notion that "it is *only* that way" or "it is *nothing* but that." Preemptive thinking points to the most profound kind of simplistic and absolute literalism, a kind of concreteness that Kelly did not expect to find in pure form. Another kind of thinking could also have literal implications. In constellatory thinking, relationships between ideas are tight. Although conceptions within constellations of ideas might be complex, more complex than in preemptive thinking, there is rigidity in the construction complex in regard to what fits or does not fit within the complex. Kelly refers to both preemptive and constel-latory thinking as instances of concreteness. In contrast to these modes of thinking, Kelly posits the propositional construction. Propositional thinking implies a freer type of construction that does not preempt elements for its exclusive use. Thus, one may apply a construction to an event and at the same time apply other constructs to the event or, at least, allow for the application of other constructs to the event. Propositional construction does not necessarily imply loose thinking. In employing a precise description of some event from the perspective of a particular propositional construct, one simply does not assume that one's particular construction is the only construction of the event, or that it is even the ultimately best construction.

Using Kelly's construct of the ball, the statement that "a ball is just a ball and nothing else," points to the most simple form of literal thinking. The statement that "a ball is a number of things, but definitely not anything else" points to a constel-latory thinking, a more complex type of construction which might be seen as literal, but not to the extreme of preemptive thinking. The statement that "a ball tends to be round, but may be described in other ways as well, including ways that we have not thought about," represents the purest form of nonliteral construction. One can define the ball in several respects without limiting oneself or others to the particular definition. One can change his mind about the definition if its suits his purposes. He may also apply other constructions. In using propositional construction, one may be operating within a perspectivist framework—but not always! This point will be elaborated in the next section.

Shifting to the process of decision making, we will now see how Kelly's C-P-C cycle has important implications for understanding the nature of literalism. This cycle begins with circumspection, followed by preemption, and then control. Cir-cumspection is the stage at which the person looks at the elements of a situation in propositional and multidimensional ways. At this stage, the person is most open to experience. At the second stage, preemption, the person focuses on some dimension or aspect of the situation. Finally, at the control stage, the person makes his choice in the direction of greater elaboration, definition, and extension of his system. In the context of the C-P-C cycle, Kelly defined impulsive behavior as the foreshortening of this cycle. In other words, the impulsive person quite immediately enters the preemptive stage which leads to a final choice. The impulsive person makes little use of propositional or multidimensional thinking. He does not take perspective within a broader framework for understanding the situation. The impulsive person can be described as a literalist.

Quite obviously, Kelly's C-P-C cycle does not emphasize the exclusive use of propositional or multidimensional thinking. Kelly states (1955), "Moreover, if a person attempted to use propositional thinking exclusively, he might have consider-able difficulty in coming to any decision as to what the relevant and critical issues were in any situation" (p. 155).

In regard to preemptive thinking, Kelly states, "Preemptive thinking, in a mo-ment of decision, is essential if one is to take an active part in his universe. But preemptive thinking which never resolves itself into propositional thinking con-demns the person to a state of intellectual rigor mortis. He may be called a 'man of action,' but his actions will always follow well-worn ruts" (p. 156).

Implied in these statements is the idea that both more and less literal ways of thinking are useful. It is the exclusive use of one or the other mode of thinking in a situation that points to problems of adjustment. Applying Kelly's C-P-C Cycle to the concept of perspectivism, it is the flexible and integrated use of both expanding and constricting modes of feeling, valuing, and behaving that is most desirable. A person caught at either the circumspective or preemptive stage would be seriously handicapped. The person whose perceptual universe is constantly expanded or expanding would likely suffer from confusion. The person whose perceptual universe is constantly restricted or restricting might have some moments of security, but his constricted perception of the world would ultimately lead to a devastating anxiety. In the extreme case, both excessive fragmentation and excessive focus would progress to the stage of depersonalization and alienation from one's social world.

The foregoing discussion of Personal Construct Theory as related to the issue of *perspectivism vs. literalism* may be summarized as follows: First of all, the higher order conceptualizations of the perspectivist can best be viewed as process rather than final product. Second, the perspectivist can integrate his more concrete, literal modes of understanding with his more elaborated and encompassing construction. Finally, an important implication for the investigator of perspectivism is that it is unnecessary for him to define the personal construct in a way that would restrict its content. In particular, one may investigate the literal relations of feeling, value, and behavior within a personal construct. This kind of elaboration of the construct seems consistent with Personal Construct Theory.

TAKING PERSPECTIVE ON FEELING, VALUE, AND BEHAVIOR

Sometimes linguistic forms become so real that people forget that words such as "behavior," "value," and "feeling" are constructs—that is, they are convenient ways of pointing to kinds of phenomena that persons may commonly share. Sometimes this reality of construction takes the form of emphasizing one of these words to the exclusion or diminution of another one. For example, one may state that the psychologist only measures behavior. This being the case, words like "feeling" and "value" become meaningless or, at best, are only mirror images of behavior. Although feeling and value may seem important, they are not really the basic stuff of life as it is understood within a scientific psychology. In contrast to this view, one may state that a capacity to value is that which makes the person truly human. It is this capacity to state preferences which allows him to appreciate sequences of time and to create structures that do not presently exist. One may also take the position that feelings and emotions provide the major impetus for all endeavor. The strength and persistence of one's values and behavior are dependent on underlying feelings which often are masked, not only to outside observers, but to the person as well.

Each of these three positions, reflecting the greater significance of one or another aspect or construction of life, has adherents within the academic community. Our own position points to the importance of all three constructions—feeling, value, and behavior. They are important as interpretations and ways of understanding experience. In this context, it is unnecessary to assume that a feeling, value, or behavior is most real. Although the person or psychologist may focus on one or another member of the constructive triad, turning more inwardly or outwardly, it is assumed that feelings, values, and behavior are all personally experienced and interpreted. The position is also taken that objectivity in regard to these three frames of knowing begins with personal awareness, experience, and interpretation.

In proposing that psychologists study how feeling, value, and behavior are interrelated, it is assumed that a dimension of personal awareness—that is, the personal construct—may consist of all three of these components. In some instances, one of these components may have greater importance than the others for the individual. In some instances, the individual may deny or seem to deny the importance of one of these components, yet function "as if" the component has great significance for him. In other instances, the individual may equate or seem to equate a feeling with a behavior, a feeling with a value, or a value with a behavior. It is also possible that the individual may function "as if" feelings, values, and behaviors are interrelated, but not intimately so. For example, a feeling might have implications for how one values, but not always. A feeling might have implications for how one behaves, but not always. A value might have implications for how one behaves, but not always.

Our purpose is not to argue the case for a feeling, value, or behavior. Instead, we want to study the implications of the person's understanding of and functioning within this triad. Does it make a difference when the person either denies or seems to deny one of these components, or does not function in regard to one of these components? Conversely, does it make a difference when the person tightly relates or seems to tightly relate two or more of these components? Restating the issue, can the conceptions of literalism and perspectivism be applied to the ways in which persons seem to relate or not to relate their feelings, values, and behaviors?

Although feeling, value, and behavior can be used in highly idiosyncratic ways, it is conceivable that psychologists and many of their subjects might be willing to accept the following definitions: *Behavior* refers to what is outwardly observable in one's functioning—that is, acts, gestures, or speech, described without implying preference, value, or underlying feeling. *Value* refers to more stable and important ways of understanding which are evaluational—that is, positive and negative, preferred and not preferred, or good and bad. In other words, value refers to more vital judgments about that which is worthwhile. *Feeling* is used in the sense of moods and emotions of the moment.

RELATING AND SEPARATING FEELING, VALUE, AND BEHAVIOR

Although a relationship between value and feeling, value and behavior, and feeling and behavior is assumed when viewing persons in the aggregate, persons may differ from one another, and markedly so, in the ways they personally construe these relationships. When persons equate one of these conceptions with another one, or perceive all three as equivalent, one may speak of literalness in the way in which these ideas are related to one another. A person may reason that a particular feeling definitely shows what a person really values; that a particular feeling is as bad as actually doing it; or that a particular behavior points to what one really values. Of course, literalness can also be shown by denying the possibility that feeling, value, or behavior can be interrelated. Thus, a feeling is a feeling, a value is a value, and a behavior is a behavior. One could assert that self-identity is nothing but one's feelings, or values, or behavior. The fact-boundness and literalness of construction is as obvious in this latter example where there can be no relationships as in examples where feeling, value, and behavior are tightly bound.

The person who equates feelings with behavior and socialized values may be constricted to two modes of reaction at the point of a "bad" or "dangerous" feeling. He can refuse to acknowledge his feeling or he can impulsively act out his feeling. In the first instance, he shows overcontrol. In the second instance, he shows undercontrol. The so-called "psychopath," not differentiating between feelings and behavior in the context of egocentric values, may simply act out with little concern about control. The person with more socialized values may suffer intense feelings of guilt, either as the result of his acting out or, alternatively, in reaction to "bad" feelings which he experiences as anxiety or physical distress. The person who equates feelings with values may brand himself as a "bad" person because he has "bad" feelings. He is terribly afraid of his feelings even though he may not act them out. He behaves as if he has done all manner of horrendous things.

Previously it was stated that literalism can also be inferred when persons seem to believe or act as if feelings, values, and behavior are unrelated. This inference can be made when the person denies his feelings, thereby reducing the relationship between feelings and values, or feelings and behavior. This inference can also be made when the person declares that only feelings, or values, or behaviors are important. For example, it is possible to focus on the validity of one's feelings to such an extent that value and behavioral implications are sharply reduced from awareness. The person who is true to his feelings, being unconcerned about what is being valued or what is implied by his behavior, could act out impulsively.

One might also state that it is only what a person values that really counts. Personal identity is a matter of what one believes. If this emphasis on value is extreme, the person may give only scant attention to how he feels or how he behaves. This overemphasis on value, in its most pathological form, can be linked with highly destructive behavior. The moral zealot who cruelly punishes others into good behavior certainly exemplifies the exaltation of one's values to the point of ignoring the feelings of others or the implications of one's own behavior. Consider the following biblical passage from Proverbs 23:14. "Thou shalt beat him with the rod, and shalt deliver his soul from hell." Finally, in regard to behavior, a person could declare that there is only behavior over which he has no control, and that feelings and values which he does not personally understand are but extensions and reflections of behavior.

This reduction of relationship within the triad of feeling, value, and behavior can be further illustrated by a therapy client, a young, male adult who was apprehended for sexual exhibitionism. This client, who was reared in a stereotypic middle-class, religious family, asserted at the beginning of treatment that he did not experience feeling. His composure in the face of acute social criticism certainly suggested that his feelings were not experienced at a high level of awareness. Although denying feelings, he firmly stated his "good" value system and his belief that he was a moral man. He treated his "bad" behavior as though it were a mystery. He seemed to separate his unexplainable behavior from values, and his feelings were separated from values and behavior by not admitting to his feelings. His composure seemed primarily anchored in having good values. His behavior, which was treated as a mystery, did not seem to invalidate his view of himself as a moral man. Moreover, he did not seem to feel any intense guilt over his behavior. Nevertheless, he did state that he was "glad to be caught" and would cooperate fully in the treatment process. It can be said that he did cooperate in therapy; however, he found it most difficult to associate feelings with his exhibitionistic act and the recital of his social history was clear, highly organized, and unemotional. This highly organized picture of his background emphasized fine parents, friends, success in school, and a curious lack of troublesome behavior. His background and behavior were properly and perfectionistically middle-class. In this context of "good background" and exemplary past behavior, he could not comprehend his "bad" act. Not surprisingly, the first two months of therapy were singularly unproductive. In some desperation, the therapist decided to ask him about dreams in an attempt to "loosen him up." Unfortunately, this client never dreamed. Undaunted, the therapist suggested that he place a notebook and pencil on his night stand and instruct himself, each night, that he would dream and would eventually begin to remember bits and pieces of the dream. Three weeks later, the client wrote several words in his notebook. Several weeks later he was reporting a dream almost every day. The therapist asked the client to review these dreams and to locate themes. At first, the client did not see any themes. It was all meaningless. Later, he reported on two major themes, one of "freedom" and the other of "hostility." The dream of freedom is illustrated by his old auto which sprouted wings and flew around the world. The dream of hostility is illustrated by a scene in which he was performing surgery, assisted by his wife. One of his rubber gloves split at a crucial moment and he asked his wife for another glove. Although his wife had access to a barrel full of gloves, she continued to frustrate him by giving him a glove for the wrong hand. He became enraged with her and awakened. In addition to the dream discussion, which focused on feelings of wanting to be free and feelings of hostility, the idea that feelings "don't bite" was introduced into the discussion. Finally, exhibitionism was not treated as "just" sexual. This client had exhibited himself in other, nonlethal ways which suggested a more general desire to express himself. Using this more general and nonliteral construction, he was assisted in learning how to express himself more fully, not only sexually, but also in other ways. The therapy, which lasted 6 months, apparently helped this client, since he was doing well in his marriage and in his profession five years later.

Summarizing this case within the context of literalism, this client initially denied any relationship between feelings and behavior when he did not associate sexual feelings with his "acting out." Later, he did associate both sexual and hostile feelings with his behavior. Regarding his strong value system, it was not "just" a defense against guilt, although by focusing on the importance of his values and the mysterious nature of his behavior, he did protect himself against guilt feelings. In the treatment process, no attempt was made to undermine his values, a primary source of his identity. Rather, an attempt was made to assist him in developing a more sensitive and less absolute application of his system. In particular, he was encouraged to become less literal about his feelings and also more resourceful in their expression.

The foregoing examples demonstrate how either sharply separating or equating feelings, values, and behavior can result in a disabling literalism. It becomes clear that literalism should be defined in a curvilinear fashion, placing perspectivism in an optimal position between the two poles of literalistic function.

In contrast to the literalist who either equates or separates the "triad of knowing," the perspectivist is aware of both linkage and separation of feelings, values, and behavior. The person, as perspectivist, does not immediately leap to absolute conclusions about his or others' behavior. He neither hides from his feelings nor necessarily acts on them. His value system, serving a guiding function for him, does not lead him into excessive guilt about his mistakes or his feelings. His feelings, which do not "bite" him, can serve as a source of imagination, inspiration, and fun. His more negative feelings, even as they can be intense, do not overwhelm him as he takes perspective from the vantage point of his values. At the same time, the monitoring from his values does not preclude learning from experienced behavior or from his feelings.

The perspectivist can consider his feelings, his behavior, or his values from the vantage point of one or another of the conceptual triad. He can consider his behavior within the superordinate (at the moment) position of feelings. He may reverse the process and reflect on his feelings within the superordinate context of his behavior. He may also reflect on his values within the higher order context (of the moment) of his feelings—feelings which can link him to both wisdom and folly. Restating the case, it is possible for the perspectivist to employ different orders of importance, meaningfulness, and hierarchy as he views one aspect of himself from the context of another one. It is hypothesized that the "schizophrenic," the "neurotic," and the "psychopath" are incapable of taking such perspective, a perspective which implies both the capacity to relate and to differentiate within the triad of feeling, value, and behavior.

PATHOLOGY AND LITERALISM

Applying this idea of literalness to adjustment processes, it is argued that a literal stance in regard to how feeling, value, and behavior are related points to difficulties in self-control. Focusing on the concept of self-control as a major problem in adjustment, it is hypothesized that over- and undercontrol or problems of "repression-avoidance-denial and impulsiveness," are related to a literalness in functional relatedness of feeling, value, and behavior.

Beginning with several biblical passages, consider the implications for problems in self-control implicit in the following quotations from the Book of Proverbs (17:17; 6:27; 20:11; 30:17):

"A friend loveth at all times. . . ."

"Can a man take fire in his bosom, and his clothes not be burned?"

"Even a child is known by his doings."

"The eye that mocketh at his father, and despiseth his mother, the ravens of the valley shall pick it out, and the young eagles shall eat it."

The first quotation, emphasizing the literal relation between value and deed, lays the groundwork for repression-denial of one's negative feelings. It could also precipitate one's acting out in uncontrolled rage when significant others fail to give consistent love. The second quotation stresses the literal relatedness between a feeling and its consequence. In this instance, feelings become dangerous. The third quotation emphasizes behavior to the exclusion of feelings and values. Such an overemphasis could lead to an ignoring of the experiential base of behavior—particularly in others and possibly even in self. When a behavioral focus is extreme, one may avoid the feelings and values associated with the deed. The fourth quotation also stresses the literal relation between bad feelings and their consequences. "The eye that mocketh" is a frightening conception designed to promote an absolute control over wayward feelings.

The clinical literature on behavior pathology abounds with descriptions of persons who have suppressed or impulsively acted out their feelings. Freud, more than any other theorist, focused on the problem of self-control. His work brought him into daily contact with the impulsive demands of the id and the restrictive counterdemands of the superego. Although Freud's experience engulfed him in examples of literalism, he did not write directly on the issue of *literalism vs. perspectivism*. His intense interest in symbolism might account for it.

A few quotations from the literature, much of it Freudian in context, point up the issue of literalism in severe maladjustment: "He must . . . protect himself against the intrusion into awareness and behavior of explosive contrary impulses and feelings . . ." (Millon, 1969, p. 280). "As for the lack of discrimination between wish and deed, it is a commonplace of psychoanalytic investigation that the superego threatens punishment for the one nearly as severely as for the other . . ." (Brenner, 1973. p. 133). "It is noteworthy that bad thoughts are much more likely than good thoughts to be equated with behavior. For instance, not even the most stringent fundamentalist preacher would assert that the thought of helping a friend in need is the same as actually helping . . ." (Lehnhoff, 1976, p. 45).

Turning now to more specific illustrations of how literalism is related to pathology, a most striking example of a problem in self-control is found in the behavior of the male exhibitionist. The impulsive acting out of his feelings suggests that feelings have immediate deterministic power over his behavior. For him, feelings must either be expressed or suppressed. He cannot simply acknowledge his feelings and think about them. He must act in regard to them.

The person who is hospitalized because he hears voices that command him to "kill" also may be suffering from a problem of literalism. Suggested here is the possibility that the person experiences feelings of anger which do not fit with his values. In his effort to avoid these angry feelings, he may perceive his feelings as emanating from a source external to himself. When the voice becomes too demanding, he may identify it clearly as that of a good and powerful person, perhaps God.

In this context, the feelings that he experiences may be acted out, since he does not have to take responsibility for the act. His values remain intact as he acts directly on his feelings.

Panic may be experienced by the literal-minded person. In another example, a woman experienced feelings of an episodic nature, feelings which she identified as love for other women. To love other women meant that she must be a homosexual, a thought that frightened her. These feelings of panic were reduced when she was helped to understand how her feelings might be viewed more broadly as "affectional needs" in the context of past and present affectional deprivation. In other words, it was unnecessary for her to construe these feelings as "nothing but" homosexualism. In the context of this "less literal" approach to her problem, she was able to settle down and become less fearfully involved in the therapy process.

Literalism may also be illustrated by the adolescent boy who became terrified by the horrible faces he saw in his mirror. During the treatment process, the therapist introduced the concept of an "omnibus of feelings" which most persons experience as they struggle with their lives in a complex and sometimes frustrating world. The client was also encouraged to role-play while looking at a mirror. He was asked to deliberately make faces, which then were labeled as "feelings that can't bite." Also discussed with him was the idea that parents and others may unwittingly teach that a feeling is exactly the same as a behavior or a value.

Sometimes literalism may be evidenced in contexts in which an individual is desperately seeking greater maturity. For example, an adult male, usually described as "schizy," suddenly asks a girl to marry him after a brief and superficial encounter. The impulsive proposal of marriage terminates in his violence when the girl cannot respond favorably. His uncontrolled outburst of anger can be linked to the idea that the girl's refusal to marry him constituted a complete invalidation of his struggles for growth and new experience. In this illustration, the male could only respond in relation to his own feelings of the moment and to one interpretation of the interaction. He could not step back and take a broader perspective on the nature of human relationships. Rather than trying to understand the viewpoint of another person, he assumed one reason for her refusal—a total rejection of him as a person.

Another kind of literalism is found in persons who seemingly must "get worse" before they get better. In this example, "real" emotional sickness is tightly related to the feeling of *not* being responsible. One's behavior is a matter of sickness rather than responsibility. The person who equates serious illness with not being responsible may deteriorate psychologically, rapidly, and forcefully, thereby warding off feelings of guilt and bad values. After the person has shown to himself and to the world that he is really sick, he can return to a more normal existence. The person has "just" been sick. This kind of example is most provocative since it tends to question the literal aspects of the "mental health movement." One may ask to what extent has the equating of "problems in living" with "sickness" encouraged drug treatments in lieu of talking relationships.

This tight linkage of "real" sickness with a lack of responsibility can be illustrated by a young woman who saw herself in the role of the attractive, popular, and successful older sister. In contrast to this role, she perceived her younger sister as an "ugly duckling" who was unattractive, unpopular, and unsuccessful. When the "ugly" duckling" was hospitalized with a psychosis, the older sister sought therapeutic assistance. During the first therapy interview, she expressed some guilt about the plight of her sister. However, this feeling was quickly replaced two days later with feelings that she also was becoming psychotic. She was unable to sleep, was restless and agitated, and complained of strange thoughts and experiences which she did not share with the therapist. This seeming deterioration in her adjustment was somewhat incongruent with her past history. Nevertheless, she persuaded a hometown psychiatrist to hospitalize her. Once hospitalized, she recovered most rapidly.

There are several possible interpretations of her behavior—for example, competition with her sister. However, the clinician felt that her "becoming worse" was a way of circumventing the intensity of her guilt feelings. She did not have to assume any direct responsibility for her bad feelings and actions toward her sister. In this case, it can be hypothesized that sickness was the alternative to taking a complete and literal responsibility for her sister's troubles. If the older sister had been less literal about the nature of her responsibility, she might have remained in therapy. Her literal equating of sickness with lack of responsibility helped her avoid the struggle for a broader perspective on the relationship between herself and her sister and between herself and her parents. Follow-up information indicated that she quickly resumed her career as an attractive, popular, and successful person.

Shifting to the area of heterosexual relationships, conflicts generated by a literal definition can precipitate psychotic reactions. In one instance, a young man had a brief affair outside his marriage. Although, from an objective view, this encounter could not be seen as a threat to his marriage, the young man believed that the affair was conclusive proof that he did not really love his wife. At the same time, he stated that he cared for his wife. However, he reasoned that he must really love the other woman. Why else would he have had an affair with her? When the other woman pressed him to leave his wife, he developed symptoms of withdrawal which were serious enough to warrant hospitalization. Psychotherapy with him focused on his literal interpretation of heterosexual behavior and the fundamentalistic religious background which supported it.

"Putting all one's eggs in one basket" presents an interesting illustration of literalism. In this case, there is one particular value which must be implemented in only one way. Ed is 37, married, and has three children. For many years Ed worked in an industrial plant where he received a moderate income. Although his life was not unsatisfactory, he wanted to "make more of himself." To implement this value, he impulsively moved his family across the country and enrolled in a university. Sickness, financial problems, and study difficulties brought him to a mental health clinic where he demanded assistance in being permanently hospitalized. Ed stated that he was obviously insane and should be put away. When the clinician replied that he had problems which should be worked out, but he was not insane, Ed became very angry. His problem solution was hospitalization. He had tried to do something more with his life and had failed because of his own inadequacies. Only a crazy person would have made his kind of decisions. Moreover, there was nothing else that could be done. He had lost his previous job, a type of work he understood but did not wish to continue. Now he was blocked in doing what he really wanted to do. He could not go back; he could not go forward. At the moment, the value uppermost in his mind was a vocational one which he could not implement. Accompanying this frustration was intense guilt over what he had done to his family and a profound sense of inadequacy about what he could do for himself or for them in the future. Obviously, only a "nut" would have done what he did. Therefore, the only answer to his problem was immediate hospitalization. An impulsive decision to enter a particular university program was now followed by the impulsive decision to enter a hospital.

In these foregoing illustrations, which link pathology to literalness, the client or patient role has been emphasized. However, roles that may seem most different from that of client or patient also can be literal or have literal implications. The next two sections will highlight the literal aspects of the role of mental health professional.

Professional Valuing and Behaving

The professional mental health worker sometimes reveals a literalism in his diagnostic approach to clients or patients. In the context of his "diagnosis," the knowledge that his patient has a lower socioeconomic background may encourage the use of labels connoting greater disturbance. When lower class becomes linked with the term "schizophrenic," a patient may be viewed as being less accessible for treatment, especially if that treatment emphasizes the person and his experiences. Restating this example in value-behavior terminology, the value term "social class" may have fixed deterministic implications for what the professional does. Professional value and behavior then become so intimately linked that the image of the patient as a whole person is lost.

Taking another example of the literalistic linkage of value and behavior, diagnosticians sometimes have avoided the term "depression" in their clinical reports because the term "depression," when used in hospital settings, invariably led to shock treatment for the patient. This literal relationship between depression and shock, in the absence of sophisticated theory or careful research, suggests that depression may have had a most negative value for some physicians. Possibly, they had to "knock hell" out of that depression as quickly as possible. It is also conceivable that the value of "doing something actively" and "immediately" was construed as being preferable to the value of "doing nothing," "thinking carefully," or "planning and carrying out complex studies." In this illustration, the singular "badness" of a symptom and the essential "goodness" of actively doing something may have led to the impulsive overuse of shock treatment.

In another type of clinical setting, the term "homosexual" was avoided in clinical reports and "problems in psychosexual development" was substituted. This recasting of the problem circumvented a literalistic administrative approach in which the strong negative valuing of homosexual behavior led to immediate and punitive consequences for those caught with this label. In this instance, the literal approach ignored the person as an individual and the possibility that he really wanted help with his problem.

A sad commentary on the growth of literalism among professional mental health workers is provided by Paul:

Paul, a sixteen-year-old black boy, was officially diagnosed as a Criminal Psychopath. During an initial diagnostic staffing, Paul was questioned about his involvements in auto theft and drug "pushing." He also was given the opportunity to talk about his activities in the hospital. In the latter context, he produced a thick notebook in which he had written an autobiography of his life, a document which he continually updated. Following this interview, staff discussion focused on Paul's emotional instability, long criminal history, and impossibility of rehabilitation. These conclusions, reached quickly and with finality, were questioned by one person who admitted that he was curious about Paul's literary efforts. He was intrigued by the idea that an uneducated black boy should make such an effort to find order, meaning, and a sense of personal identity through writing about his life, and suggested that psychotherapeutic intervention might be appropriate in his case. Granted, it was a long shot, but it might be interesting. These comments astonished the other staff members. How could a professional be so naive, absurd, and impractical? After all, this boy was black, uneducated, a criminal, unstable, and a liar. He was a Criminal Psychopath. (Landfield, 1975, p. 7)

A fifth illustration focuses on the objective role of the professional. Diagnosticians value their professional training as objective observers. They may also understand and value the idea that patients "have the problem." In this context of valuing, the professional may be oblivious and even avoidant of the possibility that his interpersonal feelings for the patient could have an impact on what the patient says and how he says it. In other words, the values linked tightly to the professional role may seriously restrict how the clinician listens to his patient and responds to his behavior. The professional becomes stereotypic in his diagnosing. Paradoxically, he becomes most subjective when he may be feeling most objective and secure in his "scientific" role.

A most interesting application of literalism to the therapeutic role is found in the attitude of a few therapists and counselors who stereotype their helping roles as acts of benignness which preclude vigorous interaction with their clients. In the role of accepting therapist, one never questions or challenges his client's thinking or behavior. In this instance, acceptance, warmth, and a nonmoralistic attitude are rigidly defined by a set pattern of therapist behavior. The idea that one might be showing more warmth, real concern, and helpfulness within certain contexts by employing greater degrees of lead, interpretation, and even confrontation would be unthinkable.

Although the early nondirective therapist sometimes behaved as a literalist, implementing his humanistic value with a precise degree of "lead" and noninvolved warmth, the new generation of client-centered therapist reveals a much greater role of freedom than his predecessor. Even as the basic humanistic value is retained, the value can now be implemented in numerous ways by the client-centered therapist. His greater perspective allows him to implement his caring with an enlarged repertoire of techniques. It is now possible to envision a variety of therapist styles as democratically and warmly directed. Even more active responses by a therapist may be construed as enhancing the client's willingness to actively work on his problem. This active style, of course, presumes that the therapist is acutely aware of how his client is feeling and thinking. Moreover, the more active style does not preclude careful listening and an acute appreciation of the client's struggles for his own life.

In using the "nondirective" illustration, we are in no way being critical of Rogers's early work since his approach has evolved, allowing greater freedom of movement for the therapist. Nevertheless, some nondirective practitioners tended to reify the Rogerian, humanistic value by equating it too closely with a particular technique. Unfortunately, too often the followers of a major theorist tend to ritualize a theory rather than elaborate it. Whereas the security of the follower may be in "knowing for sure," the theorist's own feeling of well-being may be more intimately tied to his inquiring mind, his sense of challenge, and his playfulness.

Client resistance in psychotherapy presents another intriguing illustration of literalism when we focus on the therapist's construction of his client. When the therapist perceives his client actively resisting his interpretations or refusing to follow his recommendations, it is easy for the therapist to think of his client as "just" resistant. Client behavior which is "obviously" most uncooperative points directly to and only to a particular therapist interpretation and value—resistance. The alternative hypothesis, that he has not listened carefully to his client, does not understand him, and is foisting his own values on him, may not occur to the therapist.

In this section, we have seen how the literalism of mental health professionals can dehumanize patients. In the next section, suggestions will be made about how one may employ several well-known psychological treatments in literal ways.

Professional Literalism and Training in Contrast

Almost any psychotherapy procedure can be construed as promoting conditions of contrast. Professionals know that such contrast-inducing methods can help their clients. However, not all people benefit from these experiences and for many reasons. One reason might relate to the literalness with which the professional or his client comprehends a particular procedure. Taking a few examples of therapy procedures at random, we will discuss "assertiveness training," "rational-emotive therapy," and "relaxation techniques" with regard to how they could be used in a literal fashion.

Assertiveness training is designed to help persons become more self-expressive. In the process of becoming more self-expressive, a person gains greater confidence in himself as a problem-solver and may achieve a heightened sense of his identity as a person. One might conceive of the outcome of this training as a way of counteracting one's passivity. In this context it could be seen as training in contrast.

Although this training in contrast to one's passivity can be a valuable experience, it is possible that some professionals and/or their clients may understand what they are doing in most literal ways. Assertiveness is literally defined as being very active in behavior and the person now becomes quite aggressive and consistently so in all of his life transactions. Unfortunately, the replacement of a chronic passivity with a persistent aggressiveness may not represent a heightened interpersonal discrimination. The person has not gained the freedom to appropriately choose when to be more and less active. He simply has become more perpetually active. In so doing, he may have traded one set of problems and literalisms for another one. Whereas people may have ignored him in his passive ways, they may now recognize him, but hostilely. Of course, this is not the intent of assertiveness training. However, in the hands of the very aggressive or untrained professional, assertiveness training could become most literal.

Another type of training in contrast is illustrated by Ellis's rational-emotive therapy. In this approach, the therapist encourages persons to substitute logicalness and knowledge for illogicalness and myth-making. It is possible that a neophyte therapist within this system could challenge in his client anything that is highly imaginative and beyond scientific fact. For example, the therapist could question with some logicalness the illogicalness of hope. It could be done directly or more indirectly by challenging the person's religious beliefs. In the process of questioning certain religious myths which might seem to underlie a neurosis, the therapist might also undermine a hopeful aspect of the religious belief. Again, we are not suggesting that Ellis would be insensitive to this problem. However, a therapist with little talent and a special gripe against theology might fail to perceive certain supportive features of a particular religious belief.

Finally, techniques of relaxation may produce contrasts to one's "uptight" feelings. Training in relaxation would seem an unlikely candidate for literalistic misuse. Nevertheless, it is possible to elaborate relaxation to such a point that one ceases to be involved in any serious, challenging, or frustrating reflection or enterprise. One could focus on relaxation in such a single-minded way that one "drops out" of life.

Summarizing these examples of useful treatment approaches which can be carried to the point of literalism, one may conclude that training in contrast is most helpful to the extent that it does not alienate the person from his past, nor restrict unduly his freedom of choice.

In the previous sections, our discussion of literalism has largely been devoted to clinical cases and professional roles. In the next section, illustrations will be drawn from "everyday life." However, the maladaptive aspects of literalism will still be in evidence.

ILLUSTRATIONS FROM EVERYDAY LIFE

Our first illustration of literalism from "everyday life" is so extreme that one might hypothesize a generalized literal style. A group called Posse is comprised of persons who refuse to pay income taxes. Posse takes the stand that since the Constitution does not demand that they pay taxes against their wishes, there is no reason for them to pay taxes. One member stated that he would pay taxes if his income were in real money, silver or gold, rather than in paper currency.

In contrast with the first example, the next illustration is very much in the context of everyday life. The assumed relation between extroversion-introversion and vocational success is a common one. In the past, extroversion was intimately tied to sales ability. If one could not develop the rapid patter of the extrovert, there would be few financial rewards in the occupation of salesman. Today, the absurdity of this assumption is well accepted. Another vocational literalism is presented by a law student who felt that he could not participate in the "mock trials" because he talked too slowly and deliberately. His problem was serious to the extent that he wanted to drop out of law school. At the same time, he really wanted to become a lawyer and had done well in his other course work. In the context of counseling, he was assisted in understanding that lawyers come in many packages. He was encouraged to read short stories about a slow-talking but clever country lawyer whose atypical courtroom behavior was most unnerving to the opposition.

Another type of literalism may suggest perspectivism, since the person tends to perceive every side of an issue. However, this literal-minded person is unable to make decisions within his more concrete, nonhierarchical system. He reminds one of the university administrator who seems open to all positions, yet acts in behalf of the status quo. His benign, fatherly, and supportive role, which suggests an openness to all positions, is misleading. In truth, he is closed to all positions. This closedness can be observed in relation to a variety of statements. In confidence, the administrator could admit that he becomes confused with the many different positions. He might also forcefully assert that all positions are of equal value or are equally valueless. Again, he might state that there is no way one can evaluate a new position. Therefore, it is best to stick with current procedures. Even as these statements can vary, they appear to have a common denominator. They all reflect an inability to choose a position and to experiment with it. This inability to "try it on for size" points directly to a closed system, a kind of system deficient in hierarchical structure.

To elaborate a bit on this type of administrator, we see that he may have perceived that only a few subordinates are involved with any particular issue. This being the case, his support of the status quo can be viewed as a majority opinion—that is, the silent majority of disinterested people. It is conceivable that such an administrator might conceptualize himself as democratic. However, his interest in the opinions of others is more contrived than empathic. His decisions are more reactive than chosen. His life may not be very exciting, but he can survive.

The administrator who has just been described should not be confused with another breed of literalist. The next administrator is neither confused nor passive. His game is power. He too plays the benign and fatherly role. He too listens calmly to all sides of an issue. However, in this process, he manages to encourage such confusion and conflict among his subordinates that he is never pressed by a majority to try out a new alternative. He appoints endless committees and cleverly suggests problems with any issue, but not directly to the supporting faction—only to the opposition. Whereas the primary role of his subordinates may be that of resolving shared problems, the primary role value of this administrator is maintaining control. The art of control is to manage change, and the best way of managing change is to prohibit all change and maintain the status quo. This kind of administrator is a most single-minded fellow whose literalness may be fully demonstrated only at the point of crisis, when his literal definition of stability is threatened by change. At this point of crisis, the administrator may lose his "cool." If the situation is really serious for him, he could impulsively and desperately try new solutions—from the bottle, in physical illness, in extramarital sex, or in some other avoidant response.

In these examples of the literal administrator, it has been noted that the art of controlling others in the literal style is to *appear as if* one is really open to alternatives. Thus, we may speak of the "closet literalist."

In this section, literalism was illustrated by the values and behavior of an offbeat, ultraconservative minority group, the constricted interpretation of the implications of introversion and extroversion, and, the footdragging of administrators. In the next section, literalism will be viewed within the context of a fundamental assumption about human nature: The person searches for unity in a dialectical world, a universe of countless alternatives—a contrasting universe most apparent between persons, and most avoided within the person.

Literalism, Contrast, and the Search for Unity

It is theorized that a central theme in man's psychology is his oppositional nature in contrast to his persistent search for unity. Gibson (1970) and Singer (1966) conceptualize the search for certainty and consistency. Rychlak (1968) focuses on the theme of dialectical man—his oppositional and interpretive nature. Kelly (1955) clearly states the case for the duality of the person's construct system. Kelly's argument is elaborated by Landfield (1977) when he hypothesizes thus:

It is man's nature to seek unity and certainty. However, even as unity and certainty allay man's feelings of anxiety, his dissatisfactions and boredom, coupled with his curiosity, lead to questioning those unities and certainties which contribute to his security. Unity provides the comfortable context within which meaning is stabilized. Contrast performs a dual function of providing a context for change in that unity as well as a dimensional framework within one may comprehend his particular position. (p. 131)

In regard to dichotomous thinking which has been associated with literalism, Landfield (1977) states:

Such men as Korzybski (1933) and Johnson (1946) opposed the idea that duality could have a constructive purpose. They tended to equate the dichotomy with primitive, unscientific thinking which implied absolutism, simplicity, rigidity, and absence of change. The amusing aspect of this controversy over Aristotelian dichotomies and Galilean gradations was the rigidly dichotomizing behavior of the general semanticist as he outlined the evils of the dichotomy. In this context, Korzybski's publishing company carries the interesting title, the International Non-Aristotelian Library Publishing Company.

The modern general semanticist, such as Weinberg (1959) or Hayakawa (1949), has assumed a more moderate position on the dichotomy. Hayakawa understands the motivating nature of the duality, perceiving that strong positions and commitments are necessary to initiate important undertakings, and that final decisions often involve dichotomies. . . .

Kelly (1955), even as he focused on the dualities of man, did not believe that dichotomous thinking is necessarily absolute, although a person can use his dichotomies in this way. He also did not assume that dichotomies are simple, although one might think, feel, and believe in simple, dichotomous ways. Within Personal Construct Theory, one can think like a Galilean or an Aristotelian, yet share a feature common to all men, that feeling, thinking, and behaving are intrinsically matters of contrast. (pp. 237, 238)

Within a complex universe of unity, contrast, and change, the person makes his decisions. However, in this process of decision, the person may deny the importance of the alternative to his choice. If the person changes from his original position, he may deny importance to his first decision by simply stating that he was in error. He does not probe why he made his first choice. He may also minimize the difference between his first choice and the new decision, a strategy guaranteed to prop up his ego and circumvent any need to reflect on his earlier decision.

In a previous section on Personal Construct Theory, it was noted that final decisions are single-minded and literal at the moment of decision. Nevertheless, once the decision has been made, it is still possible to step back and reflect on it. Rather than assuming that a decision is absolutely and eternally correct, one may employ the decision as a hypothesis from which one generates experience that may suggest how to construct improved decisions. Unfortunately, just as scientists sometimes cling to their old formulations, the person may behave like an automaton. Although all persons are literal at the point of decision, they may be differentiated as to whether their concrete decisions become anchored to literal assumption.

The search for unity and the process of change often take place within the same dimension. This may be illustrated by our educational and parental philosophies which seem to move from the permissive and fluid to the authoritative and fixed, then back again to the permissive and fluid. We behave like pendulums, swinging from one alternative to its contrast. Until we step back from our pendulum, taking perspective on the situation, we fail to perceive that both ends of the stroke define the motion. This perception of unity in contrast might well facilitate some appreciation that both poles of contrast may have value. Such perception could facilitate a more complex, integrative, and flexible position, particularly if the person attempts an elaboration of his contrast. The elaboration I have in mind is much like dropping two pebbles in a stream and watching the ever-widening and overlapping circles. This type of elaboration would seem to fit well within the role of perspectivist. Practice with this kind of elaboration would seem a most likely antidote for the literal assumption that one's opposites, once they are posed, must remain entirely and absolutely incompatible.

In the foregoing discussion, the position has been taken that a literal approach to contrast and unity will likely impede man's development. If so, it will be of value to investigate how three creative persons, a biologist, a psychoanalyst, and a novelist have confronted this issue.

Perspectives of Three Authors

Bertalanffy (1967) asserts that the person actively creates his perceptual world.

Since early times . . . psychology of cognition and epistemology were dominated by what Kaplan saucily called "the dogma of immaculate perception." The organism is a passive receiver of stimuli, sense data, information . . . coming from outside objects. . . .

. . . modern psychology has shown that this is not so. In a very real sense, the organism creates the world around it. . . . (p. 91)

He then questioned formal conceptual models which are used as "reals" rather than as useful interpretations.

Every model is a conceptual representation of certain traits or formal structures of empirical entites. It leads to intellectual disaster when the model is made into metaphysical reality. This is true of any model, whether it be the billiard balls of mechanistic atomism, Descarte's animal machine, robot man of American psychology, the Freudian model of personality, culture "organisms," or whatever other model concept. If we take the theories of history as working models permitting us to see certain regularities—and, at present, very immature and contradictory models—we shall be more fair, even admitting that different models are possible and pertinent. (pp. 108–109)

That Freud (1952) struggled painfully with the problem of unity seems apparent in the following quotation.

I do not aim at producing conviction—my aim is to stimulate enquiry and to destroy prejudices. . . . You should only listen and allow what I tell you to make its own effect upon you. Convictions are not so easily acquired, or, when they are achieved without much trouble, they soon prove worthless and unstable. . . . You are not for a moment to suppose that the . . . view which I shall lay before you is a speculative system of ideas. . . .

Some people have ignored my corrections of myself altogether and still today criticize me in respect of views which no longer mean the same to me. Others positively reproach me for these changes and declare me to be unreliable on that account. No one who changes his views once or twice deserves to be believed for it is only too likely that he will be mistaken again in his latest assertions; but anyone who sticks to anything . . . , is obstinate or pig-headed, is it not so? What is to be done in the face of these self contradictory criticisms except to remain as one is and behave as seems best to me . . . and I am not deterred from remodeling and improving my theories in accordance with later experience. I have so far found nothing to alter in my fundamental standpoint and I hope this will never be necessary. (pp. 256–258)

Even creative thinkers are not free of literalisms. In the following quotation, Freud seems most concrete and preemptive.

Only later does the impulse of love detach itself from egoism; it is a literal fact that the child learns how to love through his own egoism. (p. 214)

The next quotation, from Pirsig (1977), clearly shows how a less concrete reflection on the nature of life and self may provide a sense of unity within oneself and with nature.

This is the understanding that whether you are bored or excited, depressed or elated, successful or unsuccessful, even whether you are alive or dead, all this is absolutely no consequence whatsoever. The sea keeps telling you this with every sweep of every wave. And when you accept this understanding of yourself and agree with it and continue on anyway, then a real fullness of virtue and self-understanding arises. And sometimes the moment of arrival is accompanied by hilarious laughter. The old reality of the sea has put cruising depression in its proper perspective at last. (p. 68)

Although each of these three persons has commented differently, each of them has sought his unities in a world of contrast and change. Von Bertalanffy seems to find some comfort in defining the person as active, creative, and open. His biology is that of the open system. There is structure, but the structure changes. Freud states that he is willing to change his ideas, but he hopes that his most fundamental conceptions will not change. Implied here is the idea that one can encompass change as long as certain essential beliefs remain stable. Pirsig asserts the validity of the person no matter what form it takes. One recognizes and accepts the contrasts of life. Pirsig states, "When depression is seen as an unavoidable part of one's life, it becomes possible to study it with less aversion and discover that within it are all sorts of overlooked possibilities" (p. 68).

Each of these well-known authors, in his way, has attempted to take perspective on the human struggle to create meaning and the problems that are inherent in the process. Each, in his way, has taken a firm position on the nature of persons, a firmness that does not preclude creative learning, elaboration, and change.

SUMMARY

Literalism refers to a way of thinking, feeling, or doing which implies the restricted and absolute interpretation of an event or a relationship. Restated, literalism means a fixity of construction and a lack of exception to how one understands a particular event or relationship. Literalism points to a rigid and preemptive codifying of experience which, used in excess, discourages the creation of complex hierarchies of meaning and impedes the process of reconceptualization and the reordering of events. A pervasive literalism suggests a rigid, unyielding kind of interpretive structure which, on the one hand, can be related to narrowness and authoritarianism; and, on the other hand, to impulsiveness and suddenness of behavioral change. This impulsiveness and suddenness of behavioral change which may seem out of character for the person can be seen as a switch to an opposite role. Within the theory of personal constructs, this literal switching to an opposite along a personal dimension is called "slot rattling." Others may refer to this phenomenon as "the closeness of opposites." At some point of crisis, the person simply shifts to the opposite of his original choice. He does so without perspective.

Chaotic fragmentalism refers to an unorganized complexity of thinking, feeling, or doing which implies an unrestricted, loose, undirected, and shifting interpretation of an event or relationship. In the extreme, life is experienced as an array of parts which have little coherence or stability of meaning. The lack of organizing focus perpetuates a concreteness and instability of conception and response which is associated with profound kinds of personality disturbance—characterized by a lack of hierarchical structure and difficulties in anticipating events.

Whereas the fragmentalist's unorganized nature subjects him to the vicissitudes and capriciousness of his internal and external environments, the literalist, with his rigid internal structure and a greater availability of support from his environment, may more readily cope within its restricted view of reality. Restating this latter point, people, preferring unity to chaos, tend to be more receptive to a person who is definitive.

Both the literalist and the fragmentalist tend to function impulsively and literally in response to certain cues; however, the tightly organized system of the chronic literalist restricts that which is attended to and stabilizes its meaning. One may regard the chronic literalist as having greater consistency of behavior, except at the point of crisis and personal invalidation. In this context of crisis, he may "slot rattle" and behave to the opposite. The chaotic fragmentalist, although behaving kaleidoscopically, may be seen as a literalist "of the moment."

Perspectivism points to a less preemptive, but not loose, interpretation of an event or relationship which facilitates order and relatedness without sacrificing the potential for new interpretation. A generalized perspectivism suggests a flexible, but not fluid, kind of structure, a system that provides some security of meaning without closing out the impact of new experience. The perspectivist, although less certain about the specific nature of life, does not experience the vulnerability of a pervasive fragmentalism. Although he may at times experience more anxiety than the literalist, his system is less open to the sudden invalidation which may occur to the literalist.

Perspectivism can be distinguished from literalism in regard to the flexible employment of hierarchical structures which serve as guidelines to further experience. For the perspectivist, relationships between personal meanings, viewed either ordinally or in unileveled ways, allow for exceptions. This greater sensitivity to and less fear of exceptions, when matched with a propensity to integrate—to value similarity and relatedness—creates a context in which observed relationships become hypotheses to be explored rather than assumptions to be clung to. The perspectivist is open to experience, but not to the extent of being overwhelmed by it. In contrast, the literalist does not make flexible use of hierarchical structures. Although he may seem to employ ordinal structures, his more encompassing or more abstract conceptions suggest a mechanical coding of experience in which higher order abstractions are nothing more or less than the lower order observations which gave rise to them. The abstraction tends to be a literal recitation of its elements. The tight relationship between the abstraction and its elements does not facilitate exploration and hypothesis. The literalist tends to be closed to experience. When the chronic literalist does change, it is most likely that he has merely reverted to an opposite position which is held in the same firm, literal ways. In contrast to both the literalist and perspectivist, the profoundly fragmented person has neither the security of literal assumption nor the hope of hypothesis. He is truly vulnerable.

It might be difficult to locate a person who approaches all areas of his life in either a literal or nonliteral fashion. Although this may be the case, it seems reasonable to believe that some persons may have strong tendencies toward one or the other mode of relating to himself and to his world. It also seems reasonable to believe that a person might be strongly literal in only one particular area of his life. In line with this reasoning, some of our illustrations suggested a more general problem with literalism, whereas other examples seemed more specific to a particular problem or issue. An interesting implication of this rather complex conception of literalism is that persons who can take perspective in some areas of their lives may be more open to change. To have an idea or feeling about how to take perspective in one area may enable one to more easily assume a less literal stance in a problem area where one is not taking much perspective.

The literal person searches for unity and wards off the threat of uncertainty by his absolute approach to events. Systems of thinking which are tightly organized give one that firm sense of knowing. If simplicity of thinking is a mark of literalism, then the literal person might be expected to use a simpler system of personal constructs—that is, dimensions of awareness—simplicity being defined by having fewer different constructs as shown by the very tight relationships found among his "different" ways of thinking. His "seemingly different" expressions of meaning are shown not to be different because they have the same implications. Although this simplicity of construction can be linked to literalness, it is also possible that a large number of orthogonal constructions may point to literalism. The confused person, experiencing life in unorganized and fragmented ways, makes little overall sense of his life, tending to approach it in bits and parts. Whatever meaning or certainty is achieved occurs at the expense of giving up the attempt to develop more encompassing hierarchical and nonliteral life positions. The confused person, behaving in fragmented ways, tends to react tropistically to internal and external cues of the moment. He cannot step back and take perspective within another context of time or content. In regard to this illustration, one does *not* assume within Personal Construct Theory that it is "just" the large number of orthogonal constructions which point to literalism. Rather, it is the inability to place these constructions within more encompassing and nonliteral structures and themes of meaning. This capacity to place one's different ways of understanding within hierarchical systems of meaning is called ordination. It is hypothesized that the person with much orthogonal construction and little ordination will approach his life in literal ways. Likewise, the same hypothesis will hold for the person with few orthogonal constructions and little capacity to ordinate.

Having defined the concepts of perspectivism and literalism in general ways, it is now possible to focus on a particular kind of literalism within the context of Personal Construct Theory. However, this particular theoretical focus requires an assumption. It is assumed that a personal construct can be comprised of three aspects, which will be called feeling, value, and behavior. In regard to this assumption, it is now hypothesized that either the excessively tight or the excessively loose relationships within the triad of feeling, value, and behavior point to literalism which has implications for the problem of overcontrol and undercontrol of behavior. Overcontrol and undercontrol is commonly associated with serious psychological disturbance.

Several kinds of measurements of literalism within the "triad of knowing" immediately come to mind. Leitner (1979) employed a measure within standard personal construct research methodology. Using a form of the Rep Test, dimensional descriptions of acquaintances are elicited from subjects. Then, an inquiry follows in which each construct given on the first Rep Test is reconstrued by the subject into component dimensions of feeling, valuing, and behaving. These data are then formed into three rating grids: one for feelings, one for values, and the third one for behavior. The subject rates each of his acquaintances on the feeling, value, and behavioral dimensions. Grids are then analyzed by noting the degree of similarity across the grids of the three aspects of each construct. In this analysis, patterns of acquaintance-ratings are used as operational definitions of feeling, valuing, and behaving aspects of each personal construct. In other words, each personal construct is defined as a triad, and excessively tight or loose relating within each triad is noted.

Leitner's research has given support to the following hypotheses:

1. Both highly disturbed and better adjusted persons can verbalize feeling, valuing, and behaving components of a personal construct dimension. For example, a person who understands others in relation to *friendly vs. unfriendly* may transform these descriptions into: feels warm versus cold; values closeness to others versus dislikes other; and, gives a helping hand versus turns his back to others.

2. Subjects described as neurotic or having character disorders tend to be literal relaters of the feeling, valuing, and behaving components of their constructs—that is, a feeling equals a behavior; a feeling equals a value; or a value equals a behavior.

3. Subjects described as psychotic tend to be literal separators—that is, feeling, valuing, and behaving components are unrelated.

4. Better adjusted persons tend to relate their feelings, values, and behaviors in less literal ways.

5. Persons may have little insight about whether they literally relate or separate the components of their personal constructs.

Leitner's findings have exciting implications for psychotherapy. His methodology may allow the therapist to more quickly pinpoint areas of literalism and ways in which his client is being literal. Rephrasing this latter point, the therapist may locate areas in which his client is assuming, hypothesizing, and fragmenting in relation to the feeling, valuing, and behaving components of his life.

It is obvious that Leitner's procedure does not require the subject to be aware of how he is or is not relating his feelings, values, and behavior. This inference is made by the investigator. An alternative to this procedure is to ask the person whether he believes that feelings either are or should be directly related to values and behavior. He also is asked what he believes about the relatedness, actual or idealized, of other aspects of the triad. Although this method has possibilities, its usefulness is limited by the extent to which persons know how they function. A third method, less direct than the previous one, involves the use of standard personality questionnaire items coded for literalism and perspectivism. The problem with the last method relates to the assumption that subjects understand questionnaire items in the way the investigator intended. A further assumption requires the investigator to believe that his questions are most relevant for the experience of his subjects. Elaborating on this assumption, he must also assume that that which all test takers share in common is more important than that which is more idiosyncratic or shared by smaller subgroups.

A CONCLUDING STATEMENT

In opposition to the *literal* search for unity in a world of contrast, Morgenau (1963) states a perspectivist position in his sophisticated view of science.

Science recognizes eternal questions but spurns eternal answers. Its challenge is not in the discovery of truth that is as dead as a known fact. The scientist is inspired by an idea of truth that is elusive, forever changing while warming his heart in affording him the conviction that his reach is coming closer and closer to his ideal, even though he knows he will never hold it fully in his grasp. (p. 17)

Unfortunately, we tend to literalize our important decisions, using them as facts of nature, rather than as hypotheses or springboards to further exploration. When confronted with failure, we either cling to our facts or shift to the opposite decision. When we shift to the contrast, we tend to anchor ourselves, forgetting that we were quite certain about the previous decision. And so the pendulum moves, laterally and literally. Our hope lies in becoming aware of the human duality—within ourselves. Taking perspective means stepping back from the one alternative, placing it within the oppositional context, and finally, clearly recognizing one's choice as interpretation rather than literal fact.

REFERENCES

Brenner, C. *An elementary textbook of psychoanalysis*. New York: International Universities Press, 1973.

Frankl, V. *Man's Search for Meaning*. New York: Washington Square, 1964.

Frankel-Brunswick, E. Intolerance of ambiguity as an emotional and perceptual personality variable. *Journal of Personality,* 1949, **18,** 108–143.

Freud, S. *The Standard Edition of the Complete Psychological Works of Sigmund Freud.* Vol. 21. London: Hogarth, 1929.

Freud, S. *A General Introduction to Psychoanalysis*. New York: Washington Square Press, 1952.

Gendlin, E. *Experiencing and the Creation of Meaning*. New York: The Free Press of Glencoe, 1962.

Gibson, E. J. The ontongeny of reading. *American Psychologist,* 1970, **25,** 136–143.

Hayakawa, S. I. *Language in Thought and Action*. New York: Harcourt, Brace, 1949.

Johnson, W. *People in Quandaries: The Semantics of Personal Adjustment*. New York: Harper, 1946.

Kelly. G. A. *The Psychology of Personal Constructs:* Vols. 1 and 2. New York: Norton, 1955.

Kelly, G. A. The psychology of the unknown. Unpublished manuscript, 1963.

Kelly, G. A. Humanistic methodology in psychological research. In B. Maher (Ed.), *Clinical Psychology and Personality: The Selected Papers of George Kelly*. New York: Wiley, 1969, pp. 133–146.

Kelly, G. A. A summary statement of a cognitively oriented comprehensive theory of behavior. In James Mancuso (Ed.), *Readings for a Cognitive Theory of Personality*. New York: Holt, Rinehart & Winston, 1970, pp. 27–58.

Korzybski, A. *Science and Sanity*. Lakeville, CT: International Non-Aristotelian Library Publishing Company, 1933.

Landfield, A. W. The complaint: A confrontation of personal urgency and professional construction. In D. Bannister (Ed.), *Issues and Approaches in Psychological Therapies*. London: Wiley, 1975, pp. 1–25.

Landfield, A. W. Interpretive man: The enlarged self-image. In A. Landfield (Ed.), *The Nebraska Symposium on Motivation, 1976, Personal Construct Psychology*. Lincoln, NE: University of Nebraska Press, 1977, 127–177.

Lehnhoff, J. Literal determinism as a personality construct. Unpublished Ph.D. dissertation, University of Nebraska, 1976.

Leitner, L. The relationships between emotional, evaluational, and behavioral implications of personal constructs. Unpublished Ph.D. dissertation, University of Nebraska, 1979.

Maddi, S. *Perspectives on Personality*. Boston: Little, Brown, 1971.

Millon, T. *Modern Psychopathology*. Philadelphia: Saunders, 1969.

Morgenau, H. The new style of science. *Yale Alumni Magazine*, Feb. 1963, 8–17.

Pirsig, R. Cruising blues and their cure. *Esquire*, May, 1977, 63–68.

Rychlak, J. F. *A Philosophy of Science for Personality Theory*. Boston: Houghton Mifflin, 1968.

Singer, J. F. Motivation for consistency. In Shel Feldman (Ed.), *Cognitive Consistency: Motivational Antecedents and Behavioral Consequents*. New York and London, Academic, 1966, pp. 47–73.

Von Bertalanffy, L. *Robots, Men and Minds*. New York: Braziller, 1967.

Weinberg, H. L. *Levels of Knowing and Existence: Studies in General Semantics*. New York: Harper, 1959.

Name Index

Subject Index

Abstractness, 289, 295, 296
Acceptance, 149
Accumulative fragmentalism, 4, 293
Active cognizer, 274
Adventure, 24
Alpha level, 217
Anticipation, 5, 25, 27, 29, 57, 60, 63, 66,
  112, 128, 275, 277. *See also* Prediction
Anxiety, *see* Emotion
Assumptive level, 26, 128, 132, 135, 318
Attention control, 228
Awareness, levels of, 11, 12, 37-39, 48, 93,
  124, 125, 143, 146, 162, 193, 300, 301

Behavior: absoluteness, 292
  acting-out, 302, 304, 305
  aggressive, 196, 198, 199
  amok, 256-258
  compulsive, 145, 244
  dependent, 109, 147, 148, 157, 292
  enuretic, 180
  exhibitionistic, 302, 304
  as experiment, 63, 138, 185, 203
  homocidal, 106
  homosexual, 174, 307
  impulsive, 13, 108, 115, 131, 298, 301,
    303, 304, 307
  indecisive, 13, 108, 113, 145, 298
  laughter, inappropriate, 106
  nail biting, 179
  neurotic, 303
  passive, 79, 80, 83, 109
  phobic, 218
  psychopathic, 301, 303, 308
  psychosomatic, 133, 136, 244
  psychotic, 222, 306
  rating, 278, 285
  schizophrenic, 11, 223, 303, 307
  suicidal, 106
  theoretical, 295
  therapy, 79, 181

  thumbsucking, 179
  traits, 55, 211
  truancy, 131
  versus feeling and value, 289-319
Beta level, 217
Bipolarity, 8, 124, 125

Category: conjunctive, 215
  relational, 217
Change, 9, 43, 273
  application, 15
  attitude, 177
  behavior, 273
  chaotic, 62
  construct shift, 15
  construct use, 14
  contrast reconstruction, 14
  dimensional, 15
  experimentation, 69, 107, 113, 115, 117,
    178
  impulsive, 298, 315
  loosening-tightening, *see* Construct
  new construction, 14, 15, 33
  new reference axes, 174, 175
  permeability, 9
  process, 62, 211, 313
  propositions, 168
  psychological, 169
  psychotherapy, *see* Psychotherapy
  range of convenience, 173, 174
  reconstruction, 14, 58, 59, 105, 163, 177
  slot, 14, 154, 170, 171, 315
  sudden, 315
  system, 14, 15
  transition, concepts of, 12, 198
Chaotic fragmentalism, 293, 315
Child: arousal, 284, 286
  autistic, 170
  construct system, 44, 179, 275, 276, 286
  construes situation, 276, 277
  knowledge, 44

Psychology and Psychiatry in Courts and Corrections: Controversy and Change
  by Ellsworth A. Fersch, Jr.
Restricted Environmental Stimulation: Research and Clinical Applications
  by Peter Suedfeld
Handbook of Clinical Neuropsychology
  edited by Susan B. Filskov and Thomas J. Boll
Personal Construct Psychology: Psychotherapy and Personality
  edited by Alvin W. Landfield and Larry M. Leitner
Handbook of Clinical Behavior Therapy
  edited by Samuel M. Turner, Karen S. Calhoun, and Henry E. Adams
Mothers, Daughters, and Grandmothers: Personality and Child-Care in
Three-Generation Families
  by Bertram J. Cohler and Henry U. Grunebaum
Further Explorations in Personality
  edited by A. I. Rabin, Joel Aronoff, Andrew M. Barclay, and Robert A. Zucker
Hypnosis and Relaxation: Modern Verification of an Old Equation
  by William E. Edmonston, Jr.